CAUGHT IN
THE CURRENT

THE DAVID J. WEBER SERIES IN THE
NEW BORDERLANDS HISTORY

Andrew R. Graybill and Benjamin H. Johnson, editors

Editorial Board

Juliana Barr
Sarah Carter
Maurice Crandall

Kelly Lytle Hernández
Cynthia Radding
Samuel Truett

The study of borderlands—places where different peoples meet and no one polity reigns supreme—is undergoing a renaissance. The David J. Weber Series in the New Borderlands History publishes works from both established and emerging scholars that examine borderlands from the precontact era to the present. The series explores contested boundaries and the intercultural dynamics surrounding them and includes projects covering a wide range of time and space within North America and beyond, including both Atlantic and Pacific worlds.

Published with support provided by the William P. Clements Center for Southwest Studies at Southern Methodist University in Dallas, Texas.

A complete list of books published in the David J. Weber Series in the New Borderlands History is available at https://uncpress.org/series/the-david-j-weber-series-in-the-new-borderlands-history.

CAUGHT IN THE CURRENT

Mexico's Struggle to Regulate Emigration, 1940–1980

IRVIN IBARGÜEN

THE UNIVERSITY OF NORTH CAROLINA PRESS

Chapel Hill

© 2025 The University of North Carolina Press

All rights reserved

Set in Scala, Scala Sans, Sentinel, and Irby
by codeMantra

Manufactured in the United States of America

Cover art: faded blue background © Adobe Stock/Robert Hoek

Library of Congress Cataloging-in-Publication Data
Names: Ibargüen, Irvin author
Title: Caught in the current : Mexico's struggle to regulate emigration, 1940–1980 / Irvin Ibargüen.
Other titles: David J. Weber series in the new borderlands history
Description: Chapel Hill : The University of North Carolina Press, 2025. | Series: The David J. Weber series in the new borderlands history | Includes bibliographical references and index.
Identifiers: LCCN 2025019226 | ISBN 9781469689579 (cloth alk. paper) | ISBN 9781469689586 pbk alk. paper | ISBN 9781469684659 epub | ISBN 9781469689593 pdf
Subjects: LCSH: Foreign workers, Mexican—United States | Labor supply—Mexico—History—20th century | Mexico—Emigration and immigration—Government policy | Mexico—Emigration and immigration—Economic aspects | BISAC: HISTORY / Latin America / Mexico | HISTORY / United States / State & Local / West (AK, CA, CO, HI, ID, MT, NV, UT, WY)
Classification: LCC JV7401 .I23 2025 | DDC 325.72—dc23/eng/20250708
LC record available at https://lccn.loc.gov/2025019226

For product safety concerns under the European Union's General Product Safety Regulation (EU GPSR), please contact gpsr@mare-nostrum.co.uk or write to the University of North Carolina Press and Mare Nostrum Group B.V., Mauritskade 21D, 1091 GC Amsterdam, The Netherlands.

To the denizens of the bookstacks

CONTENTS

List of Illustrations · ix
Abbreviations · xi
Naming Conventions · xiii

INTRODUCTION · A Fluid Situation · *Outlining Mexico's Management of Out-Migration* · 1

1 · Proper Channels · *The Promises and Perils of a Planned Migration, 1942–1953* · 17

2 · Against the Current · *Mexico Meets Public Pressure to Contain Out-Migration, 1953–1954* · 42

3 · An Uncontainable Flow · *The Escalation and Demise of Mexico's Migrant Demobilization Campaign, 1954* · 69

4 · Turning the Tide · Part One · *Mexico Engineers the Internal Exploitation of Migrant Labor, 1955–1958* · 102

5 · Turning the Tide · Part Two · *Mexico Desists from Exploiting Migrant Labor Internally, 1958–1963* · 127

6 · A Flailing State · Part One · *Mexico Searches for Migratory Solutions after the Bracero Program, 1968–1975* · 151

7 · A Flailing State · Part Two · *Mexico's Failed Search for a Migratory Solution, 1975–1980* · 173

CONCLUSION · Caught in the Current · *Mexico Surrenders to Out-Migration, 1980–Present* · 195

Acknowledgments · 209
Notes · 211
Index · 249

ILLUSTRATIONS

FIGURES

Migrants trapped behind a closed border gate in Mexicali · *43*

Migrants relocated to La Paz to establish settlements · *94*

Close-up of migrants in Mexicali · *97*

Migrants rush toward the United States
unimpeded by Mexican authorities · *98*

US authorities contend with a crowd of migrants · *100*

An armed Mexican guard watches over migrants · *118*

Mexican authorities retrieve migrants · *119*

MAPS

Mexicali-Calexico borderlands region · *79*

Migrant destinations in Sonora, Mexico · *108*

ABBREVIATIONS

AFL-CIO American Federation of Labor and Congress of Industrial Organizations
ANC Asociación Nacional de Cosecheros
BIP Border Industrialization Program
BP Bracero Program
CI Comisión Intersecretarial
CMCT Comisión Mixta de Control de Trabajadores
CNC Confederación Nacional Campesina
CTM Confederación de Trabajadores de México
DAAC Departamento de Asuntos Agrarios y Colonización
DOL US Department of Labor
IBP internal Bracero Program
INS US Immigration and Naturalization Service
IRCA Immigration Reform and Control Act
MORENA Movimiento de Regeneración Nacional
PAN Partido Acción Nacional
PCME Programa para las Comunidades Mexicanas en el Exterior
PRI Partido Revolucionario Institucional

NAMING CONVENTIONS

In accordance with common academic practice, I use both paternal and maternal surnames when first introducing Latin American political figures—for example, *Adolfo Ruiz Cortines*. However, thereafter, for consistency and brevity, I refer to them by the more distinctive of their two surnames—for example, *Cortines*.

INTRODUCTION

A FLUID SITUATION

Outlining Mexico's Management of Out-Migration

In 1942, at the prodding of its northern neighbor, the United States, Mexico signed a bilateral guest-worker agreement. The Bracero Program (BP), as it came to be known, was grand in its scale and the breadth of its possible consequences. Through it, Mexico would send tens of thousands of Mexican nationals to toil in the United States, harvesting season after harvesting season, predominantly in fruit and vegetable crops such as carrots, lettuce, and peaches. The participating migrants, traveling and working with formal contracts to be supervised by both states, were assured baseline nutrition, housing, and compensation.

For Mexico, the upside of the initiative was clear: relatively well-compensated work for the part of its citizenry that gravitated to agricultural labor, and closer political ties to a United States on the verge of achieving global military, economic, and geopolitical hegemony thanks to its leading role in World

War II.¹ Yet, for all the potential benefits, Mexico's orchestration of mass migration also carried significant risks, three of which were immediately foreseeable. One, by agreeing to send Mexican workers to the United States, Mexico could weaken parts of its economy reliant on cheap labor. Two, by encouraging exit, Mexico could overwhelm the resources of Mexican border towns with large concentrations of migrants looking to depart as guest workers or, failing that, as undocumented migrants. Finally, by enabling the exodus, the Mexican government imperiled its reputation. Should a pattern of migrant abuse emerge in the United States despite the protections offered by the BP, public opinion in Mexico would likely ascribe some blame to the Mexican presidencies facilitating the migration.

The Mexican federal government—controlled by a single ruling party, which from 1946 onward was known as the Partido Revolucionario Institucional (Institutional Revolutionary Party, or PRI)—anticipated these problems. To combat an excess loss of labor, it restricted the number of Mexicans who could participate in the program. It pegged each municipality's participation to its specific unemployment rate.² To attenuate the swelling of border towns and border cities, it spread migrant-processing centers widely across its northern region.³ This way, the demographic impact of Mexicans moving through its northern settlements would be softened. Finally, it adopted a hardline posture in BP negotiations, wresting robust guarantees from the United States on everything from migrants' wages to their diets; left unspecified, these areas could lead to mistreatment by US growers and disrepute for the Mexican government.⁴

Mexico's cautious approach could only limit the impact of migration to a certain extent. The social, economic, and political fallout of the bracero migration was unpredictable and could be worsened by various factors. For instance, a Mexican industry, such as cotton manufacturing, experiencing a labor shortage because of out-migration might find itself in need of more workers if the climatic conditions it operated in suddenly improved. US agribusinesses, for their part, could cut production and slow the admission of Mexican guest workers during the harvesting season, causing more desperate emigrants to gather in tightly packed Mexican border towns, waiting to cross into the United States. On the cultural front, the release of news stories, books, songs, and movies portraying mistreatment of migrants in the United States could rile the Mexican public's indignation.

Caught in the Current: Mexico's Struggle to Regulate Emigration, 1940–1980 explores how Mexico navigated these choppy waters. Specifically, it chronicles the multiple complications that BP migration brought for Mexico's ruling PRI regime, both during the guest-worker program's operation and in the years following its discontinuation. Focused on the 1940s to the early 1980s, this account shows how Mexico periodically responded to the vulnerabilities created by migration by exploring and selectively instituting policies to restrain the very migratory current it helped unleash. This is the first systematic study of such "mitigatory migratory policies"—initiatives crafted or considered by Mexico to intercept, slow, or even terminate the migratory flow, and thereby blunt its deleterious side effects. Ultimately, it shows that the Mexican government struggled to arrest the migratory flow when it so wished. Mexican officials thought they had inaugurated a controllable migratory stream when they agreed to send guest workers to the United States. But over time, they found themselves trapped in a powerful current that left them little room to maneuver. In the end, the migration grew out of their control, overwhelming them and their attempted countermeasures.

Until now, academic studies have showcased how Mexico facilitated the movement of Mexicans to the United States and leveraged it.[5] Its migratory countermeasures have been downplayed. Historians are aware of instances in which Mexico espoused a desire to restrict migration. But they regard them as mere chest-thumping and "bluster": the theatrics of a government seeking to improve the treatment of its migrant guest workers by impressing upon US authorities that it could close off the migratory flow if it so wished.[6] An analysis of internal-facing government records and deliberations, however, reveals that Mexico's contramigratory politics were not merely performative. On a number of occasions, Mexican leaders conjured designs to constrain out-migration because of the blowback it generated. They felt pressed, in short, to explore and prepare alternatives. Their search led them to gradualist solutions, aimed at slowing or reducing out-migration. And also, to extreme ones, aimed at outright terminating the exodus. Previous analyses have asserted that Mexico was never at all conflicted about whether there "should be any emigration whatsoever."[7] But, periodically, as the migration generated challenges for Mexico's federal leaders, this was precisely the question that confronted them: Was it worthwhile to continue sanctioning out-migration and, if so, to what extent?

Scholars have understated Mexico's ability to operate in dual registers—catalyzing and countervailing migration—because they have pigeonholed it as a sending state wedded to out-migration. Indeed, Mexico's migration policy has often been called a safety valve. Mexico, the argument goes, purposefully released its populace to the United States to alleviate social and political tension resulting from insufficient economic growth and job opportunities.

By permitting and even prodding its nationals to migrate to the United States, Mexico dissipated social conflict.

This depiction of Mexico is based on the intuitive premise that Mexican statesmen serve their own interests. But it falters in not being cynical enough. Despite being drawn to migration and the relief it offered, Mexican leaders were also attentive to its dangers. They understood that at any point it could surge with complications for the PRI regime—through an internal labor shortage, unrest at border crossings, or reports of migrant abuse. Their approach thus easily morphed from countenancing migration to searching for ways to restrict it. The purposefully blasé governance implied by the safety valve theory was not practicable for an authoritarian one-party state that, ever attentive to its self-preservation, kept a watchful eye on mass migration to the United States.[8]

Rather than hew to one specific, well-defined approach, Mexico's migration policy was characterized by continuing adaptation throughout the twentieth century. Mexican leaders constantly hedged their bets. They craved the benefits of out-migration yet wanted to be able to modulate it and impede it altogether, if and when its downsides became untenable. In their ambiguous and waffling behavior, they were joined throughout the twentieth century by sending states the world over. Italy, China, India, and Eastern European countries also did not solely wield migration as a blunt instrument to suppress gestating domestic problems. Like Mexico, they balanced an openness and a reluctance to out-migration. Consequently, their policies could slip from encouraging migration to restricting it through punishments, incentives, or a combination of the two.[9]

The particulars varied from place to place. For some states, such as India and China, a trampled national image was the main cause of concern driving them to impede migration; for Eastern European nations, the loss of military-age men loomed as the threat. However, what they shared beyond these differences was a sense that migration was not an uncomplicated cure-all. On the contrary, it generated acute problems of its own. And these demanded monitoring, calibration, and, under sufficiently pressing scenarios, the curtailment and even cessation of the migration in question. In short, these sending states approached migration as a volatile phenomenon that demanded fluidity, not rigidity, in their policymaking.

In the case examined in this book, Mexican political leaders believed they could control out-migration—activating, deactivating, and adjusting it at will—because to them it was not an inherently international process animated solely by external factors, such as US labor demand. On the contrary, they saw it as a primarily domestic phenomenon rooted in the relationship between the Mexican state and its mobile citizens. They believed the causal chain behind mass migration began with Mexico's economic sphere, including the federal government's waning support for communal landholding among the Mexican peasantry. This being the case, the migration could be adjusted. With the right kinds of economic interventions—such as policies more supportive of peasants—Mexico could demobilize migrants, or at least restrict their mobility.

A series of Mexican presidential administrations also believed out-migration to be within their control because they possessed an authoritarian faith in their ability to negotiate acceptable outcomes with discontented interest groups. As historians have shown, the PRI monopolized state power in the postwar era by bargaining with grumbling constituencies, or failing that, violently repressing them.[10] Migrants were not straightforwardly suited to this system of governance. They were a mass social group that lacked a center of political gravity. Indeed, save some small trade unions, they had no coherent organization or leadership. Nevertheless, Mexican leaders approached migrants like any other troublesome faction. They presumed they could achieve an acceptable outcome, which in this case meant rerouting migrants away from the United States and stewarding them within Mexico when needed. To achieve this, Mexican leaders surmised that all they had to do was brainstorm, tinker with their policies, broker with migrants, and, if all else failed, intimidate them with violence.

In practice, Mexican officials overestimated their ability to seamlessly reposition their policies away from endorsing out-migration to restraining it. They were limited by internal and external factors. First, Mexican leaders were exceedingly complacent with the migration and its ill effects. They allowed them to fester. They tolerated out-migration's downsides because they wanted continued access to its boons. Hence, when out-migration resulted in crises—be it tumult at an overpopulated northern border crossing, a domestic labor shortage, or incidents of migrant mistreatment in the United States—they opted to be patient. They hoped such problems would dissipate on their own or with minimal intervention, and thus spare them from having to reformulate their original embrace of out-migration.

Their wait-and-see approach, however, allowed out-migration to grow more entrenched and resistant to Mexico's delayed adjustments. Specifically, the BP ingrained the United States as Mexican workers' desired site of employment. Vice versa, it accustomed US authorities to seeing Mexican laborers as a desirable economic input of which they could make liberal use to harvest American crops. Whenever Mexico attempted to slow the migration, it encountered this growing symbiosis between Mexican migrant labor and US capital. In the end, its pattern of belated engagement made it difficult for Mexico to slow or halt a migration that acquired volume and momentum while only loosely restrained.

Mexican leaders not only lacked timeliness. Each time they went against the current and tried to contain out-migration, their actions were frenzied. Their policymaking was sloppily experimental, guided by a desire to do anything to deal with emergent migratory crises. Born of such haste, their contramigratory interventions suffered from underdeveloped plans for implementation, oversight, and funding. Moreover, Mexican officials lacked commitment to their spur-of-the-moment ideas. They understood they were merely guessing at how to contain the migration. So, when their countermigratory ploys faced complications, they backed away from them, instead of pursuing them to their full potential.

While Mexico's mitigatory migratory measures were debilitated by the tentative approach of PRI leaders, other actors stymied them as well. In particular, when Mexican officials took an interest in restraining migration, they were vexed by the adversarial non-cooperation of two key sets of actors: US political leaders and Mexican migrants. The United States was an ever-present limiting factor. Scholars have asserted that Mexico's relationship with the United States in the post–World War II era was characterized by "cooperation and accommodation," albeit vaguely "shadowed" by an imbalance of power in favor of the United States. In this chronological arc, the United States was more "aggressive" and "uncompromising" with Mexico before World War II. Most notably, Mexico lost large swaths of land to the United States in the 1846 Mexican American War.

Certainly, after World War II, the US military did not openly intervene in Mexico and displayed a more cooperative ethos. The BP itself exemplifies a marked shift toward binational coordination. But US power following World War II was more than a mere specter looming behind an otherwise cooperative relationship. The United States definitively expressed its might and imposed its will when it looked unfavorably upon Mexican policies. It was particularly aggressive when Mexico's ruling elites deviated from sending Mexicans to the United States and mulled migratory countermeasures.

Mexican leaders hoped their American counterparts would respect their countermigratory initiatives. At their most hopeful, they believed the United States could partner with them to bring to a heel the migration they jointly catalyzed. But whereas the United States was amenable to collaborate to bring migrants to America, it sabotaged Mexican efforts to mitigate out-migration. The United States expressly derailed Mexican policies or simply refused to support them. During the supposed era of US-Mexican "cooperation," the United States hampered Mexico's countermigratory designs to ensure that the migration of cheap labor would continue, regardless of its concerning effects for Mexico.[11] The United States may have outgrown military interventionism in Mexico, but it remained willing and able to dismiss Mexico's perspective and undercut its policy-making. Mexican leaders were better able to cope with US power projections in other areas, especially by using anti-communism to repress dissent domestically. When it came to migration, they remained beholden to the United States' posture—specifically, its brazen entitlement over Mexican migrant labor and its heedless dismissal of Mexican countermigratory ploys.[12]

The United States was not the only party to inhibit Mexico's countermigratory measures. When Mexico rolled out policies to slow or halt migration, it also experienced pushback from Mexican migrants. They generally accepted Mexico's involvement in migration, as long as it was to channel them to the United States and support their labor rights as outlined in bracero contracts. For instance, through consuls, they asked Mexico for help to pursue grievances against specific employers. But when Mexico deviated from this role, questioned the sagacity of a loosely restrained out-migration, and moved to slow or impede the exodus, Mexican migrants, like the United States, reacted with limited tolerance for Mexico's attempted adjustments. They rebuffed Mexico's efforts to impede their mobility. They complained to local and national press outlets, protested in front of government buildings, and, when desperate, engaged in violent action against agents of the Mexican state.

Mexican migrants were unreserved when contending with Mexico's impingement on their mobility. They were Mexican citizens, animated by a sense that they could negotiate how the government regulated their movement. When contending with Mexico, they stood on familiar ground. They spoke the dominant language; understood the various levels of government involved in migratory regulation, from municipal presidents and local police forces on up; were not shy about contacting authorities, either in person or in writing, to protest unwanted policies; and, finally, knew how to draw in Mexican media outlets when they were dissatisfied with Mexico's intrusive handling of out-migration.

Scholars have shown migrants to be powerful practitioners of a subtle micropolitics: the small-scale, understated ways in which they negotiate their work and life conditions throughout the US-Mexican migratory circuit. For instance, they have shown that migrants developed strategies, such as writing letters to their loved ones, to endure the isolating and strenuous nature of farm labor in the United States. And they have shown how migrants delicately carved out spaces of personal autonomy by engaging in leisure activities even as US and Mexican authorities were trying to reduce them to their labor inputs.[13] However, while migrants certainly tapped into strategies of forbearance and carefully constructed spheres of personal freedom—especially in the United States, where they were politically delimited as guest workers and undocumented laborers—as Mexican citizens they were outwardly assertive and unabashed when confronted with Mexican policies that frustrated their passage to the United States. They repudiated such contramigratory policies and, by doing so, contributed to their breakdown.

TRACING MEXICO'S CAPITULATION TO OUT-MIGRATION

In retrospect, it is clear that Mexican leaders set themselves on a challenging path when they agreed to convey workers to the United States under the BP. They sent braceros off, believing they could make extemporaneous adjustments to their migration policy whenever necessary to protect the nation and party from its repercussions. This included limiting out-migration and ending it altogether. But the logics of facilitating and restricting out-migration were fundamentally at cross currents. And it was perennially difficult for Mexico to undo what it had wrought.

Spanning four decades, *Caught in the Current* traces how Mexico was gradually overcome by the migratory phenomenon it helped stimulate. In particular, it shows how Mexico lost faith in its ability to course correct and direct migrants internally. The book moves through three eras of Mexican migratory policy, from its peak confidence as an orchestrator of movement after World War II to its vanished conviction by the end of the century.

The first era explored by *Caught in the Current*, 1942–54, is the period of "autonomous flexibility." During this time, Mexico approached migration as if it held full, ultimate sovereignty over it and had the latitude to alter it by calibrating its domestic policies. The basis for Mexican leaders' enlarged sense of autonomy was the bilateral agreement that established the guest-worker program in 1942 as well as the negotiations leading up to it. President Manuel Ávila Camacho rebuffed various US entreaties for a guest-worker accord, deeming them to have insufficient labor protections. After negotiations, he assented to the first of several treaties that constitute the BP. Each of the individual treaties, however, was programmed with a termination date and depended on Mexico's express consent for their reestablishment. Neither Camacho nor the presidential administrations to follow forgot this, or the broader principle that Mexico's consent to guest work was contingent on the migration's avoiding the excessive externalities that the worker protections aimed to prevent.

Despite Mexico's caution, during the first twelve years of the BP's operation, the largest recurring problem for the PRI was precisely the mistreatment of Mexican workers in the United States. It undermined the party's image as a champion of Mexico's peasantry and common people. For this reason, in 1948 and more decisively still in 1954, Mexico leaned on its autonomy and decided not to renew the treaty behind the BP. Scholars have read these two moments mostly through the lens of negotiation, as interregnums during which Mexico attempted to secure more reliable protections for Mexican workers in a renegotiated guest-worker agreement. Such an outcome was indeed palatable to Mexican officials. But because the United States was unwilling to make sufficient concessions, they also explored the need to end the migration altogether, especially in 1954.[14] On this occasion, Mexico did not just rely on diplomatic channels to gain bolstered migrant protections. Given the extent to which migrant mistreatment in the United States had become a politically damaging trope in Mexican music, movies, and journalism of the early 1950s, the government explored a future without mass migration.

For Mexico, there was no inconsistency in exploring diametrically opposed possibilities: a revamped BP agreement or the ending of migration. The prospect that US negotiators would agree to sufficiently strengthened protections for Mexican migrants was tenuous. Mexico's most-desired change, the ability to suspend abusive American employers unilaterally without having to consult the United States first, was not welcomed by American growers or their political allies. A vast increase in Mexico's disciplining power over growers would, in their view, inject too much uncertainty into what was supposed to be a predictable and fluid system of labor exploitation propped up by the BP. Given US reticence, Mexican leaders thus gravitated toward nixing migration. In speeches and public remarks, they assumed responsibility for integrating Mexicans within the country. In terms of policy, they began to consider and implement the kinds of measures they argued would root Mexicans internally and reduce their desire to leave. In this way, Mexico could present itself as a polity that did not idly tolerate abusive migration.

The scope of the Mexican government's contramigratory exploration was particularly pronounced, privately and publicly, in 1954. Among the key highlights, the administration of Adolfo Ruiz Cortines considered establishing a new federal agency whose sole purpose would be to remove Mexicans' underlying need to emigrate. The private consideration of this and other measures was complemented by the Cortines administration's publicly unveiling of a campaign dubbed "The Braceros of Mexico for the Fields of Mexico." It aimed to create avenues of permanence for Mexicans by bolstering domestic public works programs that would provide jobs for migrants. It also launched internal resettlement campaigns through which migrants could settle into state-supported colonies. As the initiative's name suggests, the PRI also tried to mobilize nationalist sentiment, and not just incentives, to generate a migratory countercurrent moving within rather than outside of Mexico. With its rhetoric, Mexico attempted to make permanence within the country into a patriotic virtue. Ultimately, it also used its army to contain migrants forcibly and violently at key ports of exit, principally in Mexicali, Baja California, in keeping with its "soft" authoritarian strategy of intermixing incentives with repression.

Mexican attempts to be flexible, and promote rootedness and internal mobility, instead of signing a new BP accord, came to naught in 1954. Key factions in the United States and among migrants opted not to comply with Mexico's efforts to circumscribe migration. In their recalcitrance, they showed Mexico the limits of its presumed sovereignty to adjust its domestic policy and keep migrants in Mexico. Specifically, the US Department of Labor (DOL) and later the US Congress protected growers in Southern California who, due to the nonrenewal of the BP, were in peril of losing their lettuce crop. To urgently acquire workers, the United States waived customary border inspections of migrants and allowed US companies to hire them without Mexico's consent or involvement. This loosening of admission and hiring standards was dubbed unilateral hiring by the United States. Mexico regarded it as the institution of a malicious "open-border" policy.

Whatever the nomenclature, the US decision in 1954 prompted thousands of Mexican migrants, especially at the Mexicali border with Southern California, to challenge Mexico's restrictions on their mobility and its proposition that it could find a place for them within the country. Using the governor of Baja California, a former migrant himself, as a mediator, the Cortines administration attempted to calm Mexican migrants. But after repeated violent clashes between the migrants and a combined outfit of Mexicali police and federal military personnel, Mexico relented. Cortines dispatched Mexico's Ministry of Foreign Affairs to work intensively on reestablishing the BP and thus end the embarrassment of migrants rejecting the PRI's nationalistic discourse and migrant-demobilization program to instead submit to degrading work in the United States. The episode revealed Mexico's premise—that it could control migration at will by relying on its resources and machinations—to be a chimera.

The buildup and climax of Mexico's era of "autonomous flexibility," spanning the years 1942–54, are described in the first portion of the book and include chapters 1–3. Chapters 4–7 chronicle the next period in Mexico's mitigatory migratory politics: the era of "dependent channeling," which lasted from 1954 to the early 1980s. Some historical accounts have seen this as a period of decline. In this view, after 1954 Mexico slid into irrelevance as a migratory regulator. After the United States strong-armed the Mexican government into a new treaty, it sidelined it and disregarded its concerns, supposedly obviating it as a force in the migration.[15]

Certainly, Mexico's contramigratory policies would never again reach the nationalistic zenith they did in 1954. But Mexico's agency over migration was transformed rather than dissipated following its clash with the United States. PRI presidencies from 1954 onward continued to believe they could modulate the migration to soften its fallout. However, whereas in 1954 Mexico challenged the United States and sought to build up its internal strength—politically, economically, and militarily—to retain Mexican migrants, after 1954 it accepted its weakness vis-à-vis the United States, and attempted to develop countermigratory measures that acknowledged and even leveraged the power imbalance between Mexico and the United States.

The first major initiative marking the onset of the era of dependent channeling was inaugurated in 1955, a year into Mexico's presumed slide into irrelevance. At the behest of cotton growers operating in Northern Mexico, President Cortines unveiled a program that would redirect US-bound braceros to harvest cotton within Mexico. The cotton growers had long complained that it was difficult to recruit workers to Northern Mexico. In their telling, migrants only journeyed through the region, not to the region, their desired destination being the United States. For this reason, growers reacted optimistically when Mexico suspended the migration in 1954 and seemed poised to promote countermigratory reforms. They supposed Mexico's adopting such measures might bring an end to their alleged labor shortage.

After Cortines capitulated to a new BP following the open-border incident, growers advocated for a workaround. It would leave the renewed guest-worker program and the United States' supply of migrants undisturbed yet still solve their labor problem. With the help of powerful political allies, such as Governor Álvaro Obregón Tapia of Sonora, they successfully pitched their solution. The federal government could encourage migrants to work in Northern Mexico by promising them expedited bracero contracts to the United States if, in exchange, they worked a stint domestically. Migrants were to toil for two weeks in Northern Mexico, or until they harvested twenty-one kilos of cotton. When they were finished, the cotton grower would provide them with a document attesting to their service. With that paper, Mexican officials at bracero migrant processing centers were to give those migrants priority exit to the United States by bumping them up in the lists of guest workers due to depart. With this ploy, Mexican officials harnessed the US-bound migratory flow to counteract a localized domestic labor shortage.

The Cortines administration was particularly receptive to helping Northern Mexico's cotton companies with an internal Bracero Program (IBP) because the mid-to-late 1950s witnessed a rise in global demand for cotton and the end of a drought that had previously constrained productivity. Notwithstanding these tailwinds, the initiative was mired in issues that would lead President Adolfo López Mateos, Cortines's successor, to shutter it in 1963. This time, the United States was not the immediate cause for the failure of Mexico's mitigatory migratory measure. American growers continued to receive their allotment of braceros, so they had no motive to derail Mexico's program. Nor did another plausible culprit, cotton growers, introduce problems for the Mexican government by falling into patterns of migrant abuse.[16] Their reliance on Mexico's intervention encouraged them to keep their behavior in check. President Mateos discarded the initiative because of mismanagement and corruption by local staffers and federal appointees, which rendered the IBP a source of aggravation and disrepute for his administration.

Migrants, sometimes acting as individuals, sometimes as groups, were front and center in critiquing the IBP and the unfairness they felt it introduced to their lives. Communicating with officials they imagined might be responsive, and with regional and national newspapers, they complained of broken promises. Migration officials, they alleged, systematically failed to honor the agreement to send them to the United States as braceros following their service to Northern Mexico cotton growers. Corrupt authorities sold spots in the guest-worker program to whomever could pay their price. In addition, migrants lured internally to Sinaloa, Sonora, Baja California, and Tamaulipas by the promise of eventual passage abroad bemoaned the cold, hunger, and sickness they had to endure in Northern Mexico cities that were ill-prepared for their arrival and prolonged stay. Prior to the IBP's existence, many migrants spent only a short time in Northern Mexico before departing to the United States with a bracero contract or, failing that, as undocumented migrants. With the more protracted stay implied by their participation in the program, they came to depend more heavily on the social services of the borderlands, which were in very short supply. Despite attempts by the Mateos administration to tighten oversight of the IBP and amplify social supports for migrants, their complaints continued. By 1963, President Mateos's administration reasoned growers should furnish themselves with workers rather than externalize that task, its perceived headaches, and the public relations blowback to the federal government.

Despite Mexico's travails with the IBP, its operation speaks to the government's openness after 1954 to orchestrate migrants internally for the sake of Northern Mexico's businesses. The IBP also shows Mexico deviating from its chest-thumping nationalism of 1954 and instead pragmatically adapting to its economic subordination. Mexico accepted the United States as migrants' desired destination, only seeking to incorporate Northern Mexico as a pitstop.

The IBP's accommodationist spirit was immediately echoed in the well-known Border Industrialization Program (BIP) of 1965, continuing Mexico's era of dependent channeling. Through the BIP, Mexico recruited foreign companies, mostly from the United States, to open factories in Northern Mexico cities, such as Tijuana and Ciudad Juárez, by offering them tax abatements and easy access to cheap labor. Mexico's aim was to provide jobs for the surge of idle workers that developed in Northern Mexico following US termination of the BP in 1964. The BP was terminated by the US Congress because high-profile labor abuses made it unpopular. But its end provoked a new humanitarian and political crisis, albeit in Mexico. Migrants, no longer able to enter the United States as braceros, increasingly concentrated along Mexico's northern reaches. They meandered there, looking for a way into the United States, with limited personal resources. Their increasingly long stays, numbers, and immiseration led to concerns in Northern Mexico that they were dirty, criminal, reliant on social services, and potentially restive. Hence, Mexico opened up industrial parks in Northern Mexico and invited US manufacturers to occupy them, hoping to provide jobs for the Mexican migrants who arrived in Northern Mexico after the BP's termination.

Caught in the Current does not undertake a narrative history of the industrialization program, which has been well chronicled by scholars. They have analyzed how American manufacturing was lured by the BIP, leaving US industrial cities to languish. And they have analyzed how the BIP contributed to a feminization of Mexico's industrial workforce because US companies hired women and not just the unemployed men Mexico was concerned with.[17] What this project does is convey the BIP's context. In the literature, it appears as a free-floating, one-off policy to address the end of the BP. But, in truth, it was connected to a larger genealogy of mitigatory migratory measures. Like the IBP before it, it belonged to the era of dependent channeling, during which Mexico sought to soften migration's downsides by leveraging, instead of defying, its economic subordination to the United States.

To close the period of dependent channeling, the book reappraises the history of Mexico in the 1970s and early 1980s. Chroniclers have argued that Mexico toggled to a safety valve strategy during this period, accepting out-migration without qualification. Indeed, it is said that a political culture supportive of out-migration flourished in Mexico.[18] In contrast, this account argues that what flourished during this period—in which the BP was no longer active and undocumented migration boomed—were sensationalist reports in Mexican and US media of migrants being mistreated in the United States. These reports intimated that migrants to the United States were subject to more extreme forms of exploitation when not under the protection of a guest-worker program. This backdrop of constant migrant suffering in the United States foreclosed Mexico's ability to embrace out-migration.

Certainly, Mexico intermittently lobbied the United States for a new guest-worker program to see if it could protect migrants that way. But Mexican leaders quickly realized their US counterparts had no interest in a new BP. The program had ended in disrepute and advances in mechanized agriculture had eased US agribusinesses' need for a mass guest-worker program. Faced with abuse of migrants and US disinterest in a rehashed BP, Mexican leaders explored countermigratory alternatives. They formulated ideas to promote the rootedness of Mexicans. And, befitting the era of dependent channeling, while they looked to their domestic policy levers, they also sought to enlist US help.

Luis Echeverría's presidency, beginning in 1970, was key. His administration sporadically lobbied for a guest-worker program on the off chance the United States might agree. But following various rejections, his administration focused more on how to convince Mexicans to stay in Mexico, understanding that inaction and reliance on a US change of heart would not suffice to deal with publicized cases of migrant abuse. Most notably, the Echeverría administration performed a much-trumpeted, multiyear assessment of Mexican migration to ascertain its demographics and underpinnings. Mexican officials tasked with the inquiry repeatedly articulated that their mandate from Echeverría was to eradicate the migration and thus the indignities suffered by Mexicans abroad. Responsible officials offered public updates to signal that the administration was continually attentive to the need to taper off migration. Their main findings specified localized economic need as the core issue prompting Mexican nationals to depart. So, they recommended that Echeverría institute reforms to expand economic opportunities for peasant and working-class people in Mexico, focusing on key locales. Only in this way, they argued, could Mexico neutralize the perennial economic attractiveness of the United States to migrants.

Yet to achieve that economic revamping of working-class and peasant conditions, officials ultimately underscored that Mexico would have to draw on US economic power and collaboration. This affirms the book's narrative that Mexican policies to contain the migration from 1955 to the 1970s existed within a context of dependency. Specifically, President Echeverría and his successor, José López Portillo, aggressively sought tariff relief for Mexican exports to the United States. They made trade policy into migration policy. They argued that Mexico could only absorb its migrant population if Mexican goods became more affordable in the US market. In this logic, lower tariffs would heighten US demand for Mexican products and justify increased production, resulting in plentiful better-paying jobs in Mexico.

Given the extremity of some cases of migrant mistreatment, Mexican officials sometimes pretended they possessed full autonomy over migration and could stymie it—and the associated humiliations—through self-reliant policies. But, by and large, by the mid to late 1970s, Mexico admitted a need for US cooperation. The only path to a deep-reaching economic transformation to moor migrants internally, Mexican leaders conceded, was to rely on the United States. However, despite varied entreaties, their attempts to enlist the United States as an economic partner to counteract mass migration were largely fruitless. The Nixon, Ford, and Carter administrations were not particularly interested in banding together to create jobs in Mexico through pronounced tariff adjustments.

US leaders favored a more draconian approach to contend with the migration they, like Mexico, had once promoted through the BP. They increasingly militarized the border and persecuted migrants with the Border Patrol. Through these punitive deterrence strategies, they signaled to the American public their supposed seriousness about defending America's borders. Not only did the United States not aid Mexico economically, but it also added to the humanitarian spectacle Mexico hoped to avoid when it entreated the United States for binational economic reforms.

By the early 1980s, Mexico moved out of the era of dependent channeling and into an era of "disembodied manipulation." This period, well-studied in the social sciences, is narrated in the book's conclusion. Facing numerous domestic crises, including inflation, a peso devaluation, and a demographic boom, Mexican presidents from Miguel de la Madrid onward abandoned the idea that bending migrants back toward their homeland was possible or desirable. More unabashedly than their predecessors, they accepted the necessity of mass migration from Mexico, whatever its undersides.

However, even though Mexico gave up on moving people about, its mitigatory policies did not fully collapse. Mexico latched onto the more abstract aspects of migration it could still toy with. To capture part of the income generated by its diaspora in the United States and use it for societal improvements, Mexico encouraged migrant remittances back home. Through its so-called two-for-one program, it promised to supplement every peso sent by a migrant back to their municipality with a peso of federal support. This money was to fund improvements in infrastructure, local resources, public spaces, and the like, such that mass migration might bring the improvement rather than erosion of local quality of life in Mexico.[19]

Put differently, Mexico tried to limit the ever-increasing migration from becoming a drain on the country by setting aside any idea about cajoling back the departing populace and focusing on the more feasible plan of repatriating their earnings. In the last era of Mexico's mitigation policies, the country's focus shifted to manipulating the flow of remittance money, straying far from the state's earlier focus on corporeal migrants—their physical presence, their patterns of mobility, and the policies needed to marshal them within the country. In effect, Mexican officials largely surrendered to the migratory flow and no longer treated it as a navigable phenomenon. They were caught in the current.

CHAPTER ONE

PROPER CHANNELS

The Promises and Perils of a Planned Migration, 1942–1953

Mexico and the United States share a long, tortured history of managing the migration of Mexican people. The first formal entreaty by the United States for Mexican nationals came during World War I. The departure of American men to join the fighting depleted the American Southwest, in particular agricultural and railroad industries, of available laborers. The United States thus turned to its southern neighbor, seeking to import Mexican males to the United States. Mexico acceded. The BP of 1917 represented the first agreement between the two nations for the allotment of migrant workers to the United States.[1] The recruited migrants were to work in agriculture and railroads, as well as in public utilities, including roads and military labor camps.

Because tumult plagued Mexico in the late 1910s—the Mexican Revolution was being fought intensely—the groundbreaking agreement was negotiated not by a sitting president but by Mexican consuls in US border states.

It fell under the management of Venustiano Carranza once he was elected president under the Mexican Constitution of 1917. Carranza disapproved of exporting Mexicans to the United States, given reports of US anti-Mexican sentiment, poor working conditions, and the drafting of Mexican nationals into the US Army. Mexicans' fear of being enlisted in the US Army was strong enough that it drove many of them to abandon the United States in 1918. Meanwhile, Carranza's government discouraged migrants from departing by warning them that travails awaited them in the United States. It also encouraged migrants living in the United States to voluntarily repatriate.[2] Nonetheless, the guest-worker program endured through the war, bringing 75,000 Mexicans to the United States, more than half of whom stayed permanently.[3]

The Mexican population produced by the first BP expanded following Mexico's 1920s Cristero War, a conflict between western Mexican peasants and the state that led to mass dislocations in Mexico. Mexican settlements germinated across the US Southwest, concentrated in marginalized urban areas, such as the unincorporated community of East Los Angeles in California and the West Side in San Antonio, Texas, and in rural outposts near agricultural fields, including near the Sacramento, San Joaquin, and Kern Rivers in Central California.[4]

This burgeoning Mexican presence was stifled by the United States in the 1930s. It deported 2.5 million Mexicans back to their presumptive homeland. Its expulsion campaign often made no distinction between foreign-born Mexican nationals and their US-born children who possessed US citizenship. The mass expulsion of Mexicans was motivated by the Great Depression. With the United States gripped by economic malaise, the American public and elected officials used Mexicans as scapegoats. Calls to deport Mexicans predated the Great Depression, but it was only then that growers who benefited from their labor proved unable to rebuff nativist pressures to repatriate people of Mexican origin.[5]

The 1930s amounted to a moratorium on Mexican migration to the United States, one that ended only once US interest in Mexican workers was rekindled by World War II. In an echo of World War I, intensified US wartime production and enlistment of American men into the military called for a reorganization of the nation's labor force. At this time, women entered the workforce en masse, memorialized by the "Rosie the Riveter" archetype of a young white woman donning blue-collar clothes and soldering. Rosie was a stand-in for women carrying out "men's work," such as welding, assembling, and machine operation in industrial factories and shipyards.[6] This gendered reorganization of the labor force was not enough. The United States invoked Mexico to ally with it in the war against Nazism and fascism by providing it with male laborers.

As in World War I, Mexican laborers were once again sought to work as temporary guest workers in railroads and agriculture, primarily harvesting crops such as tomatoes, lettuce, strawberries, sugar beets, lemons, melons, asparagus, grapes, bush berries, and dry beans.[7] This time, however, the US-Mexican agreement was negotiated and administered by the ruling party that had consolidated power after the Mexican Revolution. The party originated in 1929 under President Plutarco Elías Calles as the Partido Nacional Revolucionario (National Revolutionary Party). It was renamed the Partido de la Revolución Mexicana (Party of the Mexican Revolution) in 1938 and finally became the PRI in 1946. During the presidency of Lázaro Cárdenas (1934–40), the party solidified its control through a corporatist model in which key interest groups were formally recognized by the state and, in return, operated within its framework, channeling their demands through controlled negotiations rather than open opposition.[8] This more consolidated Mexican government was wary of sending laborers to the United States, sharing much of Carranza's earlier apprehensiveness. But it ultimately assented to the United States' request, framing it as a temporary contribution to the Allied effort in World War II. The first guest workers to participate in the BP understood its existence in these terms. They boarded trains to the United States flashing smiles and "V for Victory" gestures. Their loved ones bid them farewell as heroes.[9] The Mexican government added that the program would catalyze Mexico's economic modernization, holding the first selections of migrants in open-air stadiums to underscore their importance.[10]

Despite Mexico's bold rhetoric regarding the BP, it was cautious. Mexican negotiators sought to limit the extent to which leasing workers to the United States could hurt either the country's socioeconomic order or the ruling party's image. On the first count, Mexico limited the source and number of men who could partake in the BP. It sought to ensure that none of the nation's pillars—industrial production, commercial agriculture, and peasant communal landholding—would be harmed by out-migration. On the second, Mexico curtailed US growers' ability to abuse migrants. Mexican officials, foreseeing unfavorable publicity, mandated that employers obey minimum standards in food, lodging, compensation, and insurance for migrant workers.

Despite the safeguards Mexico erected to limit peril to its economic order and the party's standing, the BP inspired discontent. Dissatisfaction with the migration emanated from multiple focal points in Mexico's socioeconomic order, including labor unions, communal landholders, large agribusinesses, and the Catholic Church. In the migration's first decade, the nominal leaders of these sectors used their perches to critique it. The most notable countervailing forces to migration, however, came from none of these sectors, which emphasized migration as a particular problem for them and the interests they represented. Instead, the most important critics were those who worked in politics, cultural production, and the media. They criticized the BP and the undocumented migration it fomented from a moral perspective, decrying the substandard treatment of Mexicans in the United States.

These critics decentered the Mexican social and economic order as the object of concern. Instead, they spotlighted Mexican males, sometimes real, sometimes fictional, toiling away in the United States under American employers who flouted the BP's labor protections. Their moralistic critique of out-migration disabused the Mexican public of both governments' grandiose framing. Moreover, their insistence that the migration besieged the nation's dignity provided Mexicans with a shared, emotional basis from which to oppose out-migration.

Over time, outrage inspired by the emasculation of migrant workers rendered it increasingly indefensible for Mexico. Newspaper exposés of how US growers handled Mexicans—and their echo in cultural products such as movies and songs—destroyed the grandiloquent framing of the BP and left standing a lurid picture of migratory tribulations. By the mid-1950s, the metamorphosis of the BP from a program of migrant exaltation to one of migrant humiliation would lead the Mexican state to question whether it could continue facilitating out-migration. The question would trickle down socially, with concerned Mexican observers issuing calls for Mexico to embrace pro-permanence policies.

ON GUARD

Mexico's accession to the BP was studied. Prompted by US interest in a guestworker program, the Mexican president during most of World War II, Manuel Ávila Camacho, ordered a study of the benefits and potential downsides of institutionalizing out-migration. The Mexican government's guardedness had many reasons. Given that the government was well established and enjoyed popular support, it had little need to send Mexican men to the United States and risk creating the damaging perception it could not provide for them. Moreover, there was a sense in the ruling party that Mexico would soon need to use its labor capacity. Though unemployment remained a problem, the Camacho administration believed the modernization and mechanization of agriculture would transform the peasant and commercial agricultural economies and require all hands on deck. This was the argument made by Undersecretary of Foreign Affairs Jaime Torres Bodet to US ambassador to Mexico George Messersmith in early 1942 when Mexico turned down the first US request for migrant labor. Mexico could not release them. Soon enough, he assured the United States, they would be employed internally.[11]

Mexico was only to become amenable to the BP once it became a US ally in World War II. In the early years of the war, Mexico embraced strategic neutrality. Camacho's predecessor, Lázaro Cárdenas, who governed Mexico from 1934 to 1940, had expropriated and nationalized oil fields in Mexico from foreign entities, including from the United States and Great Britain. To keep them from retaliating, he had left the door open to an alliance with the Axis powers. His strategy worked. US president Franklin Delano Roosevelt resisted pressure from affected American oil companies, which lobbied for a reversal of Mexico's oil nationalization or a reimbursement for their losses. Mexico was able to hold off for years on paying restitution to the oil companies. Whereas Mexico expropriated oil fields in 1938, the final repayment agreement was reached in 1942, with $9 million to be paid at once, and the other $20 million in installments.[12]

By not bullying Mexico into immediate repayment, FDR aimed to display amicability and keep Mexico from drifting to the Axis. The success of oil nationalization was important to Mexico's ruling party, which used it, alongside programs of land redistribution, to cement its popular rule. But it was only when Mexico was hit by the Germans later in 1942—much like the United States was struck by the Japanese at Pearl Harbor in 1941—that it united with the United States in World War II and entertained its entreaties for Mexican labor. The Germans pushed Mexico and its resources toward the United States unintentionally. Hitler's regime had also sought an alliance with Mexico. But it spoiled any potential for that when it inadvertently struck Mexican oil operations. On two consecutive occasions in May 1942, German U-boats sank Mexican oil tankers carrying petroleum off the Atlantic coast. Mexico had obtained the tankers during oil nationalization. In both cases, the Nazis misidentified the flag flying on the ships. The attacks drove Mexico to declare war against the Axis powers and add its contribution to the war effort, migrant labor included.[13]

Betraying a lingering trepidation, President Camacho assigned a commission to again study the US proposal for a temporary guest-worker program. The commission highlighted two upsides. One was the elevation of Mexico as a country making a substantive contribution to the fight for democracy against fascism, giving a sheen to the Mexican government's image. Second was that migrants, upon returning from the world's most advanced economy, would bring with them trailblazing farming techniques, which they could use to improve production in Mexico.14

On the negative side, however, the commission reiterated the enduring jeopardy of out-migration. One was the potential for mistreatment of emigrants in the United States, which would harm the Mexican government since it would be held responsible for their debasement. The committee stressed the lingering memory of the mass expulsion of the 1930s, as a sign of the low regard in which Americans held Mexicans and what could be expected now if US employers were not held to strict safeguards. The second hitch was that migration could retard Mexican economic development. While the committee thought the migration could be good for each individual migrant, their household, and their yearly earnings, it seemed that leaking a large swath of the nation's population and redirecting it from other potentially useful activities in Mexico, such as work in fields, could inhibit the aura, vigor, and development of some parts of the Mexican economic fabric.15 The concerns were shared by the Mexican secretary of labor and the secretary of agriculture, who advised against inaugurating the migration.16

But the allure of collaborating with the United States to defeat the escalating Nazi threat, and the plan's seemingly temporary nature, drove Mexico to accept the US request to arrange a guest-worker migration in support of American agricultural industries suffering from a labor shortage. President Camacho reached an accord with FDR in the summer of 1942. At a press conference about the BP on October 20, 1942, FDR announced that the provision of Mexican laborers was an "important role that our Mexican allies can and are taking in the war of production. . . . The inevitable success of our military program depends [on it]."17

But Mexico's accession was not without reservation. Mexico did not wish to be powerless to address migration, as it had been during the 1930s mass repatriation.18 Key requisites and protections for migrants were enshrined in the final agreement. Migrants provided by Mexico were exempted from onerous restrictions applied to the entry of outsiders into the United States, including the screening of individuals who were "likely to become a public charge" because of a lack of savings or mental incapacity.19 Moreover, Mexico was to conduct the background assessment of BP candidates. US border personnel would focus on containing communicable diseases.

In addition to a lightened entry process, the contours of migrant work were defined to limit their exploitation. Workers were guaranteed work for 75 percent of their contract's duration, which was set at six months. They were assured the same wages as US citizens working in their particular industry and region. They were, in no case, to be paid a wage less than thirty cents per hour. They were promised housing, arranged either privately by the farm operator or by the Department of War, and to be given hygienic living conditions. They were to receive medical attention on-site, with a physical facility present at each labor camp. And they were covered with worker's insurance, in case they should suffer a work-related injury.[20] It surprised Mexican officials that they should have to ask for the last protection—worker's insurance—since this was mandated in Mexico's labor law.[21]

Finally, to shield Mexican migrants from grave mistreatment, Texas growers were initially excluded from the BP, given their record of discrimination against people of Mexican origin. Mexican negotiators were firm on this count, even as growers, their representatives, and the US State Department tried to lure them into reconsidering. The Texas Legislature passed a law offering protection to Mexican people regardless of country of birth. Called the "Caucasian Race Resolution," or the House Concurrent Resolution 105, it passed the Texas State Legislature in 1943 and bestowed protections to Mexicans as a white group, banning discrimination against them in "all public places of business or amusement."[22]

Thanks to the wartime context, the United States entered the BP agreement without much public debate. Discussion was limited to cross-departmental conversation, with the DOL and State Department contributing opinions.[23] They too stressed that Mexican migrants should be protected. The DOL sought to prevent the importation of a vulnerable workforce, so attractive to growers that it would permanently displace US workers. It figured the contractual obligations to braceros would make the BP play out as a reasonable response to a temporary labor scarcity, and not as a permanent dislocation of American laborers. Meanwhile, the State Department wished for braceros to be treated in accordance with treaty protections. Mistreatment could unnecessarily alienate Mexico as a hemispheric ally.[24]

The second layer of defenses woven into the BP concerned Mexico's economic system. Mexico was watchful not to compromise the country's major economic workings. One consideration for Mexican officials was that the migration not be a permanent population drain. The Mexican government directed municipal governors, who handled the enrollment of Mexicans into the BP, to give priority to family men. The presumption was that Mexicans with wives and children were likelier to return to Mexico when their contract was finished, instead of violating the agreement's terms and becoming permanent undocumented migrants.[25] The Mexican state withheld 10 percent of migrants' wages, to be released to them upon returning to Mexico.

In addition to promoting migrants' eventual return, Mexico restricted the enrollment of Northern Mexicans. It sought to leave intact the pool of laborers available to enterprises based in the states of Baja California, Tamaulipas, Coahuila, and Sonora, a region specializing in labor-intensive agricultural commodities. Indeed, growers and corporations based in Northern Mexico cultivated crops similar to those in Texas and California, including fruits, vegetables, and cotton. However, they offered meager wages and struggled to attract laborers. The exclusion of Northern Mexicans from the BP in theory protected the region's enterprises. The Ministry of Labor and Social Welfare was charged with overseeing this stipulation.[26]

Members of communally held lands, known as ejidos, could not enroll in the program. Aspiring emigrants had to offer proof they were not members of an ejido. The ejido was a system of land tenure and redistribution in Mexico that was institutionalized following the Mexican Revolution (1910–20). Through it, the government gave stewardship of specific parcels of land to groups of Mexican citizens. They were to live on their allotment and exploit it. The ejido was the flagship program of Mexico's ruling party. Its claims to being "revolutionary" were in large part based on offering peasants a change of fortunes after decades of living under a system that accumulated lands in the hands of a few powerful landowners who controlled vast estates known as latifundios.

Cementing the centrality of the ejido, prior to the BP, President Lázaro Cárdenas carried out an extensive campaign of land redistribution during his term (1934–40). He sought to fulfill the promise in the Constitution of 1917 to "break up latifundios, develop smallholding, [and] create new centers of agriculturally based people."[27] In effect, the governing party was discursively and programmatically tied to the ejido when the BP was inaugurated. Migrants wishing to become braceros would need official proof, obtained from their local municipality, that they were not members of an ejido, and thus not abandoning the crux of the postrevolutionary order to become migrant wageworkers.[28]

Finally, the emigration was largely limited to Central Mexican states. Mexican officials thought these states, unlike northern ones, could afford to temporarily release Mexican laborers. Nonetheless, they wanted the seepage of laborers to be controlled. In particular, recruitment was to be related to unemployment figures in Central Mexico, specifically to that of each municipality. Municipalities were made responsible for this calculation and for determining how much manpower they could afford to release. In this way, the migratory lane the BP opened up was designed to relieve unemployment in the area without depleting the regional labor pool available to industrial manufacturers.

Mexico was wary of undermining its industrial manufacturing. Starting in the 1930s, amid the Great Depression, the sector became a leading national economic engine. From 1930 to 1940, industrial manufacturing accounted for 38 percent of the country's economic growth, thanks to countercyclical measures adopted by Mexico during the Depression. Mexico stimulated needed economic activity by increasing the money supply and running budget deficits. Domestic manufacturing also blossomed because of a devaluation of the peso in the 1930s. As imported goods became more expensive, Mexican demand for domestically produced industrial goods increased.[29] Historically, Mexican industrialization is associated with President Miguel Alemán and his eventual 1946 project of import-substitution industrialization, which intensified Mexico's support for domestic manufacturing by weaning the country off select imports. But Mexican industrialization was well underway by the 1930s and, on paper, its rise was not to be imperiled by the BP excessively depleting Mexico of its laborers.[30]

Mexico thus fashioned for itself a role as a cautious broker of outmigration. By guarding against the mistreatment of Mexican workers and possible economic harms, the Mexican government could trumpet its upsides: the BP would help democracy survive and bring Mexico close to modernity. In its directives to municipalities, the ruling party mandated that these aspects be underscored to potential recruits. By their stoop labor, migrants were to become agents of Mexican modernization and the world's struggle for democracy, their labor turned into an engine of history.[31] FDR, meanwhile, framed the BP for his US audience as he reported the arrival of the first Mexican migrants: "With great enthusiasm, [they] have marked their trains with banners expressing their eagerness to serve the democratic cause."[32]

MIGRATION AND ITS DISCONTENTS

Given that Mexico's leaders were torn about the BP's merits, it is little wonder it inspired social discontent, despite its protections for guest workers and various parts of the national economic fabric. The state-sanctioned migration drew disapproval from the nominal leaders of union, ejido, and business sectors worried about its practical economic impacts. Meanwhile, activists, journalists, and cultural producers looked past the migration's veneer to expose braceros' substandard work conditions. By the mid-1950s, the second vein of criticism would bring the PRI-led government to reconsider its backing of a migration that harmed its propeasant image.

Displeasure with the migration appeared in sporadic fashion in the years following the BP's inauguration. The nominal leaders of religious, business, agrarian, and labor sectors were most prominent in their criticism of the exodus, which they saw as dangerous to the interests they represented. Major players in Mexico could hardly miss its scale. It was a scene that began in Central Mexico, the country's major expulsive region, and its capital, Mexico City. Once the BP was underway, migrants who had been selected in their hometown municipality would arrive in Mexico City by the thousands, line up at selected locations, and meet with Department of Migration officials to be formally inducted into the BP. From there, the "spectacle," as newspapers often described it, moved to the border, as migrants were shuttled to recruitment centers to be doused, examined, and transferred to the United States. Migrant demand for the BP—exemplified by the long lines and waits at protocolary stops—turned the migration into a slow-moving, hypervisible national parade.[33]

Leaders of the Catholic Church in Mexico voiced displeasure with the country spilling its population into the United States. The church was not only a cultural paradigm; its centrality was literal, with Catholic churches dotting town centers, exerting a looming influence over townspeople and everyday life. Though the church did not exert formal political power—those days were long gone after the clerical fights of the early twentieth century—it still held sway, as a voice of moral sanction for the actions of Mexican people and the Mexican government. It also maintained communication with Mexican officials.[34] The church's position was that conveying throngs of men to the United States was imprudent because it weakened Mexican families. The departure of males, who were often heads of household, left families without leaders. The church was not critical of migrants choosing to emigrate. Its displeasure was with a federal government it alleged did not exploit the nation's resources properly. It bewildered church leaders that in "a country like ours, with so many unexploited resources, our sons have to leave their fatherland to look for work in strange lands." There were realistic bases for "all to have employment"—and for Mexican families to have present, male leaders.

The church also castigated employers for their role in enfeebling Mexican families, maintaining that employers were unnecessarily parsimonious in sharing their bounty with Mexican workers. Thinking only of themselves, alleged the church, employers "discuss work like it were a mere piece of merchandise and the worker himself like he was a mere source of energy." With this thinking, it was no wonder they lowballed workers, and left them yearning for the wages that might be earned in the United States. The government and employers alike needed to recognize "the eminent dignity of the worker" if the Mexican male-led family was to endure.[35]

Meanwhile, the country's chief labor union was not in favor of the BP either. Founded in 1939, the Confederación de Trabajadores de México (Confederation of Mexican Workers, or CTM) derived its prominence and power from its institutional affiliation with the PRI. The PRI—or more accurately, the Partido de la Revolución Mexicana (Party of the Mexican Revolution), its forerunner—sponsored the CTM's formation and consolidation in the late 1930s. Representing 15 million workers at its peak, its purpose was to serve as a go-between for the Mexican government and the umbrella of labor organizations under its wing. It was supposed to bestow Mexican workers with a sense of incorporation into the state. And it provided the state with a mechanism to respond to and absorb organized labor's critiques.[36] In a controlled pluralist model, such as Mexico's, the CTM was central to the stability of its authoritarian—purportedly democratic—one-party rule.[37] Though more leftist elements provided a challenge to the CTM's hegemony on occasion, rallying workers to break off into new confederations, the union enjoyed its special access to the Mexican government and remained throughout the postwar era one of the organs the PRI sought to balance as it governed. That said, its influence was contingent on the numbers of workers under its helm, hence the CTM's concern with emigration.

The CTM worried that releasing Mexicans to the United States would shrink the number of its dues-paying members and hamper the functioning of the Mexican economy. For this reason, Fidel Velázquez, who had been the CTM's secretary-general since its inception, sought to shame Mexican men into staying, claiming that "braceros [had] all forgotten the fatherland that saw their births and raised them." His casting migration as an act of ingratitude and national disloyalty failed to slow the exodus, which hastened throughout the 1940s. The CTM could do little to affect it, save denying membership to those who departed.

Elaborating further on the view of Mexican labor unions under his dominion, Velázquez called the exodus "extremely prejudicial to Mexico's economy."[38] The CTM worried that in leaving, workers were abandoning the marriage of industry and workers necessary for the Mexican economy to function. Industry needed workers to manufacture goods, and workers needed industry to earn a living. As two parts of a whole, they ensured production and employment in the country. Unlike the church, the CTM cast blame on migrants themselves. Velázquez believed there were plenty of options for working-class Mexicans. They just had to make a more earnest effort to look within Mexico, and not search beyond its borders, "fishing for the golden dollar."[39]

Despite its critique, the CTM remained faithfully subordinate to the Mexican government. It declined entreaties from the American Federation of Labor and Congress of Industrial Organizations (AFL-CIO), the largest federation of unions in the United States, to join it in a binational stand against the BP. The AFL-CIO sought to connect with the CTM as part of its political efforts to unravel the BP. Its main worry was that the imported Mexican workers, and the undocumented migrants who followed behind them, were undercutting US farmworkers in the labor market and degrading their work conditions. Despite being critical of the BP, however, CTM leadership was not willing to defy the PRI's authority by launching a coordinated campaign with the AFL-CIO.[40]

Leaders of the communal peasant or ejido sector also disapproved of the BP. The ejido was the policy backbone of the dominant party's revolutionary lore. To create ejidos, Mexico initially took land from rich latifundios and broke their possessions into smaller communal landholdings to be run and operated by groups of campesinos. Campesinos were to hold, administer, and exploit their land in small collectives. They did not acquire ownership of the land, since Mexico retained ultimate ownership. But they enjoyed indefinite rights of usage so long as they complied with ejido stipulations. They could also pass their entitlement to family members. The ejido provided campesinos with substantive claims over land, which before they accessed as wageworkers or under debt peonage.[41]

The ejido was dependent on campesinos' toil to turn their parcels of land into viable islands of production. Bracero migration, as far as ejido leaders were concerned, threatened that by luring campesinos to abandon their allotted lands. The Confederación Nacional Campesina (National Confederation for Peasant Farmers, or CNC) formally represented the interests of the ejido sector before the Mexican state and functioned analogously to the CTM. Representing 3 million peasants, the CNC opposed the departure of *brazos* (farmhands). The CNC alleged that the exodus could retard the ongoing development of Mexico's ejido sector by increasing the numbers of absentee campesinos, who, lured by the promise of wages, left their communal land unattended.[42]

For the CNC, the culture of mass departure conflicted with the role of the peasantry as the engine of Mexico's agricultural power. The organization advocated for years that the government instead undertake colonization in Northern Mexico, through which Mexicans would be granted land and supported financially to establish ejidos. That way, they would have no need to migrate and would no longer set a bad example for other Mexican peasants.[43] María Guadalupe Urzúa, a leader of the female branch of the CNC who eventually rose to leadership positions within the PRI itself, offered regular public reports on the departure of campesinos as braceros and the dangerous abandonment of the ejido.[44] Though the government technically barred ejido members from leaving as braceros, it could not stop them from trying their luck as undocumented workers.

Smaller campesino confederations also made clear their distaste for the migration. The Unión de Federaciones Campesinas de México enrolled 100,000 peasants across ejidos nationwide. It offered a dour assessment of Mexico as "a nation that is malnourished, seminaked, and semibarefoot . . . with only half our population that can read and write." The organization, which would play an important role in the elections of 1952, maintained that Mexico needed to better attend to "the problem of land tenure, from which are born all the other problems of our people." It argued that Mexico's and migrants' problems would be resolved by committing to, not abandoning, the ejido.[45]

Though national ejido organizations took the lead in critiquing the BP, the migration's impact varied by region. In the sending state of Guanajuato, for instance, the mid-to-late 1940s brought an epidemic disease that devastated locals and precipitated a statewide economic downturn. The state began to hemorrhage migrants to the United States as both braceros and undocumented migrants. Included among these were ejido members, known as ejidatarios, who fled their parcels to work for wages. The public health crisis plaguing their region propelled them outward, and so they went, at the risk of losing their ejido stake. According to federal statute, members of an ejido were mandated to meet residency requirements. They had to remain on their designated parcel for the majority of the year. But this did not stop migrants from leaving Guanajuato.[46] Some ejidatarios mitigated the risk of losing their land by asking fellow ejidatarios to sign their names as present at meetings. Thus, from the individual migrant's perspective, ejidos and wagework could be hybridized and were not necessarily mutually exclusive.[47]

The situation concerned President Miguel Alemán. It seemed proof of ejido leaders' fears that the migratory pathway opened by the BP would weaken the ejido sector. Under the prodding of the CNC and other groups, Alemán's administration began to offer colonization programs in Northern Mexico—that is, resettlement schemes for afflicted ejidatarios from Guanajuato. Guanajuato's government followed in kind, launching brigades to convince ejidatarios "against migrating" and threatening tighter surveillance of their departures. It warned that anyone found in the United States would forfeit their parcel of land. "The agrarian law," announced the government, "would be respected."[48]

Of all the social sectors to develop an interest in the migration, however, the organized arms of major industries made the most earnest entreaties for the migration to be curbed. Agricultural and cotton producers based in Northern Mexico were the most critical. They continually lobbied the Mexican government for contramigratory measures. Companies and growers in Northern Mexico experienced the migration as a dire threat. The laborers Mexico ceded to the United States were ones they needed for their own production. They found it unacceptable that Mexican laborers should pass through Northern Mexico on their way to the United States without first contributing some of their work in the region.

Northern Mexico companies and growers tried to convince the federal government to bend the migration in their direction. They acted through associations, rarely independently, because this enabled them to pool their resources and consolidate their efforts. The greatest pressure came from growers in Baja California and Tamaulipas, two large states respectively situated in Mexico's northwest and northeast corners. Their location put them along the path of the migration. Baja California growers saw migrants depart north to Southern California, most voluminously through the frontier city of Mexicali, which shared a border with Calexico, California, and opened into the Imperial Valley, a center of commercial agriculture in the United States. Tamaulipas growers saw the migratory flow dribble out through the natural barrier of the Rio Grande to nearby cultivation areas in the Lower Rio Grande Valley, which specialized in cotton growing and made liberal use of migrant labor.[49]

The Mexican agribusinesses driving the Mexican government to stanch the migratory flow did not cohere into a single, united front. They organized their advocacy along regional and crop-specific interests, reflecting different harvest calendars and the varying needs for migrant labor of their enterprises. The production landscape for one agribusiness cluster did not map neatly onto the next, based on the specific crops being harvested, prevailing weather patterns, access to labor-saving machinery, total lot acreage, and so forth. This contributed to the development of localized business networks, each operating separately from the next. Thus, for instance, vegetable producers in the state of Sonora lobbied against the BP and sought remedial action independent from cotton producers in Mexicali, Baja California.

What they shared, however, was a disagreement with the Mexican's government's migration policy. The emigration, they agreed, crippled their "vital" economic sector: "el agro mexicano"—that is, Mexican farmland dedicated to commercial exploitation. The growers pointed to the lost economic potential by routinely highlighting the crops that were wasting away: spoiled vegetables and cotton not picked or sorted in time for release to national and international markets. They blamed this state of affairs on a lack of workers—a lack with direct roots in Mexico's offloading migrants to the United States.[50]

Northern Mexico's growers did not just want the BP gone. They wanted the country to commit federal military troops to surveil surreptitious crossings at the border. They understood better than most that the departure of guest workers went hand in hand with the rise in undocumented migration. The departure of Mexicans as undocumented migrants was a latent danger, given that the Río Bravo could be crossed on foot and that stretches of Baja California were inadequately fortified against migrants willing to find a roundabout exit. Should the migrants be able to afford it, they could also cross with a coyote, or human trafficker. Growers, unlike the leadership of the CTM and CNC, placed no hope in restricting migration by shaming migrants or offering them economic incentives. They tended to favor more forceful mechanisms, including narrowing plausible avenues of exit and enhancing military surveillance, to stymie migrant mobility. While other industries in Mexico, particularly in the central part of the country, also sought to reduce the outflow of Mexicans, their levels of concern did not approximate the endemic affliction that northern growers claimed plagued their operations.[51]

The Mexican government in the 1940s and early 1950s did not accede to growers' desire for mass, military-led surveillance of migration. It settled for presenting growers with the promise to enforce the ban on Northern Mexicans leaving as braceros. This approach, however, included no provisions to keep residents from slipping away as undocumented migrant workers. It addressed only those migrants who sought formal channels of exit. Nonetheless, when Northern Mexicans requested special permission from Mexican presidents in the 1940s and early 1950s to enroll as braceros, they were typically rebuffed. They were given the protocolary runaround and referred back to what was for them square one, the municipal president of their town, who was given the final authority to make or deny exceptions. Tying up Northern Mexicans in bureaucracy and denials was the most the Mexican government was willing to do to curb migration. In addition to keeping Northern Mexicans captive as a laboring population, the government did not systematically pursue measures to end Northern Mexico's labor shortage, at least not in the 1940s.[52]

An open historical question is whether these businesses truly suffered from labor shortages. Evidence suggests that their antimigratory discourse was at least partially contrived to expand the labor pool in their region. Their end goal may have been to depress wages and increase workers' vulnerability. Workers in the area sometimes complained to the Mexican government that northern businesses used the labor-shortage narrative to deceive them. Several groups of workers reached out to the federal government for help, alleging that northern businesses drew them from nearby towns claiming they would offer competitive wages because they were short of working hands. The protesting migrants included in their letters flyers that had been posted in their towns describing the growers' urgent need. When they arrived to claim their jobs, however, they found the advertisements to be fiction. Migrants reported that companies were scarcely hiring and had used the labor-scarcity pitch to lure them and create a larger pool of laborers who would compete for even lower wages than usual.[53]

At times, such strategies enabled growers to overcome their alleged labor shortage. In 1951, Mexican news media reported that growers had lured so many recruits to Matamoros, Tamaulipas, that its streets teemed with people willing to pick cotton, including families and small children, who roamed about searching for food. The paper predicted that Northern Mexico would, for the season at least, experience an overabundance of labor, the opposite of its traditional problem.[54] Ultimately, whether or not growers exaggerated the labor shortage, they felt a need to compel more workers to their region by a variety of means and regarded the BP as anathema.

Concern with out-migration went beyond major organized groups. It continued to exist within the Mexican government itself. At the state level, governors of major sending states disapproved of the exodus. The governors of the three largest such states in Mexico—Michoacán, Jalisco, and Guanajuato, which formed what sociologist Douglas Massey has called the emigrant "heartland"—were in the vanguard of opposition to out-migration. Politicians from these states had expressed antagonism toward migration since it first intensified in the early twentieth century. Even though it was a nascent process in 1909, the governors of these sending states complained to the central government that it was creating labor shortages. Now, with the BP formalizing Mexicans' exit anew, their concern was reanimated. Governors from the heartland worried that migration depleted their regional industries of manpower. The governors of Michoacán, Jalisco, and Guanajuato banned the contracting of braceros for the 1943–44 hiring period to address a labor shortage. They relied on a federal statute that gave state governors plenary powers in emergencies.[55]

As growers in Northern Mexico could attest, the problem with the BP was not just the out-migration it endorsed but the undocumented migration it catalyzed. For every guest-worker contract slot advertised by the Mexican government there were twenty aspirants, all suddenly triggered to see the United States as a realistic destination.[56] The governors of heartland states thus saw the BP and the migration it induced with trepidation. Guanajuato's government undertook colonization projects and public consciousness campaigns in the late 1940s and early 1950s. Meanwhile, the governor of Jalisco announced he would seek to stanch the "immoderate flow of braceros." The state, he asserted, had to act to "protect productive activities . . . as it has become increasingly noticeable that in agricultural work, in skilled work, and in the factories, there is a growing scarcity of human resources that would guarantee the filling of local demand."[57] Whether or not the BP truly impinged on the economy of the migrant heartland, these state governments certainly blamed it for a "noticeable . . . scarcity" of laborers.

Mexican governors outside this zone also sought to diminish out-migration. The governor of the state of Veracruz instituted economic development programs after World War II and reduced the number of migrants the state allowed into the BP.[58] Other states resorted to more Machiavellian tactics. Officials in Oaxaca demanded that braceros pay them 100 pesos if they wanted to be released from their *faena* obligations to work instead as braceros. The faena system obligated locals to work in public utilities, such as road building and public building construction.[59] By charging migrants a fee, Oaxaca disincentivized out-migration and sought to preserve the laboring population available for public infrastructure projects.

THE DISCOURSE OF INDIGNITY

The migration critics surveyed so far operated from a material or niche perspective. Activists, artists, and journalists on both sides of the border framed the migration's ills more transcendentally. They conveyed that out-migration was a matter of national import in Mexico, cutting across internal divides because it involved the wide-scale, systematic abuse of Mexican nationals. Despite not being centrally organized or perfectly aligned, their narratives cohered enough to overturn the celebratory portrayal of the BP by both the Mexican and US governments. They introduced the notion that migration was an indignity for Mexican males and an embarrassment for the Mexican state sponsoring it.

In its first decade of operation, the BP was assailed with revelations of its inner workings and allegations that work standards failed to meet contract stipulations. Its key critic was Ernesto Galarza, secretary of the National Agricultural Workers Union in the 1940s and early 1950s. The union advocated for US farmworker rights and opposed what it saw as the loosely governed importation of Mexican workers. Galarza and the union eschewed traditional organizing tactics and focused on "action research." This involved exposing migrant work conditions to reveal the wanton power of American business and the allegedly infrahuman conditions it imposed on undocumented and bracero workers. The goal was to turn public opinion against the BP in the United States. But public consciousness was more quickly raised in Mexico, as Mexican papers—*El Universal, Excélsior,* and others—picked up on migrants' ordeals.[60]

Galarza regarded the BP and undocumented migration as two aspects of the same problem. His exposés collapsed distinctions between the two and cast the whole phenomenon in ignominy, placing much of the implicit blame for it on Mexico. As he recalled years after his work with the National Agricultural Workers Union, "Our view was that the so-called wetback [like the bracero] is a product of the social and political conditions of Mexico." As a result, he explained, "we favored a campaign of publicity, confrontation, documentation, protest and so on that would zero in not on the wetback as a person, but on the Mexican government and its policy in Mexico that created such terrible poverty conditions that the wetback [and the bracero] was a natural product of."[61]

Over the first decade of the BP, the experiences of select migrants, whether sourced from Galarza or elsewhere, repeatedly appeared in Mexican periodicals, appearing as fact-filled blurbs regarding US farm operators and their abuse of migrants. The disillusioning stories rained down in a sprinkle, but their power lay in hitting out-migration from every angle. During the BP's first decade, Mexican news media reported on the nonpayment and delayed payment of workers; excessive deductions from workers' paychecks by growers who charged them whatever they wished for food, lodging, and amenities; the lack of medical facilities for migrants beyond an occasional first aid kit somewhere on the farm; barracks that stacked migrants on bunks and were not climatized for weather extremes; failure to honor a migrant's injury insurance, including fatal injuries, as some growers refused to pay for the transport of deceased migrants back to Mexico; food that amounted to a morning sandwich that migrants had to stretch for the day, or even canned dog food; and the violence of "bestial" growers like T. L. Parker of Calexico, who cracked two migrants in the forehead with a shotgun. For all the labyrinth of regulations crafted by Mexico, it seemed there was a grower somewhere flouting them.[62] The exposés hit the Mexican government precisely where it tried most to protect itself: the treatment of migrant-workers.

The pattern of migrant maltreatment worsened to such an extent that by the early 1950s observers regarded the BP as a farcical cover for migrant exploitation. Texas civil rights activist and editorialist Adela S. de Vento wrote to the Mexican government to denounce growers who "hacen lo que se les da la gana" (do as they wish) with their braceros. She argued they created a race to the bottom in work conditions by pitting braceros, undocumented migrants, and Mexican Americans against one another. A strong proponent of bilingualism, de Vento wrote articles that rehearsed these and other critiques of the migration in both Mexican and US newspapers. Lest Mexico need more evidence, she furnished the president with the book *Are We Good Neighbors?*, written in 1948 by her collaborator and mentor, the civil rights activist and League of United Latin American Citizens president Alonso S. Perales, which chronicled Mexicans' troubles, from discriminatory bans from public accommodations to distressingly low wages.[63]

Other activist organizations joined the critique of the BP as a failure that trampled on Mexican workers' dignity. Writing to President Adolfo Ruiz Cortines in 1953, the Committee of Mexican-American Workers in Los Angeles reported on "the violations, abuses, and inhuman conditions" at the worksites of the Johnson Company in Santa Barbara. Among the irregularities facing braceros, the Committee of Mexican-American Workers enumerated an increasingly predictable list: "1. violation of food and lodging agreements. . . . 2. incomplete payment for work realized. . . . 3. deductions not authorized. . . . 4. a lack of assistance and medical attention. . . . 5. intimidations." Having been given power of attorney by the workers, the committee requested immediate medical attention for braceros who had been injured while working and were writhing in pain. It urged an investigation by Mexican authorities and shared this story with the media. These specific remedies notwithstanding, the organization believed the program must be dismantled. Why, it asked, would Mexico allow the "outright exploitation" of its own citizens?[64]

In 1953, the dour portrayals of the migration seem poised to continue. Antonio Díaz Soto y Gama, a participant in the Mexican Revolution who became a noted newspaper columnist for the national newspaper *El Universal*, wrote to his friend, Secretary of the Interior Enrique Rodríguez Cano, that he was ready to publish a long feature on the migration. It focused on the "infamous agricultural field of Salsipuedes, California," of ill repute among migrants because of the chronic abuses they experienced there (the hamlet's name means "Get out if you can" in Spanish). The journalist centered his story on Trinidad Guzmán López, a migrant who worked in Salsipuedes and became a leader of braceros decrying abuse there. He noted that his desire was to build support for Trinidad, who was injured and removed from the BP without financial assistance for his medical care. Soto y Gama also wanted to help others who suffered similar fates. "Our wish at the paper," he assured Rodríguez Cano, "is that justice be served for our compatriots."[65] The columnist was careful not to directly critique the Mexican state, instead offering that he was merely helping it keep track of specific violations so it might fix them. That a columnist should give a top PRI official advance notice of his exposé, along with a clarificatory note, reveals how prejudicial and sensitive such news was becoming to the Mexican government.

The migration's ignominy would be cemented via popular culture. The migration's development coincided with the golden age of Mexican cinema. A handful of movies released in the late 1940s and early 1950s portrayed the suffering of Mexicans in the United States. The cinematic foundation for such a portrayal came from director Miguel Contreras Torres. His 1922 silent film, *El hombre sin patria* (The man without a homeland), followed the life of Rodolfo, the young son of a wealthy Mexican family. Upon being kicked out of his house and disinherited by his father, Rodolfo emigrates to the United States.[66] He works menial jobs and faces discrimination. His fall from grace is punctuated by his boss physically assaulting him. Rodolfo eventually kills the boss in self-defense. He flees back to Mexico and finds redemption. He marries, forms a stable home, and does not return to the United States. The movie, the first major release to portray migrant misery, would enjoy runs in Mexican theaters even after World War II and the BP's inauguration, with sound added.

The idea that an ordeal awaited migrants in the United States was mobilized by other films. *Adiós mi chaparrita* (Goodbye my little one), released in

1939, three years prior to the launch of the BP, centered on a migrant who abandons his beloved. In the United States, he is tormented by a Mexican American overseer who picks on recently arrived Mexicans. The message is that the United States is dangerous not just because of Anglos but because Mexican Americans were oppressive too.[67]

When the BP began in 1942, Tin-Tan, the iconic Mexican comedic actor, second only in popularity to Mario Moreno Cantinflas, took to portraying migrant life. He embodied the figure of the pachuco, the slick-talking transborder individual capable of mixing English and Spanish, sartorially defined by his zoot suit and fedora hat. In portraying the role, Tin-Tan drew on his own experience as a sojourner. In his 1940s movies—*El hijo desobediente* (The disobedient son, 1945), *Hay muertos que no hacen ruido* (The dead are sometimes silent, 1946), *El niño perdido* (The lost child, 1947), and *Música, poeta y loco* (Musician, poet, and madman, 1947)—he encounters misadventures in which Mexican migrants or ex-migrants appear in the background as immiserated individuals in need of his comic or economic relief.[68]

The 1947 *Pitó Pérez se va de bracero* (Pitó Pérez leaves [Mexico] as a bracero) zoomed in more directly on the bracero experience. It repurposed the iconic character of Pitó Pérez, created by Mexican author José Ruben Romero in the novel *La vida inútil de Pitó Pérez* (The foolish life of Pitó Pérez). In the movie, Pitó enrolls as a bracero. He experiences farm labor as brutal, back-breaking work that leaves migrants with untreated injuries. His misery prods him to relinquish his bracero contract and work as an undocumented immigrant washing dishes. He again finds the work is too difficult and poorly paid. He resorts to trafficking undocumented migrants, in cooperation with the saloon owner for whom he washed dishes. But he is caught by the police, the migrants scatter, and he is deported to Mexico. He vows never to return to the United States. The movie's message was that no amount of cunning and job-switching could help migrants avoid suffering in El Norte.

With the bleak picture of the United States well established, other films established migration as a tragedy because of its impact on Mexican households. In films such as *Primero soy mexicano* (I'm first a Mexican, 1950), *Yo soy mexicano acá de este lado* (I'm a Mexican here on this side, 1951), and *Acá las tortas* (Get your sandwiches here, 1951), migration is a disaster not just because migrants are exploited but also because they abandon their proper role as family men. Emigrants are made whole only by returning to Mexico, accepting traditional Mexican clothing, marrying a Mexican woman, starting a nuclear family, and settling down.[69]

The film that best dramatized out-migration during the golden age of Mexican cinema was *Espaldas mojadas* (Wetbacks, completed in 1953), which blended various migratory tropes. Its story centered on Rafael, a young Mexican from San Luis. He appears at a bracero recruitment center in Ciudad Juárez looking for work as a tractor driver, his specialty. But he is told braceros are only wanted for stoop labor. The film thus suggests that migration is repressive from the start. Since migrants are needed as farmhands, their talents and aptitudes are irrelevant.

Rafael realizes that he lacks supporting documents anyway, so he tries his luck as an undocumented migrant. He tries to sneak across the Rio Grande, aided by a labor recruiter employed by Mr. Sterling, an American magnate who owns several agricultural and railroad enterprises stateside and relies on migrant labor. During their attempted passage, Rafael and fellow aspirants, one of whom he has befriended, are caught by Border Patrol agents and shot at. They all fall wounded or die. Before passing, the friend gives Rafael the money he carries and asks him to place his body into the river so that it can return home.

Rafael tries again to cross as an undocumented migrant, after learning Mr. Sterling needs agricultural workers. He succeeds but finds the rewards wanting. He enters the circuit of migrant labor, including stints washing dishes in Texas, picking crops, and on "la traca" (the railroad) laying tracks. In these places, he and other Mexican migrants—bracero and undocumented—are surrounded by owners who work them nonstop as beasts of burden, Mexican American overseers who regard them with disdain, and migration officials asking for "papers!" The migrants lead overworked, isolated, and paranoid lives.

The movie builds to its climax when Rafael comes to the defense of a migrant Mr. Sterling is berating. Rafael rebukes the owner and earns the ire of the all-powerful businessman. Rafael runs off and finds refuge in a Texas eatery while the police search for him. But he is saved by María, a waitress who hides him and has a heart-to-heart with him. "[Socially] we are in a worse place than [American] Blacks," she tells him. "They stick together and are not attracted by another country. We Mexicans are not truly wanted here and Americans look at us with contempt." After commiserating, the two resolve to leave the United States. They agree to go to Ciudad Juárez, each of their own accord, and marry there.

But Rafael's return and redemption prove elusive. On the way back to Mexico, farm-labor recruiters attempt to poach him back into the migratory farm labor circuit. Then, when he arrives at the border to return to Mexico, the Mexican Border Patrol harasses him because he lacks papers. Without them, they cannot tell what he is, they claim. "Many people are brown, . . . Italians, Greeks, *pochos* [Mexican Americans]," laying out a racial epistemology and the shakiness of Rafael's belonging based on looks alone. The agents of Mexican migration ask Rafael when he and other migrants will realize the problem they cause by leaving Mexico. "Have you all no dignity?" Rafael responds that what he lacked was food, not self-respect.

Rafael's frustration finds cathartic release when he stumbles into Sterling at a bar in Ciudad Juárez and confronts him with a group of migrants. Rafael reaches for Sterling, who commands, "Don't touch me, you Mexican Greaser." The migrants, incensed, give Sterling a beating and throw him into the river. Sterling has to swim upriver and is shot by US Border Patrol officials, who mistake him for an illegal immigrant. While the fictional story ends with poetic justice, it is clear-eyed about the pitfalls facing Mexican migrants.[70] The film won six Ariel awards, a cinematographic prize roughly equivalent to the Oscars in the United States, including for Best Original Story and for Film of Greatest National Interest.

Espaldas mojadas reveals that by 1953 the creative milieu in Mexico was seeded with extensive tropes of migrant travail. From these germinated the screenplay. But it also offers insights into a Mexican government that felt threatened by out-migration and by negative depictions in film and news media. Fictional as he was, Rafael crystallized the ordeal Mexicans endured in the United States and that Mexico sanctioned through the BP. The movie was also completed at a sensitive time. The BP accord was set to expire in January 1954. And President Cortines believed the release of *Espaldas mojadas*, with its pessimistic depiction of migration, would unnecessarily heighten the public's interest in BP negotiations, especially labor protections. Cortines's administration censored the film, postponing its release to 1955.[71]

The Mexican government may have gained some breathing room by suppressing *Espaldas mojadas*. But the PRI's censors either missed or could not suppress one offshoot of Mexico's golden age of cinema. Pedro Infante was an iconic actor who doubled as a singer. His characters would sometimes incorporate singing, such as when he sang "El jacalito" (The hut) in *También de dolor se canta* (One also sings from pain). In 1953, Pedro Infante released a song, written by Rubén Méndez del Castillo, called "Canto del bracero" (Song of the bracero), that summed up migrants' woes. The lyrics are from the perspective of a forlorn migrant. He goes to the United States undocumented because he does not have "palancas en migración" (any personal connections to enroll in the BP). Traveling through many places—Arizona, Texas, Louisiana—the singer tells us,

Siempre sentí la falta de estimación	I always felt a lack of esteem [in the United States]
Que es que dicen que es discriminación	This is what they call discrimination
Ay, qué triste es la vida	Oh, how sad is the life
Qué triste vida es la del bracero	How sad the life of the bracero
Ay, cuánta decepción	Oh, how much disappointment
Cuanta desolación	How much desolation
. . .	. . .
Si tú piensas ir, detente	If you're thinking about going, do not
O si estás allá regresa	And if you're already over there
Donde está tu terruño y está tu gente	Come back [to Mexico] where your native soil and people are

The song affirms the sadness of migrant life. By the song's end, the singer assumes the role of sage counselor, and his counsel is to not migrate. Though the song parts from a focus on undocumented migrants, it critiques out-migration as a whole, imploring migrants to remain rooted to their homeland. According to one migrant memoir, Infante's song became an "anthem" among them.[72]

TO TINKER OR TRANSFORM?

As the exigencies of World War II receded and the BP matured, unfavorable critiques of out-migration flourished. To contend with these, Mexican presidents in the 1940s and early 1950s believed they could tinker with the BP. Mexico's best chance to improve the BP framework, including its domestic economic impact and the treatment of contract workers, came whenever the accords underlying the BP expired. In theory, during such moments Mexico had the power to prolong the BP if the United States offered satisfactory modifications. Or, it could choose not to continue the BP and instead halt its exportation of migrants.

At two points prior to 1954—when the agreement lapsed in 1948 and 1951—Mexico still unequivocally favored revising the BP. Jettisoning it was not in the realm of imagined possibilities, despite mounting domestic concerns. In the lead-up to the BP's expiration on February 21, 1948, for instance, Mexico focused on ensuring that Mexican consuls could inspect all places where braceros worked and lived, to ensure adequate conditions. Meanwhile, leading up to the BP lapse in 1951, Mexico was so invested in successfully renegotiating the BP that the Ministry of the Interior sent two agents to intimidate Ernesto Galarza and suppress his action research. Mexican leaders worried that his activism might undermine talks with the United States by pressuring Mexico to make excessive demands.[73]

Before 1954, the closest Mexico came to discontinuing the migration was in October 1948 when it unilaterally annulled the BP. It did so because the US Immigration and Naturalization Service (INS) opened the US-Mexican border without its consent, so Mexican migrants could enter Texas through Ciudad Juárez, Chihuahua, to provide cotton growers in New Mexico and West Texas with labor. Mexico's efforts to keep out-migration from depleting Northern Mexico of labor relied on not making certain sites in Mexico, such as Ciudad Juárez, sites of migrant contracting and processing. Mexico was also particular about which cities could accommodate migrant demand, given their infrastructure. Ciudad Juárez was not one of them. The INS's dismissal of Mexican precautions irritated Mexico enough for it to abrogate the BP. However, contracting itself was not significantly interrupted. Mexico agreed to continue exporting Mexican workers without a BP, while US and Mexican negotiators hashed out a revised agreement. The US State Department had helped soothe Mexico by admitting that the INS actions were rogue and "illegal."[74]

In none of the BP lapses prior to 1954—whether scheduled or impromptu—did it appear plausible that Mexico might shutter the BP, either to members of the Mexican government or to outside observers. But as we will see in subsequent chapters, the 1954 BP lapse was distinct. By then, the tide of public and political opinion was turning against out-migration. The BP had lost its sheen. And adjacent political events, including the US coup in Guatemala, made Mexicans more responsive to migrant suffering in the United States. By 1954, both Mexican politicians and scores of interested Mexican organizations believed there were merits to terminating the BP, demobilizing Mexican migrants, and brainstorming policies to root them to their homeland.

CHAPTER TWO

AGAINST THE CURRENT

*Mexico Meets Public
Pressure to Contain
Out-Migration, 1953–1954*

On January 15, 1954, the binational agreement underpinning the BP expired. Out-migration came to a standstill. Mexico could have collaborated with the United States to extend the agreement well before the deadline. But the BP had inspired too much popular revulsion in Mexico, and the United States offered too few concessions to fix the agreement. Hence, Mexico refused to re-sign the BP. The immediate symbols of Mexico's decision were the orderly, snaking lines of migrants that formed in Mexican border cities. They quickly became disorganized crowds, as more migrants arrived, hoping to cross to the United States. They would find not just a defunct BP but Mexican military patrolling the border to prevent them from leaving. Migrants were left to wait for the possibility that the United States and Mexico would find common ground, sign a new BP, and put the transnational labor chain back in motion.

Migrants trapped behind a closed border gate in Mexicali, Baja California, following the Bracero Program's expiration, ca. 1954. *Courtesy of the Los Angeles Times Photographic Collection, Library Special Collections, University of California, Los Angeles.*

They could then get back to working in US agricultural fields, instead of staring at a chain-link fence twice their height, topped by barbed wire.

Migrants gathered at border crossings might have wished for a quick resolution, but their government showed no signs of relenting. Though the BP had lapsed before, Mexico's stance seemed to have become uniquely adversarial. During the 1948 lapse, US and Mexican diplomats expected to renew the BP following negotiations over specifics. At no point in 1948 did Mexico explore alternatives, such as the promotion of greater rootedness among its citizenry. No internal deliberations or initiatives were undertaken or public statements made to that effect. Mexico's overriding interest was simply to polish the BP. In 1954, Mexico's position was different; it wanted to do more than simply negotiate a better BP.[1]

During the 1954 lapse, Mexican federal officials conferred on and off with the US State Department. But, while doing so, they also turned their internal discussions and public pronouncements toward the idea that Mexico needed to encourage permanence and not simply promote migration. Meanwhile, socially, the notion that Mexico should impede out-migration spread beyond the Catholic Church, the CTM, the CNC, and Northern Mexico business conglomerates. Ending the migration became a cause célèbre. A wide cross-section of Mexican citizens and organizations regarded the demobilization of Mexican migrants as core to preserving the nation's dignity. Moving in sync with civil society, the government launched a campaign to anchor Mexican migrants internally, partly drawing on ideas for rootedness that were floated by interested Mexican observers.

Historians have not articulated the extent of Mexico's countermigratory stance in 1954. They have moved too quickly past the 1954 lapse, perhaps because the most explosive part of the crisis, a series of confrontations between entrapped migrants and Mexican soldiers, lasted but a few weeks.[2] Historians have also downplayed it because Mexico eventually re-signed the BP, realizing it could not contain the migrants gathered at the border. Yet to judge this moment by its duration or its final result is a mistake. While it lasted, it was interpreted in Mexico as a highly charged moment of possibility. By rejecting the BP and impeding its citizens' exit, Mexico had issued a sovereign pause on the migration. And within that pause, Mexican leaders and interested observers alike believed they had open-ended leeway to envision a new, countermigratory direction for the country. These visions did not come to fruition (Mexico remained a large source of migration to the United States), but we must ask why the country's most pronounced attempt to correct the course of its migration policy failed.

During the migratory interregnum of 1954, Mexico quickly moved from sanctioning the migration to restraining it. It was a hyperaccelerated transformation, hastened by Mexico's own acceptance that the nation's dignity was on the line. By acknowledging the BP breakdown as a transcendent national issue, the government solidified the public's interest and created high expectations for a positive outcome—expectations it then felt obligated to meet. Initially, the government simply knew it could not re-sign the BP because the United States had failed to acquiesce to its proposed reforms. When it first began to deploy countermigratory controls, including military patrols of the border, this was to strengthen its bargaining position by keeping migrants from the United States. Its idea was simple: the United States would concede to BP reforms if it could not obtain Mexican migrants without Mexican involvement. However, as the conflict elapsed and it became evident that the United States would not yield, Mexico pivoted. It no longer sought just to keep migrants momentarily away from the United States but also to root them internally through long-term measures. As BP negotiations remained stalled, the Mexican government began to trumpet a new ideal: that Mexicans should be able to find stability within Mexico. It unveiled pro-permanence initiatives to permanently demobilize aspiring migrants. Through fits and starts, Mexico arrived at a decidedly contramigratory position. It determined this to be the path to national dignity.

The most well-rounded account of the 1954 episode has noted the unique intensity of the US-Mexican migratory impasse. But rather than explore Mexican policymaking in detail—in particular, how its mitigatory migratory politics quickly evolved from the protean to the more fully formed—it treats Mexico's actions solely as moves and countermoves in diplomacy.[3] But, for Mexico, 1954 was not just a frantic, hair-on-fire, international diplomatic squabble over the BP. As it unfolded, Mexican politicians and observers approached it as a referendum on the overall desirability of out-migration. Indeed, the question that came to dominate Mexican society was not how to fine-tune the BP. Instead, it was what the Mexican state and even ordinary citizens could do to begin an enduring turn in Mexican politics toward permanence, or keeping the country's citizens in Mexico.

This chapter and the next work together to produce a microhistory of the 1954 breakdown of the BP. They center Mexico's evolving ambitions, aiming to pinpoint precisely when, why, and how Mexico deviated from facilitating out-migration. The present chapter tracks two stories. First, it shows that US imperial intervention in Latin America intersected with Mexico's migration management. Specifically, the specter of US intervention in Central America in 1953 and 1954 turned Mexico's handling of the BP into a litmus test of its sovereignty. Would the United States allow Mexico to question and abandon a binational policy that trampled over its prerogatives?

Second, this chapter explains how Mexico's decision not to renew the BP created not just an international chasm with the United States but a sovereign pause in Mexico, a deliberative space for Mexicans, and their government, to reflect, draw conclusions about the migration, and possibly remap the country's relationship to out-migration. A wave of optimism swept over Mexico, as a gamut of interested parties—including ejido associations, trade unions, business councils, social organizations, and political insiders—wrote to the Mexican president to support his disavowal of the BP. They took it as a moment of patriotic self-defense, with Mexico finally repudiating the debasement of Mexican laborers in the United States.

Galvanized by the nonrenewal of the BP, these groups volunteered to act on the front lines to ensure that no migrants attempted to leave the nation. They also pitched ideas about how migrants could be demobilized permanently. They believe the episode should trigger far-reaching political transformations aimed at the systemic issues that stimulated migration. Mexican federal officials noted the sentiments of these respondents, their disposition to contribute, and some of their countermigratory ideas. The government would tap into all three during the US-Mexican impasse of 1954.

MIGRATION AND EMPIRE COLLIDE

The exploitation of Mexican migrants in the United States was a particularly sensitive topic for President Adolfo Ruiz Cortines. His campaign for president in 1952, while successful, had seen allegations that he was a lackey to the United States. The BP's impending expiration on January 15, 1954, was thus tricky. Cortines could hold the United States to account for its mistreatment of Mexican migrants and thereby cleanse his image. But being overly aggressive with the United States could lead to unpredictable reprisals.

President Cortines's controversial relationship to the United States first surfaced during the 1952 election campaign. His political adversaries affirmed that he had assisted US forces that invaded Veracruz in 1914 amid the Mexican Revolution. US president Woodrow Wilson had launched the incursion to bring down President Victoriano Huerta, who was perceived as too repressive to secure American interests. His strong-arm rule had caused constant civil strife in the country.[4] President Huerta's forces defended Veracruz because it was a gateway for them to receive arms and munitions. Without it, Huerta feared he could not replenish his stockades and fend off political adversaries. Mexican civilians joined in to support Huerta's forces and repel attacking US soldiers. But, poorly prepared for battle, Huerta's forces and supporting civilians lost Veracruz to the US Navy. The United States seized infrastructure, utilities, and communications centers, including the power plant, railroad terminal, telegram office, and customshouse. The United States only relinquished the port city seven months later, once it had helped install a new president, Venustiano Carranza.

After the invasion, the soldiers and civilians who defied the American invasion were glorified in Mexican political culture; those who assisted the United States were maligned. A payment ledger left at the Veracruz customshouse partly revealed who helped the Americans. One name listed was "Adolfo Ruiz C.," then a little-known accountant, but whose role supporting the invasion would take centerstage, as Cortines became a leading candidate for the Mexican presidency in 1952.[5]

Francisco Mugica, an important political figure from the Mexican Revolution, took aim at Cortines. Mugica had disappeared from national politics in the late 1930s, after then-president Lázaro Cárdenas declined to make him his political heir. During his presidency from 1934 to 1940, Cárdenas had spearheaded the Partido de la Revolución Mexicana (Party of the Mexican Revolution), the PRI's direct forerunner, helping to shape its corporatist model. When searching for a successor, he passed over Mugica, his mentee, whom he once thought could guarantee the Revolution's promise to uplift Mexico's peasantry, but whose politics he came to find too extreme to bring stability to Mexico.

President Cárdenas's Partido de la Revolución Mexicana had ushered in a corporatist national model in Mexico, in which the government juggled various constituencies. It established patron-client relationships with labor, agriculture, military, and miscellaneous popular sectors. To manage this assortment of interest groups, Cárdenas, and any of his successors, had to juggle their various demands and requests, without deferring to any particular one.[6]

To the left of Cárdenas on most issues, Mugica helped shape and defend propeasant policies in the Constitution of 1917. Among these was Article 27, which gave the federal government the right of ownership over all the lands, waters, and natural resources in Mexico. This empowered Mexico to appropriate and redistribute property rights, thus facilitating the transfer of property from large landholders to landless peasants. Mugica then worked for Cárdenas as secretary of the economy.[7]

But by 1940, with the rise of challengers on the right, Cárdenas grew cautious. He calculated the party would be on stabler ground in the hands of a more centrist leader. Someone like Mugica, zealous in pursuit of improvements for peasants, might provoke a counterrevolution that would undo the delicate balance of Cárdenas's corporatist regime. Cárdenas anointed Manuel Ávila Camacho to be Mexico's next chief executive and relegated Mugica to governor of Baja California Sur.

Mugica resurfaced in the 1950s—his popularity and pedigree intact—having grown disturbed by the moderation that came over the political establishment once Cárdenas left office, as the PRI shifted to tightening its hold on the federal apparatus. He forged the Constitutionalist Party and re-entered national politics through this vehicle. He did not campaign himself. Rather, he joined the Federación de Partidos del Pueblo (Federation of Parties of the People) in support of the presidential candidacy of General Miguel Henríquez Guzmán, who ran on a propeasant platform. Mugica was a chief strategist for the campaign.

Mugica's plan centered on tearing down the reputation of the PRI candidate, Adolfo Ruiz Cortines. Taking advantage of his high standing in Mexican politics, he cast Cortines as undeserving of office. He alleged Cortines assisted the US occupation of Veracruz during the Mexican Revolution. The accusations were based on the payment ledger found in the Veracruz customshouse that included the signature of "Adolfo Ruiz C." for undisclosed assistance to the occupying US Army. Henríquez Guzmán's campaign cast Cortines as a traitor who had abetted an intrusion on Mexican sovereignty.[8] Though Cortines won the election thanks to the PRI's institutionalized power, he emerged tarnished as a facilitator of American overreach. That the claims originated from a leader like Mugica, with stature, moral authority, and lasting involvement in Mexican politics, only made them more adhesive.

Cortines's questionable relationship with the United States would prove salient because just as he was beginning his mandate in 1952, the United States was considering interventions in Latin America, ostensibly to contain communism. Mexicans had certainly warmed to the North American business presence by the 1950s, but direct US military intervention was another matter, still inspiring widespread hostility.[9] To be associated with it, as Cortines was, provoked the need for image-control. Worse still for Cortines, by 1953, US interference centered on a case close to home: neighboring Guatemala. Rumors circulated in media and government channels that US secretary of state John Foster Dulles was looking to depose Guatemalan president Jacobo Arbenz, who was undertaking land redistribution in Guatemala. Arbenz was appropriating land held by the United Fruit Company, a US-based company with direct ties to Secretary Dulles.[10]

The US-Guatemala situation gave weight to questions about Cortines's independence and his relationship to US imperialism. Two sets of characters helped draw awareness to Guatemala's struggle. One was a host of activists, pamphleteers, and protestors, spearheaded by college students in Mexico City. They demonstrated in the capital's streets throughout 1953 to decry North American imperialism. US actions in Guatemala also owed their notoriety to former president Lázaro Cárdenas. He remained an iconic political figure, recognized for his role in shaping Mexico's governing party and leading a land-redistribution program in 1937. Naturally sympathetic to Arbenz's program, he condemned US meddling. These strands of civic activism and critiques would keep American imperialism at the forefront of public consciousness. Cortines's administration thus assiduously tracked developments in Guatemala and the reactions of the Mexican public.[11]

The imperial milieu of 1953 made it imperative for Cortines to manage his dubious patriotic credentials. He thus refrained from policies or opinions that might validate the suspicions that he was beholden to the United States and disloyal to Mexico. He kept US officials at arm's length. Cortines avoided meeting with President Dwight Eisenhower, and even for the most part direct communication with him. Similarly, he declined to meet with Francis White, the newly appointed US ambassador to Mexico, other than for formalities.

At times, he attempted to take suspicions about his loyalties head-on. In speeches to the Mexican Congress, he delivered odes to patriotism and self-determination. Then, when he finally agreed to meet with President Eisenhower on October 19, 1953, for the dedication of the Falcon Dam, he took advantage of the fact that it was a public setting, and not a private one, to create more of a separation between him and the US government. In a speech in front of thousands, he underscored "self-determination" and "sovereignty," and the need to reject "any form of external hegemony." The only way to ensure positive relations between states, he argued, was to respect people's "indeclinable right" to be "governed by those whom they choose, in the economic system they prefer." Though framed as a universalist proclamation of any nation-state's theoretical right to manage its own affairs, it was a subtle critique of US imperialism and the destabilization of Arbenz's government.[12]

By 1953, however, oblique defenses would hardly suffice when dealing with the exploitation of migrants in the United States. Mexicans were well aware of the abuse faced by their compatriots, and since Mexico voluntarily engaged in the migration, it was hard for the Mexican government to exonerate itself as a partially responsible party. It plainly held the power to remedy the situation, either by making changes to the BP or disbanding it. The ill repute of the BP owed to the ongoing work of journalists, cultural producers, and migrants, surveyed in chapter 1, who framed the mistreatment, underpayment, and discrimination faced by migrant workers as a national shame. As a headline in *El Heraldo* from the summer of 1953 put it, "The life of an animal is worth more than that of a bracero."[13]

Top-level Mexican officials could not deny the challenges endured by Mexicans because they themselves faced discrimination when visiting places with institutionalized bigotry in the United States, such as Texas, where in addition to onerous labor, people of Mexican origin endured a system of social apartheid. Like African Americans, they suffered from separate and

Against the Current

unequal schooling and were denied entry to restaurants, pools, and other common public accommodations. One Mexican official offered that his anti-Americanism stemmed from his time as a student in the United States, where he was denied housing because of his Mexican origin.[14]

Cortines was accountable for at least those Mexicans migrating as guest workers. Their migration was governed by the international accord set to expire on January 15, 1954. With its termination looming, he could re-sign it and allow the compromising migration to continue without much complaint, or he could stand his ground in defense of Mexican workers. It was a binary choice that would show his mettle, or lack thereof, vis-à-vis the United States, and he could not postpone it, avoid it, or merely obliquely address it.

Contemporary chroniclers and observers understood that the BP's pending lapse was a reckoning point for Cortines vis-à-vis the United States. José Lázaro Salinas, a journalist who covered the migrant contracting center in Irapuato and conditions for migrants there from 1953 to 1954, produced a series of articles that noted the way Guatemala and migration cases bled into one another. "The attempt [by the United States] to consummate an intervention in the internal affairs of Guatemala," he wrote, was an act of "foreign aggression" that was becoming intertwined with Cortines's consideration of whether to continue sanctioning out-migration through the BP. Moreover, the conflation of the two storylines intensified the drama of bracero exploitation. As Salinas explained, "This coincidence of conflicts—that of the braceros and that of Guatemala—contributed undoubtedly to Mexican public opinion following with sincere passion all the incidences of the bracero case."[15]

With the United States throwing its weight around in Central America, Cortines aimed for a credible victory against his northern neighbor. He did not forswear negotiation. His Ministry of Foreign Affairs sought significant concessions from the United States. Chiefly, Cortines sought the power to bar from the list of eligible employers any US businesses presumed to violate bracero rights. Mexico would not have to prove wrongdoing first. Under the existing agreement, Mexico and the United States investigated businesses and mutually determined whether they had transgressed. Only then could they be blacklisted. This slow system gave American employers ample time to use Mexican workers while flouting the international agreement.

In Cortines's proposed streamlined system of unilateral blacklisting, his government would dictate which corporations and growers could hire braceros. This was a design he could credibly sell as a victory, for it meant Mexico would have final say over the migration. His Ministry of Foreign Affairs offered it to the United States as a take-it-or-leave-it proposition. But this was to no avail. The DOL argued that braceros needed no such exaggerated protections, for they were privileged with enviable benefits, from insurance, to wage controls, to food guarantees.

President Cortines was faced with the option of caving and re-signing the BP, at the risk of being criticized in Mexico for acquiescing to the United States, or stating the mistreatment of Mexicans to be an intolerable affront to the nation. For Mexico it was not a moment of imperial reckoning on par with what Guatemala was experiencing under the beleaguered Arbenz administration, but for Mexicans and Cortines it was a test of the president's autonomy and backbone. With the specters looming of American intervention in Guatemala and his own collaboration in one such intervention years before, Cortines chose to pursue redemption. He notified the United States that he would not sanction the BP as presently constituted.

Out-migration came to an official halt on January 15, 1954, when the BP expired. Figuratively wrapped in the flag, Cortines affirmed he was turning away from a situation beneath Mexicans' dignity and standing up to the United States. He maintained he would only open negotiations if the United States negotiated on Mexico's terms.[16] He acted out an identity that had proved elusive: the fearless patriot.[17] Indeed, since he stepped into the office, he had promoted patriotic culture with jingoistic verve. One of his prized accomplishments had been the re-creation of a popular radio show featuring live-broadcast dramatizations of seminal events of Mexican history. Its aim was to kindle in Mexicans a heroic national pride.[18] But throughout his presidency, he had been beset by American imperialism and his long-standing association to it. Now, at last, he could bring a tangible international victory to the Mexican people and burnish credentials as a patriot of the first order. Perhaps, in his thinking, he also was creating his own seminal moment of drama in Mexican history.

In addition to declining a new BP, Cortines blocked emigration at key points along Mexico's northern frontier, summoning local police, municipal politicians, and Mexican migration authorities as the frontline enforcers. The exit at Mexicali in Baja California drew the government's special attention. Crowds of Mexicans were already in Mexicali or headed there in January to look for work in the soon-to-begin harvest in Southern California's Imperial Valley. Mexican municipalities followed Cortines's orders to warn residents not to attempt to emigrate. They were told federal forces would be vigilant and that migrants would suffer "innumerable penalties" should they attempt to cross. The government was clear that contracts for guest work were no longer being awarded, and that no workers, period, were to be allowed exit. The argument made by Cortines's administration was that Mexican consuls in the United States could not handle the volume of grievances that would inevitably result from more Mexicans choosing to live in the United States.[19] Altogether, Cortines signaled an initial willingness to impede the migration by cordoning off key points of exit and dissuading prospective migrants.

It was unclear what might occur next. What was certain was that Cortines was stuck in an adversarial position. Unless he could gain robust concessions from the United States—unlikely given the way the United States dismissed his request for unilateral blacklisting power—he could hardly resume the flow of migrants without resurrecting the questions about his mettle and national loyalty he intended to quell. President Cortines's choice to enter a standoff with the United States effectively opened a realm of possibilities in Mexico's migration policy.

A SIMPLE MORATORIUM OR A MOMENT OF RECKONING?

Cortines found wide support for not renewing the BP. Interested onlookers deemed his decree patriotic, founded on dignity and self-respect. That it should come against the United States deepened nationalistic pride. This was manifested by an array of Mexicans: doctors, lawyers, schoolteachers, students, parent associations, and small-business owners (the "miscellaneous groups" of Mexican society, as labeled by the PRI); as well as ejidos, unions, and large business associations (the groups most crucial to the corporatist order); and government officials, party officials, and competing political parties (the political spine of the country). The breadth of this outpouring was without precedent in prior lapses of the BP, when only party minions had bothered to communicate with the president. No one understood those lapses as a national turning point for Mexico, just a chance to renegotiate a stronger BP.[20]

In contrast, over 500 letters sent to the Mexican government during the 1954 lapse survive. They illuminate Mexicans' emotional investment in the migration following exposés and cultural productions regarding migrant travails. Fueled by the indignity of the migration, letter writers offered to serve on the frontlines of the effort to encourage Mexicans to remain in place. And they were driven to brainstorm. They proposed policy designs to root migrants internally. This section explores one-sixth of these letters, selected based on the writers' prominence, the extent of their mobilization, the depth of their mitigatory migratory ideas, and the extent to which their messages did or did not resonate with Cortines's administration.

Analysts have observed that Mexicans historically harbored an "ambivalence" toward out-migration, recognizing its advantages and disadvantages. While this characterization holds true as a general statement, at certain times, such as 1954, political opinion swung in an unequivocally negative direction. Mexicans offered clear-cut, full-throated critiques of emigration, and brought noteworthy intensity, intellectual depth, and mobilization to the question of how to invite domestic rootedness.[21] The Mexican state took note of these elements of the social response. Indeed, three days after Mexico allowed the BP to expire, even periodicals remarked with a hint of surprise just how popular Cortines's stance seemed to be. "It has been years since we have seen such a unification by all groups and by parties close to the state," editorialized *La Opinión*. Cortines's actions "have earned the approval of all, both groups addicted to his regime and those who have otherwise stood in opposition to it." An American reporter confirmed the sentiment in a wire to the Associated Press, claiming that not since the "nationalization of oil [effected by Cárdenas] had there been such a unity in public opinion."[22]

In the next chapter, I will analyze more thoroughly how Mexico's countermigratory politics evolved during the 1954 lapse. But I begin that process here by underscoring that Mexico's policymaking was limited from the start. Despite the earnest, at times elaborate, and varied mitigatory migratory ideas emanating from different corners of Mexican society, the government constrained its focus to peasants. More narrowly still, it gravitated to one remedy suggested by contributors: granting arable land to landless peasants. By following such a narrow vision of reform, Mexico forwent the multipronged, deep-reaching change collectively sketched by members of the public.

A bottled-up antagonism toward the United States for its neglect of Mexican migrants was apparent in Mexicans' response to President Cortines. The sentiment was powerful enough to bring people into the streets. In the state of Tamaulipas, people took to public roads by the thousands, cheering the president for his "decisiveness." The celebrants in Tampico Madero consisted mainly of peasant associations, trade unions, and women's groups, and numbered around 10,000. They cheered Cortines for refusing "to sign an agreement that was injurious to our compatriots." In their estimation, the BP violated migrants' dignity. Their *vitoreos* (cheers) were also for the state's governor, Horacio Terán, who publicly declared his support for the president's stance.[23]

Indeed, far from seeing migration as a desirable safety valve, many Mexicans felt pride and power in President Cortines's bringing it to a standstill. To them, this was an act with profound symbolism that signified Mexico was standing up to the United States and championing respect for its nationals abroad. One letter writer who described himself as a humble man who had never before reached out to a president wrote that "all fibers of my enthusiasm vibrate with the knowledge that at last there is a president" who "truly [*deveras*] wants to defend our country." His message, however, came with a warning that suggested the high-octane energy fueling this moment in Mexican political history. He cautioned that the "spirit of the times" in Mexico was perhaps overexcited and driving toward a "wholesale redress of countless problems in Mexico" that indeed "need fixing" but could not be addressed "all at once."[24]

Meanwhile, an association of small-business owners (*comerciantes*) in Guadalajara, Jalisco—who seemed to share very little material interest with migrants—wrote that they were so stirred they were willing to offer up "the blood in their veins" as "obligated patriots" to defend their country and "its rights in this matter" to keep Mexicans from leaving for the United States. As the source of their animus, they pointed to the "arbitrariness and outrageous abuses" that "our best workingmen" were subject to in the United States.[25]

Such was the language and tenor of those moved by the migration's suspension. The stoppage seemed to be an achievement in itself. "With the step you have taken to block the emigration of Mexico's children of the fields, you fully vindicate the dignity of our country, painfully humiliated by the exportation of slaves, who are our compatriots," wrote one. Letter after letter expressed a sense of how Mexicans deserved to be treated, and what treatment they did not deserve. Whereas some respondents saw the treatment of Mexicans as a form of slavery, others, such as a group of aviators from the Air Force, underscored that it was unacceptable for migrants' "human rights" to be disrespected in the United States.[26]

Even a major newspaper, *Excélsior*, ostensibly tasked with reporting, stepped outside the veneer of objectivity to express "ecstatic feeling" and support for the government's denial of migrant workers to the United States.[27] *Novedades*, another major national newspaper, did the same.[28] So did La Cadena García Valseca, publisher of thirty-seven state and local newspapers across the country, including *Esto, El Sol de León, El Diario de Durango, La Voz de Chihuahua, El Correo Cd. Juárez*, and *La Tribuna de Monterrey*.[29]

The comments of Mexican people indicated that many of them felt themselves in a curious relation to time, seeing the end of a social ill that had plagued Mexico for too long and on the cusp of a solution to migration that would reverberate far into the future. "You are redeeming the dignity of our nation, painfully humiliated by the exporting of slaves, who are our brothers of race," wrote observer Salvador Azuela. "Today, the nation all respects and admires you, [President Cortines]."[30] However, while the moratorium on the migration itself offered a taste of redemption, this would only be fully savored when Mexicans were permanently rooted. "National sentiment is on your side, for the attitude you have taken with respect to Mexican braceros, [President Cortines]," communicated one Guillermo Ruiz V. But "the [Mexican] federal government and state governments ought to solve absolutely this national problem [of migration] by creating job sources in the country through farms, land parcels, and ranches."[31]

With migrants at a standstill at the border, it was possible for Mexicans to imagine the end to out-migration. Artemisa Xochitl Sáenz wrote, "As an old-timer, revolutionary, pioneer of the political social feminist movement, and as a Veracruzana, I congratulate your serene, patriotic attitude to bring this exodus to a close once and for all."[32]

Even ultranationalistic associations that placed high standards on patriotism poured in support of Cortines's closing of the northern border. The Defensores de Veracruz en 1914 (Defenders of Veracruz in 1914), famed for repelling the US intrusion in the port city of Veracruz during the Mexican Revolution, congratulated Cortines for finally taking an "absolutely correct" and "patriotic" stance by denying Mexicans to the United States.[33] Their support was notable given the claims that Cortines had helped facilitate the US intervention in Veracruz that the Defensores had fought to prevent. The symbolism and substance of Cortines's decision was allowing him to overcome his ill repute as a pawn of US power.

The fascist paramilitary group Acción Revolucionaria Mexicanista (Mexican Revolutionary Action), also known as Los Dorados, also expressed its support. Boasting 100,000 members, the last time Los Dorados had made an appearance in national politics was in 1952, when a band of armed Los Dorados members attacked a popular annual festival for workers in Mexico City, leaving injuries and fatalities in their wake. They associated the festival with communism and treason, even though workers agreed to march with a Mexican flag, after years of only marching with a red and black flag to signify worker solidarity across national boundaries. Workers' groups had also framed their event as a tribute to President Miguel Alemán Valdés for advancing the interests of working-class people. All of this was not enough for Los Dorados to accept that festival-goers were loyal Mexicans. Now, two years later, in the midst of the BP lapse, the executive committee of Los Dorados expressed pride in President Cortines's nationalistic assertiveness. Colonel Aniceto López Salazar praised the government's "patriotic attitude." He put the Dorados' armed strength at his service. "Our loyalty is yours across this territory," he said, "in whatever is necessary," portending the open-ended conflict that might be necessary for Mexico to battle out-migration.³⁴

Outside of the extremes, the tamer core of Mexican civil society was also drawn into nationalistic agitation. A parent's association, the Sociedad de Padres de Familia Escuela DF Sarmiento, reported to the Cortines administration, "Yours is a virile defense of the sovereignty of Mexico, before the aggressive and absurd attitudes of the US government."³⁵ The Federación de Estudiantes de Guadalajara (Guadalajara Student Federation) also celebrated the attack on "wicked exploitation abroad." "Your government's act," the federation avowed, "lights a fire of patriotic sentiment in us, the youth of Jalisco."³⁶ Another student group, the Comité Nacional Confederación Jóvenes Mexicanos (National Committee of the Confederation of Young Mexicans), was similarly riled up: "We will fight as a nation behind your decision."³⁷

A group of 6,000 students at the Universidad Nacional Autónoma de México (National Autonomous University of Mexico) not only extoled Cortines's patriotism but mobilized 800 social workers in training to go out into country and orient migrants to stay. Like Pedro Infante in "Canto del bracero," they instructed migrants that nothing but "privation, exploitation, and misery" awaited them in the United States.³⁸ The Federación de Organizaciones Populares de Jalisco (Jalisco Federation of People's Organizations), an umbrella group based in the historically sending state of Jalisco that unified various popular sectors outside of the labor, peasant, and military establishments, convened a meeting to cheer Cortines's action as one that "safeguarded" Mexican interests. Operating in one of the hotspots of migration, it reported itself ready to be mobilized for next steps, including door-to-door discussions with migrants.³⁹

The bent toward patriotism and problem-solving also emerged from core sectors, including peasant groups, landless people, labor unions, and business associations. They reported to Cortines their supposedly disinterested hope in seeing Mexicans no longer emigrate, detailed their efforts to that effect, and recommended policies to demobilize Mexican nationals. They all agreed that Cortines's migratory suspension preserved the nation's dignity and opened up avenues for reform. But they differed in that each believed their corner of the Mexican economy held the key to solving mass migration.

Business groups celebrated the BP's lapse and offered policy directions. Their basic idea was that if Mexico wanted to keep Mexicans from emigrating, the best way was to offer them employment within the country. Throughout the 1940s and early 1950s, they had lobbied the PRI to preserve the domestic labor pool instead of sharing it with the United States. Now, recognizing the migratory lapse as a fertile moment for policy generation, business groups built on their case. The vehicle that organized business turned to in 1954 was the Asociación Nacional de Cosecheros (National Association of Harvesters, ANC). An agglomeration of 620 local, regional, and national agricultural producer associations in the country, the ANC formed autonomously in 1947 because growers wanted to have a united body through which to lobby the government when they had sector-wide concerns. The PRI supported its creation because it likewise wanted a consolidated awareness of agribusinesses' concerns. Indeed, upon its creation, the ANC was invited to the presidential palace in Los Pinos. ANC officials presented President Miguel Alemán with a parchment that made him "lifetime president" of the organization.

Prior to the ANC, local growers operated independently in their political efforts. They behaved as the economic bourgeoisie in their own localities, instead of constituting a national elite. They thus "lacked a unique representation in the national realm," as one scholar has written. This disunity was purposefully seeded by the Mexican government. The old agrarian economic elite of the 1910s had organized through large regional organizations controlled by latifundistas, or large landholders. When the government appropriated their lands to redistribute them, it forced them to disband the regional organizations through which they wielded influence. With latifundistas' organizational structure dismantled, a cascade of smaller associations formed in their place. The new business associations organized around location and crop harvested—hence, there was an association of cotton producers in Sonora and one for vegetable growers in Baja California.

In 1947, these more discrete organizations decided to band together as the ANC to see if they could replicate the influence on national policy that organized labor and organized ejidos seemed to possess.[40] They still lobbied through their local organization when they had a very particular issue, such as insufficient workers during a specific growing period. But when their concern was broader—shared beyond locality and crop—they operated under the ANC to build strength in numbers.

Even before the Mexican government's decision to block Mexican migration, growers anticipated the BP's impending deadline and urged Cortines to reconsider whether out-migration was healthy for the country. Using the ANC as their vehicle, they claimed they had been hurt by the scarcity of hired-hands. They framed it as a national issue, particularly acute for producers in the North. The exodus of Mexicans as braceros and undocumented workers left their areas depleted of labor.[41] These agricultural producers, they maintained, were left unable to regularly satisfy their labor needs. Only government intervention, they argued, could fix their chronic labor shortage. The looming deadline of the BP offered an opportunity to address their systemic woes. As they saw it, by not re-signing the BP and denying the US access to Mexican workers, Mexico could severely limit options for migrants, who would then be compelled to settle for work in Northern Mexico once the United States was eliminated as a realistic destination. The ANC argued that discontinuing out-migration represented a "defense of our national economic interests," conflating their interests with those of the country at-large.

After Cortines rebuffed US entreaties to renew the BP, the ANC continued to press its case. It argued that stanching migration—and increasing Mexican growers' supply of workers—would increase the country's wealth. On the day of the suspension, they delivered a white paper on migration to President Cortines, laying out the schematics of the migration, the major problems caused by it, and ways forward.[42] The principal crisis, as they saw it, was not the BP but the ease with which Mexicans could leave as undocumented migrants.

Based on their experience, they observed that easy passage through the border region encouraged an unyielding migration and created a continual shortage of labor across the country, most acutely in the North. For agricultural enterprises, this resulted in higher costs of production. They had to dedicate time and resources to securing a labor force domestically. This involved commissioning labor recruiters, entering agreements with far-flung municipalities, and transporting workers from disparate locations. More damaging still, the ANC claimed, the steady stream of workers to the United States doomed growers to a "ruinous" wage competition with American corporations. They had to bump up wages to woo Mexican migrants. By their account, it was an unwinnable competition, for they could not match US wages. Such was the dilemma the ANC perceived in a world with insufficient barriers between them and the United States. Hence, in addition to supporting a complete end to bracero guest work, the ANC advocated for the institution of aggressive border controls to repel undocumented exits.

Yet holding onto workers was more than a matter of narrow self-preservation, or so the ANC alleged. Retaining Mexican laborers would sustain the national economy. As they saw it, the country was developing based on a strategy of import-substitution industrialization and the promotion of domestic manufacturing. Under such an approach, allowing Mexicans to leave for a foreign country was counterproductive. Mexican nationals who migrated were workers, yes, but they were also potential consumers of the domestically produced goods on which the country was pinning its hopes of economic modernization. When Mexicans left the country, they took not just their labor but also their purchasing power. By ANC calculations, the 1.6 million Mexicans living in the United States, either without papers or as guest workers, represented a loss of 5,840 million pesos that could otherwise be in circulation in the Mexican economy. This figure was based on a hypothetical worker income of ten pesos per day. In sum, the ANC anticipated two changes from the demobilization of Mexican nationals. Northern Mexico enterprises would no longer have to compete much for Mexican labor. And with a greater pool of Mexicans consuming goods produced domestically, industrial development in Mexico would accelerate.

Building on its economic theories, the ANC offered plans to ensure that migrants—and their economic value—stayed in Mexico, beyond removing the BP and policing undocumented migration. The true crux of Mexicans' itineracy, argued the ANC, was not the erosion of the ejido system, general landlessness, or unattractive wages and work conditions in Mexico. Rather, it was that agricultural jobs, including in Northern Mexico, were cyclical, with harsh off-seasons. This forced Mexicans to have to seasonally relocate, including to the United States, to sustain themselves and their families.

The ANC welcomed a partnership with the Ministry of Agriculture to find ways to "root campesinos to the land through work that is more permanent and remunerative." The ANC's constituent members offered to cede fields they used in commercial agriculture, so that select campesinos could harvest them year-round. These fields, granted by business to the federal government to control, should be dedicated to the "rational exploitation of livestock, poultry, and eggs." Since each of these three ventures was nonseasonal, Mexicans would have "permanent occupation" and be less likely to move abroad.

ANC members stood to gain by encouraging a contramigratory culture. But they fashioned themselves as noble patriots forswearing "sectarian interest." Regardless of what path Mexico chose, they vowed to "help the government and fellow citizens put into play the constructive energies indispensable to increasing production." The point was "to improve the lives and lots of Mexican workers" not to correct their labor shortage. That would just be a welcome by-product.

The ANC's constituent members expressed support for President Cortines independently but left policy formulation to the association. The Cámara Agrícola Ganadera del Norte Coahuila (Agriculture and Livestock Chamber of North Coahuila), an association of agricultural producers and cattle ranchers, for instance, adopted the theme of national self-respect. It lauded Cortines, claiming to be inspired by his "patriotic" attempt to "safeguard the national dignity" unfairly trampled by the BP.[43] The business sector's discourse shows how "dignity" became a unifying framework for various stakeholders who had previously operated in silos. The same tone was struck by various other local or regional associations, including the Confederación de Asociaciones Agrícolas del Estado de Sinaloa (Confederation of Agricultural Associations of the State of Sinaloa) and the Cámara de Comercio de Hermosillo (Hermosillo Chamber of Commerce).[44] The latter convened "in a meeting and resolved to express solidarity with your [Cortines's] patriotic attitude to confront the bracero problem to protect the interests of our conationals, the dignity of the country, and the vigor of its institutions."[45]

A bevvy of trade unions also made their solidarity known to the Mexican government, emphasizing themes of manliness, the inhumanity of bracero work in the United States, and the prospect of improving salaries and conditions for Mexican wageworkers. As the Trabajadores de Recursos Hidráulicos of Jalisco (Jalisco Water Resource Workers) put it, their "compatriots" had been leaving for the United States in absolutely "humiliating conditions." It was only right that Cortines assume a "dignified, virile posture" and set the stage so that "we can all work together and develop better working conditions in Mexico."[46] They believed the *engrandecimiento* (greatness) of Mexico was within reach with policy reforms that focused on working-class Mexicans.

The Confederación de Trabajadores de Tabasco (Tabasco Workers Confederation) was proud of the "utmost patriotism" of Cortines. In line with other trade unions, they began to orient *obreros* (workers) in their state to "abstain from seeking to cross the border to the United States."[47] The Federación Regional de Trabajadores de Soconusco (Sononusco Regional Workers Federation) did the same in Chiapas, advising enrolled Mexicans to respect the migratory suspension. They acted "so that migrants do not leave for strange lands." "Arms and effort," they reasoned, "are what Mexico needs for its uplift."[48]

Meanwhile, the Sindicato Minero (Miners Union) mourned the violations of Mexican workers' "human rights." It praised Cortines's "valiant effort," which lifted "enthusiasm in any Mexican who was well-raised." The union believed defending Mexican workers abroad would open a path to internal reform, including improved wages and work conditions.[49] The Federación Revolucionaria de Obreros y Campesinos (Revolutionary Federation of Workers and Campesinos) praised "the step, so firm, you have taken by not allowing any Mexican workers to go to the United States." "Our Federation," it remarked, "which has the aim of fighting for the betterment of the country and the well-being of our workers . . . will continue to seek better salaries so that Mexicans can crown their struggle and their faithfulness to work." With reforms friendly to working-class people, they envisioned Mexicans would no longer "abandon work in this country and their families."[50]

The executive committee of the Federación de Trabajadores de Sinaloa (Sinaloa Workers Federation) also perceived great possibility: "We are proud that the destiny of our nation is in the hands of a man like you, who has lifted up Mexico's name." It imagined a future in which migrants no longer went "to the United States to earn starvation wages, be extorted, and be treated like beasts by the growers." All that was left was to "germinate plans" favorable to workers and bring Mexico "great relief" from its historical migratory woes.[51]

Mexico's most influential labor federations mobilized to exert a countervailing effect on the migration as well. The CTM, the largest confederation of labor unions, with direct ties to the PRI, maintained its opposition to the migration and celebrated the development. As we saw in chapter 1, the CTM's leader Fidel Velázquez sporadically criticized the migration publicly in the 1940s, worrying mainly about the effects it would have on the CTM's enrollment and the strength of organized labor. Now the CTM trumpeted the dignity, valor, virility, and promise of Cortines's decision, heralding it as a "transcendental position."[52] Members of the CTM were given the instruction to abide by the migratory suspension and remain in Mexico.

The constituent bodies of the CTM at the state level affirmed this direction. The CTM in Nuevo León reported that the "proletariat celebrates your manly and patriotic attitude defending the dignity and interests of the Mexican people," and relayed that it was impressing upon workers the magnitude of the moment, which represented a defense of Mexicans and, possibly, a springboard to working-class reform.[53] The CTM chapters in Jalisco, Tamaulipas, Sonora, and other states, as well as CTM affiliates organized by profession, similarly extoled the political possibilities opened up by the BP's termination.[54]

The CTM's peers in the Confederación Regional Obrera Mexicana (Mexican Regional Workers Confederation), another influential union, formed commissions at the state level that traveled to municipalities throughout Mexico, voicing the potential latent in this moment.[55] In Puebla, for instance, the Confederación Regional Obrera Mexicana commission went to the regions of Huejotzingo, Cholula, Puebla, Atlixco, Matamoros, Tehuacán, and San Martín to visit with workers. It reminded them that to "abandon Mexico is to abandon their duty to [their country] . . . and renounce their share in the betterment of Mexico." Cortines, they explained, was making gestures to improve working-class people's "quality of life." And he might do more if they fell in line and stayed home.[56]

Other organizations interested in seeing out-migration curbed pointed to Mexicans' ability to subsist on arable land as the key area of reform. Two forms of land ownership were common in Mexico but were decreasingly supported financially, as the PRI moved away from "el campo," an agrarian economy, and embraced the modernizing promise of urbanization and industrialization. The first was private parcel ownership by campesinos.[57] The second was communal landholdings, or ejidos, administered by communal landholders, ejidatarios.

The ejidos were historic instruments of social change. The Mexican state established them after the Revolution by appropriating the lands of latifundistas, monopoly landholders, who for decades had amassed the country's fertile land, forcing campesinos to work for immiserating wages or in debt peonage. The Mexican state gave selected groups of Mexican campesinos stewardship of seized plots, which they were to farm communally. Article 27 of the Mexican Constitution empowered the government to conduct this measure. It was the "original owner" of all land and water within the national domain and could expropriate land for public utility, provided that the original owners received an indemnity.

The government did not transfer full ownership to ejido beneficiaries. It kept final claim over expropriated lands. Nevertheless, ejidos endowed Mexican campesinos with cultivation and use rights, contingent on continuous land use, with no more than a two-year break in cultivation. In theory, campesinos just needed to band together and submit a request to use part of an existing large property as their parcel. After some bureaucratic procedures, it would be apportioned for them to use indefinitely. Their stake could be passed to their children.

One perennial problem for ejidatarios and their advocates, however, was convincing the government to adequately increase financial support for ejidos—mainly by way of government credits and loans. Otherwise, they were left to rely on their own capital. The other issue was spurring the government to create more ejidos out of extant large, monopoly landholdings throughout Mexico.[58] Though the PRI moved toward an embrace of industrialization following World War II, the lore of the ejido system and the rhetorical weight still given to it by officials gave some campesinos and their associations a lingering faith that the ejido and "el campo" could still act as bastions of permanence.[59] To the leading campesino organizations that communicated with Cortines, the ejido and rural life remained alive, and there was reason to hope migrants could be anchored to regimes of agrarian production.[60]

Campesino associations were enthused by Cortines's migratory suspension. Acción Política Ganadera Mexicana (Mexican Livestock Political Action) published a spread in the national newspaper *Excélsior* exhorting campesinos to stop migrating and commit to the fields, either in ejidos or the private parcels in their possession. The dually targeted ad was fitting as most campesino organizations admitted both private landholders and ejidatarios.[61]

Campesinos Mexicanos Confederados (Confederated Mexican Campesinos), for its part, issued a circular to all of its members in which it similarly underscored the importance of campesinos' committing themselves to their fields. The confederation reported to their members that the government was acting in the defense of Mexicans and the Revolution. However belatedly, it was rescuing migrants "who suffer vexations and whose lives are in danger . . . and bringing an end to a series of outrages that had gone unpunished by the Mexican government." The communiqué to enrolled campesinos stressed that such a course merited their collaboration. "The parcels our government, born of the Revolution, has given us are not to be abandoned under any circumstances. You must cultivate them with determination and faith to improve our agricultural production."[62]

The Liga Nacional Campesina de México (Mexican National Campesino League) similarly publicized its antiemigrationist, proagrarian resolve: "We stand in solidarity with your government. . . . We have sent circulars to our delegates in border regions to tell workers accustomed to emigrating that, for their own safety and personal dignity, and out of pride in their Mexicanness and the Revolution, they should refrain from crossing the northern border, for it would be a betrayal of the nation." They pledged to Cortines, "We are under your orders, ready for any emergency" that might arise from the "enslaving inclinations" of the "Northern Colossus."[63] Meanwhile, the Campesinos Mexicanos Confederados (Confederated Mexican Campesinos) reported, "our regional delegations from both coasts have met to provide ample instructions to the campesinos in our organization on their duty to farm more Mexican land and take advantage of agricultural possibilities in this country."[64] Campesino organizations were in lockstep in advertising the importance of guaranteeing permanence to migrants.

The CNC, the most established organization for campesinos and the one affiliated with the PRI, joined the contramigratory impulse. Though Mexican ejidos could be part of other autonomous associations, the PRI required that as part of their charter they maintain membership in the CNC. The CNC formally represented their interests before the PRI, in theory acting as an intermediary between ejidos and the government. This was part of the postrevolutionary state's larger plan to stabilize rule by granting key sectors, such as campesinos, an organ through which to communicate.

As we saw in chapter 1, the CNC viewed the BP and out-migration unfavorably, fearing they would draw Mexicans away from cultivating their individual or ejido landholdings. The opposition held firm at this moment, with the executive committee of the CNC expressing that it "welcome[d] the patriotic measure you [Cortines] have taken. We consider that this measure can be highly beneficial to our country. We support your determination on this matter and will support their enforcement." The CNC vowed to do so by passing any subsequent resolutions by Cortines to its chapters and by insisting that CNC members adhere to his initial order not to emigrate.[65]

The support was seconded directly by the constituent state bodies of the CNC, or *comités regionales* (regional committees), such as the CNC in the State of Puebla, which "applaud[ed] without reservation [Cortines's] decision to prevent the departure of Mexican braceros from our country."[66] It stressed that the government should not stop there but should instead see to the "opening of new ejido *lands* and sources of activity, so that [Mexicans disposed to migrate] may progress with dignity." The CNC affiliate in the state of Veracruz joined the chorus, agreeing that Cortines's determination would "benefit the national economy."[67] Similar sentiments were expressed by CNC bodies throughout Mexico. A CNC affiliate in the state of Sinaloa wrote that "the feeling of the campesinos organized by this entity is that we are to respect your patriotic stance on the problem of migration." It added that its members would police one another to make sure no one attempted to abandon the nation.[68]

Less influential organizations also submitted their adhesion. The Confederación Campesina de la República Mexicana (Campesino Confederation of the Republic of Mexico), for instance, proclaimed that "national rehabilitation requires the effort of all the sons of Mexico." It urged Cortines to undertake policies to vitalize the agrarian sector.[69] The Confederación Revolucionaria de Obreros y Campesinos (Revolutionary Confederation of Workers and Campesinos), a then-ascendant organizing force for campesinos and workers, was celebratory but also recommended policy. It wanted to "take advantage of the moment to request that you [President Cortines] order the Ministry of Agriculture to resolve favorably the petitions we have been making that idle or empty lands be placed at the disposition of our organization's members in order to increase agricultural production." With such fields properly exploited, "Mexicans will have the opportunity to remain in the country with new sources of jobs.... It would create in them the same highly patriotic spirit that animates you, Mr. President."[70]

Antonio Cabrera Valdés, president of the Liga Nacional Campesina (National Campesino League) that represented 300,000 campesinos, concurred that Cortines should expand "the depth and scope" of federal support for campesinos.[71] The Coalición de Agrupaciones Revolucionarias de México (Mexican Coalition of Revolutionary Associations), a coalition that included ejidatarios, took a similar position. It communicated to Cortines, "In representation of our campesinos, we support your decision. In the migrants lie our most precious capital: our men." The coalition no longer wished to see "our brothers" be "subjected to inhumane exploitation in the United States." To that end, the "precious capital"—the migrants—should be better kept in Mexico by "a political recommitment" to the country's agricultural economy.[72] For another organization, Ejidos Confederados (Confederated Ejidos), the issue was plain to see: the "illusion of the dollar" was impelling Mexicans to abandon their country, and instead of simply reveling in its decision, the PRI needed to renew its support of the ejido to find the "most natural" and obvious solution to the problem of Mexicans abandoning their homeland.[73]

Generally speaking, the campesino organizations that engaged with the migratory moratorium of 1954 avoided making particularized claims, arguing for support of their own ejido. Their calls were by and large for reinvigorated support of the ejido system and "el campo" as a whole. The Federación Nacional de Agrupaciones Campesinas de México (National Federation of Campesino Associations) was representative of this point. An organization that drew its membership from ejidos in areas of high out-migration, it argued that ejidos were languishing under technological backwardness and banks' restrictive lending practices and needed systemic overhaul. The government could remedy the situation by "making it easier for agriculturalists to obtain physical and financial resources."

Beyond a need for loans and machinery, the Federación Nacional de Agrupaciones Campesinas de México maintained that ejidos were hindered by bureaucratic red tape. It complained that the government made ejidos wait a long time, sometimes years, to turn their temporary ejido assignments into permanent ones and underscored that this created a sense of precariousness among provisional ejidatarios and left them open to emigrating. The organization advocated tightening of timelines, and immediately making all temporary ejido assignments permanent, so that ejidatarios would feel safely attached to their land and able to resist the temptation to migrate.[74]

To the extent ejidos stressed the particulars of their situation to President Cortines, instead of the importance of broader reform, it was only when the challenges they faced seemed insurmountable. For instance, the Comité Municipal de Defensa Revolucionaria (Municipal Revolutionary Defense Committee), based in the high-migration zone of La Barca, Jalisco, singled out maladministration by employees at the Department of Hydraulic Resources, who for five consecutive years denied their claims to acquire land by Lago de Chapala with specious justifications. Even there, however, the aspiring ejidatarios connected their experience to a more general phenomenon of administrative corruption in the management of ejidos. They revealed that not just they but also applicants from nearby Ocotlan and Jamay were being denied access to cultivate in Chapala by administrators happy to keep those lands amassed in the hands of businessmen, priests, judges, politicians, and "even compadres of these people." To these aspiring ejidatarios, this was lamentable, for it led directly to their need to migrate. Mexico, they asserted, should "never let working people, so needed in our country, leave to create wealth for our neighbors."[75]

Whereas ejidatarios advocated for their particular form of land usage, landless Mexicans begged to receive any land at all. Contemporary sources indicate that of the 300,000 Mexicans who left annually as guest workers, as many as 100,000 were without land.[76] Their lack of ownership could have been due to any number of factors: the checkered history of land redistribution; the failure of their own ejido or privately held land; or simply their choice to prioritize other forms of income generation, including work as migratory laborers. With no claim on existing agricultural property, this segment of the population used this opportunity to levy claims that the viability of Mexicans staying in Mexico depended on their being able to access land. They exhorted the government to undertake land allocation and colonization. Like other sectors, they celebrated Cortines, while underlying the necessity of reform.

Landless citizens reached out to the government both on their own and through larger campesino associations. To them, it was plain that Mexico's migratory woes owed to the inaccessibility of landownership for many campesinos. The Coalición de Agrupaciones de México, for instance, stressed the numbers: "THERE WERE ONE MILLION TWO HUNDRED THOUSAND CAMPESINOS WITHOUT LAND," they wrote in capital letters, each of these campesinos prime candidates to depart the country. In their own organization, there were hundreds, particularly in the northern states of Sonora, Tamaulipas, and Sinaloa, who had put in requests for ejido land and three years in had yet to receive approval. This provoked in them a "reasonable desperation" and a desire to migrate. The organization thus advocated emergency measures to cut through the red tape and approve the requests of as many landless Mexicans as possible. Only in this way would the government be able to deal with the "lacerating" situation of braceros and migrants subject to "inhumane exploitation" and "preserve within the country the most precious capital of a nation: its working men."[77]

The landless also offered clear ideas of where Mexico would find the land they needed. The Comité Regional Campesino (Regional Campesino Committee) asserted that lands should be appropriated from large landholders. To minimize controversy, they argued the government should first target absentee landowners whose land was farmed by hired hands and staff. Moreover, to avoid creating more monopoly landholders going forward, the government should set a limit of twenty hectares per landholder. With more land freed, Mexico would be able to engage "in a redistribution of land that is fair" and "tackle" the "primordial issue" animating the "abusive migration." Once a Mexican had his ejido land through this redistribution, "it would hold him, and create in him an unmovable love for the country that gave him life."[78]

Groups of landless migrants who left every year for the United States wrote directly to President Cortines. Interestingly, of all the groups that wrote to Cortines, including the ANC, which represented 620 growers' associations, the chronic migrants were the ones the administration took most seriously. The migrants urged Cortines to undertake *colonización* projects at once. Colonization was the process whereby the Mexican state sponsored new settlements, or colonias; opened them up to be populated, providing residents with everything from communication infrastructure to irrigation; and eventually transferred ownership to the beneficiaries. Migrants saw colonias as a straightforward solution that would "immediately disincentivize" out-migration. Cortines's cabinet made special note of these communiqués by landless people as "proposals" to avoid *la fuga de campesinos* (the flight of peasants). Whereas with many other respondents, Mexican officials highlighted supportive sentiments and mobilizations, they flagged letters from landless migrants for their policy import.

The letters of landless migrants served other functions too. President Cortines's administration did not just highlight the idea of shuttling migrants to state-supported lands. Cortines personally instructed his staff to forward some of the messages from landless migrants to Secretary of Foreign Affairs Luis Padilla. Padilla could then show them to US negotiators to convey that not even Mexican migrants wanted to keep going to the United States. They backed Mexico and were open to remaining in it, so long as Mexico could provide them with oases of settlement.[79] Cortines attempted to convince US negotiators that Mexico was operating from a position of strength.

Yet, ultimately, this was not merely a negotiating bluff. By highlighting migrants' interest in domestic attachment, Mexico intimated to the United States a direction to which it was prepared to commit itself. After all, what Cortines needed was to emerge from the BP lapse of 1954 with a political victory and an aura of strength and vigor vis-à-vis the United States. That could be achieved through a new, fortified BP, or by trailblazing long-term outlets for Mexicans internally and embracing a future without migration.

The next chapter will take us more fully inside Mexican government circles. Mexican officials joined the buoyancy and brainstorming filtering through Mexican society. In fits and starts, they would give shape to a pro-permanence platform in 1954. But by focusing on the social response to the migratory interregnum, as this chapter has, it is possible to see how Mexico's efforts to mitigate the migration were compromised from the outset. In a rush to deal with the migratory crisis, the authoritarian state would give primacy to colonization schemes, relegating the perspective of Mexican respondents who advocated for other types of systemic reforms to make the country hospitable year-round.

Concerned citizens, business groups, labor syndicates, and ejido organizations wrote to Cortines based on their experience and expertise. But, for all the reform they imagined possible, the range of change was delimited from the very beginning. Cortines would seize on colonization as the most viable way to stem out-migration, shunting aside the possibility of more thorough reform. Under the PRI's autocracy, federal leaders took stock of public opinion but presumed they had the unconstrained power to decide which voices to heed and which to ignore. Indeed, in early 1954, Cortines officials were still confident as architects of migration and movement.

CHAPTER THREE

AN UNCONTAINABLE FLOW

The Escalation and Demise of Mexico's Migrant Demobilization Campaign, 1954

Chapter 2 spotlighted President Adolfo Ruiz Cortines and the context for his decision not to renew the BP, as well as the immediate social response to the moratorium he imposed on out-migration. The present chapter explores the further buildup, crescendo, and conclusion of the US-Mexican impasse. Rather than focus exclusively on one set of actors, I will show how the Mexican state, Mexican migrants, and the United States converged in a pitched conflict to shape the short- and long-term future of Mexicans' managed mobility. Toggling among these actors, we will see their different reasonings and imperatives throughout the 1954 migratory stoppage. This entangled social and political history reveals the interpenetration of Mexican state power, US international power projection, and migrant agency. These actors were not straightforwardly powerful or subaltern; rather, they tested and negotiated each other's strengths and weaknesses.

Because Mexico most consistently animated the conflict—by disavowing the BP and exploring countermigratory possibilities, tentatively at first, more aggressively later—this chapter gravitates toward it. We will begin with the Mexican state, moving through its various levels, from state and national legislatures, to state and municipal governments, to regional committees of the PRI, to political insiders in the orbit of federal officials. Throughout the Mexican political machine, its constituent elements mirrored the social buoyancy explored in chapter 2.

Mexican officials, claiming to be gripped with patriotic fervor, offered to use their power to preclude migrants from leaving and began to consider long-term means to root migrants internally. Their buy-in to the migratory moratorium was significant. Because they were in positions of authority, they were the ones most involved in broadcasting or implementing President Cortines's immediate campaign to deter out-migration, and eventually his longer-term efforts to demobilize migrants too.

The chapter then offers insights into top-level Mexican policymaking. It shows how Cortines's team took advantage of the sovereign pause it issued on out-migration. Mexican leaders understood that their decision not to renew the BP had opened space for deliberation. They could programmatically rethink the state's relationship to out-migration. Specifically, the Cortines administration debated which means to use to deter migrants from leaving: violent repression, appeals to patriotism, incentives, or a combination thereof. Cortines ultimately favored a mix of immediate deterrence, such as the deployment of military personnel along the border, and long-range reforms to stanch out-migration. His administration, for instance, formulated explicit plans to programmatically distribute land to migrants, so they might create state-supported colonias and remain in Mexico.

Cortines's administration largely ignored the United States as it formulated its policy position. It presumed itself powerful enough to bend the migration to its will, irrespective of the United States. The United States, however, was not to be rendered invisible. Just a week after Mexico chose to deprive it of migratory labor, the United States opened its southern border. It allowed any Mexican male laborer who wished to cross into the United States unregulated entry. Faced with the US challenge, Cortines was emboldened.

He set aside any remaining hesitation and definitively and publicly embraced a countermigratory stance. He also launched contramigratory measures, mostly based on creating colonias for migrants.

Despite shifting its countermigratory campaign into high gear, the Cortines presidency would struggle with the US deregulation of its border. Its strategy aligned perfectly with many migrants' wish to move about without impediment. Thousands of migrants answered the US call and crossed the open border. They preferred immediate mobility and existing higher wages in the United States to waiting for President Cortines's projects of migrant rootedness to mature. Faced with the irrepressible recalcitrance of migrants—namely, the way they fought with Mexican militiamen patrolling the opened border—Mexico relented. Cortines returned fully to diplomacy to reinstate a modified BP. The episode put an end to Mexico's conceit that it could control the migration—or even impede it altogether—with the domestic tools at its disposal.

IN AND AROUND THE STATE

President Cortines's migratory moratorium touched a nerve, not just socially but within the Mexican political system. Cortines could adjust the government's approach to out-migration, but the constituent elements of Mexico's political class were the ones who would have to implement an antiemigration political program. The bases of the PRI—governors, representatives, congressional bodies, and associational organs in Mexico—declared themselves galvanized, itching to launch the state machinery, from police forces to incentives, to impede migrants' exit and root them within Mexico.

Congressional lawmakers exemplified how easy it was for Mexican politicians to slip between opposing the BP, opposing out-migration altogether, and supporting pro-permanence reforms. Representative Jacobo Aragán Aquillón of Oaxaca exulted, "You have defended with sincere care and singular patriotism the sovereignty of Mexico, a norm of conduct that all the nations of the world are watching unfold in the case of the bracero, before the shameful insistence of the United States [on migrant workers]. We must stand with resolve."[1] "All of Mexico values your effort to serve the nation," wrote Representative Jesús María Suárez, adding that President Cortines should "create room in Mexico for thousands of families" through land-grants.[2] Representative Emmanuel Palacios of Guadalajara echoed this recommendation.[3]

Representative Pedro Ayala Fajardo had other ideas: "I hasten to convey my sympathy and solidarity with your patriotic stance in zealously defending our national dignity against the aggressive US empire." But "at the same time I respectfully request that a national emergency be decreed." This emergency should "bring immediate protection to the rural citizens who run away from the country because they are exploited by fierce caciques, municipal authorities, and ejidal authorities." Only by taking on its own corrupted elites could Mexico "promote guarantees to the campesino and intensify cultivation in the fields" and "make life more livable in Mexico."[4]

While some officials made recommendations, others merely applauded Cortines and deferred to his judgment. Senator Miguel Osorio Ramírez, a three-time member of Congress, wrote, "I am honored to submit myself as a Mexican to your high authority for the patriotic position you have taken concerning emigrant workers," and offered to drum up support for any subsequent Cortines policy.[5] The Congress of the State of Campeche, the Legislative Power of Tlaxcala, and other state bodies met to declare the centrality of "denying exit" to Mexicans by any means necessary.[6] Regional executive committees, in charge of locally mobilizing the party's resources, convened as well. The party's regional executive committee in Mexico City extoled Cortines's "patriotic and revolutionary defense of the interests of the workingmen of Mexico."[7] The regional executive committee in Culiacan, Sinaloa, reported that it carried out a "campaign to orient campesinos to respect the patriotic decision you have taken, for it will eventually increase the probability of their finding work in Mexico."[8]

State governors broadcast Cortines's migratory suspension, enlisted civic organizations and government bureaucrats in support, and pitched their ideas for containing out-migration. For instance, Coahuila governor Román Cepeda Flores launched a "high-intensity" campaign that enlisted civic organizations and state authorities in his state to "orient migrants to stay [in Mexico] and to ensure that they do."[9] The governors of Sonora and Jalisco, roused too in support, began to plot even further, offering to scout lands where Mexicans could be resettled, seeking to fix the migration issue by promoting permanence.[10] Agustin Yáñez, governor of Jalisco, wrote that in the meantime his administration would "undertake a campaign of publicity and persuasion to keep people in place."[11]

Through an intermediary, President Cortines learned that the governor of Veracruz was "enthused . . . and had identified vast virgin territories that could be populated, especially in Veracruz's southern region, where a virgin mountain zone could be offered to form settlements." The governor of Veracruz expressed this was "no egotism, no exaggeration . . . simply whatever was needed to establish settlements of migrant workers."[12] Governor Efraín

Aranda Osorio of Chiapas professed his "indefectible solidarity," offering to lead a "consciousness-building" campaign among would-be migrants to inspire them to remain in Mexico.[13]

Víctor Meno Palomo, the governor of Yucatán, carried out such a campaign: "I have widely announced [the Cortines decision] via municipal authorities so that workers here know their importance to the nation."[14] The governor of Tabasco, Manuel Bartlett Bautista, enthusiastically committed to launching initiatives: "We will considerably increase our [labor] demand by initiating public works programs in road-building and hydraulic works."[15] Though each communiqué was unique, all seemingly understood the necessity of communicating with migrants, who, the writers admitted, would have to be convinced to stay through nationalistic pleas, jobs programs, or land grants.

Meanwhile, on the frontlines of the battle against migration, Braulio Maldonado, the governor of the border state of Baja California, reported, "My government has invoked civil and military authorities in the region, as well as trade unions operating here, and we have arrived at a series of joint agreements." Among the resolutions was unreserved support for migration authorities, local police, and highway patrol to surveil disobeying migrants seeking exit; an "ample" newspaper and radio "information campaign" to discourage migration; and the formation of teams tasked with identifying migrants roving about Tijuana, Tecate, Ensenada, and the Valley of Mexicali—essentially, northern Baja California—to instruct them to return to their place of origin. The creation of such a team was confirmed by the PRI Municipal Committee in Mexicali, which reported that it established a special delegation specifically to "orient people present in our jurisdictions" back to their homes.[16]

It was imperative that Mexico make Baja California a dead end for migrants. The state bordered Southern California, with its impending harvests, and would be the heaviest corridor of migration in January 1954. Cognizant of Baja California's strategic importance, its governor, Braulio Maldonado, told President Cortines that his measures were entirely provisional. They were designed to buy the executive time to find "the programs and reforms possible" to achieve "the spiritual and economic rooting of our compatriots."

Finally, military men, who might be called upon for coercive methods, volunteered their support. Coronel Manuel Durán proclaimed that "there can be no good Mexican that does not at this moment respond in solidarity."[17] "We applaud you without reserve," celebrated General Eduardo G. Garci, "for pursuing a humane resolution to the migration issue."[18] Meanwhile General José Ricardo Pacheco Iturribaria made remarks in the Military Zone of

Tabasco regarding the "posture of dignity" assumed by the government, meritorious of a supportive mobilization by Mexicans.[19] General Valle Jordán, a commander stationed near the border whom Cortines was to task with patrolling to prevent unauthorized exits, offered his "unconditional support behind this patriotic policy." He perceived Mexico was "at long last proceeding with dignity on the problem of migration."[20]

Even opposition parties reported themselves as having "surrendered" to Cortines's rejection of the BP. They made statements calling for unity and cross-ideological alignment. The Partido Popular (People's Party), founded by prominent leftist Vincente Lombardo Toledano, had repeatedly agitated against the PRI and CTM for being sclerotic, nonrevolutionary in spirit, and weak on the United States. The party now said it was "in communication with members, explaining to them the urgency of unifying across party lines to defend the interests of the nation."[21] The Partido Social Integralista (Fundamentalist Social Party) also rallied in support, asserting that "the supreme wealth of any nation is the work of its men." Cortines, they wrote, deserved praise for defending the nation's "treasure."[22] The Partido Político Nacionalista de México (Nationalist Political Party of Mexico) also supported the BP's nonrenewal.[23]

Close allies of the administration were also galvanized, perceiving the nonrenewal of the BP as a springboard for deeper reform in Mexico. Bartolomé Vargas Lugo, who enjoyed a long career in the PRI, used his direct line of communication to Cortines to steer him toward a full pro-permanence agenda. Lugo possessed authority in matters of migration, governance, and agrarian economic development. Earlier in his career, he had been governor of the state of Hidalgo; secretary-general of the Partido Nacional Revolucionario (National Revolutionary Party, the progenitor of the PRI); head of the National Commission on Agrarian Affairs; and director of the National Bank of Agricultural Credit. He had a degree in agricultural engineering. During the early bracero period, he was a chief adviser to the Department of Agrarian Issues.[24]

Lugo urged Cortines to understand the historical gravity of the 1954 BP lapse. It represented an unmissable, potentially last-of-its-kind, opportunity to stamp out migration. Out-migration was growing in intensity, constituting a steady "current that has not stopped flowing [since World War II]." The data supported his prose. In 1953 alone, 1 million Mexicans emigrated, 800,000 without government-sanctioned contracts. He estimated that there were 2.5 million or more "wetbacks" in the United States. Mexico, he argued, must spearhead solutions. No matter how high these numbers climbed, the United States would not tackle the phenomenon. The prosperity of US agriculture depended on an abundance of labor, whether undocumented or not. The glut of migrant labor allowed growers to drive down wages by spurring competition between undocumented migrants, guest workers, and US citizens.

To keep Mexicans from moving north, argued Lugo, Mexico should orient its efforts around the ejido. Prosperous ejidos, he posited, offered the blueprint to permanence. They enabled Mexican families to remain rooted with "little thought of going to suffer abroad." Yet, of 17,500 of ejidos in Mexico, only 7,500 had sufficient resources to produce rice, sugar cane, coffee, cotton, alfalfa, and wheat. The other 10,000 ejidos lacked the capital needed to consistently cultivate these crops. They offered Mexicans no basis for fixed settlement.

In his view, the PRI abandoned ejidos, excommunicating them from the "Mexican family." PRI presidents had gradually defunded the Banco Nacional de Credito Ejidal, SA de CV, established in 1935 to support small producers of scant means. President Lázaro Cárdenas gave the bank a budget of 20 million pesos. But his successor, Ávila Camacho, allocated half this amount, 10 million pesos. Moreover, what funds were available were directed overwhelmingly to ejidos set on "good, quality land." The bank lent to them because they promised a safer return on its investment. Mexico's ejido policy thus elevated better-off ejidatarios but left others to languish. Finally, the ejido was mired by corruption. Functionaries of the Agrarian Bank syphoned funds and enriched themselves, not the peasantry.[25]

Lugo proposed a constitutional amendment to set aside 300 million pesos for ejido credits and to prioritize stability in Mexico. Ejidatarios could use the credit to purchase tools, seed, plows, and work animals. Moreover, each ejidatario would be granted five to seven pesos daily, a guaranteed basic income to sustain his family. To ensure that officials would not pilfer this money, Lugo provisionally recommended the appointment of specific trusted personnel. But, to truly mitigate against corruption, he advised that the national ejido bank be disbanded and replaced with regional ones controlled by councils composed partly of campesinos themselves.

Lugo urged Cortines to act before the window of opportunity closed. Foreign companies were buying swaths of land throughout Mexico and the country's population was booming. Within two decades, Mexico would fall into a "demographic disaster," with no arable countryside to sustain its population. It behooved Mexican leadership to act proactively to create rural oases of settlement, citizenship, and belonging. Should Cortines want to be particularly aggressive, Lugo proposed restricting foreigners' ability to buy property larger than twelve acres, and restricting ownership privileges to natural-born citizens, naturalized citizens, or foreigners married to a Mexican woman.

Lugo thus envisioned a future in which Mexico's "strong, young, healthy men" could "grow their own country with their labor," never to leave Mexico as "wetbacks" or under the veiled exploitation of contract labor. With these migrants integrated into "the Mexican family," a new, proud era of Mexican history would begin, closing "a spectacle so sad it should bring remorse to any of us who have ever served in the public realm."[26] President Cortines thanked Lugo for his ideas on how to reinvigorate the ejido and foster permanence.

Top government officials grappled with this dissatisfaction with the BP, evaluating how to best promote permanence in the short and possibly long term. Their chief concern was that migrants would not abide by the moratorium on out-migration. They knew that simply declaring the border closed would not, by itself, deter migrants. What migrants wanted were jobs, with or without a BP framework, and with or without Mexico's authorization. Mexican officials thus wrestled with how to prevent the flight of Mexican nationals through coercion, economic incentives, and appeals to patriotism.

President Cortines began by endorsing recommendations from the Junta Federal de Mejoras Materiales (Federal Board of Material Improvements), a government agency overseeing public works programs, including those tending toward economic modernization and job creation, especially in port areas and frontier regions.[27] The chief administrator of the agency in Tamaulipas advised that whatever set of policies Mexico used to treat out-migration, these should be "packaged in a propatria, pro-Mexican" messaging. In his letter to Cortines, the administrator argued that to "counter Mexicans' migratory impulse," the country would need a "psychological campaign" that conveyed unity and created a patriotic "social mystique" around permanence. Though Cortines concurred that a psychological operation was needed, he mandated that the Junta Federal de Mejoras Materiales immediately expand local public works programs. Action, not just discourse, he asserted, would be needed to "counteract the migratory tendencies of campesinos."[28]

Andrés Napoleón Molina Enríquez Rodea, a PRI political insider thanks to his father's hand in drafting the Constitution of 1917, and a self-described friend of President Cortines for over three decades, urged him to embrace pro-permanence reforms. Addressing the "central reasons for the flight of the *indio* and *mestizo*," he affirmed, would be "[your] government's most glorious piece of work." Enríquez indicated that he was in contact with Gustavo Díaz Ordaz, a high-ranking official in the Ministry of the Interior, and a future Mexican president, to impress upon him that the state should not "promote sedentarism through violence." He believed he had made some inroads convincing Díaz Ordaz away from his preference for strong-armed action. Whatever the truth, what is notable is that Mexico's top brass and elements close to it were gravitating to a goal—"sedentarism"—and discussing appropriate strategies.[29]

Pedro de Alba, Mexico's permanent ambassador to the UN International Labor Organization, a body dealing with international labor standards, wrote in Mexican periodicals *El Nacional* and *Novedades* to enunciate President Cortines's updated position. He conceded there "existed perhaps no more tragic problem for us [Mexican political leaders] than that of the emigrant workers of Mexico." It reflected "a failure of our social and political organization, with long and deep roots." "At stake" in remediating it, he maintained, was the "decorum and dignity of our country and the prestige of the Mexican Revolution." The time for permanent solutions had arrived, for the situation of these "rootless" workers had acquired a "tragic character that no Mexican has the right to ignore." It was "urgent that we [federal officials] find a formula to root them to the country . . . at any cost."

The material uplift of migrants would be key. It was the "instabilities and anxieties of our economic realm" that produced a "mobile wave of workers unable to find subsistence or tranquility [domestically]." "Theories and words would not be enough," he argued. Mexico would have to rely on "effective technical economic measures." Federal leaders were on the task, he told his Mexican readership. "We must think of a politics of rootedness" that understands as "essential the surefooted opening of new routes to permanence." At the crux of the policymaking would be "the Secretaries of the Interior, Foreign Affairs, Health, Agriculture, Hydraulic Resources, Work and Social Provision, and Agrarian Affairs," working to "formulate a coordinated plan so that the exodus of Mexican workers is stopped" and migrants' "love for their homeland is aroused."[30]

Evidence suggests that Mexican officials searched for such "effective technical measures." A proposal generated internally by the Cortines administration after the BP's collapse hypothesized a new federal agency to counter migration. The *anteproyecto* (proposed blueprint) referred to the agency as Comisión Colonizadora para Trabajadores Emigrantes (Colonization Commission for Emigrant Workers). Its aim would be to settle migrants in state-sponsored colonias. Through it, the Cortines administration envisioned delivering its first comprehensive solution to mass migration. The creation of colonia settlements was presented as an opening salvo "to begin to bring an answer . . . to the economic causes that engender migration." Other methods—such as long-term investment in ejidos—were not off the table, but they would require more time to develop. Colonization schemes, in contrast, would immediately expand avenues to permanence and could be more readily propped up, monitored, and vitalized by the state. Cortines's cabinet thus regarded them as the ideal solution to the "lack of permanent opportunities to work and subsist in the country."[31] Colonization would "create, in zones that fundamentally produce this migration, new centers of agricultural work." And it would be a vehicle for the government to steer migrants to "other parts of the country," thus achieving a healthy "gradual demographic redistribution."

There was no ambiguity that the Comisión Colonizadora's task would be to foment permanence. Its goal would be to anchor "groups of migrant populations" in stable communities by offering them wraparound support to maintain their agrarian settlements. The land upon which migrants would establish their homes and neighborhoods would be granted to them for a provisional five-year term. These assignments would become permanent if the settlement was successful. Migrants would thus have an incentive to work their land for the long haul. Individual parcels would be twenty hectares, "large enough to guarantee economic yields." And migrants would receive credits from the federal government to cover capital expenses, including for machinery and fertilizer.

The Comisión Colonizadora would dispense land to migrants by turning existing properties into colonization zones, including large holdings, privately or corporately held, and the government's own lands, or *predios*. The Cortines administration postulated that it could establish the Comisión Colonizadora as a new, permanent, federally funded body under the Colonization Law of 1946, which granted the Mexican state power to create colonies to establish new population centers and increase agricultural production. Lands that were not "properly exploited," according to the law, were eligible for repossession and redistribution by the state.

The administration worried about initial results. Applicants would be screened tightly to improve the odds that colonias would succeed and become a popular policy instrument. A points system would be used, with migrants judged by their age, marital status, savings, and occupational background. The administration was aware that "diverse methods" were needed to stymie migration. But it believed the Comisión Colonizadora, "with experience," would fine-tune the program and ably promote permanence.[32]

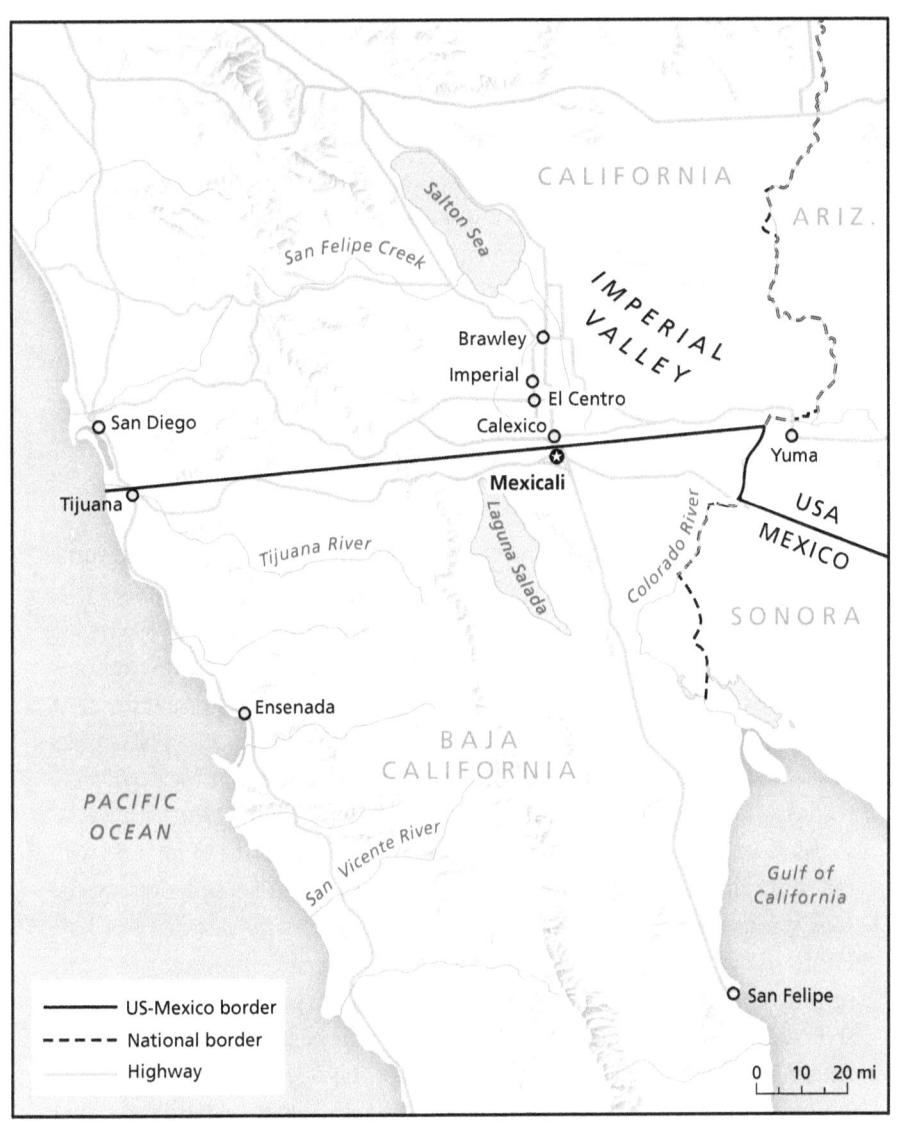

Mexicali-Calexico borderlands region. The Mexican border town of Mexicali was the epicenter of the 1954 US-Mexican impasse and the chief site of Mexico's migratory blockade. Mexican migrants were intent on crossing over to the Imperial Valley where the American lettuce harvest was underway.
Courtesy of Erin Greb Cartography.

As the week of January 15 developed following the BP lapse, Mexico's contramigratory intentions were publicly voiced and privately formulated but had not yet been substantially implemented. In terms of policy, Mexico's immediate attention was on a surge of migrants who gathered in Mexicali. They hoped to leave Mexico for the lettuce harvests of Southern California's Imperial Valley. Nine thousand migrants arrived in the border town after January 15. They streamed in, despite the BP lapse, and despite the ban Cortines imposed on out-migration after arguing that consular officials could not handle any more complaints from émigré Mexicans. Tulio López Lira, the head of the local immigration office in Mexicali, oversaw the arriving migrants there. Mexico deemed it imperative to control these migrants. It was a critical first step toward the two political alternatives at hand: to pursue a politics of rootedness or to pressure the United States to improve the BP by depriving it of labor.

Border crossings, such as the one in Mexicali, typically maintained some semblance of order during the BP. But this was only because migrants who arrived at border processing stations usually had to wait only a few days before being released to the United States. The BP gave migrants a sense they would be contracted eventually, abating the incentive to go around the state and migrate without sanction. However, with no BP in effect and talks of its renewal at a standstill, the migrants, 9,000 and counting in Mexicali, were restless—reluctant to idly wait while politicians determined their future.[33]

Mexican officials initially leaned heavily on national pride to contend with the Mexicali migrants and those who might join them. Serendipitously, the Mexican government's main messenger to migrants in Mexicali was Baja California governor Braulio Maldonado, a sharp critic of Mexico's inability to provide internal outlets for Mexican nationals. A migrant worker himself until his mid-twenties, Maldonado saw himself as championing the "most humble class" of Mexico—the proletariat—and against its "natural enemies."[34] He rejected the PRI's claim to faithfully represent the values of the Mexican Revolution. "It should cause us [politicians] great shame," he commented prior to the 1954 episode, "to call ourselves revolutionaries" when Mexico's working people—the people who "made the revolution"—"do not have salaries, or lands, or schools, or bread for their children, or guarantees of work."[35] He described the PRI's unwillingness to fight the "bankers, industrialists, and commercialists full of avarice" as a disgrace. Most of all, Maldonado condemned the PRI and the BP for subordinating Mexicans to the United States. How, he asked, could the PRI "in the twentieth century still lease and sell our people to American imperialism, which has neither scruples nor limits in its ambition and economic voraciousness"?[36]

Before the 1954 BP lapse, Governor Maldonado had buttressed his anti-guest work, pro-permanence rhetoric with action. In the early 1950s, he attempted to eliminate what he called "bracero slavery." He invoked braceros to help him launch a "modest rural and urban colonization effort in Baja California."[37] Families came by the hundreds, he later recalled, to claim a parcel of land, even though most of it was arid and difficult to till and live on. "Our peasants," he remembered, "wanted a piece of land and it didn't matter where. They ardently desired to own property and feel free, even it was in the middle of the desert."[38] Governor Maldonado was thus at the vanguard in using targeted policies to encourage permanence. Few politicians, with the exception of the governor of Veracruz—a mentor of his—championed land reform to abate mass migration prior to 1954.

Now, with Mexicali situated in Maldonado's state, he was summoned to explain to gathered migrants the stakes of the 1954 BP lapse. He joined migration officials in Mexicali, including López Lira, to deliver stump speeches to migrants. He underscored the transformative possibility: Mexico's conversion from a country of emigrants to a country of rootedness. If they were honorable, dignified Mexicans, they would support this fragile moment by respecting the government's order and refusing to migrate. As he described his intent to President Cortines, the point was to "spiritually and economically bind" migrants to Mexico by "appealing to their civic and patriotic sentiment."[39]

Federal officials echoed these sentiments in print media. Not yet able to make an economic case for migrant rootedness, they appealed to patriotism and love of self: if Mexicans were loyal to their nation, they would not abandon it, especially not to go to the United States to be debased. The Cortines administration sought to ensure that would-be migrants received its message. Recognizing that illiteracy might work against its nationalist appeals in newspapers, President Cortines called on state officials to spread the word through municipal authorities. Municipal presidents should stress to their residents that leaving the nation was tantamount to disloyalty and lacking proper love for their homeland.[40]

The Mexican government stood ready to use force against disobedient migrants. Ordinarily, at most, local police were called in to impose order among braceros in Mexicali. But with the border closed and no BP in sight, migrants gathered in numbers beyond what local authorities could handle.

And the fence separating Mexicali from the United States was not going to contain migrants through its presence alone. Hence, President Cortines mobilized the Mexican Army to guard 150 kilometers of the border. After a week of surveillance, General Valle Jordán, the head of the operation, claimed that thanks to his unit's watch not a single Mexican had crossed the border and circumvented the migratory stoppage.[41] It remained to be seen whether he could maintain that success once the United States began to aggressively recruit the migrants clustered in Mexicali.

MEXICO UNDER THE IMPERIAL GAZE

The lapse of the BP was well received in Mexico. Meanwhile, within the Mexican government itself, confidence seemed to abound, as officials contemplated the possibility of not just temporarily but permanently containing out-migration. On the US side, elite political and economic actors invested in the migration system viewed the BP lapse with similar confidence. They trusted that Mexico's will to hold onto its nationals, whether as bargaining chips or a catalyst to broad reform, could be broken. With the exception of the US State Department, these state and corporate elements agreed to flout Mexico's migratory freeze to maintain the US grip on Mexican migrant labor.

The DOL was pivotal in framing Mexico's migratory ban as an overreach. In particular, it presented the ban as the last of a series of Mexican excesses that had begun when President Cortines took office. The DOL was prepared to respond aggressively, even with what could be interpreted as attacks on Mexican sovereignty. Capturing the full, detailed DOL perspective is elusive, given that its records for this episode were destroyed. But a surviving internal memo provides the broad contours of its internal narrative: that it was Mexico, with its excessive grievances and demands, that imperiled the BP; strained growers' and the DOL's patience; and made itself an unreliable—and thus disposable—partner in migration management.[42]

By the DOL's account, President Cortines began his unreasonable demands in 1953. As a condition for a renewed BP, he insisted that migrants be provided nonoccupational insurance. Occupational insurance covered migrants for injuries suffered on the job. Nonoccupational insurance would extend that coverage off the job. Going further, Cortines wanted growers to purchase this insurance from a list of vendors vetted by Mexico. The DOL objected because of the measure's cost and because it seemed unreasonable to hold US businesses liable for injuries suffered outside the workplace.

What alarmed the DOL, however, was that Mexico by late 1953 sometimes flouted BP protocols and binational consultation. Mexico acted as if it had unilateral control over a potent BP tool: the power to permanently blacklist employers who flouted bracero protections. Mexico had previously followed a protocol of "joint determinations" specified in the BP to achieve blacklisting. When Mexico was concerned with an employer, a binational joint probe assessed claims of employer wrongdoing and determined redress.[43] For Mexico, these investigations often took too long, were inconclusive, and spared employers from blacklisting. So, by late 1953 Mexico decided to purge the BP of offending growers on its own. It empowered migrants to report offending businesses so it could bar them unilaterally.[44]

The United States complained of Mexican overreach, but Mexico defended itself with a semantic argument. Article 13 in the BP stipulated bracero contracting was to be "supervised" by representatives from both governments. Mexico argued that the verb "supervise" meant the DOL needed an additional, final permission by Mexico before releasing workers in US reception centers to employers. Previously, Mexico's say over day-to-day contracting ended once migrants crossed into the United States at the border. Now, complained the DOL, Mexico was operating with unlimited supervisory powers.[45]

Under these new conditions, American employers arrived at hiring centers to collect their expected allotment of workers only to find out that Mexico had blacklisted them. Mexico would offer them a chance to comply with its demands. It demanded banned employers accept a wage rate unilaterally set by the Mexican secretary of foreign affairs to get off the blacklist. Less frequently, Mexico demanded individual employers make an additional advance subsistence payment to workers, so they could buy food, clothing, and other necessities while they waited for their first formal BP paycheck. This was a new expense for growers. Ordinarily, migrants themselves covered the cost of personal provisions needed during their first days on a job through deductions from their paycheck. The DOL, moreover, complained that Mexico set the subsistence payment at an "unjustified rate."[46]

The DOL was alarmed that Mexican interventionism was peaking when there was an "urgent" need for workers in the Imperial Valley to bring in the region's lettuce harvest in the waning months of 1953.[47] More than that, Mexico's posture threatened the entire initiative. Growers, concerned with bottom lines, found the BP alluring if it worked reliably. But if every time the Cortines administration had a complaint against a specific employer, it could immediately cut them off and impose financial demands over them, such as nonoccupational insurance or subsistence payments, the BP lost its appeal. At any given moment, Mexico could withhold migrants' labor and undermine growers' ability to reliably and profitably plan ahead.

Beyond the added unpredictability, Mexico's expanded authority made participation in the BP "substantially" costlier for growers. The greatest financial burden for growers was the need to "retain leased or chartered transportation equipment for relatively long periods."[48] Blacklisted employers, that is, had to keep the vehicles they hired to transport workers on standby, in case Mexico—upon consideration—relented and allowed renewed contracting by the employer. The transfer of migrants from border sites to job sites, cost-efficient when it flowed smoothly, was less so when Mexico interrupted it by fiat.

By October 1953 the DOL determined it would be "firm and unyielding."[49] The US State Department, however, stressed the need for continued amicable relations with Mexico and sought to restrain the DOL by advising diplomacy. Playing along one last time, the DOL informed Mexican officials that the BP did not entitle Mexico to unilaterally interrupt contracting by blacklisting employers. In a somewhat condescending tone, they outlined to Mexican officials what each step of the process was supposed to look like, underscoring that once Mexican laborers crossed the border, Mexico had limited say over them and whom they worked for.[50]

Mexico dismissed the DOL's clarification and continued to assume unilateral blacklisting power. It also began to insist that US employers cover the transport of deceased laborers back to Mexico. The DOL lost faith in diplomacy and the reasonableness of its Mexican counterparts. By late 1953, the DOL decided it would act unilaterally to overrule Mexico's blacklisting of particular employers. The BP was enlisting a record number of employers, and the DOL surmised they would turn to undocumented workers if it tolerated Mexican interventionism. As the DOL explained, undocumented workers truly had no protections and would certainly debase American labor standards. The DOL decided that, with "regrets," it would have to continue contracting Mexican laborers to businesses Mexico had banned.[51]

This snub cemented President Cortines's decision not to renew the BP before its January 15, 1954, expiration. Though not privy to all the details, Mexican commentators saw the US unwillingness to grant Mexico major concessions in the BP as creating a deep, potentially unbreachable fissure between the two countries. *La Opinión*, a Mexican national newspaper with wide circulation, described "a heavy atmosphere of disagreement between [the United States and Mexico] that in recent years, since Roosevelt's Good Neighbor Policy, had been collaborative and fruitful."⁵² Papers reported that Mexico was "not willing to renew the bracero agreement" unless the United States granted Mexico vast unilateral control. So, by January 13, 1954, the DOL decided it would have to obtain Mexican workers for American agribusiness without Mexico's consent. It consulted with the Department of Justice to find a legal framework to allow Mexicans into the United States without the BP, just as Mexico was considering the opposite: how to contain Mexicans and prod them toward internal settlement. *La Opinión* condemned the US intent to sideline Mexico as unscrupulous. It lamented that the United States was willing to obtain migrants "at any cost."⁵³

When the BP finally lapsed and President Cortines decreed the border closed, migrants were momentarily cut off from American growers. The 9,000 migrants gathered in Mexicali were a sight both tantalizing and aggravating for planters in the adjacent Imperial Valley of Southern California. They needed at least 3,000 laborers to harvest their lettuce. By late January, they would need more for the carrot harvest as well. American growers searched for ways to bring trapped migrant laborers to their fields. They felt pressed for time, as they claimed their crops were spoiling. They also heard rumblings that Northern Mexico business were recruiting migrants gathered in Mexicali to work in Baja California, thus creating competition for the stagnated labor pool.

Growers in the Imperial Valley thus decided to skirt the DOL, which was busy with the Department of Justice, figuring out a legal architecture to bring migrants across the border without Mexico's involvement. During the week of January 15, employers first focused on retaining some of the migrants already working in their fields. Hundreds of braceros, having completed their contract, were supposed to report back to Mexicali to be transported home by Mexican authorities. Planters made a bid to keep them. They told migrants they could stay. They would provide "higher salaries, first-class food, adequate housing and even lump-sum payments." Lured by the extragovernmental promise, many braceros broke their contractual promise to return to Mexico.⁵⁴

Planters also sent Henry Hicks, a recruiter from Las Vegas, and two other labor recruiters to talk personally with migrants gathered in Mexicali. Into early February, the three recruiters spoke to the same gathered Mexicans that Governor Maldonado was trying to stir to permanence with nationalistic speeches. They snuck into Mexicali every day before dawn to recruit Mexican people and bring them surreptitiously into the United States. Mexico had long experienced foreign labor recruiters entering the country. Their activities were illegal. So Mexican police eventually were able to arrest the three recruiters. The head of the Mexicali immigration office, Tulio López Lira, heralded this as a victory in the "battle" to defend Mexican labor from the designs of American farmers who held no regard for Mexican sovereignty and the sanctity of Mexico's borders. But, to continue his metaphor, the activities of the recruiters were just the opening salvo in a conflict that was to further test Mexican authorities.[55]

On January 23, the DOL, after completing its consultation with the Department of Justice, moved to establish a transnational system of labor exploitation based on direct, unmediated connection to Mexico's working masses. The agency relaxed border policing and issued an open invitation to Mexican workers to cross into the United States without Mexico's involvement. The DOL only required migrants have no active police records. In most cases, it even bypassed medical examinations. It called it an "emergency program" of unilateral hiring. Mexico saw it differently. It was the institution of open borders and a flagrant assault on its sovereignty.[56]

The US Border Patrol used the open-border program to provide immediate amnesty for undocumented migrants in US fields. It brought twelve undocumented migrants to the border, had them place a foot back in Mexico, dragged them back to the United States, and rushed them to agricultural fields. Through the exercise, they were legally permitted to work, since they were now lawfully authorized entrants sanctioned by the emergency program.[57] This small-scale legalization was easy enough for US authorities to carry out. The trickier question, however, was how to reach the more than 9,000 migrant laborers trapped behind the Mexicali-Calexico border gate, now that Mexico, not the United States, was patrolling it with force.

Cortines's administration lambasted the new program of unrestricted migration. The migrants who participated, Cortines bemoaned, would have no labor protections whatsoever. US-Mexican discord had been grave in 1953, but diplomacy remained within grasp, as the two governments grappled over semantics, principally whether the BP's promise of binational "surveillance" over contracting entitled Mexico to blacklist employers without US participation. The open-border program now activated by the United States, in contrast, openly challenged Mexican authority. Mexican officials demanded "full human rights," such as life insurance for migrants, and unilateral control over braceros, to even consider reestablishing conversations. Mexico considered that it must control the opening, closing, and adjustment of migratory flows in accordance with its needs; otherwise, it was better off exploring alternatives, such as promoting the fixity of its populace.[58]

Mexico's governing and business elites were alarmed by the relaxed US border controls. They imagined apocalyptic scenarios. A huge number of Mexicans might abandon the nation and economically eviscerate the country. Even before the US open border, some PRI politicians worried about a "bracero psychosis" driving Mexicans to the United States and depleting Mexico of manual labor. Offering the case of his home state of Jalisco, for instance, Governor Agustín Yáñez complained that the number of Jalisciences emigrating undermined local agricultural activity. In particular, it compromised grain production. Jalisco was indeed a major sending state, often competing with Michoacán for first place. Yáñez wrote that some areas of Jalisco had become inert as zones of production.[59]

The deregulated US border sent fears of a migrant-driven economic collapse into overdrive. Business consortiums in Central Mexican states, such as Jalisco, organized to support the arguments of their state governments. They warned the lax US border program would be cataclysmic. Already, they were struggling to recruit sufficient laborers, even before the US innovation. Now, the problem would be aggravated as local laborers would be wooed by US permissiveness. The issue lay in replacing local laborers. To find supplementary labor, businesses held they had to rely on labor recruiters to search throughout Mexico. They then had to cover the transportation of far-flung workers to job sites, usually by bus. This pattern, they worried, would only deepen after the US action.[60]

Similar prognoses of the economic devastation streamed in from Northern Mexican states. In Coahuila, for instance, a group of leading businesses and politicians banded together to declare that the permissive US border policy would "undoubtedly cause our [Mexican] agriculture and our national economy to collapse." Attempting to galvanize the federal government to aggressive counteraction, they claimed that the United States was imperiling the PRI's import-substitution industrialization program. They predicted that the open border would cause a massive labor drain, as migrants would ignore Mexico's migration moratorium and head for the United States. Faced with a critical labor shortage, Mexican business would underperform, unable to satisfy either national or global markets. Mexico would then be forced to "import three times as much grain as it does now."[61]

These dire projections were inspired by the uncertainty of how many migrants would respond to the open-border call. A political-business junta in Tamaulipas, a northeastern border state, was pessimistic. It worried that Cortines's existing public strategy—of policing the border and invoking nationalism—would not be enough to prevent the coming exodus. The junta urged Cortines to accelerate plans for industrialization and economic growth, the end goal being to create well-paying jobs for Mexicans. A "patriotic call to contain the exodus" they affirmed, "can only work when in this country there are jobs that disenchant Mexicans from the illusion of the dollar."[62]

It was not clear whether the scenarios of economic calamity imagined by Mexican political and economic elites were farfetched. Cortines thus recognized a need to intensify the countermigratory campaign. In addition, regardless of its economic ramifications, the US decision to disregard the Mexican government as a regulator of Mexicans' mobility was an affront to Mexican sovereignty. And Cortines, with his checkered past, could not let it proceed uncontested. Building on the inflamed national feeling chronicled in chapter 2, President Cortines sought to stoke patriotism further to restrain migration throughout Mexico. He emphasized to potential migrants the direct connection between staying in Mexico and being loyal to it. Cortines enlisted municipal authorities to spread the word to local residents that internal fixity was paramount. Addressing the public, Cortines asked all good countrymen to mobilize in a grassroots antimigratory campaign to "properly orient" aspiring migrants to remain in the country.

In response, throughout the country, members of different social classes came together and formed what newspapers described as "citizen brigades." They visited ranches and fields, appealing to patriotism to dissuade people from migrating. In Aguascalientes, for instance, groups composed of ordinary citizens and local political, religious, and civic leaders went door-to-door and spoke to the men they encountered in each household. They became intimate salesmen of a new Mexican nationalism that made permanence and love of one's nation synonymous.[63] The work of these brigades complemented the earlier work, chronicled in chapter 2, of trade unions, peasant associations, and other social organizations that held meetings asking their members not to leave.

Municipalities buttressed efforts stemming from civil society. In Irapuato, Guanajuato, residents were handed a government-issued flyer. "No peasant, honored to be a Mexican," it read, "should cross the northern frontier without a contract authorized by our state. . . . To leave without the consent of the government," it unambiguously concluded, "is to betray your fatherland."[64] To support this clamoring for loyalty, President Cortines empowered state authorities to take and advertise "measures that will impede [out-migration]." *La Opinión* relayed the government's emphatic message, as well: "Not a single Mexican peasant must leave."

Cortines granted that social pressure and patriotism, no matter how intimate or persistent, could only go so far in counteracting the allure of an open border. His administration thus prepared to expand the use of force and incentives, especially in Baja California—ground zero of the impending exodus. Federal envoys were dispatched to meet with Baja California governor Braulio Maldonado and representatives of the region's business sectors. They agreed that the "president of the republic, the members of the army and the local police will become auxiliaries to the office of migration" for the purpose of patrolling the border. The federal government thus articulated a chain of command that consolidated its force behind Tulio López Lira, the head of the immigration office. Beyond that, the group agreed to persuade Mexicans gathered in Mexicali to stay by involving them in local projects and giving them a tangible path to permanence. Governor Maldonado would be in charge of enrolling interested migrants.[65]

Zooming out from Mexicali, President Cortines laid out a broader vision for how Mexico would break from its migratory identity once and for all. He announced a new national program to ensure that all Mexicans could remain within the nation's borders. He called it "The Braceros of Mexico for the Fields of Mexico." The political tagline alone was significant. Cortines was fully reframing the stakes of the 1954 BP lapse. It was no longer in any way about diplomacy and securing a better BP. Now, it was a matter of domestic transformation: of striving toward a culture of mass rootedness.

Beyond his nationalism, President Cortines offered the broad contours of a plan to moor Mexicans internally. His administration would focus on campesinos by supporting ejidos and colonias, that is communal landholding and rural settlements. Campesinos, or peasants, were seen as the demographic most susceptible to out-migration.[66] The first element of Cortines's Mexicans for Mexico initiative was to augment credits for ejidos to aid ejidatarios farming their collectively held parcels. The PRI largely deprioritized this sector of the Mexican political economy in favor of industrialization and urbanization following World War II, while continuing to extol its importance rhetorically. By underlining a need for intensified financial investment in the ejido, Cortines implicitly admitted that the PRI's neglect of ejidos had exacerbated peasant immiseration and mass dislocation. Cortines imagined that peasants would again be married to their land once provided with founts of government support. The government's outlay, he held, would pay for itself, since migrants would "expand the cultivation of grains" and reduce imports. Significant as it was that Cortines admitted the government's responsibility for the out-migration crisis, he failed to specify the extent to which credits for ejidatarios would be expanded and when they would be disbursed.[67]

Cortines was a touch more specific in his second plank for how to reserve "the braceros of Mexico for the fields of Mexico." In addition to supporting ejidos, Cortines envisioned using colonias as clusters of settlement. His government, he explained, would open up state-supported colonias for peasants to settle there at once; it would expand already established ones; and it would search and improve areas to house colonias in the future. In speeches delivered after the US opening of the border, he bragged of the short- and long-term transformation these colonias would bring. Speaking of the Comarca Lagunera, a region spanning Coahuila and Durango, he gloated that "no fewer than 15,000 peasants" would find a place to live and work there, once the secretary of hydraulic services launched irrigation projects to remedy the usually dry and unproductive land.[68] Commentators in *La Opinión* responded by lauding the president's vision "to dry the migration current" at its source. The Comarca, they predicted, was the first of many projects that would root Mexicans by empowering them with "land ready to be exploited."[69]

Unlike the Comisión Colonizadora hypothesized by the Cortines administration in a white paper when the BP lapsed, the colonization effort announced by Cortines after the opening of the border was not clear regarding the application and approval processes. With the Comisión Colonizadora, the Cortines administration imagined it would carefully enroll applicants, ensuring their eligibility based on an explicit point system, and that it would monitor recipients of land grants to ensure that they were on track to create viable bases of settlement. The point of cautious selection and continual oversight of colonia participants was to ensure the commission's good reputation as it worked toward its goal of eradicating out-migration. The deregulation of the US border made Mexican officials panic. Instead of instituting a slow but careful bureaucratic body, they rushed to unsystematically offer immediate economic palliatives, in the form of ejido credits and colonia investments.

Perhaps Cortines surmised he would have time to flesh out his promises of invigorated ejido and colonia support. If so, he was mistaken. Indeed, while Cortines extoled his proposed path to anchoring Mexicans, shrewd commentators wondered out loud whether Mexico, despite its rush and bombast, was arriving to this moment in history with an offering for its peasant class that was too little, too late. As one editorialist wrote in response to Cortines's program, absent some radical, expeditious transformation of

Mexico, it will be "difficult to convince [migrants] that patriotic fervor can substitute for [the] tortillas or beans" they could afford as migrant workers.[70]

In case that was true and migrants did not wait for his promised economic tinkering, President Cortines intensified the use of force, sending additional reinforcements to the border. General Valle Jordán lined his men across a thirty-eight-kilometer stretch, spanning from one end of Mexicali to the other.[71] The migrant crowds, however, would grow in size too, despite Cortines's attempts to steer them internally. They promised to complicate Valle Jordán's mandate to impose order.

MIGRANTS AND MOBILE RESISTANCE

Migrants reacted poorly to Cortines's efforts to prevent their departure to the United States and contain them in Mexicali, despite his promises of reform. They lashed out at being effectively trapped in the border town. Acting individually at times, collectively at others, they sought to surge past the impediments devised by Mexico—mainly the closed border gate and the stationed militia. Their unwillingness to be pinned down had two consequences. First, they discouraged Mexico from maintaining its countermigratory stance. Cortines could not anchor migrants while they demanded to be released. Second, Mexican migrants overwhelmed US authorities too. The open-border proclamation provoked a migrant stampede into Southern California that proved to the United States the merits of controlled guest work.

Migrants rebelled against the Mexican and US governments because their usual strategies of adaptation were rendered useless in 1954. Migrants survived as workers and sojourners in the borderlands by acquiring information—experientially or secondhand—regarding opportunities and dangers in their way. On that basis, they could envision their movement through different ecosystems, work conditions, crops, bosses, and jurisdictions to limit personal danger and wear and tear on their body. In effect, the basis of migrant power was their ability to move—to find viable nooks for themselves. The BP lapse of 1954 constrained their mobile power, as Mexico's federal government allowed them no further than the Mexicali border gate and vaguely suggested that domestic possibilities were in the offing, if not quite available yet. Facing a truncated field of possibility, migrants turned to violence against the state and against each other.

Migrant agency was premised on understanding different crops, climates, wage scales, and managerial styles and using this information to orient movement. A migrant speaking to Governor Braulio Maldonado about his plight assured him that migrants feared and generally avoided the Imperial Valley. The picking of beets was particularly strenuous, "the heaviest job one can imagine," as well as agonizing: "You have to be bending down for hours and even days at a time . . . sometimes on your knees." Even worse was "the incredible heat of the Imperial Valley." The migrant said few farmworkers could adapt to these working conditions; most left within a few days.

Other environments were similarly distressing. Drawing from his own experience as a child migrant, Governor Braulio Maldonado described picking cotton in Texas. He recalled seeing a young man unaccustomed to either cotton or the Texas heat. As an inexperienced farmhand, he lacked proper technique and the stamina to crouch all day long. He made only twenty-seven cents per kilo of cotton, so he could barely afford to feed himself.[72]

The rattlesnakes in Texas cotton fields, recalled Governor Maldonado, only made matters worse. Migrant Luis Chávez recalled seeing them as the "most bitter experience" of his life, and reported that many migrants fled Texas because of them. "Better to come back to Mexico than to get bit by a snake," he concluded. Chávez understood the centrality of experience and knowledge to migrant life. He said he was blessed to have visited Texas, rattlesnakes and all. For "we [migrants] went, familiarized ourselves, worked for a bit," and "experience, which is the University of life, has allowed us to learn." He avoided Texas thereafter.[73]

Sometimes, migrants did prioritize pure and simple wage earning. The lettuce crop was thought to be the best paying, causing many to follow its harvest. Migrant Adolfo González trekked to multiple locations in Texas, Colorado, and even New York state. This was not part of his bracero contract but work he found chasing his own leads. That his harvest-hopping was in violation of his contract and technically illegal did not deter him. Once he was in the United States, he believed he was "free to go wherever, free."[74]

Higher wages did not render migrants oblivious to work conditions. Though more lucrative, the lettuce harvest could be daunting, as could picking cotton or beets. Migrant Alfonzo Ceja, who entered the BP precisely in 1954, blamed the arduousness of lettuce harvesting on farmers. They supplied workers with short hoes that forced workers to stay close to the ground to pry the lettuce from the stalk.[75]

Navigating human relations was no less important than gauging crops, climates, or wages. Migrants avoided certain bosses and overseers. The common wisdom was that it was preferable to work for a Japanese or white American. The Mexican American *pocho* was to be avoided like a Texas rattlesnake.

When interviewers asked him about discrimination in the United States, the lettuce-hopping Adolfo González responded excitedly, "Yes, listen, yes, all the time. Those damn pochos, well, they could not even look at us. . . . That is the saddest thing [about migration], that your same race . . . does not want [you]."[76] In his opinion, Mexican Americans tended to work migrants harder than other overseers and bosses.

Movement itself was not straightforward, even with both countries facilitating transport through the BP. The BP's popularity led to the rise of crooks who posed as state authorities to rob migrants. "Don't think that we get [to the United States] so easily," said one migrant. He was victimized by a man who arrived in his hometown claiming to be a PRI representative. The man charged 300 to 400 pesos for formal enlistment in the BP. So the migrant sold his house, his father's house, and some mules to cover the cost. But the fraudster disappeared, with the money.[77] The migrant lamented the false promises migrants had to weed through just to earn a living.

By sharing the lessons of their experiences with one another, migrants positioned themselves to succeed. When Luis Chávez went back to Mexico, he described the sharing of migrant tribulations as a sort of social ritual of return. "How did it go for you?" acquaintances and relatives would ask returning migrants. "Well, I ended up in such and such place," the migrant would answer, narrating their itinerary. Chávez, for instance, let it be known that he "had to return because things were difficult there," referencing the heat and rattlesnakes of South Texas.[78]

The key to migrant adaptability, however, was mobility itself, what migrant Adolfo González referred to as the freedom "to go wherever." Without it—knowing about the *pocho* overseer, the better-paid lettuce harvest, the rattlesnakes of Texas, the sun of the Imperial Valley—meant little. Migrants could assess which crops paid the highest wages, could be picked with less risk of physical injury, and exposed workers to the mildest weather, but that strategizing was irrelevant if migrants could not travel within Mexico and the United States with relative freedom.

Thus, when Mexico moved to block their passage, migrants' well-honed adaptability was hampered by their own government. It did not matter that migrants knew lettuce and carrot growers in the Imperial Valley were in urgent need of workers; it did not matter that they had met labor recruiters who specified the wages and stipends they were to receive. Their knowledge was irrelevant as long as Mexico impeded their exit. To be sure, Mexicans were accustomed to facing obstacles to enter the United States. For instance,

The Mexican government relocated migrants to La Paz, on the southern end of the Baja California peninsula, to establish settlements, ca. 1954. Courtesy of Fondo Adolfo Ruiz Cortines, leg. 11, 12, exp. 548.1/122, caja 893, Archivo General de la Nación, Mexico City.

migrants recalled they sometimes had to bribe low-level, gatekeeping Mexican officials, even when they had bracero contracts. But they had never encountered such a mobilization of Mexico's state machinery to keep them from leaving. With the PRI's force, nationalistic admonitions, and policy promises bearing down on them, migrants were severed from the world of concrete, familiar possibilities they knew existed in the United States.

President Cortines's administration had hoped peasants would keep away from Mexicali, despite the deregulated US border. However, by January 23, thousands more had streamed into the border town, with more arriving each day. Mexican authorities thus intensified the "efforts to persuade the groups of peasants who have gathered in Mexicali from the Mexican interior, so they might stay and work in the ranches and fields of Baja California."[79] For those not persuaded by the offer of wagework in Mexico, the government offered that "virgin lands ready to be colonized" were available throughout Baja California, ready to absorb the gathered migrants. Governor Maldonado, operating as the point person for on-the-ground federal efforts, believed such overnight colonia settlements would bring a final solution to the problem of "migratory workers who have to flee their country in search of new horizons."[80] Photographic evidence suggests only a few migrants took interest in the all-new colonias established near La Paz, Baja California, and settled there.

The unyielding exodus imagined by concerned Mexican observers did not materialize, but Mexican authorities were nonetheless overwhelmed by the crowd of migrants that amassed in Mexicali, impervious to their demobilization campaign. This group of migrants saw Mexico's attempt to bind them to their homeland not as a tempting proposition but as an intrusion on their mobility. So, they experimented, individually and collectively, with forms of resistance, in order to leave for the United States.

Migrants attempted to leave Mexicali without authorization. One tried to climb over the border fence even though the Mexican Army was right in from of him. A soldier shot and wounded him.[81] Migrants overwhelmed the soldiers when they acted in unison. A group of fifty migrants repeatedly attempted to climb over the gate. Fights broke out between them and the armed Mexican forces grasping at their clothes. Some of the fifty migrants were severely beaten once they were on the ground. This inspired hundreds of the more peaceful migrants to join the melee against the Mexican soldiers, who backed down. Eight hundred migrants managed to charge through the army and the border gates.[82] US Border Patrol officials, operating under an open-border policy, did not stand in their way. Indeed, they welcomed the migrants. The Mexican Army managed to regroup, bringing the other 7,000 or so migrants to a halt and pushing them back from the border fence. They arrested the most belligerent migrants in order to calm the crowd.[83]

Mexico had not expected such migrant rebelliousness, but it effectively subdued the first wave of insurgency in the days that followed. Bob Porter, a recruitment contractor for the Doña Ana Farm Bureau, described the effectiveness of the military. He reported that "three or four truckloads of Mexican soldiers arrived" as reinforcements. Ready to restore order, they arrived at the border with battlefield artillery. They "got out of the trucks, and they were giving orders to line up with bayonets. And they got that crowd under control, this massive crowd.... It, it was sad because all these people wanted to come across and there just, there wasn't any opportunity for them."[84]

Prevented from crossing the border, migrants also lacked the money to return home. The common practice for migrants was to arrive at the border crossing point with enough money for a few days while they awaited permission to enter the United States. With the BP lapse dragging on indefinitely, migrants became entirely reliant on the goodwill of locals and emergency provisions doled out by Mexico. Porter, the labor recruiter, recalled the "massive wave of humanity" "without money and food" waiting desperately on the Mexicali side.[85]

The migrants' partial success against Mexico's barrier led them to take further united action. Following the mass skirmish with soldiers, 500 migrants marched to Governor Maldonado's palace to protest the government's use of patriotic rhetoric and violence to keep them from leaving the country. As redress, they demanded that sufficient food and work be made available to all the migrants immediately and indefinitely.[86]

The government responded with nationalism and greater violence. Soldiers fended off the protestors with firehoses. Governor Maldonado delivered an address to the protestors, telling them that Mexico needed them and offering free transportation home as well as an opportunity to work in Baja California. Only a few men took him up on his offer; most of them were determined to emigrate.[87]

By the end of January 24, Mexican officials were reeling. The bracero insurgency threatened to become a fiasco, with injuries to migrants and soldiers alike. Mexico could not use its army to forcibly contain its nationals and seriously question the US exploitation of its workers. An editorialist who at first had cheered Cortines now condemned his government for cornering migrants into working for Mexican industries, a practice he described as "neofeudalism."[88] Cortines launched a newspaper campaign denying that violence had occurred at the border, dismissing reports to the contrary as American propaganda.

But he also retreated. Cortines ordered soldiers to desist from abuse and to allow some hundred migrants to exit to the United States every day. Only a portion of the gathered migrants would pass on any given day. But Cortines figured their recalcitrance would subside if they had a hope of eventually crossing to the United States. By their sheer bullheadedness, migrants had forced the Mexican government to renounce its attempt to fully seal the border. In the interest of crowd control, it would allow the migratory flow to seep daily into the United States.

Los Angeles Times photographer Frank Brown captured images of migrants as they stormed through the open border, taking advantage of Cortines's order that the army strategically allow some of them through. They appear, for the most part, ecstatic. The jubilation evident on their faces suggests the

Migrants despondent when trapped behind the
border gate in Mexicali, Baja California, ca. 1954.
*Courtesy of the Los Angeles Times Photographic Collection,
Library Special Collections, University of California, Los Angeles.*

liberation they felt upon finally arriving in the United States. They no longer appear despondent, as they had when the gates were closed and heavily policed by Mexico, compelling them to accept a long and uncertain wait. Now, they could mobilize their knowledge about crops, weather, tools, bosses, and wages to their benefit. During their ecstatic arrival in the United States, American border patrolmen stood aside.

During the following days, migrants did not relent. Mexico was on the back foot, unwilling to use violence and allowing a few hundred border crossers every day. So migrants continued to harness their mobile power. Every day, when Mexico allowed some of them to pass, migrants avalanched toward the border. Cortines's order on January 24 was that Mexican soldiers allow no more than 500 through per day. But migrants—refusing to be contained—blew past that metric. By January 26, the immigration office in Mexicali conceded it was difficult to only gradually release the migrant crowd. It estimated more than 2,000 Mexicans had crossed over.

Migrants' steady success left Cortines's administration in a predicament. Officials feared the triumph of the transgressing migrants would accelerate a massive exodus. In a last-ditch effort, Mexico hired buses to transport

An Uncontainable Flow

Migrants are jubilant as they approach the United States unobstructed by Mexican authorities in Mexicali, Baja California, ca. 1954.
Courtesy of the Los Angeles Times Photographic Collection, Library Special Collections, University of California, Los Angeles.

Mexicans back to the interior and granted them a lump-sum payment of 500 pesos to stay in their home country. Some migrants took the offer. But they were outnumbered by the hundreds more who came daily, seeking to cross the open border.[89] On January 28, there were 14,000 migrants in Mexicali seeking passage, galvanized by the success of the earlier waves.

On January 27, a defeated Cortines ordered on-the-ground forces to stop regulating Mexican emigration. The command was not widely circulated so as to not inspire more Mexicans to head north. López Lira at the office of migration scaled back supervisory activities.[90] Overwhelmed officials warned Mexican citizens that they could not protect them if they left without bracero contracts. Migrants had officially won their battle against a Mexican nationalism that was insufficient in its material promise and overbearing with its military force. Their mobility had bested their government's attempts at control.

MIGRANTS IN CONFLICT WITH THE UNITED STATES AND EACH OTHER

With Mexico no longer stemming the tide, the United States feared its open border would lead to a torrent of migrant arrivals. The DOL's problem was no longer how to pry migrants from Mexico but how to prevent them from pouring in all at once. Images of unruly crowds of Mexicans running past an unguarded border symbolized an ungoverned stream of migration, and were at odds with the agency's mandate to secure foreign labor in a controlled, measured way that did not adversely impact US laborers. The DOL thus abandoned its unlimited open-border policy and adopted a new admission system. It determined to allow only 500 migrants through per day. The US Border Patrol, back by Calexico and county police, would open the gates once daily, allowing migrants to jostle to enter the United States. Reacting to the DOL plan, planters and hiring managers arrived early every morning at the Mexicali-Calexico border crossing to collect successful migrants and claim their share of the migratory flow.

For migrants, the enemy impeding their passage was now the US Border Patrol rather than the Mexican Army. Yet the migrants were also competing with one another as rival laborers hoping to secure one of the 500 spots allocated by the DOL. Given this dual reality, during the following days, migrants alternated between unified action against US authorities and fighting one another. The situation was reminiscent of contracting seasons in which the number of workers dispatched by Mexico to border-crossing stations overshot the amount requested by US growers, leaving many migrants in limbo. Migrant Juan Abasta recalled one such overpopulated situation, "In the patio [adjacent to the border crossing] there were 12,000 or 13,000 migrants scattered around. One had to stand all day, others leaned on the fence. And so everyone stood like that, one behind the other.... Then ten, fifteen, or more people would start pushing when contracting began.... The pushing left us disoriented, some with bruises. Others appeared dead."[91]

Migrants were not pacified, even after rumors spread among them that Cortines was to reinstate the BP to stop the border drama. When the Border Patrol opened the gate each day, migrants jostled for position and pushed forward. They were so strong, according to a US patrolman, that "the steel posts swayed like branches in the wind." Photographs from those days show migrants not only pushing collectively toward the gate but also climbing on top of one another, stepping on shoulders and faces to reach the opened gate. Thirty-year-old migrant José Rodrigo Reyes from Durango, Mexico,

US authorities try to pluck out migrants from the crowd and impose control in Mexicali, Baja California, ca. 1954. *Courtesy of the Los Angeles Times Photographic Collection, Library Special Collections, University of California, Los Angeles.*

was crushed in the chaos and taken to a local Mexicali hospital with serious injuries.[92]

Migrants unable to push their way into the United States remained frustrated in Mexicali. They worked together to impede traffic on the main thoroughfare leading from Mexico to the United States. They lifted cars and buses full of passengers and shook them. The migrants threw rocks at journalists and photographers, who took refuge on the rooftops of nearby buildings. Crowd members cheered whenever they hit a reporter perched above them. Some migrants added to the chaos by setting off firecrackers.[93]

In the midst of this, US officials initially maintained their target of 500 daily migrant admissions. However, with Mexico no longer patrolling exits, migrants were free of that counterweight. They rushed toward the border each time US agents unsealed it at dawn. They thrust their bodies forward and into one another, hoping to ride the human surge to their desired destination, even if it meant bringing the gates down with them. It was difficult to tell where the individual ended and the group began. Migrants who failed to make it through became increasingly angry. Fights broke out between them.[94]

The persistent scenes of unruliness from Mexicali made clear that the United States did not have a handle on the migratory flow it invited. *La Opinión* called it an "avalanche." In all, by February 6, an estimated 10,000 migrants had crossed, well in excess of the US goal of 500 daily admissions. Migrants and their willingness to both compete and coalesce trumped the US attempt at gradual admission. Their chaotic surge into the country prompted the DOL to renew attempts to reestablish of the BP through the US State Department. Mexican officials were amenable to a reset and a return to the BP. Pressure on Cortines to push back against the United States had eased. Migrants themselves had spurned Mexico's campaign to integrate them internally and protect them from US exploitation. According to some Mexican media outlets, migrants were "Mexican filth"—hardly worth further consideration.[95]

Following meetings between Mexican and US envoys, it was resolved on February 11 that the binationally coordinated passage of Mexican laborers would resume immediately, while the two governments negotiated a new BP. The final, revised agreement slightly augmented baseline protections for braceros. It included, for instance, guaranteed subsistence allowances sufficient to cover a diet "necessary for persons performing arduous labor." But Mexico did not emerge with strengthened power to police the treatment of migrants. The United States agreed to "expedite" the blacklisting process for "grave" discrimination, including "physical mistreatment, abuses, or threats" against migrants.[96] But the meaning of "expedite" was left undefined. Moreover, the agreement maintained joint deliberations had to govern any Mexican grievance. The agreement contained no semantic ambiguity that could allow Mexico to unilaterally intervene in the contracting of braceros, as it had done when it instigated the 1954 conflict. Mexico was thereby confirmed as the reservoir of cheap labor for the United States and the Mexican government was relegated, for the moment, to being a mere conduit.

CHAPTER FOUR

TURNING THE TIDE

Part One

Mexico Engineers the Internal Exploitation of Migrant Labor, 1955–1958

The United States emerged from the 1954 conflict with a certain dominance over Mexican migration. The new BP, set to last until 1959, entitled it to seasonal shipments of Mexican laborers. Mexico's ability to mitigate the migration and its adverse impacts would remain constrained by the obligation to provide labor when requested by the United States. However, a spirit of defiance lingered in Mexico's relationship to the United States. In March 1954, Mexico was one of only two nations at the Inter-American Conference in Caracas to reject US entreaties for a joint declaration to condemn "communist Guatemala." Mexico was not enticed by the "millions of dollars in concessions on oil, coffee, military aid and debt forgiveness" offered to other Latin American nations. Instead, Mexico included language in the summit's final declaration that affirmed each nation's sovereign right to "live its own social and cultural life."[1] Notwithstanding Mexico's disapproval, the Central Intelligence Agency toppled Guatemala's government in June 1954, ending Jacobo Árbenz's land redistribution program.[2] As the DOL had shown Mexico just months before when it pried Mexican laborers from its grip, some matters of US national interest were not negotiable.

As 1954 developed, Mexico thus settled into a less antagonistic stance vis-à-vis the United States. President Cortines's rhetoric from January 1954 that he would guide Mexicans away from the United States and to "the fields of Mexico" disappeared. On the Guatemala front, Cortines provided Árbenz's supporters asylum and staved off pressure from Secretary of State Dulles to extradite them to the United States. But, by and large, Cortines backed away from sharp criticism of US interventions. Moreover, he forced the resignation of Narciso Bassols, an adviser, who according to the US ambassador to Mexico, Francis White, had influenced Mexican officials in 1953 and early 1954 to respond forcefully to bracero exploitation and intervention in Guatemala. Bassols was particularly close to Mexican secretary of foreign affairs Luis Padilla.[3] Cortines's tidying up of his administration was interpreted by Ambassador White as a sign of Mexico's submission to the United States.

In addition, Ambassador White reported to President Eisenhower that the Mexican president was no longer making himself inaccessible, as he had in 1953 and early 1954. After several private meetings, White concluded that Cortines was no socialist and could be worked with. Mexico's pliability was confirmed by its tepid response to Operation Wetback in the summer of 1954. Operation Wetback was framed by Eisenhower as a mass roundup of undocumented migrants, whose numbers had ballooned in the postwar era. Migrants unable to secure bracero contracts in the United States had simply entered without authorization; others had overstayed their contracts. The operation was spearheaded by Joseph R. Swing, commissioner of the INS, who viewed it as an opportunity for his agency to win greater visibility and congressional funding.[4] Bombastic numbers and visceral images of large migrant roundups followed. Swing invited journalists to cover and photograph selected raids.

Historian Kelly Lytle Hernández has shown that the United States overstated the scope of its dragnet operations, its purpose being more performative. But in the moment, it appeared to be a historic deportation campaign, rivaling that of the Great Depression. Cortines's administration did little to deter the United

States. It heeded the lessons offered by Guatemala and open-border situations of that year: standing in the way of US unilateral actions offered limited upsides.

Since the work of Manuel García y Griego, historians have regarded 1954 as a watershed moment for Mexico's management of migration. The year allegedly marked the crumbling of Mexico as a force in the governance of out-migration. According to this narrative, under the new bracero agreement, Mexico lost influence over the conditions of migrant-labor in the United States and accepted its role as simple purveyor of migrant labor. Its migratory politics fell into dormancy.[5] But this chapter and those to follow show that Mexico did not implode as a force in migration policy. The impacts and lessons of 1954 were important less because they completely eroded Mexico's power than because they transformed it. Mexican officials continued to believe themselves capable of redirecting and steering the migration internally when pressed by political or economic exigencies. But they no longer supposed they could do so while relying solely on domestic policy, such as adjustments to the ejido sector or colonization schemes. Nor did Mexican officials believe they could profitably defy the United States. Their countermigratory ploys from 1954 onward were largely based on acknowledging and leveraging US power to restrict out-migration.

Not long after 1954, Mexico revisited its relationship to out-migration. To be sure, the bracero accord President Cortines signed under duress limited Mexico's ability to shape migratory policy. Mexico would have to satisfy US orders for migrant workers for the foreseeable future. Besides, the hostile US reaction to Mexico's asserting itself over the migratory flow gave Cortines good reason to pause before considering any subsequent migratory policy. But cautiousness is not inertia. And the Mexican state did not cower from adjusting out-migration. After 1954, the Mexican government remained selectively interested in channeling migrants internally to safeguard its image, national economy, and social order.

Mexico unveiled a new contramigratory policy in 1955. It consisted of providing Northern Mexico's growers with migrant labor en route to the United States. I refer to it as the internal Bracero Program (IBP), because Mexican officials tied it closely to the existing BP. Specifically, Mexico made migrants an offer. If they first worked in the Northern Mexican states of Sonora, Baja California, Tamaulipas, or Chihuahua picking cotton, either a certain amount—2,000 kilos—or a certain number of days—fifteen at first, later twenty-one—they would be granted priority on waiting lists for international guest-worker contracts. The internal labor regime sought to address Northern Mexico growers' long-standing complaint that they lacked labor internally.

The existence, logic, and scale of the IBP speak to the enduring ambition of the Mexican state in the aftermath of a disastrous 1954. Through it, the Mexican government showed it was not simply resigned to pushing its population toward the United States. It believed Mexican migrants could be coaxed internally to increase cotton production and drive economic development in Northern Mexico. Partially because of the IBP, cotton production and profits increased exponentially into the 1960s.

This chapter and the next center the program's rise but focus mostly on its demise. Why did the Mexican government discontinue the program in 1962, after just seven years, given its economic success? What did Mexico learn about its limitations as an internal purveyor of labor? Why was this government—widely acknowledged by historians for its adaptability—not able to overcome the challenges that surfaced in the IBP?[6]

Scholarship focused on the IBP is scant, even though it offers a key window into Mexico's evolving migratory politics. The most thorough existing analysis is by historian Luis Aboites Aguilar in a section of *El Norte entre algodones*. He treats the IBP as a small but important part of Northern Mexico's long economic history. As a whole, his book emphasizes two themes: how the Mexican government coddled Northern Mexico's industry throughout the twentieth century; and how growers, thus empowered, consistently exploited workers. Along those lines, *El Norte entre algodones* argues that the IBP came into being because of the federal government's subservience to the cotton industry, and that it ended because of the excesses of growers. "Se les pasó la mano," Aguilar declares. That is, they overplayed their hand by mistreating Mexican workers allocated to them under the IBP.[7]

Aguilar's account leans heavily on class dynamics to explain the IBP's eventual termination. The present account, by contrast, argues that the IBP's programmatic dysfunction and frailty were rooted in the behavior not of growers but of the government officials who managed the program. They were ill-prepared to handle the housing of Mexican migrants in Northern Mexico. Additionally, many officials were corrupt and demanded bribes from migrants in exchange for expedited contracts. Finally, they did not move with urgency to alleviate either the logistical woes or the corruption within the IBP. They thus provoked migrants' ire and activism.

The IBP became an indefensible policy as news outlets learned of migrant suffering, particularly in the depots where the Mexican government housed migrants entering the IBP. Newspapers described migrants as suffering from deteriorating health because of a lack of proper shelter and medical facilities, starving because of poorly provisioned mess halls, and living in unsanitary conditions due to insufficient lavatories. Migrants themselves complained to media outlets, especially about the corruption in the IBP. They could not tolerate the culture of bribery that pervaded the program, given all the other privations they were subject to.

This chapter and the next focus on the state of Sonora. The IBP operated in several Northern Mexican states, but Sonora was key. It received the highest number of workers. And its governor, Álvaro Obregón Tapia, was able to leverage his family's connection to the PRI to initiate the program. Other states subsequently joined the IBP. Sonora is also important because *El Norte entre algodones* uses it as a case study to argue that the IBP was derailed by grower maltreatment of workers, rather than by the government's own mismanagement.

Methodologically, the chapters focus on flareups in the IBP's operation. These tended to originate from the government's chronic incompetence, rather than from growers. This chapter begins with the emergence of Mexico as an internal, rather than solely international, steward of labor. While it acknowledges the ambition of the Mexican state, it shows that even in the first few years of the IBP's operation, the Mexican government's shortcomings as a steward of labor became evident both to government officials themselves and to growers, who hurried to help the government improve its custody and management of domestic laborers. The next chapter captures the later years of the IBP's operation, when the Mexican government's repeated failures discouraged it from further coaxing migrants into Northern Mexico.

THE EMERGENCE OF AN INTERNAL LABOR REGIME

In Baja California, Sonora, Sinaloa, and Tamaulipas, cotton growers were among the producers who had long clamored for the federal government to address out-migration and improve their access to labor. They favored an end to the BP and increased surveillance of undocumented migrants. As detailed in earlier chapters, they were part of the business contingent that cheered the 1954 moratorium on out-migration and pressed the government to bring migrant workers to them. However, President Cortines's countermigratory plans during the 1954 BP lapse focused on promoting permanence among Mexicans through colonias and ejidos. He did not advocate the internal exploitation of migrant laborers as a solution to out-migration. In the end, Cortines's romanticized emphasis on rural settlement failed to keep Mexicans grounded as the United States beckoned them with an open border.

Cortines might have avoided tinkering with Mexico migration policy given the negative experience of 1954. But northern growers and their notion that out-migration needed to be addressed were buttressed by an important ally in 1955. Northern Mexico gained influence with the ascent of Álvaro Obregón Tapia to the governorship of Sonora. The son of former Mexican president Álvaro Obregón, he was well-connected to PRI power circles. Obregón convinced Cortines to establish a mechanism to funnel Mexican migrant labor to Sonoran growers, instead of letting it dribble out entirely to the United States. In a series of private meetings, Obregón and Cortines formulated the IBP's broad contours. If migrants picked 2,000 kilos of cotton, or worked for fifteen days in Northern Mexico, they would be given priority on waiting lists to depart as guest workers. The program would operate on a year-to-year basis, and the federal government would have to assent to its yearly renewal.[8]

Thirteen years of participation in the BP had left federal officials well acquainted with the political and administrative headaches involved in administering a migrant labor program. Among the most common issues in the international BP were the mistreatment of contract workers sent to the United States; the mistimed delivery of migrants to Mexican processing centers, resulting in backlogs, overcrowding, and migrant suffering; and persistent journalistic and activist exposés and critiques of these problems. Mexico's experiment in deploying migrant workers internally promised similar, and potentially deeper, challenges. Mexican authorities would have to mobilize workers across vast distances for onerous manual labor jobs. But they would have to coordinate with the BP to ensure they had enough migrants on hand to meet US labor expectations. The IBP was also likely to provoke migrant recalcitrance. It hinged on a cruel incentive: the promise to migrants of more work in the United States as braceros if they first worked in Northern Mexico. Moreover, unlike in the United States, where migrants were disempowered by their alienage, in Mexico they could assert themselves as part of the citizenry.

The federal government established and managed the contracting center for IBP participants in Empalme, a coastal town in southwest Sonora. There, it kept custody of migrants in a center where growers could pick them up. Growers who wanted to partake in the IBP had to first band together with fellow growers from their region or municipality and form a Comisión Mixta de Control de Trabajadores (Mixed Commission for Labor Control, CMCT). Each CMCT was stewarded by a board composed of local growers, corporate agents, and a supervisory representative from the federal Ministry

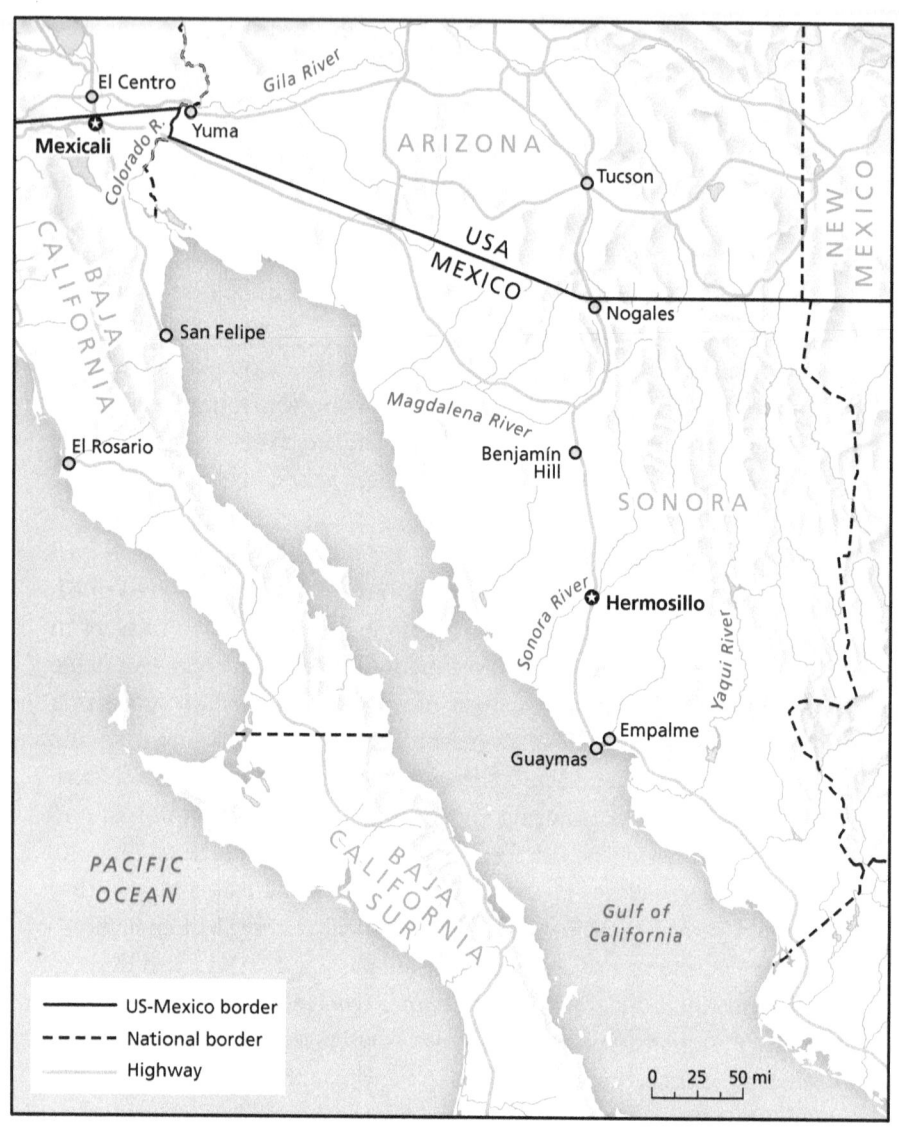

Migrant destinations in Sonora, Mexico. Mexico stationed migrants in Empalme to supply labor to Sonoran cotton growers, including those in Hermosillo and the Yaqui Valley. From Empalme, the federal government also dispatched migrants to the United States, ostensibly giving priority to those who had worked first in Sonora.
Courtesy of Erin Greb Cartography.

of Agriculture. CMCT operatives were to pick up workers from the federal government's contracting center in Empalme, escort them to growers' area of production, and return them to the contracting center when their stint was over so they could be released to work in the United States. In Sonora, the first and largest CMCT was based in the city of Hermosillo. It was run by grower Enrique Mazón.[9]

President Cortines and Governor Obregón laid out the financial blueprint for the IBP and its continual expansion. If growers from a certain town, city, or region in Sonora wished to join the program and form a CMCT, they were to notify Obregón. He would impose a tax on their cotton sales to fund the CMCT and guarantee the looping itinerary of workers: from the federally run contracting center in Empalme, to the participating Sonoran city, town, or region, and back again. What ensured the sufficient financing for the IBP was that large cotton gin operators would cover the tax payments in advance, on behalf of growers. This was essentially a no-interest loan from cotton gin operators to cotton growers.

Northern Mexico and Sonora in particular were home to many cotton gin operators. These were mostly US conglomerates with extensive operations internationally, including Honenberg, Empresas McFadden, and Anderson, Clayton, and Company; some were Mexican-owned, such as Industrial Agrícola de Hermosillo and Sonora Industrial. They were willing to provisionally cover growers' IBP expenses because they wanted them to have access to the labor the program offered. They predicted the IBP would increase the amount of cotton growers were able to collect and sell to the cotton gin operators.[10]

Cotton gin operators would be made whole at the end of the process. Growers had to bring their cotton to the cotton gin to be deseeded and shipped to market. At that point, growers would receive a *liquidación*, a lump-sum payment from the cotton gin operator that varied depending on the quality and amount of cotton provided. Cotton gin operators would deduct from that payment the CMCT tax they had paid to the Sonora government on behalf of growers. Growers were responsible for a contribution proportionate to their crop yield; bigger growers or companies paid more, smaller ones less.[11]

The financial aspect of the IBP seemed to work well initially. The CMCT in Hermosillo was so successful in gathering funds through cotton gin operators in its first year that it did not require additional funding from them the second year. Expenditures for moving migrants around had been lower than predicted.[12] Only two of the many participating growers complained that their expected contribution was too high.[13]

Logistically, the IBP was circuitous but straightforward. CMCTs from across Sonora picked up migrants held in federal custody in Empalme. CMCT operatives then transported migrants to growers' area of production. Growers housed them in depots they established specifically for IBP participants. Every working day, growers would pick up workers from their private depots, returning them when their workday ended. When migrants completed their fifteen days of service, CMCT operatives would escort them from the private grower depots back to Empalme. There they were returned to federal authorities, who held them pending final release to the United States.

The federal government was responsible for the contracting hub in Empalme, including staffing. With the advent of the IBP, it became a central artery pumping labor not just to the United States but also to much of Sonora. Mexico left the management of the private grower depots to the grower-controlled CMCTs. They had to hire their own supervisors; explain the IBP to migrants; maintain vehicles, mostly trucks, to move migrants around; and ensure that migrants received paperwork verifying they worked in Northern Mexico and were eligible for expedited departure to the United States.[14] In the IBP's first few years, this string of activities went without major incident.

Sonoran growers and their subordinates were well incentivized to run the IBP and their private worker depots competently. CMCTs featured a representative from the federal Ministry of Agriculture, who acted as a watchdog. For the large Hermosillo CMCT, this was Manuel Robles Linares.[15] Though such representatives were outnumbered by growers in each CMCT, they sat in on determinations about how much money would be spent on worker transport, housing, and care; and they communicated directly with Mexico City. Since the program was only happening with President Cortines's consent, reports of grower negligence could jeopardize the initiative.

The first signs of dysfunction within the IBP emanated from the Empalme migrant contracting hub. The city was ill-prepared to function simultaneously as a staging ground for the international BP and the domestic IBP. The Cortines administration thought it was prudent in choosing Empalme. The government had twice before unsuccessfully operated a bracero processing center in another Sonoran city, Hermosillo.[16] Bracero aspirants were held there, pending final release to the United States. The volume of workers alone proved difficult for Hermosillo's authorities to manage. Migrants often became exasperated at being warehoused indefinitely—days and weeks on end—pending a US request for workers. Moreover, the United States typically only asked for a couple hundred or thousand laborers at a time, making it difficult for Mexican authorities to clear the waiting lists at the contracting center. The number of workers was also a strain on Hermosillo locals. They complained of scenes of migrant emaciation, defecation, and urination, as migrants overstrained public accommodations. Locals also suffered theft by migrants waiting to be released to the United States who had run out of money.[17] The bracero contracting center in Hermosillo engendered strong local opposition and was shuttered in 1951.[18]

The federal government experimented with Hermosillo again in early 1955. Sonora governor Ignacio Soto, Obregón's immediate predecessor, requested that the bracero contracting center be established in Hermosillo. He wanted migrants to work for Sonoran growers while they awaited release to the United States. Sonoran growers used the braceros-in-waiting for cotton picking. But again, the contracting center ran into problems. US requests for workers were slow and at one point stopped entirely. Migrants were incensed. They felt they had been duped into working in Northern Mexico. And many had run out of resources while waiting. They protested in front of government buildings. Governor Soto relocated a couple thousand of them to Empalme. He figured that at the coastal location they would at least be able to wash themselves and fish for sustenance. José T. Rocha, a representative from the federal Ministry of the Interior dispatched to Hermosillo, recommended and won federal approval for permanently closing the center. This dashed the hopes of the migrants who remained in Hermosillo and wanted to leave as braceros. Enraged, they attempted to lynch Rocha, who had to be rescued by police and federal agents.[19]

The federal government selected Empalme as the staging site for the BP and IBP largely because of the 1955 crisis, and based on the coastal city's location. Mexico surmised that the ability to fish and bathe in the Pacific Ocean would be enough to make the IBP/BP, and any associated waits, tolerable to migrants. In reality, the Empalme coast only guaranteed migrants could bathe. They would still have to rewear their clothes after washing themselves. And to actually feed themselves from the sea, they would need fishing and cooking equipment. Finally, the coastal location could not by itself resolve other issues resulting from large migrant gatherings, including a shortage of beds, blankets, hospital capacity, and medical supplies.

Empalme's capacity was sure to be tested by the concomitant BP and IBP. A flood of migrants was bound to arrive, willing to trade their labor in Northern Mexico for expedited passage to the United States. Technically, migrants arriving without prior enrollment in the BP could not participate in the IBP, but that hardly stopped them from trying. As we will see, migrants surmised, with good reason, that they could bribe authorities into enrolling them. Adding to the overcrowding, some municipal governments in Northern Mexico sent unemployed men directly to Empalme to attempt to enroll in the IBP. Municipal authorities openly ignored federal instructions that the IBP/BP was first and foremost for migrants from Central Mexico.[20]

Besides the sheer volume of migrants headed to Empalme, there was concern that the overlap of the BP and IBP would result in chaos. Migration officials, personnel, and police would have to allocate workers between two labor systems, that of Northern Mexico cotton and that of US agriculture. They would have to oversee the deployment of thousands of workers across Sonoran cotton fields, their return to the coastal Empalme contracting center, and their release to the United States, effecting that mobilization without the delays and hiccups that had provoked unrest among migrants in years past when authorities were just handling the BP.

As soon as the contracting center began to operate early in 1956, the problems began.[21] Local authorities on the front line of managing the IBP and BP were the first to experience them. They immediately sought support from their higher-ups. On January 31, 1956, the municipal governor of Empalme wrote to Sonora's secretary of the interior that the area was already overwhelmed by Mexican migrants who had showed up wanting to participate in the IBP. He requested that state leadership petition the federal government for an apportionment of military forces to help local Empalme police and migration authorities control the arriving migrants. When his letter went without response, Empalme's municipal governor requested that Sonora's secretary of the interior at least ask Governor Braulio Maldonado to accept some of the migrants in his state, Baja California, which is adjacent to Sonora.

Governor Obregón of Sonora endorsed the idea that Governor Maldonado should receive some of the gathered migrants. The Sonora secretary-general contacted the secretary of the interior in Mexico City, first by phone, then in writing, confirming Obregón's request that Baja California take some workers for they were "creating serious problems for the municipality [of Empalme]." The emergency measure seems to have momentarily worked, as neither local newspapers nor government archives reported problems with migrant overcrowding in the weeks that followed. However, the problem would resurface continually in the months and years to come, to such a degree that even deflecting migrants to nearby states would not help.[22]

Obregón thus played a large role not just in bringing the IBP into being but also in mitigating its early problems. Indeed, growers thanked him for his leadership and involvement. His office was again called into action a few weeks into the program when the chief of coordinated services of public health and aid in Sonora discovered that the migrant contracting center in Empalme "lacked the most basic sanitary services," including bathrooms. Obregón ordered that an agent of the Services of Public Health in nearby Guaymas be dispatched to the Empalme contracting center to make sure that "appointed authorities" "immediately begin to install these services."[23]

In addition to responding to issues as they arose, Obregón tried to preempt complications. The mayor of Empalme, for instance, grew noncommittal about Obregón's plan to provide migrants with eating areas. Obregón planned to erect dining halls for them on the grounds outside the municipal baseball stadium. The mayor, however, received a request from a Mexican railway based in Jalisco to rent the grounds from the municipality. It was a lucrative offer he wanted to take, but not before consulting with Obregón. As Obregón wished, the request went nowhere. Obregón, for the moment, was more interested in the smooth running of the BP/IBP. The short-term profits from leasing stadium grounds could not compare with having a stable labor regime in support of Northern Mexico cotton. The mayor wrote back, saying he understood the priority given to the BP/IBP and the need to avoid "negatively impacting migrants" by depriving them of a mess hall.[24]

Notwithstanding Obregón's direct interventions, the Empalme contracting center quickly became rife with operational problems. Empalme's mayor wrote him a detailed letter three months into the program characterizing the issues. The overarching problem—the one that begot all others—was the oversaturation of Sonora with aspiring migrant laborers. If before the IBP, from the perspective of growers, the problem had been insufficient labor; now, from the perspective of local government, the emergent problem was calibrating the arrival of laborers such that they arrived only in the quantities desired. The mayor complained that "every day the number of compatriots in Empalme grew." "Far from diminishing," he observed, "the number [of willing laborers] increases at every moment."

As problematic as migrants' numbers were their expectations: Migrants arrived with "hopes of eventually being hired as braceros in our neighbor to the north." But "functionaries and employees responsible for overseeing hiring" could only release them to the United States if they were requested by American growers. Unfortunately for Mexico, daily US requests for laborers often did not match the frenzied pace of arrivals in Empalme, resulting in a backlog of workers at the contracting center.[25] Migrants were understandably displeased when they had to wait, given that they had been promised expedited release to the United States as part of the IBP.

Mexico's predicament was that it had deepened its attachment to the BP when it decided to use a work contract in the United States as bait to recruit workers into Northern Mexico's cotton fields. In effect, it made itself and Northern Mexico captive to the rhythms of US agriculture and the varying daily labor demands of US growers. Mexico had no influence over these fluctuations. Such was the compromised situation of Mexican officials who sought to eke out economic gain from migrant labor within a hegemonic framework in which another government, that of the United States, dictated the timing of the migratory chain, completely detached from Mexican policy.

In any case, by establishing a program that attracted more migrants than it could realistically release, Mexico invited migrant suffering. The mayor of Empalme reported to Obregón that he counted more than 10,000 braceros who "swarm the streets of the city." And the "vast majority of them, we have observed, lacked the most indispensable things needed to subsist." They needed to get to the United States immediately to start working and earning wages so they could afford food, hygiene supplies, and the like. Empalme's mayor was no zealous humanitarian. He worried that "should things continue this way, it might result in social disturbances or riots." This made him particularly "uneasy" because he did not think Empalme was in a position to control angry migrants given the "sparse elements of repression"—including police forces and migratory center personnel—"on which we count."[26] The mayor's solution was geared not toward improving accommodations for migrants and alleviating their suffering but toward finding ways to repress their predictable frustration. This buttresses the argument that it was not necessarily the growers who "got out of hand" in their treatment of migrants but various actors within government who were most responsible for the IBP's failure.

Certainly, Mexico had no way to compel the United States to take more migrants per day and alleviate migrant overcrowding in Empalme. But Mexican authorities were also not inclined to make extensive social investments in food, sanitation, and health services to make matters more bearable for migrants. Instead, the Sonora government focused on avoiding particularly damning press. The Empalme contracting station was so saturated with workers, for instance, that migrants had to spill out onto the nearby highway. In 1956, multiple migrants were hit by oncoming traffic. This came to the attention of Obregón, who ordered that the mayor build a barbed-wired fence to cage the troublesome migrants. Neither the governor nor the mayor seemed to consider that the unsightly fence might attract unfavorable press down the line. They had it built immediately.[27]

By the end of 1956, the municipality of Empalme and the Sonora government were no closer to solving the issues of migrant overcrowding, public order, and public safety affecting the BP/IBP. Once again, the mayor of Empalme—who was becoming a transcriber of everyday migrant suffering—wrote a letter describing migrants' ordeal, only this time he communicated directly with the Ministry of the Interior in Mexico City. He remarked that the contracting centers and the surrounding environs were becoming even more densely packed with migrants because many of them did not arrive with their paperwork in order and thus could not be released to participate in the program. The paperwork underpinning the BP was supposed to make matters easier for the state by standardizing the process by which authorities "knew" subjects, determined their eligibility, and managed their case files. But when the migrants did not participate well in the bureaucratic dance, it added to the turmoil and headaches by creating backlogs of workers, physically present in Northern Mexico but, legally, impossible to move along. While some simply showed up without paperwork, others arrived without the signature of their hometown mayor who was supposed to attest to their being excess laborers and not ejidatarios, two prerequisites for their enrollment. Either way, whether because of faulty or completely absent paperwork, many migrants found themselves trapped in Empalme, with no "resources of any nature" to care for themselves, or even to return home.[28]

Though the anger of the stranded migrants loomed as a threat, the more immediate and inescapable issue growing was the threat they posed to public health. As recounted by Empalme's mayor, the stranded migrants did not have shelter with a roof, and with inclement weather hitting the area, the idle men were left exposed to wet and cold conditions. Migrants developed pneumonia and the flu. The mayor claimed he provided the migrants with "great quantities of firewood and charcoal" to keep themselves warm, as well as medical attention to "avoid as much as was humanly possible the propagation of infectious respiratory illness." The mayor noted that although his interventions kept migrants from dying, the concentration of migrants was straining his government beyond its capacities. Governor Obregón, he assured the federal Ministry of the Interior, was helping Empalme provide housing and health services for as many braceros as possible, but the overcrowding of migrants seemed to outpace the government's ability to provide a "satisfactory solution."[29]

What prompted the mayor to break the chain of command by reaching out directly to Mexico City, without consulting Obregón, was that the number of sick migrants was increasing "considerably." They were afflicted by stomach illnesses, which in the worst cases were evolving into peritonitis—a disease in which the lining of the abdominal wall becomes inflamed. The result was pain, tenderness, rigid abdominal muscles, fever, nausea, and vomiting. The disease effectively incapacitated affected migrants in Empalme and left them unable to care for themselves. Worse, the disease did not go away by itself but needed to be treated with antibiotics and possibly surgery. Even with proper care, it was life-threatening. The mayor could not offload the migrants to anyone else. He could not marshal them to the cotton fields for growers to exploit and take care of, for they were unable to work. He could not return them to their hometowns, for they might die along the way. And he certainly could not transfer them to the United States as part of the bracero shipment. Stricken migrants were likely to fail the US medical examinations performed prior to a migrant's definitive admission.[30]

The outbreak of stomach maladies among Empalme migrants illustrates how unprepared the Sonora and local Empalme governments were to manage the BP and IBP in a way that valorized not just profit but life. Empalme lacked a public hospital and thus could not deal with an uptick in unwell migrants. Empalme's mayor was forced to solicit the help of the public hospital in nearby Guaymas, and also of the Pacific Railway Company, which had a private hospital reserved for railway employees and their families. The railroad agreed to share its medical personnel but only for grave cases of peritonitis. Empalme's mayor told the federal government that he had footed the bill for transporting the infirm to these two hospitals this time. But because he presided over a "small geographic area," he did not have much in the way of a tax base to draw on going forward.[31]

If stricken migrants were already straining local public health resources, the mayor predicted the crisis would only deepen once winter began. Many of the arriving Mexicans came from more temperate regions and were not accustomed to the Sonoran cold—about forty-five degrees Fahrenheit in the winter—increasing their likelihood of falling sick. If the situation in the more temperate fall—with lows hovering around sixty degrees—was already proving difficult, he expected a winter spike would be truly beyond Empalme's administrative and financial capacity. With the funds from the various CMCTs off limits—these were reserved for healthy migrants who could work, mainly to transport them to and from Empalme—the only practical solution he saw was for the federal government to construct a hospital in Empalme immediately. "Without the aid the federal government can provide," he was at a loss for how "our compatriots" could be tended to. His admission that Empalme needed to be retrofitted to properly administer the BP/IBP went without response from the federal government.[32]

The federal government thus erred doubly, first by selecting a city without a hospital, then by neglecting to erect medical facilities to safeguard migrants' health. The failure was not only a public health or humanitarian one. Failure to treat the sick in a systematic way added to the bottleneck of migrants at the contracting center. Sick migrants unable to work in either Sonora or the United States undercut the IBP's economic goals. Finally, through its inaction, the federal government compounded the issue of overcrowding in Empalme and brought migrants closer to the social unrest the mayor of Empalme warned he would not be able to handle.

The first full year of the IBP's operation revealed its dysfunction to the mayor of Empalme who, through his pleas for help, made Obregón and the federal government aware of prevailing issues. The disarray narrated by the mayor did not, however, make its way into local or national media, except for two brief articles in the local newspaper about migrant complaints about delays at the processing center and the lack of food, shelter, and sanitation there.[33] Thus, at the end of the first year, the political calculus of the federal government favored keeping the program. For not only was negative press minimal but 1956 was a superb year for cotton growing. The area produced 426,000 tons of cotton, almost double the 208,000 tons it had produced as recently as 1949.[34] Indeed, growers seemed satisfied, as they lodged almost no complaints and behaved well enough with migrants to avoid controversy. Only one Hermosillo grower complained that workers were not being equitably distributed.[35]

While that was the case in Sonora, the IBP also operated in other Northern Mexican states that signed up later. In Monterrey, Nuevo León, problems at the contracting center became sufficiently serious to attract negative press. A newspaper based in Monterrey ran a multipage story, announcing in large, bold font atop the page, "Braceros with Contracts to Work in the US Treated Like Animals: Overseers with Firearms and Batons Have Them Confined behind a Barbed-Wire Fence." It was an exposé of how migration officials at the contracting center in Monterrey handled migrants and included photographic proof. A contingent of migrants, led by Salomé Trujillo, submitted it to President Cortines to inform him about what was transpiring with the IBP in Monterrey and seek his help.[36]

The newspaper reported that contracting center personnel routinely roughed up migrants. Migrants, it showed in words and photographs, were physically organized based on their place of origin and pushed into pens

An armed Mexican guard watches over aspiring
migrants held behind a barbed wire fence, July 16, 1956.
*Courtesy of Fondo Adolfo Ruiz Cortines, exp. 565.4/91,
caja 1021, Archivo General de la Nación, Mexico.*

guarded with barbed wire. The barbed wire was run at three heights to prevent migrants from slipping beneath or between it. Additionally, personnel at the contracting center were armed with long-barrel guns and patrolled the migrants all day long. The paper suggested that the barbed wire and forced containment recalled Nazi concentration camps. Migrants, it concluded, were effectively "encaged" and "treated like animals." The paper suggested that the contracting center staff should be the ones tossed into a government-run cage—namely, a prison.37

To supplement the newspaper exposé, the migrants who wrote to Cortines added their first-person perspective. They bemoaned they were at the mercy of contracting center officials. Officials had all the power because they decided who would receive a contract to the United States. They could have migrant workers waiting for weeks at the facility. The migrants writing to Cortines had been at the center "for more than a month" and had "not gotten a US work contract." In the meantime, they specified, Sgt. Sebastián Aguilar of the Mexican Army showed up every three days to gather a contingent of

Mexican authorities retrieve migrants to
dispatch them to cotton fields, July 16, 1956.
*Courtesy of Fondo Adolfo Ruiz Cortines, exp. 565.4/91,
caja 1021, Archivo General de la Nación, Mexico City.*

migrants and bring them to work on nearby cotton ranches. They described him as the corpulent man who was seen in one of the pictures taking a "fellow migrant into a holding pen."

Sometimes Sergeant Aguilar arrived in uniform; at other times he dressed more casually but donned a *sarakof*, a hat associated with authority. In all cases, however, he came armed with "a steel rod to hit and herd us like recalcitrant animals" or a gun with which to menace migrants. The migrant Salomé Trujillo reported that these strong-arm tactics subdued migrants, producing a "constant parade" to the nearby ranches, where growers accepted the government handoff and enjoyed the labor of their captive labor pool. Trujillo expressed no concern about the labor itself; his ire was directed at the government's mishandling.

The letter to Cortines, supplemented by a newspaper account, was not the first time this group of migrants had written to him. They had sent "countless" correspondence to Cortines describing the "continuous current of men" swept into this internal labor system ruled by force. But they had received no reply. They hoped their account, corroborated now by an on-the-ground field report and visuals, would inspire the government to intervene. The migrants did not believe they deserved to be physically abused just because they were "unfortunate enough to be poor campesinos."[38]

Outside of Sonora, there was also slightly more tension between the federal government and employers regarding the latter's management of migrants entrusted to them. Problems surfaced in Tamaulipas, a Northeast Mexican state also rich in cotton production. Growers there immediately joined the IBP after Obregón convinced the Mexican government to launch it. As in Sonora, growers moved workers from the Tamaulipas contracting center to their private depots, returning them at the end of their stints. However, Tamaulipas growers cut costs by using *carros de redillas*, trucks used to haul livestock, produce, or equipment, and not designed for the safe transport of human beings. Growers and their foremen bunched migrants into a cage-like compartment in the back of the vehicle and set off on their trip, which was sometimes as long as an hour, with no safety mechanisms in place.

The Departamento de Tránsito Federal (Federal Transit Department) stepped in to police the growers, as this fell under its mandate to oversee the use of highways. Its agents detained *carros de redillas* carrying migrants, imposed fines on the growers, and ordered that they find adequate transportation for their labor supply. In addition to stuffing the trucks beyond capacity, growers had not taken out proper insurance for the people in them and were cited for this.

The growers in Tamaulipas pushed back against these regulations through their growers association. They asked President Cortines to stick by the "ample concessions you have given us to transport braceros," emphasizing that the migrant labor would save "the harvest of the region, valued at 800 million pesos."[39] In addition to reminding Cortines of the economic boon guaranteed if the Departamento de Tránsito Federal stopped meddling, growers argued they could not take out travel insurance on the migrants because insurance companies were refusing to offer them such coverage.

The department claimed growers were lying and attempting to cut costs by not paying to retrofit their trucks with seats and seatbelts or purchase travel insurance, and it argued that Tamaulipas growers should not be exempted from their financial responsibility. Even with the "extraordinary demand" for laborers, Article 127 of the Federal Constitution's Law of Road Use should be respected. It legislated that conveyers could not use federal roads in ways that brought travelers into harm's way. The Departamento de Tránsito Federal feared improper transport would result in fatal accidents involving workers.⁴⁰ Heeding the department's logic, President Cortines did not exempt growers, compelling them to fall in line with the regulations. Thus, while growers in the IBP generally left little evidence of reckless labor management, when enough money was on the line, the ones in Tamaulipas were no paragons of virtue. In such cases, the federal government and its agencies reinforced the boundaries of acceptable behavior.

In subsequent years, as the IBP matured, growers outside Tamaulipas avoided egregiously mistreating migrant workers and inviting federal scrutiny. This is not to say that work in Northern Mexico's cotton fields was pleasant. Pedro Benítez, who was from Sinaloa but had lost his parents early and thus began migratory labor at the age of twelve, had acquired a good deal of knowledge of Sonora by the time he sought to enroll as a bracero. He recalled how he had "worked for the *terratenientes* [landholders], many of whom had acquired land during the Mexican Revolution as generals, including Topete, Bustamante, Obregón. . . . Two thousand kilos is what one harvested to receive the card [confirming participation in the IBP], and from there you went to [the] Empalme [contracting center to await departure as a bracero]."

Benítez recounted the process as being difficult, even compared to his work in the fields as a child. In his experience, the Sonoran growers tended to use the workers for the "third round of picking cotton, what was known as the *culeo*." "The first picking has much cotton, . . . the second one, very little, . . . and by the third one you're just picking up little feathers off the cotton stalk." Picking one's quota of cotton by weight was thus no easy task: "It was a very sad life."⁴¹ Besides the work being hard, the nature of the exchange— work in Mexico exchanged for more work in the United States—was not lost on migrants. As migrant Rigoberto Pérez, who arrived from Michoacán, summed up the situation, "You had to work in Mexico. They were worried that people were abandoning Mexico, that there wouldn't be people to pick the crops there. So they made it a requirement that you had to have picked for so much time, or so many pounds of cotton in Mexico, in order to be able to come to the United States. It was basically a kind of racket."⁴²

Nonetheless, it seems workers accepted the transaction. Indeed, when they narrated their lives to interviewers many years later, those who worked in Northern Mexico described it quite matter-of-factly as part of the recruitment process and their transnational lives. In their mental geography of lettuce, tomato, onion, carrot, and vegetable picking, cotton was just one more crop to pick and one more negotiation to endure on their way to the United States. As migrant Eusebio Hernández, from the pueblo of Cuquío in Jalisco, recalled, "We went to Sonora, to the Yaqui Valley in Sonora. And, um . . . one had to harvest 2,000 kilos of cotton or work around twenty days, and they [growers] would give us a card to contract ourselves [as braceros] . . . just with that card."[43]

Isidro de Jésus Pérez from San Pedro Ixtlahuaca, Oaxaca, a state to the south of Jalisco, recalled that he journeyed in 1960 to "harvest cotton in Ciudad Obregón, Sonora. There we harvested 2,000 kilos of cotton so that they would release to us the card of control [proof of completing the required harvest]." He characterized the system repeatedly as "el control," the control mechanism regulating his mobility.[44] José González, from Jalisco, recounted that in his case it was the "ranchers of Boradé, Sonora," whom he was compelled to help. "They work you . . . and in exchange they give you a card and with that card the authorities would let us come here [to the United States] to work. That was the manner in which I could come." He recalls working in that situation for "three weeks."[45] Aguileo Namba from Michoacán agreed that "there was an association of growers and they gave you the *miquita* [card]." He recalled that they would "get us on a bus and drop us by twos or by threes on the ranches in the area to earn the card."[46] As long as growers held up their end of the bargain, it seems migrants were willing to accept the addition of this transactional relation and thereby advance their arrival in the United States.

Mexico's federal government understood that the core issue with the IBP/BP was not growers but the chronic overcrowding and insufficiency migrants endured in Empalme. The government thus invested 200,000 pesos in early 1957 to upgrade the facilities in Empalme.[47] The Mexican government's attempts at remediating the IBP through a one-time investment was to little avail, however. The problems at the contracting facility endured, bringing with them more incendiary headlines. The numbers of migrants seeking to secure a contract continued to overwhelm the capacity of local administrators and the public spaces of Empalme. More damaging still, a growing pattern of corruption emerged among officials at the processing center.

Migrants reported that migratory center personnel demanded personal payments—not just their labor in Northern Mexico's cotton fields—to be released as bracero guest workers. Migrants were unwilling to tolerate this misgovernance and misconduct, on top of the setbacks and insufficiencies they already had to endure. In 1957, they began more outspoken activism—directed at news outlets and top officials in the Mexican government—that would ultimately bring steady media attention to the dysfunctional processing center in Empalme. They did not always need to protest: sometimes their suffering simply spoke for itself.

As soon as the contracting began for the 1957 harvesting season, problems at the Empalme contracting center increased. Anticipating his municipality's limited ability to control the migration and forestall emergent problems, the mayor of Empalme had requested that his city not be used as the site for IBP and BP contracting in the new year. He failed largely because Empalme was a *ciudad rielera* (a rail city) to which it was easy for the Mexican government to send would-be migrants from the interior.[48]

The new contracting season was formally announced on January 10, 1957. And at once, migrants began to arrive seeking work in the IBP and BP. The announcement, however, turned out to be premature, as ten days later the Mexican government found out the United States would not be requesting workers through the Empalme zone until March, a full three months later. This left workers who had shown up to the area stranded and destitute. This mishap shows that the efficacy of the Empalme operation was dependent on proper timing with American requests for labor, which were subject to change year to year and even within a season.

Mexico was also chronically underprepared, even when it injected money into migration management. Despite the federal government's investment of 200,000 pesos to improve the Empalme facilities in 1957, migrants still found themselves living in wretched conditions. The local newspaper described thousands of migrants enduring the cold of late January without blankets.[49] The IBP continued to impoverish migrants, and only two weeks had passed since the government issued a call for laborers. The federal and Sonora governments promised gathered laborers that contracting to the United States would resume in March. This was of little comfort to stranded migrants, who had to find a way to survive in the interim.[50]

When contracting began in April, Empalme officials were again flummoxed by predictable issues stemming from the overcrowded processing center. Local news media reported that migrants in Empalme lacked potable water. The municipality did not have enough for migrants, who complained of dehydration. A potentially more explosive issue emerged that same month. Migrants reported that officials at the contracting center were extorting them and demanding side payments of 500 pesos in exchange for passage to the United States. The fact that they had gained acceptance into the BP from their hometowns and worked for Northern Mexico's cotton growers was not enough. They alleged that the corruption originated in high places, with the chief of the Empalme center, a representative of the federal Ministry of the Interior, personally selling *plazas*—spots in the BP—to the aspirants. The newspaper, *El Imparcial*, sympathized with the migrants' plight, calling the migrants' allegations "Justified Complaints" in its front-page story.[51]

By June, contracting to the United States was suspended again. US labor demands had quieted, leaving behind 35,000 workers who had rendered their services for Northern Mexico growers but now missed the cut to go to the United States. Many did not have personal funds to finance their trips back home, did not have enough public accommodations to fall back on, and had gambled on making it to the United States to earn the money they needed to subsist. They were thus left destitute by this turn of events and walked the streets of Empalme. The newspaper described the men as producing "a series of scenes and happenings that depress the hearts of Mexicans." As they searched for shade, food, and shelter, said the newspaper, they proved that "to wish to be a bracero is the most disgraced aspiration, the most tragic and the most painful." Empalme, concluded the paper's headline, was now the "Tomb of the Nation's Dignity."[52]

The federal government felt sufficiently pressured by reports of migrant suffering and official corruption that it sent representatives from the Ministry of the Interior to Empalme in June. They were to investigate the "real conditions" in the town. Of course, if they wanted to investigate the full extent of "real conditions," it would have been better to send operatives in April, when migrant claims of corruption surfaced and when contracting was actively taking place, not when contracting was paused because the United States no longer needed Mexican laborers. That way, investigators could see whether or not officials at the contracting center were selling plazas to would-be braceros who had already sacrificed much to make their way to the United States. The timing of the investigation by the Ministry of the Interior suggests a lack of sincere interest by the federal government to assess and prosecute the alleged corruption within its ranks. But since there were 35,000 migrants stuck in Empalme, investigators would at least be able to observe how overwhelmed the area was by unemployed workers.[53]

A local Sonora paper also suggested that the Ministry of the Interior focus on another issue affecting migrants: *coyotaje*. This was the practice of coyotes, human traffickers, promising migrants they could arrange work contracts for them in exchange for a payment. The coyotes were private citizens operating in the area who boasted of special access to government officials and enrollment in the IBP/BP. Their modus operandi was to spread rumors that contracting was about to begin, then promise that they could work their connections to get migrants to the United States. Many migrants, desperate to get out of Empalme, a place without adequate social services, would engage the coyotes' services. Even migrants on official bracero "lists" could not be sure of their place in line and when, if ever, they would be called, so they were vulnerable to participating in coyotaje as well.

Some coyotes honored their promise. At other times, they defrauded migrants, accepting their payment but failing to arrange work contracts for them. The migrants had little recourse, as their embrace of coyotaje meant they had stepped outside the official, legally acceptable channels of recruitment. Instead, they were left in more dire financial situations, having gambled a significant part of their savings to skip the line of workers to the United States. Workers like these swelled the problem of stranded and destitute migrants in and around Empalme.[54]

In the end, migrants were vulnerable to coyotaje because experience had taught many of them that its premise was true: beneath official circuits of BP/IBP movement there existed a parallel underworld of migratory regulation, navigable only with the help of coyotes with access to corrupt officials. The federal government, however, chose to isolate coyotaje as the reason for migrant suffering, absolving itself and its officers from wrongdoing. In a report issued three months later, Gustavo Díaz Ordaz, a senior official with the Mexican Ministry of the Interior, announced that his office had been able to find many coyotes who lied to migrants—selling the promise of work contracts to the United States, while having nothing to give them. Díaz Ordaz neglected to solve the issue, noting his office lacked jurisdiction to go after such scammers. He entrusted the matter to local jurisdictions.[55]

As the summer of 1957 drew to a close, the federal government was sufficiently concerned over the issues of coyotaje, corruption, overcrowding, and insufficient accommodations at the Empalme contracting center that it considered simply moving it elsewhere. The Ministry of the Interior proposed placing the contracting center in Guasave, Sinaloa, a town about 250 miles south of Empalme, an approximately five-hour drive. The move did not proceed because the growers in Sonora mobilized through the CMCTs and Governor Obregón to lobby against the move and its damaging effects. The main issue was the spike it would produce in costs. Enrique Mazón, president of the Hermosillo CMCT, argued that it currently cost Hermosillo growers twenty pesos per laborer to transport migrants from Empalme to their depot in Hermosillo. That cost would be doubled if they had to retrieve the workers from faraway Guasave. The IBP was attractive to growers insofar as it helped them easily tap into a pool of cheap labor. Arranging pickups from Guasave, by contrast, would make it "completely unaffordable to mobilize the workers to the fields."[56]

The federal government chose to maintain the center in its existing location. But evidently Empalme's dysfunctionality was beginning to make officials nervous. Notably, what drove federal officials to launch an investigation into the IBP and consider changes was not growers' misbehavior, of which there are no accounts in 1957 in newspaper or federal government archives. Rather, it was the chronic overcrowding, lack of resources, corruption, and coyotaje in Empalme.

The only relocation growers experienced was within Hermosillo. As part of the IBP, when Hermosillo growers drew workers from the Empalme contracting center, they took them to a private depot they had established through their Hermosillo CMCT. This depot, however, was erected on a lot on which the city of Hermosillo was completing construction of a high school. With the building completed and the school year about to begin, the center had to be moved. Led by Enrique Mazón, the Hermosillo CMCT invested money in a new lot in Hermosillo's northern edge. Within a month, they assured it would have "the water and electric services necessary," as well as "roofs for the pickers, dining tables, sanitary facilities, and so on, in order to avoid any public health issue."

Besides preparing for the arrival of next year's contingent of workers, growers sought to make Hermosillo locals more receptive to the IBP's operation. Mazón announced the Hermosillo CMCT had provided half a million pesos to help finance the recently built school, even though it would displace their warehouse for IBP workers. The message from growers was clear: they would not be the only ones to gain from migrants' arriving; the local populace would also benefit from the growers' resulting largesse. Half a million pesos was not an insignificant sum for the CMCT to dole out. To run the IBP itself, it had spent 275,000 pesos in 1955, 300,000 in 1956, and 125,000 in 1957. The local newspaper, which had decried the contracting center and its corruption for giving rise to "justified complaints" among migrants, remarked that "truly, the way in which this affair has been handled [by growers] in Hermosillo is worthy of praise [from Sonorans]."[57] As 1957 wound down, growers recognized a heightened need to responsibly manage migrant workers and to improve locals' perception of the IBP. But their actions could only go so far in rehabilitating an IBP that, as we will see in the next chapter, was to remain mired in government maladministration and would crumble within five years.

CHAPTER FIVE

TURNING THE TIDE

Part Two

Mexico Desists from Exploiting Migrant Labor Internally, 1958–1963

Chapter 4 demonstrated how the IBP that the Mexican government developed in 1955 and officially kickstarted in 1956 quickly strained its capacity. From 1956 to the summer of 1957, the program suffered from chronic government maladministration. In particular, federal authorities operating the contracting center in Empalme and their collaborators—the mayor of Empalme and the governor of Sonora—demonstrated a persistent inability to receive, care for, and transport the tens of thousands of migrants who seasonally arrived to participate in the suddenly entwined labor regimes of the United States and Mexico. The depth of arriving migrants' suffering arose from their day-to-day dependence on the Mexican government's support, including for daytime shelter, showers, restrooms, rest areas, and dining accommodations. All of these were forms of infrastructure that migrants, no matter how resourceful, could not carry with them and, at best, could only improvise, such as by washing themselves in nearby coastal waters.

Migrants who came to Empalme not only were forced to make do with limited resources but also were subjected to delays of uncertain duration at the contracting center. Indeed, a challenge for the Mexican government in appending the IBP to the BP was that the US hiring of braceros was not entirely predictable. In 1956 and 1957, the United States significantly and surprisingly reduced and altogether halted hiring. Such variations in the US pattern of labor demands made it difficult for Mexican officials to develop a coherent synchronicity between their IBP and the BP. Materially, this resulted in backlogs of workers stranded at the Empalme center, awaiting contracts in the United States after rendering their services in Northern Mexico.

The long waits migrants endured aggravated the material inadequacies they faced in Empalme. As they were kept on standby, migrants suffered nights out in the cold, with no shelter and no blankets, leading to outbreaks of infectious pulmonary diseases that the city of Empalme, which lacked a public hospital, was in no position to contend with. The Mexican government was already testing the forbearance of its migrant population by dangling bracero contracts in front of them in exchange for work in Northern Mexico. It was a "racket," as one migrant put it. The Mexican government's inability to reliably deliver on this promise, coupled with the inhospitable conditions it subjected migrants to, gave the mayor of Empalme reason to fear a rebellion among them. He begged the federal government to stop using Empalme as a staging ground for the BP and IBP, after just one year of operation.

The administration of President Adolfo López Mateos, Cortines's successor, stuck by the twin program of migrant labor exploitation and its basis in Empalme, choosing to see migrant overcrowding, underdeveloped infrastructure, and unreliable coordination with the United States as resolvable glitches. President Mateos attempted to tidy up the program by dispatching a fact-finding mission to Empalme and by providing a one-time stimulus payment to support the rehabilitation and expansion of the contracting center. Yet even as the federal government moved to better equip Empalme to process the migrant influx, the IBP/BP remained plagued by scandal.

The scandal that grew from 1957 onward was migrants' allegation that contracting center personnel extorted them. In addition to being asked to work in Northern Mexico, in addition to waiting sometimes for weeks at the contracting center, and in addition to the material privations they endured, migrants alleged that they were being asked by contracting center staff to pay for passage to the United States—either directly or through coyote networks. More than the delays and lack of suitable infrastructure at the contracting center, this distortion of the IBP and BP—which was guided by a clear quid pro quo, the exchange of work in Mexico for a contract in the United States—stirred migrants' indignation and activism. Their unwillingness to idly abide government corruption, on top of government maladministration, caused the federal government to retreat from the IBP.

GROWER OPTIMISM AMID GOVERNMENT FAILURES

As dysfunctional as the early IBP was, it was an economic boon to cotton growers, a fact not lost on either them or the federal government. In 1957, the Mexican secretary of agriculture spoke at a convention of regional agricultural producers in Reynosa, Tamaulipas, and highlighted the stimulus provided by the IBP. In 1948, well before the program began, 404,678 hectares of cotton were harvested in Mexico, producing 520,000 kilos of cotton, a rate of 295 kilos per hectare. With the labor influx represented by the IBP, results improved dramatically. In 1956, 883,000 total hectares were farmed, with a production of 1,800,000 kilos, a rate of 470 kilos per hectare. Total surface farmed doubled and production quadrupled, making Mexico "the world's leader in cotton production." Mexico was not only outpacing other cotton-producing nations, remarked the secretary. Its cotton was of the highest quality, thus earning higher prices. Whereas the cotton produced in 1948 had yielded $158,128,520 pesos, in 1956 that figure increased to $3,207,000,000 pesos.[1]

Growers and federal officials alike believed their fruitful collaboration would continue to net economic results. Enrique Mazón, grower and head of the Hermosillo CMCT, predicted the cotton bounties of the late 1950s would be the largest in Sonora's history. The climate seemed propitious and pests were under control. The federal Ministry of the Interior agreed with Mazón's forecast. It anticipated a particularly large demand in Northern Mexico for migrant labor beginning in late 1957. The office thus sent a special representative, Gustavo de Anda, to cooperate with Mazón and ensure the orderly movement of bracero workers into the fields of Hermosillo cotton growers. Mazón ordered his fellow Sonoran growers to register ahead of time and specify how many workers they needed. They would receive an allotment of migrant workers in the order their request was received.[2] By the end of the year, Mazón proudly announced that on the growers' end the program was working seamlessly, "solving with true success" Northern Mexico's long-standing labor insufficiency.³

By early 1958, however, the Empalme center under federal control was yet again saturated with workers who, unable to fit into existing accommodations, were sleeping on city streets. For food, they fished in the waters of Empalme with makeshift tools. They could not fish offshore since they had no boats. Journalists described a "painful scene." Desperate men hoped to hear their name called in Empalme, signifying they were released to work in the United States. A newspaper's headline captured the predictable weariness of the situation: "Yet Again, the Spectacle of Starving Braceros in Empalme."⁴

Moreover, contrary to the federal government's claims that coyotaje, rather than corruption, afflicted Empalme, migrants insisted that officials were selling passage to the United States. Migrants claimed it was theoretically "easy" to arrange one's passage. The challenge was cobbling together the 300 pesos that officals in Empalme charged for the service. Indeed, migrants interviewed by the local newspaper did not mention coyotes. They emphasized that it was contracting center personnel who ran the extortion scheme.

Government mismanagement and corruption of the BP/IBP reached its tipping point in 1959. What had been, up to then, a vague, faceless problem became one with a cast of named characters. This happened largely thanks to migrants. Frustrated with their experiences at the contracting facility, they began to expose their victimizers, in particular the nexus of coyotes and officials selling bracero contracts. In February 1959, a group of migrants wrote to Sonora's secretary of the interior, Francisco Enciso, asking him to investigate corruption and coyotaje in Empalme. They copied Gustavo Díaz Ordaz, who was now head of the federal Ministry of the Interior.⁵

The migrants reported that they were stranded in Empalme. They had paid a coyote, Mario López, to arrange their passage to the United States. But López was arrested by local police on charges of coyotaje and could no longer hold up his end of the deal. They felt it was unfair that they should suffer the effects of this policing. It was "an established rule" that migrants paid a bribe to Mario López in the amount of 500 pesos, and he then facilitated their passage, thanks to connections between coyotes like him and the officials at the contracting center. They suggested an interrogation of López, who was being held in the local prison of Guaymas, Sonora, to reveal the precise nature of those links and help bring "justice" to Empalme.

While migrants hoped the federal government would dismantle the network of corruption and coyotaje in Empalme, they also insisted on restitution.

They had given "all of our financial resources [to López], which were already sparse to begin with." They could neither "move forward nor turn back." López should be forced to pay them back their money. Failing that, the frustrated migrants wrote, the government should make a "special exception" for them and accelerate their exit to the United States. They argued it was "obvious that there were connections between the coyotes and contracting center officials" and they had been guilty of nothing more than operating within the actually existing, de facto channels of exit. Twenty-two migrants signed the letter. Their leader, Salvador Ramos Sánchez, asserted there was a "substantial group" of migrants in Empalme who had yet to organize but were also "victims of this misfortune."[6]

Salvador Sánchez's comment turned out to be prescient. Soon other migrants organized to unmask the corruption in Empalme. This time, they implicated by name not only coyotes but also the staff at the contracting center. A contingent of migrants showed up in March 1959 to the offices of the local newspaper *El Imparcial*, claiming they had proof corroborating the links between Sonoran coyotes and contracting center officials. Part of their anger was directed at coyotes for falsely promising them contracts. But, in practice, the decision to let people through to the United States, observed migrants, was up to contracting center personnel, who handled matters "arbitrarily." Some of the migrants who paid a bribe went through, others did not. This inconsistency angered migrants who simply wished to go north.

Additionally, migrants questioned why there should be a separate, illicit channel for contracting to begin with. In their understanding, contracting center personnel were supposed to oversee out-migration, honoring the IBP's promise of expedited exit for migrants who worked in Northern Mexico, not pick and choose migrants based on side payments. The migrants reported they were now being charged up to 700 pesos for passage to the United States. Migrants claimed the chief administrators of the contracting center were responsible for this corruption. The newspaper, after assessing the evidence presented by migrants, called for a serious federal or state-level investigation into the center's gatekeepers.[7]

Within a few days, the federal Ministry of the Interior dispatched investigators to Empalme to assess migrants' complaints. Unlike the ministry's prior investigation, which took place during a lull in contracting in the late summer of 1957, this one was undertaken while contracting was in full swing. Seven thousand migrants were present in Empalme. In the interim, more migrants contacted *El Imparcial* complaining of the corruption and singling out the chief of the contracting center as its ringleader.[8]

By April, 12,000 migrants were in Empalme, leading, "yet again . . . [to] more robberies and scandals at the contracting center," according to *El Imparcial*. The federal Ministry of Interior sent more special agents to the area to oversee contracting. The persistence with which the federal government dispatched special envoys to Empalme confirms that its concern with the IBP/BP stemmed from internal corruption at the contracting center, rather than grower malfeasance.[9]

Despite the presence of investigative federal agents, coyotes and corrupt officials kept up their money-making scheme. Migrants spoke to an investigative journalist sent by *El Imparcial*. They refused to be named in his story, believing their disclosures could place them in mortal danger. To a greater extent than any migrants prior, these interviewed migrants revealed the corrupt regime reigning in Empalme. The journalist corroborated their claims that a number of cantinas (working-class bars) operated in Empalme disguised as restaurants. There, cantina operators sold not just food and drink but contracts to whomever could pay the price. Given the heightened danger introduced by increased federal oversight, the migrants alleged, the price of contracts had increased to 1,000 pesos.

Several "restaurant" operators were identified by migrants as coyotes. The one with greatest notoriety was María Félix de Barreto. She and the others could "make a man appear in the lists of people to be contracted to the United States." Just as surely though, they could make a man "disappear from the world of the living," and for this reason no migrant spoke against them by name. According to the migrants, these coyotes operated undisturbed by local police. Arrangements between coyotes and migrants were sometimes made "in plain sight," with police standing by as "spectators" to the bribery. As far as migrants were concerned, police were in the pocket of the coyote business and Empalme was a place ruled by illegality. The contracting center personnel, including the center's chief, benefited handsomely, as they kept a portion of the thousand pesos migrants paid to coyotes.[10]

El Imparcial's special investigative reporter sought to get in contact with the new municipal president of Empalme, Ciro Arce, to ask why local police forces with direct jurisdiction were not proceeding aggressively against coyotes and contracting center personnel. The journalist declared it was imperative to put a "total end to the outrages perpetrated by the men who manage vice and fraud in the city." The municipal president denied the interview request. The journalist wrote that political authorities could not go into "hiding" forever. They would have to answer for "the vile exploitation of braceros they perpetrated." And for turning Empalme into an "Emporium of Crime . . . lost in iniquity."[11]

Against the backdrop of migrant accusations, overcrowding in Empalme persisted. The Alliance of National Workers of Mexico in the United States, a bracero-led union, received complaints from migrants in Empalme who had worked in the IBP and were awaiting release to the United States. In the meantime, they tried to feed themselves by fishing but were arrested by local police for vagrancy. Police would only release them if they paid fines of twenty to thirty pesos. The union argued it was unfair to ask this of migrants who "lacked all kinds of economic resources." The union wrote to Governor Obregón, and copied the federal Ministry of the Interior, to ask for an immediate end to the predatory policing of immiserated migrants.[12]

By June, migrants themselves complained to the Sonora governor that it was unclear when, if ever, they were going to reach the United States. One contingent described how contracting center officials were only allowing the passage of ten to fifteen migrants per day—"a rate at which the entire year might pass by and we might not be let through." The United States was requesting fewer migrants than expected per day. The migrants had already worked a couple of weeks in Northern Mexico and were promised expedited release to the United States. They lost patience with the delays and said the cards they received attesting to their service in Northern Mexico meant "nothing."[13] Another migrant told the governor he had been waiting for two months, despite having the official card provided by Northern Mexico growers attesting to his service. Contemplating the meaningless of the card, he asked, "Are we even braceros or not?"[14]

By the summer of 1959, tens of thousands of migrants were stuck in Empalme, having "already worked picking cotton in the Valle del Yaqui and Valle del Mayo." Migrants claimed their stagnation was caused by corruption at the contracting center, and not just by the low daily quotas assigned by the United States. Migrants observed that "thousands of [bracero] aspirants who have not fulfilled the requirement to [work in Northern Mexico cotton] are allowed by authorities to pass," while they were forced to wait. The angered migrants organized themselves and funded a special delegation to visit the secretary-general of the state of Sonora, Francisco Enciso, to express their frustration.

Enciso was Obregón's second-in-command. He received the migrants in his office and promised to prosecute any "arbitrariness" and injustice in the running of the BP/IBP. Following his meeting with the migrants, Enciso summoned the chief of the contracting center, Juan Cerdán Lara, and asked him to explain the irregularities at the center.[15] Two weeks later, the judge of the First Court in Guaymas issued a warrant for Lara's arrest as head of a bribery and corruption scheme that preyed on braceros. The investigation led by the state attorney general, Adolfo Harra Seldner, and supported by the federal government, found that Lara was the lead conspirator in a system that had "defrauded migrants of 40 million pesos" since the IBP's inauguration. According to the investigation, Lara, an appointee from the federal Ministry of the Interior, worked in tandem with a number of coyotes, including Gilberto Gil Macías, Elías Ángulo, Carlos Villela, Filiberto Manzanilla, and María Félix, whom the migrants had mentioned earlier that year as a key figure selling contracts out of her restaurant-bar. The judge issued warrants for their arrest too. He denied them bail and conditional liberty because, if convicted, their prison terms would exceed five years.[16]

The scandals surrounding the contracting center made the federal government consider ending the IBP. The timing of Mexico's reckoning with its corruption indicates it was the dysfunction at the Empalme contracting center, including the actions of Lara and his associates, that prompted Mexico to question its ability to direct migrant labor internally. Growers had managed their end of the IBP satisfactorily. After a month of internal, top-level deliberation, the federal government decided to hold off on suspending the IBP.[17]

In a final show of faith, the federal government doubled down on the program. It doubled the number of braceros to be contracted out of Empalme from 300,000 to 600,000. Growers celebrated the expansion of the migratory labor pool available to them. They imagined "money [would] pour in."[18] The Ministry of the Interior was confident in the IBP for two reasons. First, now that Lara and his accomplices were under arrest and awaiting trial, the ministry believed corruption at the Empalme contracting center was fully under control. Second, the Sonora attorney general had sent five special agents to investigate and prosecute any fraud in the area during the heightened contracting season. If the ongoing trials of Lara and others did not deter coyotes and corrupt officials, perhaps the looming threat of five roving officials would. The precautionary measures taken by the Mexican government are a telltale sign of where its concerns with the IBP lay. It ordered no such surveillance of participating growers.[19]

Over the next two years, the IBP did not transform into an efficient, scandal-free operation as the Ministry of the Interior had hoped. Coyotaje and corruption, not to mention overcrowding and resource insufficiency at the contracting center, remained commonplace. Migrants complained to anyone who would listen. In February 1960, a migrant contingent wrote to President Adolfo López Mateos, requesting his attention to their suffering in Empalme. They copied the Mexican secretary of the interior, the secretary of foreign affairs, the governor of the State of Sonora, and the García Balseca newspaper chain, and had their claims certified by the chief of police of the state of Sonora.[20]

The migrants in the contingent claimed they each paid "900 to 1,000 pesos" to "persons who pretended to be authorities with the power to process their documents" and make them braceros. They paid the sum out of desperation, after a two-month wait in Empalme to be contracted as braceros. They sought to bribe their way out of Mexico, even though they were certified to be part of the BP and had served their time in the IBP as well. They had only budgeted for a "two-week wait" in Empalme by "mortgaging and selling [our] meager belongings." So they were desperate to leave with the help of coyotes. Migrants asserted that coyotaje and fraud were the fault of the federal government. Insofar as migrants believed mysterious people could arrange their contracts, this was because in fact such people had existed for years and the federal government had done little to impede them.[21] The migrants may have had Lara in mind when writing the letter. In any case, their story points to the intractability of corruption: even when the federal government attempted to stamp it out, it left behind a legacy of credulity among migrants that was hard to undo.

A few weeks later, another group of migrants questioned the degree to which the contracting center had been truly reformed. They wrote to Governor Obregón but copied the new chief of the contracting center, the president, the mayor of Empalme, and the director of a newspaper, *El Diario del Yaqui*, seeking to deploy as many mechanisms of shame and accountability as might serve them. They were in their third month of waiting for a bracero contract. They had worked in Guaymas as part of the IBP to hasten their emigration. But they were not receiving any priority at the contracting center. In fact, migrants from the rest of Mexico continued to arrive and "mysteriously" were allowed to exit to the United States immediately. They suggested that a pattern of corruption continued to reign at the center.

The injustice was material to them. They subsisted on "one meal a day, sometimes not eating anything at all." Addressing all the people copied in the letter as witnesses to their plight, they wrote, "Gentlemen: we ask, is it justice that after we worked for Mexico, to help the growers in Guaymas, we are now abandoned?" They invited reporters from the *Diario del Yaqui* to come investigate the situation personally, for surely they would find many like them and confirm the ongoing corruption. They also called on any of the "government offices we have listed" to come and investigate their complaints and "agonizing situation."22

Two other migrants, Máximo García Huerta and Víctor Bedella Zavala, stuck in Empalme since January and now in their fifth month of waiting, also wrote a letter of protest to Obregón. Huerta and Zavala had worked for cotton growers in Guaymas, including the Ranch of San Antonio del Real, after traveling for days from Michoacán. Regarding San Antonio del Real and their experience working in the fields, the migrants offered no complaints. What they found inexcusable was the inordinately long wait they and others suffered in Empalme. It was all the more frustrating because the "government knows the things that go on at the contracting center." In this way, they delicately alluded to enduring corruption at the contracting center and gestured toward the government's complicity.23

During the summer months, US demand for Mexican workers was sufficient to clear out the Empalme contracting center. Migrants complained, however, that their resulting stints in the United States were far too short given how long they had to wait in Empalme. A group of migrants from Jalisco arrived in Sonora in January and worked at the Metates Ranch in Guaymas because of "the promise that we would be given the license to work in the United States." Contracting center personnel, however, questioned whether the migrants had truly worked in Northern Mexico's cotton fields. They asked the migrants to provide their services anew to confirm their eligibility for expedited exit. The migrants finally gained admission to the United States in late July. Their US contract lasted two months. Given the seven months they waited, their bracero contract was "too short to even partially justify the time we wasted in Empalme." They appealed to Obregón's compassion and asked him to guarantee them a slot in the BP for the following year. They pleaded that they needed the money. They had taken on debt to fund their trip to Sonora, which their two months of earnings in the United States would not be enough to repay. They feared they would be "sued and jailed by the lender."24

The government's management of the Empalme contracting center thus remained dysfunctional in 1960. But officials were finally joined by misbehaving growers, who had otherwise avoided notably mishandling their end of the IBP. Earlier, grower handling of the IBP had not led to notable migrant complaints through either government or media channels, other than the one early instance in Tamaulipas investigated by the Departamento de Tránsito Federal (mentioned in chapter 4). This is not to say mistreatment did not occur, but migrants accepted it, in whatever form and dose they encountered it, as a tolerable part of the transaction that would bring them to the United States. They understood Northern Mexico to be a pitstop and were more concerned with obtaining the official letter from growers attesting to their service than with publicly questioning their work conditions.

Fittingly, when growers stood accused of mistreating migrants in 1960, the complaints came not from migrants but from the Sonora Ministry of Health. The agency conducted a sanitary inspection of the CMCT migrant depot in Hermosillo and found it lacking. Whereas the federal government was responsible for the center in Empalme, growers were supposed to oversee the care of migrants allotted to them in Hermosillo. This included running a depot with dining, sleeping, bathing, and lavatory facilities, where migrants arriving from Empalme would stay while completing their stint in Northern Mexico's cotton fields. Financial records of the grower-led Hermosillo CMCT indicate it spent most of its funds on erecting infrastructure to house migrants, dedicating smaller sums to "feeding braceros."[25]

With this system in place, growers generally did their duty. But in early October 1960, Joaquín Lozano Corona, an agent of the Sonora Public Health Department, assessed the Hermosillo depot to be a failure. It was managed by Abel Martínez and under the ultimate responsibility of Enrique Mazón, head of the Hermosillo CMCT. Corona observed that the depot was completely overwhelmed by the number of migrants growers had brought in from Empalme. There were not enough latrines, so "many men—having nowhere else to carry out their physiological needs—are left to defecate out in the open." Space and lodging were in short supply too, so many migrants took shelter "under trees." Food and dining services were insufficient as well, so vendors set up makeshift establishments to hawk goods to migrants, while other vendors just walked about, leaving a stream of garbage in their wake. The food preparation practices in the depot did not meet the sanitary code. The center thus presented a "danger," in Corona's words, not just to the migrants, but to the neighborhood and to children enrolled at the Vincente Mora and Club de Leones schools nearby.[26]

Though the report was generated by the Sonora secretary of health, it made its way to the federal government. This is because Sonora governor Luis Encinas, Obregón's successor, stepped in to ask Mazón to "urgently" fix the Hermosillo depot, but when doing so, he addressed the CMCT, which was partly composed of watchdogs from the federal Ministry of the Interior.[27] The findings of the public health agent gave the federal government an opening to argue that growers were the ones who were fundamentally irresponsible and to undo the IBP on that basis.

Already, the federal government had publicly wavered from the IBP earlier in 1960 because of endemic corruption, coyotaje, and overcrowding in Empalme. Its interventions—from constantly sending special agents of the Ministry of the Interior to investigate matters, to investing in upgrades to the Empalme facilities, to prosecuting coyotes and their accomplices at the center—had softened but not eradicated Empalme's reputation as "tomb of the nation's dignity." The growers' reported misstep allowed the government to undo a program that, for all its economic benefits, surpassed its management capacity.

Since the federal Ministry of the Interior had already arranged for another year of the IBP when it received the Health Department's report, it did not discontinue the program right away. Besides, quickly withdrawing growers' access to workers could have had devastating effects on the yearly cotton harvest. The federal government decided the IBP would be terminated a year later, on October 13, 1961.

There were arguably easier ways to tackle the problematic overcrowding in Hermosillo, if that was truly the ministry's concern. It could have reduced the number of workers allotted to the Hermosillo CMCT, for instance. Such numbers were not set in stone. Indeed, the government had doubled the number of migrants destined for Sonora—Hermosillo included—between 1959 to 1960. That bump likely provoked the overcrowding witnessed by the Sonora health agent.[28]

The speed with which the federal government decided to discontinue the IBP is notable. At its own processing center in Empalme, it had tolerated outbreaks of disease, incessant delays, the growth of coyotaje, and endemic corruption. Yet when Hermosillo growers committed their first major blunder and failed to provide adequate accommodations for IBP workers, the federal government was unforgiving. It determined that Hermosillo's growers had failed to "fulfill their existing obligations to workers." The Ministry of the Interior, however, could not point to a larger pattern of specific offenses when making the indictment. Growers and their political allies were befuddled. The new Sonora governor, Luis Encinas, defended growers from these allegations in a seven-page memo to federal secretary of the interior Gustavo Díaz Ordaz.[29]

Moreover, there is evidence that the overwhelmed worker depot in Hermosillo was an isolated case, rather than an example of a widespread problem plaguing other Sonoran localities that likewise drew migrant labor from Empalme. Growers in other Sonoran regions took precautionary measures to prepare for the greater influx of workers in 1960. Migrants sent to those areas reported no problems to authorities or newspapers. For instance, in El Yaqui, growers installed 120 new latrines so migrants would not have to urinate and defecate in public.[30]

Finally, the federal government's decisiveness was jarring to growers because it is not as if they responded with hostility or reluctance to cooperate. Growers proposed to Secretary of the Interior Díaz Ordaz through Governor Encinas that their yearly tax be increased by 20 percent to fund special inspectors who would oversee their worker depots and operations at large.[31] The secretary of the interior was not interested in reforming the IBP, however; he wished to take advantage of the growers' mishandling of their Hermosillo depot to end the program.

After intensive lobbying from the growers in conjunction with Sonora governor Encinas, President Mateos agreed to extend the program one year past its announced end date of 1961. Growers and their allies emphasized to him how much the program meant for their bottom lines.[32] In effect, after the Health Department's investigation into the Hermosillo depot in late 1960, Sonoran growers could count on the IBP for two more years. The first was the grace year granted by the federal government to avoid jeopardizing Northern Mexico's cotton harvests; the second was an extension of that grace period. The federal government recognized it would take growers some time to find the supplementary labor needed to replace the IBP.

Fittingly, even in 1961, the penultimate year of the IBP, it was the aspects directly controlled by the Mexican government that remained most persistently dysfunctional. In the late summer of 1961, Empalme was overwhelmed yet again by migrants. US growers had changed their bracero order and were requesting fewer migrants than expected, making it plain to Mexico's Ministry of the Interior that most of the migrants in Empalme would not receive contracts. The agency counted about 15,000 migrants and figured most would not be able to make their way home without assistance. Their presence in Empalme could not be tolerated for long, as they were already creating a "grave problem of supplies for their care." So the ministry launched what it described as an "evacuation" of the migrants gathered, with an initial convoy sent out of Empalme on August 7. The first shipment of migrants back into the interior consisted of eighty-one boxcars, into which the Ministry of the Interior fit 4,000 migrants. The government publicly pleaded that no more aspirants come to Empalme.[33]

More headaches awaited, however. The federal Ministry of the Interior was only able to clear Empalme of migrants who were physically gathered there. Many thousands more were soon due back in the city. They had been released to work in Hermosillo, El Yaqui, El Mayo, and other towns under the IBP. They came back to Empalme after serving their stint. The number of migrants in Empalme swelled to 17,000 by early September, according to the new head of the contracting center, Francisco Gasca Muñoz.

These migrants would similarly strain the resources of Empalme. But the larger problem was that, unlike the first cohort of arrivals, these migrants had all actually worked in the cotton fields of Northern Mexico. The federal Ministry of the Interior had to be careful not to provoke their anger by telling them that there would be no contracts for their passage to the United States. The ministry sought to defuse the situation by promising the migrants that if they showed up to Empalme the following year with special slips "that corroborated their work in Sonoran harvests," their passage to the United States would be arranged with "ease." With that promise, the office was able to get migrants to comply with its plan to remove 500 of them from Empalme per day in a continued "evacuation." Their removal stretched out for thirty-four days.[34]

Coyotaje and corruption in Empalme also persisted to the end, as a group of eight migrants from Central Mexico, led by Francisco Aguilar Figueroa, learned. In late 1961, they worked for weeks in various Sonoran cotton fields, from El Yaqui to Hermosillo, in accordance with the "initiative that we first lend our services here, in Mexico," and then "cross the border to the United States as braceros." But contracting center authorities were not letting them through to the United States. They suspected official wrongdoing because even though they were at a standstill, workers from Guadalajara, Jalisco, "streamed in continuously" and were promptly shuttled to the United States. The migrants decided to launch their own investigation into the situation—intercepting and interviewing some of the migrants from Guadalajara. The migrants they interviewed admitted they had paid off officials at the contracting centers using coyote collaborators in Empalme. The migrants wrote to Governor Encinas with their reportage but specified they wanted "the federal Ministry of the Interior to be notified so that it could take proper charge of the situation."[35]

For migrants, the corruption reached peak absurdity in the fall of 1961. Migrants sought the help of the Sonora police. They alleged that contracting center personnel were selling not just bracero contracts to the United States but also ones for Northern Mexico cotton harvesting. Rodolfo Cuevas Montoya, an agent of the judicial police of the state of Sonora, tried to interview the migrants concerned. By the time he arrived, however, they were gone. According to the man who had lent them lodging and his mailing address for a fee, they had given up and dispersed throughout Mexico. Agent Montoya spoke with other migrants instead. He confirmed that there were widespread rumors that contracting center personnel, in conjunction with local Empalme police agents, were preying on migrants and selling them spots to work in Sonora's cotton harvest. These spots were desirable because, under the IBP, they theoretically entitled migrants to expedited passage to the United States, provided they first completed their Northern Mexico work stint. The agent could not establish exactly who at the contracting center was implicated in the scheme, but he was able to get the names of the police officers most deeply involved.[36]

Migrants charged that the ringleaders of the initiative were the sergeant of the Empalme police, Silvestre Castro, and Víctor Manuel López, who until recently had been a municipal transit police officer. Migrants accused Castro and his conspirators of charging them thirty, forty, and fifty pesos to join the cotton harvest. They paid the fee to Lorenza Castro, the sergeant's wife, who operated a private cafeteria inside the Empalme contracting center and had ample, close contact with migrants.

The extortive scheme did not end with the sale of spots in Northern Mexico cotton harvesting. Police also demanded an additional fifteen pesos "to transport them to the place where they will pick [cotton]." Agent Montoya noted that such transportation charges were already covered under the IBP by growers and their CMCTs. Montoya recommended to Guillermo Cajigas, the Sonora state chief of police, that he launch a more formal investigation into migrant accusations. Records indicate that Cajigas did nothing.[37]

Perhaps the state's chief of police accepted the side businesses of Empalme's police officers or did not want to bother with an IBP that was soon to expire. Either way, his inaction reflects the government's broad failure to properly administer the program. Moreover, that it was the Empalme sergeant orchestrating the scheme, when he was supposed to police corruption and coyotaje, reveals the persistent rot in the IBP. Finally, it is worth emphasizing that while growers paid to transport workers to their cotton fields through their CMCTs, their supposed allies in government—the contracting center staff at Empalme and the police—extorted migrants by levying on them a contrived transport cost. Growers could not police this; it fell to the government to police itself.[38]

At any rate, in the penultimate year of the IBP's operation, growers had to focus on their own behavior. The federal Ministry of the Interior, displeased with the program and its controversies, threatened that any migrant complaints against growers would be seriously investigated and that offending growers would have workers taken from them at once. Tellingly, the ministry sent special commissions to inspect Sonoran fields for this misbehavior, rather than relying entirely on migrants' reporting. Migrant complaints against growers had, for years, been few and far between, unlike the recurrent complaints they delivered against various entities of the Mexican government. In those cases, migrants possessed courage enough to share their grievances, even when according to them it put their lives at risk. The ministry also announced its expanded supervisory efforts publicly in the newspapers of each of the cities receiving braceros. The aggressiveness and publicity of the grower surveillance campaign helped the government signal a rhetorical commitment to worker rights, and buttress the shaky narrative that it was growers and their malfeasance that made the program unworkable.[39] The ministry's search came up empty, but the news of the campaign sufficed to meet the government's performative ends.

In the final year of the IBP, President López Mateos and the Ministry of the Interior underscored to growers that the decision to discontinue the program was permanent. The president himself communicated to growers in April 1962 that his idea, reached in consultation with state governors, was that growers should resolve their labor problem "internally within Mexican territory" by relying on local workers, "without any reference to the Bracero Program."[40] He asked growers to collaborate with nearby municipalities to find and contract willing workers. Municipal presidents would recruit workers on behalf of growers. Meanwhile, growers would cover the cost of transporting them to and from Northern Mexico's cotton fields, and the costs associated with lodging, food, and sanitation. Growers would be responsible for all logistics too. President Mateos's proposal effectively abdicated federal participation in Northern Mexico cotton production and unlatched the IBP from the BP. Municipal authorities, under the suggested framework, were to remain involved in the labor question only as mediators between growers and workers, rather than as labor suppliers. Mexico was admitting it lacked the competence needed to internally mobilize migrant workers.

It remained an open question whether Northern Mexico's cotton growers would be able to continue their financial successes without the government as chief orchestrator of their migratory labor pool. The abandonment by the Mexican government would revive many of the problems that growers had experienced prior to the IBP. First, it was unclear whether there were enough workers in Northern Mexico willing to work for inferior wages in the demanding cotton crop when the United States loomed on the horizon. The whole premise of the IBP had been that Northern Mexico's growers could not compete with US wages and needed special help from the government.

Second, even supposing there were enough workers available locally, there was a question of whether growers would be able to afford transporting them from disparate municipalities in their state and nearby states and back again. Already, when the Ministry of the Interior had proposed moving the processing center from Empalme to Benjamín Hill, a few hours to the south, the growers complained the transportation costs would become too onerous. Though slightly farther, Benjamín Hill would have still been a convenient, centralized location for growers; now they were going to have to simultaneously get workers from all over Northern Mexico, including towns many hours away.

Third, cotton growers from across the region would have to compete with one another for the same scarce labor, with the most obvious recruitment tool being improved wages, an expense the growers avoided for years with the IBP, which used contracts in the United States, not wages in Mexico, to lure workers. Overall, the government's renunciation of the IBP threatened to leave growers logistically and financially overstretched.

The other part of President Mateos's message to growers, separate from the recommendation that they rely on local and regional labor pools, was that they should stop using the BP and the promise of bracero contracts as recruitment tools. Going forward, Mateos's government wanted to prevent the overcrowding of migrants in Empalme. It intended to continue using the contracting center there to process migrants promised to the United States. To avoid chaos there, it would be helpful if migrants did not arrive in the Empalme region based on the notion that working for northern cotton growers would lead to their passage to the United States. Mateos wanted the growers to convey to migrants that work in Northern Mexico's cotton fields meant work in Northern Mexico cotton fields and nothing more. That clarity might help reduce the crowds at Empalme in future years and the problems they invited: migrant destitution, migrant desperation, the predation of coyotes, and the opportunism of corrupt officials.[41]

Heading into the 1962 harvesting season, the final season with the IBP in effect, President Mateos signaled he would not budge from ending the government's involvement in internal labor allocation. He ordered the Ministry of the Interior to slash the number of migrants allotted to Northern Mexico's growers. Sonoran growers in El Mayo, El Yaqui, and Hermosillo were originally promised 60,000 workers for the season. That provision was suddenly reduced to 20,000. Growers were stunned by the federal government's move and tried to convince anyone with high governmental power that they needed a larger allotment of workers to survive the harvesting season. Through the entire year, they wrote to and arranged for meetings with the governor of Sonora, the secretary of the interior of Sonora, federal secretary of the interior Díaz Ordaz, the federal secretary of agriculture, and President Mateos. They organized through their various commissions, as well as other collectives including the Confederación de Organismos Agricultores de Sonora (Sonora Confederation of Farmers Organizations) and the Asociación de Productores de Algodón del Noroeste (Northeast Association of Cotton Producers), to argue that the sudden and dramatic dwindling of their labor force would severely hurt their productivity and bottom line.[42]

Typical was the argument of the Asociación de Productores, which argued that the IBP had been beneficial because it had freed their productive capacity. Now they would have to match their productivity to the labor capacity of the region by reducing the size of their harvests. The association outlined a domino effect in which this diminished capacity would not just hurt the "individual growers" but the fiscal health of the state and country. Their decreased earnings, they explained, would result in lower tax revenue. Sonoran growers were well capable of articulating a sense of their macroeconomic significance.[43] However, not all expressed themselves in measured tones. As they grew exasperated with the federal government's measure, some said that if the government was going to so severely abdicate its role in supplying them with labor, the least it could do is move the migrant processing center far from Empalme. That way, the pool of workers who arrived in the area would not be so bent on working in the United States and disinclined to work for the lower wages of Northern Mexico.[44]

Their lobbying earned Sonoran growers no reprieve from President Mateos. Not one additional worker was tacked onto their allowance, leaving their total share of braceros at 20,000 workers, far short of the 60,000 workers growers expected and clamored for.[45] The federal government was firm that now was the time to transition from, not return to, the practice of syphoning workers from the BP. President Mateos's unwillingness to restore Sonoran growers' flow of migrant labor, even in part, encouraged them to follow his advice and seek to resolve their farmworker needs "internally" and "without any reference to the Bracero Program." Grower commissions contacted the presidents of municipalities in Sonora and asked them if they could help identify available workers in their jurisdiction; the federal Ministry of the Interior, in turn, asked municipalities to cooperate with growers.[46]

By turning to local municipalities, growers hoped to cover their immediate labor shortage of 40,000 workers. The state government of Sonora went a step further and began to plan for subsequent years. Of course, it had more of a financial stake than the federal government in growers' continued success since the growers represented a greater part of their tax base. Enabling growers' success meant making sure they had the labor they needed, so they would not have to reduce their production as the Asociación de Productores had threatened would be the case. So the Sonora Ministry of the Interior, acting under the direction of the governor, called upon municipalities to send any available workers to state growers. The cost of transportation, it promised, would be fully covered by the growers. Thus Sonora's leaders and growers sought to solve their labor problem "internally," in line with President Mateos's recommendation.

The Sonora secretary of the interior also specified to mayors that under no circumstances were workers to be promised contracts in the United States as a reward for working in Northern Mexico.[47] Workers should understand that from 1963 onward neither the state nor the growers would be able to offer this, as their arrangement with the federal government had come undone. In August, Sonoran growers' associations reinforced this message but communicated it directly to migrants by radio, just in case municipal presidents failed to let prospective workers know that the reward for work in Northern Mexico was wages in Northern Mexico and not also a contract in the United States.[48] Growers thus obeyed President Mateos's instructions to sort out their labor shortage without reference to the BP. President Mateos's surprise curtailing of the number of braceros worked by jolting growers and their allies toward self-reliance.

Growers returned to the federal government one more time, however, to seek its assistance. They attempted to make do in 1962 with the 20,000 workers provided by the federal government, plus whatever they could cobble together from municipalities in the state. The approach worked through the beginning of the harvest, as growers relied on the laborers provided by the federal government. They essentially frontloaded their access to the 20,000 workers, such that by midsummer they had burned through their allotted quota. Months still remained in the harvest, so the question became whether growers would be able to gather the remaining workers they needed from municipalities in the state. Growers were not the least bit optimistic and with good reason, for in losing their ability to promise contracts to the United States, they had lost their most compelling recruitment tool.

A feature report in *El Imparcial* seemed to confirm their fears. It spotlighted Sonoran locals who argued they would help the growers lift their cotton harvest only if they were given contracts in the United States. Growers pleaded with the federal government, especially in July, to reconsider its abdication of its supportive role, first sending a special envoy to meet with Secretary of the Interior Díaz Ordaz in Mexico City, then sending an envoy to the secretary of agriculture. Before both officials, they argued that the 20,000 laborers made available to them by the federal government were not enough and that the Sonoran locals they were being asked to rely on would not lift a finger unless they were promised contracts in the United States.[49] Their outreach failed, so growers formed a special delegation that went to speak with Secretary of the Interior Díaz Ordaz again, this time accompanied by Sonora governor Encinas. They remained unsuccessful. Díaz Ordaz would not grant them more workers.[50]

Growers urged Governor Encinas to remain stubborn, with the Cámara Nacional de Comercio de Ciudad Obregón (Ciudad Obregón National Chamber of Commerce), for instance, arguing that the "economy of the Valle del Yaqui and the entire state of Sonora was at imminent risk" given the lack of workers available to "save the harvest of cotton." Sonoran growers argued that they needed the federal government to intervene because people in Sonora could not be counted on to save the crop. As the chamber of commerce wrote, "The workers who come here during the cotton harvest have nothing else in mind than obtaining a certificate [from us] to allow them to contract themselves [as braceros]." "They refuse to work only in exchange for remuneration from us [growers]" and "opt to head back to where they came from," they asserted. "This situation is happening daily and can be proved."[51] The IBP had built in laborers' understanding that working in Northern Mexico was only worthwhile if it accelerated their passage to the United States.

The growers' struggle to find workers on their own and without reference to the BP was also attested to by Enrique Mazón, president of the Hermosillo CMCT, in his personal communications with Governor Encinas. He similarly confessed that the new model of local and regional recruitment was not working well. He had obeyed the governor's instructions that growers and Sonoran municipalities cooperate to save the cotton crop. Specifically, he wrote to each municipal president in Sonora to arrange for the transport of available workers. But, after an entire summer of outreach, he only received one response to his inquiries. That municipal president offered a grand total of thirty workers to the Sonoran cause, far short of the aspirations of growers when turning to local municipal presidents for a supply of workers.[52]

Growers feared that the inadequacy of federal, state, and municipal support, coupled with migrants' general disinterest in picking Northern Mexico cotton, would doom their current and future harvests. *El Imparcial* ran a series of stories on how growers were adapting to the loss of the IBP. The earliest came in the middle of the summer, when growers were still attempting to convince President Mateos to extend them access to 60,000 workers. One grower, Antonio Haro, who owned large tracts of land throughout the region, reported he was turning to machinery to save his crop. He was fed up with having to rely on the federal government for labor, and the way it reduced him and fellow growers to supplicants. So he traveled to Arkansas to purchase the latest in cotton-picking equipment designed to automate labor. He believed in this technological solution so strongly that he agreed to represent the US company in Northern Mexico as a seller.[53]

As the summer deepened, so did growers' alleged crisis. *El Imparcial* ran another story, "Cotton—Its Problems and Its Future in Hermosillo," spotlighting another large grower in the area, Alberto Covarrubias, and his outlook. He cast the labor problem as an endemic one, rooted in the fact that "thousands of migrants from the center of the country come to Sonora attracted by the possibility of contracting themselves to the United States and only agree to work in our fields when they have absolutely no other choice." On top of that, he found that these workers manifested a higher sense of self-worth because they compared Northern Mexico work conditions to US ones, and "only agree[d] to work for us once they [had] made a series of demands that border on the absurd." This generated a problem of "labor insecurity" that affected "all growers in the state."

The present crisis, stemming from the loss of the IBP, only served "to confirm that we cannot on our own procure the amount of labor needed to harvest the cotton we plant." The solution going forward was complex. First, Covarrubias reiterated that the contracting center needed to be withdrawn from Sonora. It attracted groups of workers who only had the United States in mind and would always find Northern Mexico wanting. Second, growers needed to diversify their crops. Cotton was too labor-intensive to be the region's monocrop. Growers needed to hedge against the risk of insufficient labor by growing other income-generating crops in their fields. And finally, echoing Haro, Covarrubias said growers needed to figure out a proper balance between technology and labor. He believed growers had underused machines available to increasingly "mechanize the cotton crop." Workers would still be required in ancillary roles, but one machine "does the work of 100 men" and would lower the cost of harvesting, from 370 pesos per ton with laborers to 110 pesos per ton with machines.[54]

Covarrubias spearheaded Hermosillo growers' experimentation with machinery during what remained of the harvesting season. He cautioned, however, that it would take time to figure out which machines worked best for harvesting the very "leafy" cotton plant that grew in the area. The growers had already tried out one brand of machine at the time *El Imparcial* sought Covarrubias for an interview, and they planned to experiment with others. As for the next year's harvest, the plan was to conduct a "census" in Sonora "to figure out with absolute certainty the number of men we [as growers] can count on." Growers would then "reduce the size of the harvest to match the labor supply" indicated by the census.[55]

While growers brainstormed how they would bear the loss of the IBP in the future, they still had to adapt in the present season to confront their worker shortfall. Their solution was to no longer just recruit single men but entire families. Growers reflexively favored the use of men, hewing to the dichotomy of women working inside the home and men outside of it. But, out of necessity, they stepped outside this gendered division of labor. This multiplied each household's earning potential and made cotton harvesting more attractive to Northern Mexico residents. To minimize the number of worker families the growers in Sonora had to find, they agreed to share them, such that when the worker families were finished in one area, mainly in El Yaqui, El Mayo, and Hermosillo, they were transported to the next set of fields. The practice was reported by *El Imparcial*, which described "a constant arrival . . . mostly of families to work in this cycle of the cotton harvest."[56]

Growers' shifting hiring patterns were perceived and critiqued by some migrants. Clemente García Hernández, an experienced agricultural migrant worker who had worked in the United States as a bracero on and off since 1942, confirmed that growers from the Sonoran coast were "sending buses throughout Sonora and taking people" to work, "giving preference to men who have their entire families with them." Hernández found it "disagreeable to see women and children enduring this suffering."[57] "It's not as if they are one of us [men]," he concluded, suggesting that women and children were fragile and ill-adapted to this line of work.

Notwithstanding Hernández's gendered ethics of cotton labor, growers' adaptation allowed them to obtain the labor force they needed to finish the harvesting season. "The Harvest in the Yaqui Valley Ends without a Shortage of Farmhands," trumpeted *El Imparcial*. "The shortage of workers that was feared has been avoided," with workers receiving "one peso for every kilo of cotton." This ending was not entirely satisfactory for growers. For one, global prices for cotton "danced around" in 1962 but eventually dropped from 2,200 pesos per ton earlier in the year to 2,000 at year's end, thus limiting grower earnings in the latter half of the year despite their innovation. Beyond that, it remained an open question whether their mix of strategies—from downsizing their production to match the labor force available, to mechanizing their harvest, to relying on entire families to pick cotton—would allow them to thrive financially without federal involvement in cotton production.[58]

CONCLUSION

The impact of the IBP's end on cotton growers is hard to calculate. The early to mid-1960s were marked by other developments that adversely affected them. First, in addition to the disappearance of the IBP, growers had to contend with the rapid emergence of synthetic cotton as a competitor in the global marketplace. The synthetic fiber was particularly popular in textile manufacturing and achieved a market share of 29 percent, immediately accounting for a third of all cotton sales.[59] On top of this, global prices for cotton dipped and remained relatively low throughout the 1960s compared to the 1950s because the United States, the world's biggest producer, engaged in cotton dumping.[60] Under this tactic, the US Department of Agriculture, which stored and sold cotton on behalf of commercial producers in the United States, sold its haul in one blitz at below-market prices. In years prior, the United States artificially propped up the price of cotton by holding back some of its supply. It did so partially as a favor to some nations. But by the 1960s, it prioritized selling its entire cotton supply, a move that other nations, including Mexico, regarded as cotton dumping and bemoaned for its impact on prices.

Despite their dipping cotton income, not all news was bleak for growers. Though the federal government would no longer insert itself as an orchestrator of labor, the state government of Sonora remained sympathetic to providing growers with workers. In 1964, the governor of Sonora asked municipalities to transport any unoccupied laborers in their jurisdiction to growers. Their transportation, he assured, would be covered and laborers would be paid thirty centavos for each kilogram of cotton they picked.[61] Another positive development for growers was that the BP came to an end in 1964. US public opinion and lawmakers finally turned against the BP after high-profile cases of worker abuse surfaced, including the 1963 crash in Chualar, California, in which thirty-two braceros died when the flatbed truck transporting them collided with an oncoming freight train.[62] The loss of the BP meant that tens of thousands of Mexican workers would no longer have that outlet to work legally in the United States, and would—if only out of necessity—be more open to working in Northern Mexico.

CHAPTER SIX

A FLAILING STATE

Part One

Mexico Searches for Migratory Solutions after the Bracero Program, 1968–1975

This chapter and the next offer a political history of Mexico's management of out-migration in the 1970s. This decade is particularly significant in the study of the Mexican state's migration politics. Historians have argued that in this decade, more unreservedly than in years before, Mexican politicians began accepting migration as a "safety valve" that could be used to reduce domestic ills, chief among them unemployment. Indeed, it has been said that a "political culture that acquiesced and even supported citizens' emigration flourished [in Mexico] in the 1970s."[1]

This categorical pronouncement errs in a key regard. It presents Mexican leaders as being consistent and confident in the use of out-migration as a safety valve. In actuality, Mexican politicians in the 1970s were initially quite uncertain about how to deal with the migration. They continually attempted to reposition their policies. Much like their predecessors in other eras, they approached migration not with immutable convictions but with fluidity. They invited it at times and gestured toward curtailing it at others.

In the late 1960s and early 1970s, Mexican officials worried that certain border towns continued to be overwhelmed by the arrival of prospective migrants. But their gravest concern stemmed from the fallout of the BP ending in 1965. When that legal outlet to the United States disappeared, Mexicans continued to migrate but without authorization. The proliferation of undocumented migration spelled trouble for Mexico because those migrants were more vulnerable to abuse than bracero contract workers. Mexican officials understood they were partly responsible for the migration, since they had oriented Mexicans toward migration through the BP for over twenty years.

As cases of migrant abuse in the United States surfaced in the post-BP era, Mexican officials offered all manner of solutions, even if contradictory. For instance, they proposed a new guest-worker program to reinstitutionalize protections for migrant workers. But they also floated economic reforms to substantially curb out-migration. The Mexican government's equivocal search for policy answers peaked in intensity when US and Mexican media ran incendiary exposés of migrant abuse, and when Mexican politicians met with their US counterparts. Such forums gave them natural occasions to discuss how to fix a migration they had jointly instigated.

The argument that Mexico unabashedly embraced migration to relieve domestic pressures not only glosses over Mexico's political equivocation through the early 1970s but also mischaracterizes Mexico's eventual stance. By the mid-1970s Mexico did arrive at a steadier viewpoint. But it was not to support emigration. To the contrary, given reported abuses of Mexican migrants, the Mexican government committed publicly to explore measures to mitigate out-migration and to root Mexicans internally. Mexican leaders from the mid-1970s to the early 1980s emphasized permanence as a solution to migrant travails, and only occasionally budged from that posture.

Both this chapter and the next show the crisis-solution paradigm that dominated Mexico's migration politics in the late 1960s and 1970s. Scandals emerged regarding the abuse of undocumented migrants, deportees, and internal migrants. Mexico felt pressured to address them. Its fixes proved insufficient. And so, the problems recurred, forcing Mexico to propose new solutions. Mexico became stuck in a loop of crisis and failed policymaking.

The present chapter analyzes the evolution of Mexico's migration policy up to 1974, particularly under President Luis Echeverría. His administration continually repositioned its migratory policies to respond to migrant abuse in the United States and migrant travails more generally. Three ideas recurred, however, and one came to dominate. Up to 1974, Mexico periodically proposed reinstitutionalizing guest work as an interim solution to immediately forestall the abuse of Mexican migrants in the United States. Second, because the United States downplayed Mexico's complaints and declined its proposals, Mexico resorted to small-scale interventions that it alone controlled, such as the policing of human smugglers to prevent undocumented migration. Third, given the recurrent failure of its small interventions, and the plain US disinterest in guest work as a viable interim solution, President Echeverría slowly but surely gravitated to the idea that the only lasting solution to Mexico's migratory woes was for the government to embrace pro-permanence policies.

THE CYCLE CONTINUES

Undocumented migration boomed in the post-BP era. Without a legal outlet to the United States, many migrants chose to work and live in the United States without formal authorization. Unlike braceros, however, they could count on no official protections. They were exposed to danger after danger. Traffickers lied to them about their ability to get them to the United States. Migration authorities and policemen misled migrants with promises they could get them across the border in exchange for payment. The currents of the Río Bravo could drown them. Unpredictable US Border Patrol agents sometimes allowed them to be in the United States and other times targeted them for deportation. Growers and foremen underpaid them, offered them harsh housing conditions, and psychologically or physically abused them, knowing the migrants had little recourse.

These conditions prevailed in the post-BP era, as migrants increasingly moved outside of legal channels. In turn, migrants' travails did not go unheeded by high-level Mexican officials, including the president, members of his cabinet, heads of various federal agencies, and members of Congress. They sought US cooperation to address the escalating undocumented migration. They frequently engaged the topic at the Comisión Interparlamenteria, an annual meeting between members of Congress from both nations. When there were no diplomatic meetings scheduled, Mexican officials raised the matter through private governmental channels instead. And when a case of migrant abuse was egregious enough, they addressed the matter unilaterally in speeches, declarations, and briefings. Regardless of the venue, Mexican political leaders unsystematically toggled between three sets of solutions. First, they tried small-scale measures to control undocumented migration, such as the policing of human trafficking. Second, they advocated for a return to guest work as an interim solution to migrant suffering. Third, they proposed that the most effective, long-term cure would be to root Mexicans within Mexico and bring an end to their itinerance.

In the years after the end of the BP, Mexico found itself hard-pressed to contain the migration and the suffering of migrants with the tools at its immediate disposal. For one, coyotaje, or human smuggling, outpaced the Mexican state's attempts to police it throughout the late 1960s. Local Mexican police in border states jailed traffickers who helped migrants cross to the United States without formal authorization. But these were small and occasional victories. Coyotes continued to spring up, in response to persistent migrant demand for their services.[2]

The Mexican government was also not particularly effective at policing those who offered migrants fraudulent paperwork to enter the United States. When they presented invalid documents, migrants were turned away by US authorities and left to roam penniless in Northern Mexico.[3] Mexican police investigated individual fraudsters and imprisoned some for up to two years.[4] But the government failed to dismantle an organized group that migrants alleged preyed on the vulnerable: the Alianza de Braceros. According to migrants, the Alianza posed as a union for migrant workers but was dedicated to the sale of sham US work documents.

The federal Ministry of the Interior obtained samples of this paperwork, including receipts in the amount of seventy-one pesos for migrants' "registration" as members of the Alianza, as well as *micas*, index-sized identification cards that migrants were told would grant them passage to the United States. The micas included a portrait of President Echeverría as well as the insignia of the PRI, thus wielding the iconography of officialdom to mislead migrants into thinking the micas had the force of law.[5] The Ministry of the Interior ordered an investigation by the attorney general, which found that the organization operated nationwide, including in major migration zones like Michoacán, that their victims numbered in the tens of thousands, and that the group was a "huge part of the problem" of migrant fraud.

The Mexican state was not able to prosecute the group, despite acknowledging that it contributed to "the exodus of field-workers to the northern frontier," where defrauded migrants were left to wander without money.[6] The leaders of the Alianza, Francisco Rodríguez, José Hernández Serrano, and Alberto Salinas Serrano, maintained that they were just a political action group that worked to represent the interests of migrants before the government and that the payments they received were effectively membership dues.[7] If their affiliates were misrepresenting this purpose and portraying them as purveyors of work authorizations, that was their individual deviance, not a directed and organized attempt from the Alianza leadership. With this defense, they saved themselves from prosecution, in spite of the government's three-year investigation. The Mexican government was not able to prosecute them for using official iconography either. Mexican federal law made it illegal to use the national emblem on documents not issued by the state. But the Alianza used the PRI logo, not Mexico's emblem, on micas.[8]

In addition to organized delinquent groups, the police itself, especially in border towns, contributed to the ravages of migration. Migrants alleged that local authorities were implicated in coyotaje and fraud. At times, they pressed for redress from authorities at both the state and federal levels and would explicitly leave out police departments from their communications. They were both convinced of and outraged by the corruption of low-level personnel. The Mexican government promised to investigate such matters but failed to follow through.[9]

Another concern for Mexico was the brutality migrants endured in the United States, particularly at the hands of the Border Patrol. Migrants complained to the Mexican government through its consulates, especially those in the major receiving states of California and Texas. The consulate in El Paso, Texas, reported in 1971 that the volume of complaints was distressing. Speaking to a Mexican periodical, consular officials lamented that "the treatment the Border Patrol gives Mexican citizens residing illegally in the United States is truly brutal, savage, and terribly inhumane." Consul Estela Gutiérrez Chávez described how Border Patrol agents insulted, hit, and even murdered migrants, most recently in Presidio, Texas, a town bordering Chihuahua. There, the Border Patrol shot at eleven Mexicans attempting to enter the United States. One migrant died. The Mexican consul expressed that she and the Mexican secretary of foreign affairs were working to diplomatically protest the use of lethal force.[10] Sometimes, migrants did not need to go through consulates to convey their peril. Mexican migration agents received migrants who had been beaten by the Border Patrol. Acting as first responders, they arranged for the hospitalization of injured or ailing migrants.[11]

The most recurrent issue was deportations from the United States. The federal Ministry of the Interior received daily deportation reports. The reports, which were prepared by Mexican migration authorities stationed at border stations such as Mexicali, cut to the specifics. They gave the numbers of repatriated Mexicans and regularly expressed that deported migrants were treated "inhumanely" by US immigration personnel, who manhandled them when dumping them back in Mexico.

The deportations were concerning to the Mexican government on many levels. First, the US approach of rounding up undocumented migrants meant that Mexicans, the greatest source of undocumented migration, were permanently demonized and persecuted in the United States. The second worrisome aspect was the removal conditions, including the loosely regulated jails in which migrants were held.[12] Third, the endless stream of deportees represented a strain on a Northern Mexico job market and society that went from complaining of labor shortages to an "excess" of migrant labor.

Northern Mexico began to swell with migrants following the end of the BP. Without an established outlet to the United States, migrants had to remain in the region for longer, looking for a clandestine exit. In the eyes of locals and the Mexican state, they were "unoccupied," idle workers who could lapse into chronic homelessness, crime, and potentially political agitation. Indeed, in 1965, the same year the BP concluded, the Mexican state began its BIP. It explicitly sought to absorb the "excess labor" that began to pool across Northern Mexico as soon as the BP ended. Mexico's plan was to lure foreign companies to the border region by promising them tax abatements and access to the cheap labor pooling there.[13]

Deportations cut against Mexico's attempts to mitigate its demographic crisis. The mass reinsertion of deported Mexican nationals into Northern Mexico—280,000 in 1970 according to Mexico's calculations—aggravated the region's excess labor problem post-BP.[14] The Mexican government tried to cope with the influx of labor sent back by the United States, particularly by sending the removed laborers to work in cotton production. No formal program, such as the IBP, was inaugurated to formalize this internal rechanneling of deportees. But, from Mexico's perspective, the strategy worked best when the timing of deportations aligned with the cotton harvest.[15]

In sum, the Echeverría administration sought to address each downside of the migration separately—imprisoning fraudsters, chasing coyotes, diplomatically protesting Border Patrol abuse, and mobilizing deportees to work within Northern Mexico when possible. But it also reached out to the United States to reinaugurate a guest-worker accord. For Mexico, most of the concerning aspects of migration could be blunted with a legal and political framework to regularize the movement of Mexican nationals.

Mexican outreach to resurrect the BP began in earnest in the summer of 1971. At the behest of President Echeverría, Mexican secretary of foreign affairs Emilio Rabasa took up the subject with the United States. Describing the situation of Mexicans as "worrying," Rabasa affirmed that "we have to create some legal regime to protect Mexicans." Migrants were "defenseless," especially on the US side, where in addition to all the known problems, they "worked uninsured," "could be arbitrarily fired," and "were stuck with low wages."[16] In subsequent remarks, he noted that despite the flaws of the original BP, it would be an improvement over the present situation. "It is the aspiration of the Ministry of Foreign Affairs to . . . as quickly as possible achieve the protection of Mexicans in the United States," he said.[17] Mexico wanted a speedy interim solution.

From the outset, however, Echeverría's administration did not just claim that guest work would render migration a nonissue. Occasionally, it also acknowledged a need to deal with the economic context that propelled Mexicans to move. The government was prompted to deal with migration's economic roots specifically because of the abundance of idle, dislocated laborers in Mexico. It grew concerned when itinerant people, roaming the country for work, created social disturbances. And it responded practically by providing them with material relief and opportunities. It understood that Mexicans did not migrate out of misplaced adventurism but because they sought economic opportunities wherever they might exist.

Roving populations looking to make a living, but in dire material straits, directly pressed Mexican authorities for help. In the summer of 1971, the Mexican government received word of a crisis in various cities in Central Mexico, including in Jalisco, Guanajuato, Zacatecas, and Aguascalientes. Thousands of campesinos from rural areas gathered in the streets outside railroad stations. They were set to travel to Northern Mexico to work for growers who recruited them and offered to pay their railroad passages. Yet the recruiters employed by the growers reported that they had not yet received funds to cover the ticket costs. So, in the interim, the campesinos milled about "without the economic means to provide for themselves and their families." The campesinos may have been reduced to vagrants, but they refused to leave the cities until their needs were met. The Mexican government, not wishing to see the matter escalate, paid for and monitored their passage north.[18]

Northern Mexico was an epicenter of crises stemming from idle labor. Groups of Mexicans arriving there were not content with the economic outlook that greeted them there. In Sonora, near the city of Villa Juárez, too many internal migrants from Central Mexico arrived for the harvests. Angered that growers were not able to provide them with employment, they looted local stores. Out of caution, the Sonora government and growers, with federal support, immediately began to build barracks to at least protect idle workers from inclement weather. They also promised to move them to areas where they would be needed. In addition to guiding migrants to economic opportunities, growers and officials agreed to police the Villa Juárez bank with additional guards. Rumors suggested that migrants planned to loot it because they were not satisfied with the government's intervention.[19]

The same group of dissatisfied Central Mexican migrants kept causing trouble. They looted more stores, this time in another town, Pueblo Yaqui. As the conflict wore on, their displeasure with growers and government officials grew stronger. They were promised food vouchers for subsistence but did not receive enough of them to cover the whole group.[20] In the end, growers and the Sonora government, with support of the federal government, were forced to provide 30,000 meals a day to prevent more migrant holdups and robberies.[21]

If these migrants were mollified by the business-governmental response to their anger, their counterparts in the border city of Ciudad Juárez, Chihuahua, proved more difficult to calm. The federal Ministry of the Interior's internal reports indicated that a contingent of migrants from Central Mexico were planning a *mitin* (rally) because they could not find jobs in Northern Mexico. They formed an action group they called the Pro–People without Jobs Committee and met at a local monument to Benito Juárez. Their leader, Ventura Ibarra Esparza, called on President Echeverría, Secretary of the Interior Mario Moya Palencia, as well as local and state authorities to fix the problem of unemployment or otherwise arrange a guest-worker program. Palencia urged that these migrants be taken seriously. They numbered in the hundreds and were "creating a real problem in the city." Social disturbances might break out "if their entreaties are not met." Palencia warned that migrants need not organize to cause chaos. As more arrived, "delinquency would increase significantly in the city," as destitute migrants would turn to criminality.

An unspecified number of the migrants had just returned from South Texas, where they had been underpaid by growers and forcibly returned to Mexico by bus. Secretary of the Interior Palencia noted an unspecified but "concerning" increase in delinquency following the arrival of this group in Ciudad Juárez, where they joined the Central Mexicans. Sufficiently concerned, President Echeverría dispatched envoys to meet with the Pro–People without Jobs Committee. They offered to relocate the migrants and the repatriated to Campeche, a coastal city on the distant Yucatán Peninsula, with all expenses paid. There the government would launch a work program for them.[22] If only in small ways, the government was mobilizing economic remedies to deal with mass migration.

In addition to offering specific economic strategies to placate frustrated labor migrants, Echeverría continued the BIP of 1965 and an earlier program, the Programa Nacional Fronterizo of 1961. The latter directed federal investment to the development of borderland communities, including the building of critical infrastructure. The BIP, meanwhile, sought to give employment to out-of-work migrants languishing in border areas. Workers were hired by foreign factories, maquiladoras, mainly owned by US corporations, which produced a range of goods, including electronics, toys, and clothing.

The federal government continued the Programa Nacional Fronterizo and the BIP in the 1970s. For even though these programs did not resolve the matter of unemployed migrants, they abated it. The head of the Programa Nacional Fronterizo reported that as of 1971, 25,000 Mexicans worked in 179 different maquiladoras. Taken together, the factories provided more than 200 million pesos in salaries to Mexicans, or about 12,750 pesos per worker annually. Most critically, he noted, they remained active throughout the year. This was in comparison to seasonal agriculture, which hired workers on and off through the year. The maquiladoras thus provided a stable, if insufficient, bulwark against unemployment.

Mexican officials admitted the limits of relying on such factories for blue-collar employment in Northern Mexico. The number of deportees to the area was high—280,000 in 1970. And the factories tended to hire women, rather than unemployed men. The federal government thus sought to amplify the impact of maquiladoras in the 1970s. It committed to creating technical schools to train specialized workers. The hope was that their expertise would make them coveted employees. Celso Delgado of Nayarit, president of the Congress, served as the initiative's spokesperson. The main obstacle he foresaw was simply convincing migrants to enroll in technical schools.

"The so-called braceros," he observed, "are strongly lured to the other side [the United States] by the bait of the dollar ... even though in the end they only find misery." Even while championing the schools and their promise, Delgado affirmed that Mexico and the United States needed to partner in the short term to compassionately resolve the migration they had catalyzed with the BP.[23]

President Echeverría continued to seek a guest-worker program with the United States. He appealed to US president Richard Nixon personally in the summer of 1972. Echeverría expressed to him that the deportation of Mexicans from the United States, as well as their mistreatment, "troubled the national conscience [of Mexico]." Echeverría did not emerge from his sit-down with Nixon with a new BP. He settled for a pledge that each nation would establish a separate commission to study the migration and propose solutions, both collaborative and autonomous. This was crafty US diplomacy. It neither dismissed nor affirmed Mexico's concerns. And it allowed the United States to engage with migration reform at its own pace.

Nonetheless, President Echeverría trumpeted the commission as a breakthrough. Upon his return, he established the Comisión Intersecretarial (Intersecretarial Commission, or CI), a cross-ministry commission including the secretaries of the interior, labor, public education, agrarian matters and colonization, and finance, as well as the attorney general. Each, he reasoned, offered unique insights into out-migration. He tasked them with assessing the specific local sources of migration and its root causes.

To do this, the CI traced the phenomenon back. It sampled the records of 10,000 deportees and pinpointed the "critical areas" that were sources of out-migration. The CI then visited the municipalities that contributed the highest number of migrants, including in Zacatecas, Michoacán, and Jalisco. It sought to establish the factors that "promote the exit of Mexicans to the United States."[24] The CI found that the migration was rooted in a languishing campesino or rural sector.[25]

The CI shared its findings with the media. Its conclusions were amplified by the Ministry of Foreign Affairs, which issued a special bulletin regarding migration and the CI's investigation. The CI also shared its conclusions with the equivalent body created by Nixon after his meeting with Echeverría. Publicly, the CI stated that its aim was to share the empirical bases upon which mutually beneficial solutions might be built.[26] Privately, the CI began to hedge its bets. Its members did not believe the United States would implement policies to help Mexico deal with migration. So, from 1972 to 1973, it began to formulate solutions Mexico could pursue on its own.[27]

While the CI studied programmatic solutions, the problems surrounding out-migration continued. Investigative journalist Jesús Saldaña earned a multipage spread in *El Heraldo de México* for his case study of Santa Anna, California, where migrants lived beholden to Chicano labor recruiter José Pérez, known as "Papa Joe." Above a restaurant he owned, Papa Joe provided initial lodging for migrants he trafficked into the United States. Once they established themselves and made it out into the barrio, however, it was as if they had never migrated. The barrio "looked like any of the poor areas of the Mexican republic, the only difference being that the street names are in English." Moreover, since the migrants owed their jobs to Papa Joe, they also owed him half of their wages. If they complained, Papa Joe referred them to the INS for deportation, ending their "tragedy."[28]

Special correspondent Manuel Mejido similarly published a front-page spread in the national newspaper *Excélsior*, focusing on the US Border Patrol. The lead image depicted a young girl "running away to not be beaten up by a Border Patrol member." The girl was merely playing on the Puente Negro, a railroad bridge that migrants used to cross from Ciudad Juárez in Mexico to El Paso in the United States. The newspaper also ran a photo in which a Border Patrol agent menaces the photographer "with his night stick, pepper spray, and gun." The article's message was that in or near the United States all Mexicans were treated as a threat, whether they were local children or journalists.[29]

In addition to depicting Border Patrol agents as overzealous and abusive, Mexican media also chronicled US detention practices, including the way deportees were used as labor in US penitentiaries. *El Universal* featured a couple of such stories by special correspondent Rigoberto López. López reported that Border Patrol agents in Texas sent deportees to jails if they determined them to be recidivists—that is, if they had attempted to cross the border illegally multiple times. Their sentence was commensurate with their number of attempts, and they labored in the prison while serving their time. The Mexican consul in El Paso, who visited the local jail weekly, confirmed these details.[30]

López was able to speak with migrants during a subsequent visit. They told him that prison work was laced with racial discrimination. They were relegated to menial jobs, while their Black and white counterparts labored in a workshop repairing government furniture. One migrant in the La Tuna Prison said he went on a hunger strike to protest the abhorrent food. Some complained they had been wrongfully charged but had no competent lawyer to defend them. Speaking to the outside world, one migrant mused, "Remember, even if a prison is in this gilded country, it is still a prison."[31]

US media outlets also took interest in the prisons, resulting in coverage that worked its way back to Mexican periodicals. California US senator Alan Cranston visited a prison in San Isidro to follow up on claims by a local health official that Mexicans were held in conditions like those of a "concentration camp." Cranston confirmed that migrants were "crowded together like cattle." The Border Patrol, in his estimation, lacked funding to provide "humane and adequate" treatment to the detainees. He recommended that investments be made to enlarge the prisons. The highly public visit revealed for a Mexican audience the depth of migrant misery in the United States.[32]

Though acknowledged by US leaders like Cranston, the poor, even bestial conditions migrants were forced to endure failed to inspire congressional reform in the United States. They did, however, prod elected officials in the US Southwest to launch a campaign in support of a more organized guest-worker program. Of course, they were not motivated only by empathy. Governors and members of Congress from states such as Texas, New Mexico, and Arizona capitalized on reports of migrant abuse to try to more straightforwardly secure the labor force they required.[33]

Representative Robert Price of Texas spoke before the US House promoting the "importation" of Mexican laborers. Even with his state experiencing 13 percent unemployment, "no one wants to work in the fields or ranches," he said. "Our people," he lamented, "are simply not disposed to do this work," which required "a spirit of sacrifice" inherent in migrants. Growers, he admitted, continued to hire them, in an open underground economy. So, while the cotton companies suffered some inconveniences, it was criminalized Mexicans who suffered the most, as their extralegal status exposed them to certain "risks." Price blamed the misguided liberal "idealism" of the 1960s for bringing an end to the BP, and hurting migrants and growers alike.[34]

Texas's support was auspicious for a Mexican government looking to provide immediate relief to suffering migrants, but it was unpersuasive in Congress. Speaking to a Mexican newspaper, Senator José Montoya of New Mexico echoed Price's remarks, saying, "We need Mexicans." But he pointed out that he and other supportive members of Congress were a "minority." Despite supporting Mexico's position that a guest-worker program offered the most practical, humane solution in the near term, he and his colleagues could "do nothing to amend or change [immigration] laws."[35]

Mexican officials—with only limited support in the US Congress for reinaugurating a guest-worker program—turned to the governors of Arizona and New Mexico to see if they might sway the US president to take executive action, bypassing the congressional dead end. President Echeverría hosted the governors in Ciudad Juárez. But he obtained little. They issued a statement affirming that a guest-worker program was desirable but promised no concrete action.[36]

Mexico thus had to try to reduce the migration and the travails migrants faced on its own. It continued to focus on consular support for migrants and on jailing human traffickers.[37] But its search for migratory solutions—both stopgap and long-term—intensified following bombshell reporting in the *New York Times*. The *Times* accused high-ranking officials in the United States and low-level Mexican authorities of running a multiyear bribery campaign. They invited deported migrants to pay them to remain close to the border, from where they could pursue reentry to the United States. Journalist Denny Walsh spent a year documenting and vetting his evidence. By not deporting migrants into the Mexican interior, migration authorities were essentially letting them back in, and revealing immigration control to be a sham.

According to Walsh, airplane and bus crews transporting the migrants out of the United States would inform migrants that, for a fee, the plane or bus could make a pitstop close to the border on the Mexican side, allowing them to get off. Many migrants who could afford it consented, as it saved them a trek from the interior of Mexico to pursue reentry. The money extorted from migrants was partially pocketed by the crews transporting the migrants. But it was also funneled back up to higher authorities in both countries.[38]

On the US side, Walsh implicated US attorney general Richard Kleindienst and Leonard Gilman, southwest regional commissioner of the INS as the masterminds and chief beneficiaries of this sham deportation regime. Kleindienst would resign from his position in disgrace in a matter of weeks, following his involvement in the Watergate scandal. Meanwhile, reported the *Times*, Gilman was already the subject of a Department of Justice investigation called Operation Clean Sweep, which was looking into corruption and mismanagement in the INS's Southwest Division. Details about the bit players and their interrelationships remained uncertain, but the *Times* was categorical that this "shakedown racket" of migrants had been operating for four years. Walsh calculated that up to one-quarter of all deportees were "removed" this way.[39]

The upper echelons of both governments sought to distance their state apparatuses from these allegations. This was especially the case in Mexico, where the story, thanks to the influence of the *New York Times* and the profile of the US actors involved, was placed front and center in Mexican periodicals. Major peasant and worker organizations, such as the CNC and the CTM, denounced the callous predation by US officials.[40] As the CTM declared,

"The United States has no consideration for our compatriots." Several op-eds were also published in the nation's leading newspapers. Some held the United States responsible for "turning a blind eye" to migration when it was convenient, and staging fake deportations of migrants as a domestic political spectacle. Some, however, held Mexico responsible for ending this flow, since evidently such extortion would not exist if Mexicans did not have to migrate.[41]

To insulate the Mexican state from public furor, the Mexican secretary of foreign affairs argued that deportations were handled by private companies, which the government would now investigate.[42] The secretary and the CI assured the public that Mexican migration officers behaved with "all honesty." They affirmed that anyone complicit in the fake deportation scheme was violating Mexicans' constitutional rights, particularly their right to freedom of movement within Mexico. There was no reason for migrants to pay anyone, be it a contractor or a Mexican official, if they wanted to be left close to the border.

The United States distanced itself from the scheme too, blaming Mexico for any dysfunction. Allen Gerhardt, chief of the Border Patrol in the US Southwest, sat down with a Mexican newspaper to defend his agency. He suggested that any wrongdoing could be traced to the Mexican bus company Tres Estrellas. The Border Patrol had partnered with it to carry out the deportations, at the recommendation of Mexico's secretary of communications and transportation. Gerhardt suggested that Mexico should focus on policing wrongdoing on its side.[43]

Echeverría's administration recognized that denials could only go so far in addressing this controversy. He acknowledged that Mexico needed to get a hold of the migration and address its root reasons. The CI, which prior to the *Times* report was already mulling solutions, had privately proposed its plan to President Echeverría and now shared it with the public at large. The CI proposed that Mexico foster small industry in towns that contributed most to out-migration. The CI affirmed that the main reason campesinos left for the United States was that at the end of their seasonal harvests, no profitable economic activity remained for them. Having small-scale industry to employ them locally would tide them over until the following harvest.[44] Miguel Cantón Moller, an official of the Ministry of Labor and a member of the CI, declared the administration's goal was for Mexicans to "not have a need to migrate" anymore.[45]

Shortly after the deportation controversy arose, President Echeverría began to publicize initiatives to retain rural Mexicans. He revealed that based on his consultations with the CI, he had been working with the CNC for months to devise and implement solutions to out-migration. The first plan Echeverría readied for implementation was for the federal government to hire campesinos to build roads in their rural towns. The jobs would pay at least the minimum wage and would offer the kind of supplementary support Mexican officials surmised campesinos needed at the end of their harvests to deter them from migrating.

The other part of the CNC-Echeverría partnership was to begin establishing in rural areas the small industries envisioned by the CI to provide work for campesinos between their harvests. The CNC spokesman, Oscar Santos, announced that in conjunction with the Ligas de Comunidades Agrarias (League of Agrarian Communities) they would be holding orientation meetings with campesinos in targeted rural communities and ejidos. There they intended to disseminate the president's vision: that Mexico wanted them to remain in the country and that "their [campesino] manpower is important to the development and greatness of Mexico."

At such meetings, the CNC planned to focus on the first order of business: what kind of small-scale production campesinos in particular localities would prefer to engage in. To the CNC, it was crucial that campesinos be involved in choosing the goods or commodities to be produced, and in establishing the microindustries that would hire them between harvests. Only with campesinos' buy-in, observed the CNC spokesman, would the initiative "succeed in achieving that the Mexican peasant no longer leaves as a wetback for the United States."

The CNC-Echeverría partnership made no secret about its foremost long-term goal: "To avoid that our campesinos offer their manpower to the United States and to instead use it to benefit our own country." But there was a note of caution. The CNC shared that the "bracero problem is very old, and it will take an effort of many years to say it has been [successfully] attacked. [For now] we can only say we have begun to attack it."[46]

Indeed, since its economic measures focused on abating the migratory crisis over the long term, Mexico continued to trumpet the need for a collaborative guest-worker program to prevent scandalous exploitation. Mexican officials renewed their pleas to the United States. The CI publicly laid out the rationale. Even as it advocated strategies to keep Mexicans in Mexico, it argued that guest work offered the most immediate, humane, and logical solution to migrant suffering. The United States, it reasoned, had a clear need for migrant workers. Not even Black Americans, said one CI member, wanted the difficult jobs Mexicans performed without complaint. There was no point in the United States being cruel and denying this reality. Given their irreplaceable contributions, migrants deserved a renewed BP that would provide legal protections for their work and mobility.[47]

Mexico sought to drum up support for a guest-worker agreement at a yearly meeting between US and Mexican members of Congress in late May 1973.[48] Upon arriving at the so-called Interparlamentaria, Senator Mike Mansfield of Montana, chair of the US delegation, tried to temper the expectations of his Mexican colleagues. He noted that President Nixon's predicament in the Watergate scandal made it improbable that the United States would be able to launch an ambitious collaboration to protect Mexican workers.[49] Mexico was undeterred. The Mexican delegation, composed of fifteen senators representing jurisdictions highly affected by migration, including Nayarit, Jalisco, Michoacán, Morelos, Baja California, and Sinaloa, had met repeatedly prior to the Interparlamentaria with the secretaries of foreign affairs, agriculture, commerce, and others to strategize Mexico's approach.[50] They agreed to seek a guest-worker program, no matter how much US envoys rebuffed them.

President Echeverría endorsed the pursuit of a new BP. He hosted the US legislators at his home, along with the Mexican delegation.[51] He aimed to demonstrate his goodwill by providing a more relaxed atmosphere. As officials streamed into his home, he instructed them to take off their suits and change into guayaberas, breathable summer shirts. The Americans indulged what President Echeverría presented as a Mexican custom. Mexican delegation members were puzzled by the theatrics and for a moment were unsure whether Echeverría was joking. One of them refused to wear the guayabera, feeling it was a silly and debasing attempt to ingratiate Mexican leaders with the United States. The other Mexican delegates swallowed their discomfort and participated in the groveling ritual, which Mexican media derisively labeled "Operación Guayabera."[52]

At the Interparlamentaria meetings, the Mexican delegation sought to clarify their country's position. Senator Víctor Manzanilla Schaffer, cochair of the Mexican group, told the Americans that "within the sets of problems that exist between us, there exists a special interest on our part, given its social and essentially humanitarian character, in the problem of Mexican migratory workers in your country."[53] What Mexico desired was a "framework," under which Mexican workers would be protected instead of being treated like pariahs. It would deepen the two nations' cooperation. There were already "complex agreements [between Mexico and the United States] to regulate commerce," he added, "[so] there can also be a legal framework to regulate these workers." After all, he argued, "manpower is a part of production."

Extending "humane treatment" to migrants was the duty of the United States. It was no victim of mass migration. Just as "Mexicans have a desire to work in your country . . . you too [Americans] . . . have a need for their labor."[54]

Mexico obtained only words and vague promises of collaboration from the US delegation. The Americans issued a statement that migrants' human rights were inviolable irrespective of whether they were legally admitted or not.[55] Yet, as the Interparlamentaria unfolded, the United States announced large raids on Mexican migrants. Donald Williams, interim head of the INS, announced that they were to continue "indefinitely."[56] The US ambassador to Mexico, Joseph J. Jova, lamented that it would take years to find a "bilateral solution" to migration. The gap between Mexico's aspirations and US practice could hardly be wider.

Heading into the summer of 1973, the United States foreshadowed that matters would only worsen. The US attorney general proclaimed that migration was growing at "overwhelming" rates that could only be addressed with intensified deportations. The deportations were widely covered in Mexico and followed by the Mexican government. The Border Patrol was likened by critics to the Gestapo for launching "giant raids" with "heavy-handed methods."[57]

Migrants seemed wedded to tragedy. Nine died after a bus transporting them slid and overturned on a Missouri highway. The bus lacked properly working seatbelts and the passengers were thrown onto the pavement. They were presumed by local police to be part of a contingent of undocumented migrants, since none of the survivors could speak English.[58] In the Southern California city of Orange, a detective uncovered a series of mass graves. They were victims of human traffickers, who extorted them for additional payment. Those who did not make the payment were killed.[59]

In response, the Mexican government reached for its preferred interim tools: reinforced consular support for migrants harassed by businesses, human traffickers, the Border Patrol, and others; and the prosecution of human traffickers operating in Mexican territory.[60] The Mexican secretary of Foreign Affairs reported that he was adding personnel to Mexican consulates in the United States to work on migrants' concerns. He also directed local police in Mexican border towns to interview subjects deported to Mexico. He wanted the names of smugglers who had helped migrants cross over.[61]

Pressure on Mexico to deal with migration intensified further in late summer of 1973. True to Donald Williams's promise, the deportations of

Mexican nationals continued "indefinitely." The INS reported that it had gathered 10,000 undocumented migrants in Los Angeles, mainly by raiding workplaces, and that it would have taken more if available detention centers had not run out of space.[62] Migrants took advantage of heightened media coverage to levy complaints about the deportations. Migrants in Tijuana told *La Prensa* they had been "branded" during the raids with a seal that read "Processed" across their left leg. They had warned the Border Patrol officers that they would accuse them before the Mexican consul, but this had not deterred the agents. The reporter, who interviewed migrants and saw the brands, reflected that this "treatment that can only be given to animals . . . [is] an elemental violation of the most basic human rights."[63] INS officials defended the practice as a tool to save time. It kept them from having to repeatedly process migrants' paperwork while shuttling them to different locations. What drew the ire of Mexican officials was not just the scale of deportations, or the time-saving branding practices, but that they converged with reports that the United States planned to install an electric fence along the border. Since it could electrocute people upon touch, it would make the border and borderlands even deadlier.[64]

The unilateral, strong-arm, and draconian US tactics to deal with migration turned it into a "lacerating" issue, said Secretary of Foreign Affairs Emilio Rabasa.[65] He protested that neither the deportations nor the electric fence were solutions to migration, for what was required were "deep solutions." As far as collaborative solutions went, guest work remained of interest to Mexico. But both Mexican members of Congress and the secretary of foreign affairs switched to more prickly tones. They called for the United States to embrace "realism" in dealing with this topic.[66] José Juan de Olloqui, Mexican ambassador to the United States, lamented the criminalization of Mexican workers. They had done nothing but take jobs "neither Black Americans, nor Mexican Americans, nor [workers] of any nationality or income level dare work."

Mexico obtained a meeting with US secretary of state Henry Kissinger to voice its concerns.[67] But when Emilio Rabasa met with Kissinger, the latter largely acted as if this was the first he had heard of Mexico's concerns with US migration management. He promised the United States would "study" the phenomenon and Mexico's idea of instituting a guest-worker program to conduct migration in a safe, orderly way. This approach was hardly satisfying to Mexico.[68] The United States had recommended "studying" the issue in the past. That was the whole basis of Mexico's CI, including its countermigratory ideas.

As far as Mexico was concerned, the time for studies was over. Peeved by Kissinger's response, Mexican officials grew brazen in their remarks and began to look past the United States as a partner in migration management. Mario Moya Palencia, secretary of the interior, accused US authorities of "cyclical myopia," letting Mexican migrants into their country when they needed them and then purging some of them when harvests concluded. The facts were simple, suspicious, and spoke for themselves: "Every year, even though the United States officially says it has no labor needs, . . . massive migratory currents of Mexican workers make their way past a border that is very well protected and guarded . . . and always find a place in their fields and places of production." Then, "when the harvests are over and the crops are collected, the US watchmen suddenly discover that there are half a million Mexicans working for the growers and in areas of production." Palencia stressed that whether or not a guest-worker program materialized, President Echeverría would press for "the rooting of our peasants" and was exploring direct subsidies to aid their agricultural production.[69]

Mexico made a few last-ditch efforts to convince Nixon and Kissinger into a guest-worker program. It entered a guest-worker agreement with Canada and held it up to the United States as an example of how to systematically and humanely organize the movement of laborers.[70] But Mexico's attempts were for naught. Sources close to Nixon filtered to the Mexican government that the chances of a guest-worker program were nil when unemployment in the United States remained high. It had reached 6 percent in 1973.[71] Besides, the AFL-CIO and Cesar Chavez were closely monitoring the guest-worker proposals and were ready to pounce on them as an attack on the US working class.[72]

Core elements of the Mexican government began to concede defeat. There could be no guest-worker program. In a moment of honesty, Mexico's ambassador to the United States said it would take another world war for the United States to again welcome Mexicans with open arms.[73] The Mexican Senate likewise dropped guest work as a policy alternative. The president of the Mexican Congress said the United States should at least "legalize" Mexicans who had lived and worked in the United States for five or more years, instead of demonizing, persecuting, and confining them to a life of precarity.[74]

Given that Nixon and Kissinger did not take Mexico seriously, it was fortuitous for the Mexican government when the Nixon administration crumbled in the spring of 1974. Nixon resigned following allegations he had led an illegal spying campaign against the Democratic National Committee and then attempted a cover-up. Mexico was optimistic that the new president, Gerald Ford, would be more amenable to cooperating with Mexico. Mexico greatly overestimated these prospects. This became readily apparent when Mexico's secretary of foreign affairs sent Ford a letter on Echeverría's instructions to update him on Mexico's positions and establish common ground for a dialogue. The note of June 19 said that the situation of migrant workers in the United States was one of only "two problems that permanently bother[ed] Mexico" and that were "pressing to resolve."[75] Rabasa, the note added, had tried "on repeated occasions to find recourse within every level of diplomacy" but had been unsuccessful, including of course his attempts to "immediately" fix the vulnerability of migrants through a legal framework for guest work.[76]

Ford torpedoed the chance to reset the relationship. He did not offer the minimum: a tepid promise to meet and discuss the matter at a later date. Instead, he had the US embassy put out a short, flippant statement dismissing Mexico's concerns. This was poorly received by Echeverría and the secretary of foreign affairs. They judged it to be "rough" and "out of protocol," and signaled that they would be reviewing relations with the United States as a result. For Mexico, the response by Ford went hand in hand with news that Ford's attorney general, William B. Saxbe, was publicly trumpeting more restrictive immigration laws to control Mexican migration. Saxbe declared that the "cornerstone" of Ford's anti-immigration plan would be a congressional bill to make it a crime for employers to hire undocumented immigrants. Mexico's perception was this only entrenched the paradigm of criminalizing everything related to Mexican migration, rather than acknowledging that if Mexican migrants were in the United States—legally or not—it was because employers wanted them there and would continue to find a way to employ them, regardless of out-of-touch US dictates.[77]

The confluence of these two occurrences—Ford's snub and his embrace of yet-more-restrictive and unilateral anti-immigrant policies—prodded a change in Mexico's migration politics. By the end of 1974, the Mexican government deemphasized the United States as a partner in combating the migration and its ills—at least through guest work. It underlined its own responsibility instead. The task going forward was to open viable routes of permanence for Mexicans so they did not have to go to the United States. President Echeverría began to collaborate with the Departamento de Asuntos Agrarios y Colonización (Department of Agrarian Affairs and Colonization, or DAAC) on this policy direction. Immediately after the US embassy's curt letter, he ordered the head of DAAC, Augusto Gómez Villanueva, to make a public announcement: "[President Echeverría] has ordered firm actions to liquidate *bracerismo* [migration] to the United States."

In line with the CI's original findings, President Echeverría's actions to "liquidate bracerismo" would focus on "the fields of Mexico." Villanueva outlined several targeted policies to support the peasantry and clamp down on out-migration. But he emphasized three in his public messaging. First, Echeverría said he would open 500,000 hectares of land in the Mexican Southeast to settlement by Mexicans. These roughly 1.2 million acres would welcome Mexicans wishing to stay in Mexico, so they would not have to migrate to the United States. The lands were reserved for colonization and ejido-formation. Villanueva also announced that DAAC was working to improve an additional 2 million hectares across the country that would likewise welcome Mexican peasants, following the introduction of more irrigation canals. "Combined," he estimated, the two policies would give "occupation to 90,000" Mexicans. Finally, the administration would prosecute people guilty of *acaparamientos*, illegally hoarding lands intended for the general well-being of Mexican citizens.

Villanueva announced these Echeverría directives following a nine-hour meeting with the president at the national palace. There, they formulated not only these policies but also details about how peasants would apply for land, how federal agencies would cooperate, and so on. Villanueva admitted that a lack of attention to detail had beset colonization efforts in the past. With the federal government's support and oversight, he proclaimed it would surely achieve its "unlimited potential [as a solution]" for "migrants aspiring to go to the United States."[78]

President Echeverría began to consistently extol Mexico's leading role in abating out-migration. For instance, in the lead-up to a meeting with President Ford, US ambassador Jova had determined that a guest-worker program was "impossible."[79] Rather than dwell on impractical aspirations, President Echeverría extolled the policies he had DAAC undertake. At a press conference held prior to the Ford meeting, he declared that the Mexican government was embracing the mindset that the migration problem was its own to solve. The only way to do that, he elaborated, was to look to the demographic participating in the migration—peasants—and provide them with holistic support in terms of land, subsidies, and technology. With a proper boost, they could be moored within the country.[80]

The day immediately preceding his meeting with Ford, President Echeverría offered declarations in Nogales along the same lines. He recognized that Mexico would have to increase investments in its rural economy to keep peasants from responding to what he called the "magnet" of US jobs. Reflecting on years of failed outreach to the United States, he declared that "Mexico must fight the problem of braceros alone . . . [for] there is no other way to national dignity." In his telling, Mexico would have to be ingenious to safeguard Mexicans from further humiliation in the United States.[81]

Immediately following his meeting with Ford, Echeverría reaffirmed his position, announcing that Mexico would no longer be pursuing guest work as a solution. It would instead engage in continual self-reflection and "self-criticism" to find ways to keep "peasants better rooted" within the country. He made these remarks in Tubac, Arizona, before heading back to Mexico.[82] Echeverría would maintain the same posture upon touching down in Mexico. Mexico had shifted its migration politics. It effectively disavowed guest work and embraced an independent exploration of solutions. It remained to be seen what effect, if any, Mexico's new round of mitigatory policies might have on a US-bound exodus that Mexican secretary of the interior Palencia aptly described as an "ever-growing current."[83]

CHAPTER SEVEN

A FLAILING STATE

Part Two

Mexico's Failed Search for a Migratory Solution, 1975–1980

By 1974, President Echeverría had embraced the notion that Mexico was responsible for curbing out-migration through economic reform. He maintained that this was the only viable path to address the abuses Mexicans experienced in the United States. Before then, Mexico had alternated between various solutions. These included the policing of human smugglers, the pursuit of a new guest-worker accord, and the exploration of economic adjustments, such as the development of small industries in Mexican towns that were the greatest sources of out-migration. Once it was clear that neither President Nixon nor President Ford would agree to a guest-worker program, Mexican leaders stopped their repositioning and hedging. They began to stress Mexico's primary role in eradicating Mexicans' need to depart. This political trend extended from the end of the Echeverría administration into that of his successor, José López Portillo.

While both Echeverría and Portillo foregrounded Mexico's responsibility for fostering economic development and thereby easing the migratory crisis, they ultimately vacillated on whether Mexico could truly achieve meaningful results independently. This doubt manifested briefly during Echeverría's term and then far more intensely during Portillo's. Both administrations undertook autonomous policies to moor Mexicans internally. But from time to time they felt they needed to draw the United States into an economic partnership to boost Mexico's ability to retain its population. They would be disappointed. Just as US leaders were disinterested in guest work, they were also disinclined to pursue long-term economic collaboration with Mexico to curb Mexican out-migration. If Mexican officials wanted to abate the migratory crisis through economic policies, they would have to do so mostly on their own. Under those conditions, they admitted, it would likely take some time to calm the migratory outflow.

AN ENDURING DEPENDENCY

Upon returning to Mexico from his meeting with President Ford, Echeverría grew more strident before his domestic audience. He completed his administration's about-face on guest work. At a stop in Caborca, Sonora, he remarked to gathered peasants and peasant organizations that he would never sign a guest-worker program to sanction the departure of Mexican nationals. To sign such an accord would be to recognize the migration as "necessary." In his estimation, despite its scale, the migration could be attenuated through targeted policies. Indeed, he affirmed, he was in Caborca to ensure that the DAAC was speedily effecting *dotaciones*, endowments of land to peasants, so that they could organize their colonias or ejidos and remain in the country.

Echeverría spoke standing in the fields of Caborca, under the beating sun, rather than in the town center, as if to emphasize that the solution to emigration lay in the land. He called upon peasants to do everything in their power to work Mexican land and achieve critical levels of productivity. Only then would the nation end a migration that was "injurious" given the endless string of "injustices, exploitation, and vexations" Mexicans suffered in the United States. The United States, he assured his audience, was nothing more than a "mirage."[1]

At the time of Echeverría's arrival in Caborca, 924 families were being resettled there in fields that DAAC had purchased from large agricultural operators. The price was 8,000 pesos per hectare. The fields were upgraded with wells and farming implements and readied for production for the formerly landless families. Augusto Gómez Villanueva, the head of DAAC, trumpeted next steps, including the purchase of an additional 5,000 hectares in the area. Once it secured the title to this land, he said, DAAC would expand each family's allotment to ten hectares.

DAAC purchased another 8,000 hectares in Mexicali. Villanueva reported that this land would soon be ready for settlement by landless families when DAAC completed improvements. "Mexico will be able to keep its people rooted in the country, if they are given the means to stay," he predicted. By late October, Mexico had spent more than 30 million pesos in purchasing and upgrading lands for resettlement.

That said, Echeverría was not deluded about the time these policies would take to bear fruit. Though celebratory about their ultimate ramifications, in particular their ability to moor Mexicans, he warned that the process hinged on complicated individuals. These included government officials who needed to be stripped of their "egotism, fatigue, and apathy" when it came to carrying out policy directives, such as his command to DAAC that would-be migrants be apportioned lands. They also included migrants themselves, who needed to be convinced that the opportunities being opened up for them in Mexico were worth staying for. This was no easy task, he acknowledged. They were entranced with the United States and needed to come to a "deep consciousness" that "the promises they imagined working on the other side [the United States] were a lie. . . . What awaited them there generally were bad outcomes."

Despite these cautionary words, the CNC applauded Echeverría's emphasis on the fields of Mexico as a solution to migration. The head of the CNC, Celestino Salcedo Monteón, present in Caborca, noted that the actions taken there were an example of agrarian policy that would extinguish migration.[2] Echeverría had fed such hopes not just with his specific policy of land allocation but also by signaling that this emphasis on campesinos would be "our point of departure" to create a "wall of progress" against "bracerismo." The notion of a "wall of progress" was an explicit rebuke of US policy, which was simultaneously gravitating toward a draconian border build-up.

Echeverría's remarks in Caborca following his meeting with Ford represented his most earnest formulation to date that migration was tied to the rural economy and that Mexico's economic malaise in this domain had to be remediated to stave off migration. Such a recognition might be "painful," he stated in Caborca—after all, the PRI had been founded on the idea that it would champion the peasantry, breaking it free from latifundio oppression—but it was the truth. The numbers and persistence of rural migrants to the United States were evidence of the PRI's political failing.

Campesino organizations picked up on the fact mass emigration was, at least for the moment, putting a political spotlight on the rural economy. Their perennial struggle was Mexican state officials' tendency to see economic "progress" as urbanization, industrialization, and large corporate gains, while being less attentive to small-scale landholders and the country's agricultural wealth. The Confederación Permanente Agraria (Permanent Agrarian Confederation), composed of the country's major campesino organizations, including the CNC, welcomed the chance to correct Mexico's "unbalanced development." The federal government, they lamented, had left the agrarian sector and all those who depended on it "decapitalized."[3]

Celebrating the president's "self-criticism," the confederation applauded that the policies being taken now "in the short term, in irrigation works, road building, electric energy, and education in peasant communities," and in providing campesinos with "land, agricultural subsidies, technical advisory, and capacity building," would, over the long haul, fix "the origin of bracerismo." Its representatives concluded their press conference with a line directly borrowed from Echeverría: "Mexico should not be exporting social problems but products"—including products cultivated by campesinos on their own land. Looking forward, the Confederación Permanente Agraria committed to collaborating with the federal government to "execute works that permit campesinos to utilize their labor power in Mexico and exploit their own resources." That way campesinos, especially "those without land ... would be able to establish themselves in the country and constructively channel their laboring capacity."[4]

Notably, the confederation's representatives urged the need for autonomous policymaking: "Mexicans could not wait for their problems to be resolved for them from abroad." US officials could not be counted on to address migration. They had come to see it as acceptable to enjoy Mexican labor while "exposing it to manifold risks, ill treatment, discrimination, and humiliations." So, by default, the problem was Mexico's full responsibility. The confederation established a special committee of its executive officers to follow and support DAAC's plans.

DAAC hardly seemed to need the extra support or motivation from the Confederación Permanente Agraria. The head of DAAC, Augusto Gómez Villanueva, embraced the task of mitigating migration with a renewed emphasis on agricultural policy. He believed the nation was at an inflection point in its migratory and agrarian policy: "For more than a decade, year after year, the resources the federal government allotted [to the agrarian economy] were diminishing . . . until now, perceiving a critical need, President Echeverría has corrected course to remind all us Mexicans that the peace of the nation is in its fields, that our national sovereignty is deposited in the hands of campesinos." "We have the obligation," he added, "not only to say that we are going to help them and encourage them with words, but to fundamentally show them with daily doings that their government is with them."

Heeding his own advice, Villanueva followed up on the land grants in Mexicali and Caborca, monitoring their development. At Echeverría's direction, he also convened a special gathering at Santa Rita Tlahuapan, attended by the governor of Puebla; a congressional representative for Puebla, María Martínez; CNC officials; and ejidatarios from the area. There they celebrated the opening of new lands for campesino settlement in Puebla. These had been allocated to ejidatarios by President Cárdenas in 1939, but large private interests had managed to fight off the legal order and continued to use the fields to grow pine trees. Echeverría and the DAAC intervened to end the dispute and make the 844 hectares of land the formal patrimony of the ejidatarios, an outcome they had pushed for continually for over thirty years.

At the public celebration where the formal decree was read, Villanueva extoled this as an example of the all-around resourcefulness Mexico would need to fix the problem of migration: "President Echeverría is making us realize that the grave problems we have in this country can be fixed by fulfilling laws [ensuring campesinos' right to land] and by providing them with the resources they need [to exploit that land]." With the "revolutionary, nationalistic posture" of the president, he assured, "productivity across the Mexican countryside can improve" enough that Mexico would not have to "beg the United States," or any other nation, for help solving its migration problem.[5]

As 1974 drew to an end, the Mexican government announced that it would lean harder into the bolstering of its campesino economy, namely by allotting 25 billion pesos to support small-scale farming. In 1973, by contrast, the government budgeted 14.5 billion pesos for this aspect of the economy, and ultimately spent around 20 billion pesos once Echeverría proclaimed a commitment to the campesino sector as a solution to out-migration. Underlining the importance of his government's amplified support for small-scale Mexican agriculture, Echeverría affirmed that "anything else, [any other policy], is a false door" to solving the migratory problem. This included leaning on the United States for help, for the "problem is Mexico's." What Mexico needed was to execute colonization plans and "better organize the ejido so that it is a basis for cooperative and collective work [for Mexicans in this country]." The CNC celebrated the planned increase in support for campesinos, which would lead to a "takeoff" of the agricultural economy. The head of the CNC, Celestino Salcedo, asserted that in time the financial resources committed by the government would translate into increased production, decreased unemployment, and an "end to the practice of bracerismo."[6]

In the new year, 1975, Echeverría continued to find support for his stated policy direction. A meeting of the Coordinating Committee of the Agricultural Sector, composed of representatives from Mexico's central bank, large private banks, campesino organizations, and officials from the largest migrant-sending states, including Guanajuato, Querétaro, Michoacán, México, and San Luis Potosí, honed in on out-migration. Their consensus was aligned with Echeverría's: that the fields of Mexico were far too often "producers of braceros" who could be "exploiting its richness" such that "campesino emigration" would not be necessary. The lending practices of private banks were discussed most extensively. Other representatives on the committee exhorted banks to allocate and release more private funds to campesinos as a way of lubricating the rural economy. The banking representatives agreed and committed to make the proper modifications to support Echeverría's contramigratory mission.[7]

Meanwhile, Echeverría's plans to root migrants through land tenure proceeded and were highlighted in the press. *La Prensa* offered special coverage of new settlements being opened up to show that Echeverría was giving both rhetorical and substantive backing to campesino rootedness. *La Prensa* visited the neighboring states of Campeche and Quintana Roo in the Yucatán Peninsula, where the federal government was transitioning groups of would-be migrants into settlements. The new colonia settlements included the Settlements of Álvaro Obregón, Pucté, Coyococ, José N. Rovirosa, Carlos A. Madrazo, Sergio Butrón, and Alfredo V. Bonfil.

A journalist and photographer visited a couple of these, reporting that they "give opportunity to Mexicans without employment and without land to work in their homeland, instead of emigrating to a life of hard exploitation on the other side of the border." The team deemed the settlements to be well developed. Each featured 500 completed houses, delineated roads, functioning power lines, schools and hospitals, and a town store. Fertilizer, seeds, and machinery were onsite for the resettled Mexicans to use. *La Prensa* included a picture of four tractors to be used for tilling and plowing.

Three settlements visited by *La Prensa* were already producing agricultural commodities, including Sergio Butrón which produced four tons of rice in its first year and expected that to grow to twenty tons, and Carlos Madrazo, which planted rice and safflower, as well as 5,000 tamarinds, preferring a mixed-production approach. The Mexicans and their families who settled there were reported as being in good spirits, many of them men with large families. Many had experienced migration before and came from states such as Michoacán, Guanajuato, México, Hidalgo, Puebla, Zacatecas, and Coahuila. Bulmaro Padillo Mendoza, a forty-seven-year-old from Michoacán with seven sons, thanked Echeverría and Villanueva for choosing him to be a beneficiary of their initiative to root Mexicans inside of Mexico.[8] The beneficiaries had applied for land through DAAC.

The push to address bracerismo through a renewed emphasis on campesino landholding was billed by Echeverría as part of the latest *reforma agraria* (agrarian reform), the name used by the PRI since its inception to describe the ongoing process of dismantling monopoly landholding, setting aside lands for campesinos, more equitably spreading Mexico's wealth, and, in so doing, supposedly abiding by the Revolution's aims. The Ley de Reforma Agraria (Agrarian reform law) had provided the basis for the creation of DAAC in the first place, as a "federal dependency" responsible for "applying . . . agrarian laws." And it had vested the president with the power "to freely appoint and remove" the head of DAAC, reaffirming his office's centralized authority. For the countermigratory installment of agrarian reform, the government announced it would rely on the Ley de Reforma Agraria of 1971, a statute Echeverría and the Mexican Congress had updated on April 16, 1971, specifically to refine how the Mexican Constitution's Article 27, which permitted land redistribution, could be operationalized.

In the Yucatán Peninsula resettlement efforts, Echeverría made use of updated Articles 247 and 248, which declared that "it was in the public interest for the government to create and execute regional plans when creating new centers of population." The clause favored and facilitated the regional clustering of new ejidos and new colonias because, in theory, bunching them together would better allow the government to provide them with support, including "work on their [shared] economic infrastructure (i.e., roads, electricity), technical assistance, and social infrastructure (i.e., hospitals, schools)." It was thus no accident that the new population centers being worked on and unveiled during 1975 were set in the Yucatán Peninsula and organized between two neighboring states, rather than strewn over a broader swath of Mexican territory.

Echeverría also rolled out administrative and structural changes at the tail end of 1974, while he was promoting the interconnected outposts for would-be migrants in the Yucatán. Using his executive power, Echeverría disbanded DAAC and established the Secretaría de la Reforma Agraria (Ministry of Agrarian Reform), which was to be elevated to be on par with the country's other ministries, such as Foreign Affairs and Finance. Echeverría intended the move to signal the Mexican government's deepened seriousness and commitment to supporting campesinos and abating out-migration. The head of the newly formed ministry was Augusto Gómez Villanueva, former head of the defunct DAAC, thus promoting federal government continuity during this transition. The ministry assumed responsibility for opening new settlements for Mexican people.[9]

Despite Mexico's forays into contramigratory policymaking, the exodus to the United States continued, just as Echeverría had conceded it would when he launched his program, reasoning that it would take time for both government officials and migrants to unlock Mexico's agrarian potential. PRI officials suggested it was urgent for Mexico to hasten its transformation. At an annual gathering where PRI officials deliberated and hashed out policy priorities, it was revealed that 61.4 percent of the millions of Mexicans in the United States were young people between the ages of eighteen and twenty-nine. The statistic was presented by Tamaulipas member of Congress Gabriel Legorreta Villareal. The number was jarring enough that the president of the PRI, Jesús Reyes Heroles, lamented that this showed Mexico was "wasting" the "best" of its labor force—the young and vital—"at a time when Mexico should be engaged in the greatest and most rational utilization of its natural and human resources."[10]

In light of the unyielding migration, Echeverría reached for other strategies to protect Mexicans already in the United States from their hypervulnerability as undocumented aliens. In 1974, the Mexican government lobbied at the United Nations for a charter that would protect migrants irrespective of their legal status in a particular country. Signatory countries would extend to immigrant workers protections "equal to those that they provided to their own citizens." These protections, such as the right to press charges, would become "human rights," disentangled from a person's standing vis-à-vis a particular nation-state.[11] The Mexican delegation formally presented its proposal before the UN General Assembly the following year. It succeeded, obtaining 110 votes, with the only abstention coming from Madagascar. The resolution called for all states "to respect the human rights of migratory workers, irrespective of whether their entry into a country was legal or not."[12] Whether the measure would have more than a symbolic effect remained to be seen, but Mexico had succeeded in spearheading global consent to the idea that migrants deserved baseline protections regardless of whether or not they had legal status in a country.

High-profile scandals involving migrants in or en route to the United States abated in 1974 and 1975, precisely when Echeverría escalated his emphasis on land tenure. That ended in 1976, however, as a pair of crises prompted Mexico to entrench its two main positions: first that guest work was no longer a sufficient or desirable outcome and, second, that agricultural economic uplift offered the best path to keeping Mexican migrants in Mexico.

The first crisis involved the deaths near the border of forty undocumented Mexican migrants between the months of January and June 1976. The Mexican government linked the attacks to white supremacist groups. In particular, it asserted that the American Nazi Party, headquartered in Virginia, was distributing leaflets across border cities such as San Diego, to the effect that the United States had to be "cleansed" of Mexicans. It claimed that the white supremacists were behind the murder of migrants or "at the very least" had incited them. Alan Clayton, chief at the San Ysidro border crossing, did not disagree that white nationalists were on the "hunt" for Mexicans, but he downplayed any US responsibility, arguing that border agents could barely police transgressing migrants, let alone prevent spot cases of violence by civilians.[13]

On the heels of these forty murders, Mexico admitted it might need US economic assistance if it was to expediently achieve the rooting of Mexican migrants that Echeverría had promoted after 1974. Through his Ministry of Foreign Affairs, Echeverría proposed to President Ford that he lower tariffs on Mexican imports, specifically from locales in Mexico responsible for sending the highest volume of emigrants to the United States. This would not be blanket tariff relief for Mexico but a microtargeted intervention that would boost economic prospects in the specific places designated as zones of high out-migration. Mexico reasoned that if it was easier for Mexican producers, small and large, to sell their produce and wares in the United States, economic activity in their microregions would improve enough to keep them in Mexico. The Ford administration dismissed the idea pitched by Echeverría. The Mexican president, however, was acknowledging Mexico's dependence on the United States, after years of pretending it could be self-reliant.[14]

The second set of vexations to strike Mexico in 1976 were escalated deportations. In the late summer, the United States began to deport hundreds of migrants per day both through airlifts and land crossings, with rumors of even-larger raids in the offing. Upward of 15,000 Mexicans were deported, according to Mexican outlets, through the Border Patrol's initial "'wetback' hunt." Migrants arriving to Ciudad Juárez from South Texas complained to journalists that they were "caged, without nutrition" on the US side and left to suffer excruciating stomach pangs.[15] The journalist remarked that this was a "sad" scene—the "most inhumane hunting of 'wetbacks' by the United States in recent memory." They had "only dreamed of cobbling dollars to support their families" but were instead subject to a "bestial" disposal. Migrants deported by plane also arrived in distress. Many were left penniless in Mexico City's international airport and slept on the floors.[16]

Reports also surfaced that the United States was violating the civil rights of Brown people to effectuate these deportations. A Mexican American organization, the Hermandad de Trabajadores (Workers' Brotherhood), reported to Mexican papers that the United States was arbitrarily detaining Mexicans "in churches, schools and public streets," whether or not they had papers. "Just the fact of being brown, speaking Spanish, speaking English with an accent, or living in a Mexican barrio" was enough to arouse authorities' suspicion. The United States, wrote Hermandad de Trabajadores, tacitly tolerated Mexicans when it was convenient and "persecuted" them when they were economically expendable.[17]

Mexico's secretary of the interior protested that the US treatment of deportees, from the racial profiling down to the malnutrition they endured in US jails, violated the UN accord on migrant rights. He decried the "cyclical" US practice of "using Mexicans" and then foisting them on Mexico when they had extracted their labor. The offensive US treatment of Mexico, the secretary said, was made more so by the fact that US authorities felt they could deport Hispanic peoples with "physical traits similar to those of Mexicans" to Mexico. He vowed to correct this by turning away deportees who did not have documentation confirming their nationality.[18]

Meanwhile, the ongoing deportations prompted Echeverría, who had but a few months left in his term, to remind the United States that it might not always be so powerful: "Strength does not last forever." When such a day came, it should hope for "[powerful nations] to treat it with a justness" it did not afford Mexico. He also reaffirmed the centrality of creating economic opportunities within Mexico, so "that our poor people no longer have to go to another country to be victims of abuse."[19]

Mexico adjusted to the constant arrival of deportees at the Mexico City airport. It erected an emergency shelter with hot food and beds, placing it under the authority of the capital's director of social services. Since most migrants wanted to return to their place of origin, the director provided them with funds and paid for their bus tickets, mainly to Jalisco, Michoacán, and Guanajuato. Those who reported that they did not want to go back home because limited economic opportunities awaited them were given priority to be resettled in the new colonias that the Secretaría de la Reforma Agraria was opening on a rolling basis.[20]

Both Echeverría and interested onlookers granted that some portion of the deportee flow was composed not of campesinos accustomed to working the land but of industrial workers. As the leader of the Central Campesina Independiente (Independent Workers Central) pointed out, the opening up of fields in the Southeast by the Secretaría de la Reforma Agraria would not be a solution for these individuals and families.[21] The CTM, the largest confederation of labor unions, concurred that "this [migration] is now firmly our problem and the country has to assume the responsibility for creating sources of employment" for all Mexicans, not just campesinos.[22]

Echeverría seemed to concur, affirming that the federal government needed to "crystallize" new sources of employment, so campesinos and non-campesinos alike might find their footing in Mexico. Echeverría postulated that jobs for industrial workers might be created through a collaboration between the state and Mexican entrepreneurs and businesses. Organized labor seconded this position. The Congreso de Trabajo (Labor Congress), composed of the country's major trade unions, including the Confederación Regional Obrera Mexicana (Mexican Regional Workers Confederation), the CTM, and others, declared that it was time for business operators to change their indifferent "attitude." They should urgently create jobs, with a "concern" befitting the situation of repatriated migrants.[23]

But Echeverría could not get any plans off the ground. Though they claimed they "lamented" the situation of migrants, the largest organizations representing commercial interests in Mexico used the "potential of a mass deportation from the United States" to attempt to bend both the federal government and organized labor to their will. José Luis Ordóñez, president of the Cámara Nacional de Comercio (National Chamber of Commerce), and Víctor Manuel Gaudiano, president of the Confederación de Cámaras Nacionales de Comercio (Confederation of National Chambers of Commerce), expressed that for businesses to create more jobs in the country, as was being suggested, the central bank would have to increase subsidies to their operations, at a time when the central bank was trying to control inflation and restricting credit. Meanwhile, to labor organizations commercial interests suggested that if unions wanted to see more job growth in the country, perhaps they could be part of the solution by "moderating their demands for better salaries and employment benefits."[24] Neither the Echeverría administration nor organized labor responded to these suggestions.

As Mexico fumbled for a way to respond to surging deportations, the United States promised to escalate them. Charles Hoffman, INS chief of investigations; Don Clegg, head of deportations; and Gordon Davidson, assistant director of the INS District of San Diego, announced they had the funds and resources to deport all 8 million undocumented migrants in the United States, 80 percent of whom they said were Mexican. They claimed they were just waiting on a comprehensive plan from Congress, which would include criminal or civil sanctions for employers who hired undocumented migrants. Meanwhile, the INS director in Texas denied that the migrants being rounded up in his state, about 600 per day by 80 patrol cars, were maltreated. He refused to describe the INS detention center as a "prison," even though the *Excélsior* photograph of the compound in El Paso showed it to be surrounded by barbed wire.[25]

The United States and Mexico were at odds. Jorge Bustamante, professor at the Colegio de México at the time, an expert on migration, and a figure consulted by the Mexican government on its migration policies, observed that relations between Mexico and the United States regarding migration were "in the Stone Age." Not only were US measures carried out unilaterally, without consulting Mexican authorities, but they were driven by "scandalous exaggerations" about the size of the immigrant population in the United States. He scoffed at the figure proposed by Leonard Chapman, head of the INS, that 8 million undocumented people were present in the United States. Bustamante noted that the US Census Bureau denied such a figure was possible. With his statistical malfeasance, observed Bustamante, Chapman confirmed his "lack of consideration for anyone who is not Anglo-Saxon." Indeed, as Bustamante pointed out, since the beginning of his tenure at the INS in 1972, Chapman had continually referred to the entry of Mexicans into the United States as an "invasion," an inflammatory framing that only made measured thinking and action on the topic more difficult.[26]

Yet there was room for Mexico's relationship with the United States on migration to deteriorate further. In the midst of the publicized deportations, a new case of migrant abuse surfaced involving the slow torture of three Mexican migrants by a couple of well-off brothers in Arizona. Thomas and

Patrick Hannigan, sons of wealthy rancher George Hannigan, were accused by Manuel García Loya, Eleazar Ruelas Zavala, and Bernabe Herrera, aged eighteen to twenty-five, of questioning their immigration status, kidnapping them in a pickup truck, driving them to their ranch, robbing them and stripping them naked, hanging them from a tree, burning the bottoms of their feet, scalding them with hot irons, all before finally cutting them loose and instructing them to run back toward the Mexican side of the border while the Hannigans shot at them with birdshot, an ammunition intended for bird hunting but that nonetheless can cause severe flesh wounds in humans. The accounts of the migrants and pictures of their tortured bodies made the rounds in Mexican papers. In a history marked by stories of abuse, the Hannigan case stood out because it involved a particularly macabre slow torture of Mexican migrants and was perpetrated by well-off Americans.[27]

The Hannigans were roundly condemned by Mexican members of Congress. Many called the incident a violation of human rights, or as the senator from Baja California Alberto Alvarado put it, an "affront to human dignity, an affront to the dignity of any citizen, of any country." Members of Congress called for the Ministry of Foreign Affairs and Echeverría to press for an investigation and take the issue to the United Nations, and also for a redoubling of efforts when it came to finding job prospects for Mexicans in Mexico. As Alvarado put it, the government had to figure out "how to keep Mexicans from leaving the country."[28] In a speech before Mexico's Congress, Deputy Juan José Osorio Palacios received a standing ovation for a speech in which he asked how "advanced the [American] civilization" could be if it bred men such as the Hannigans with "dark prejudices and barbarous instincts."[29]

The governor and attorney general of Arizona promised the Hannigan family would be prosecuted. But, as the days lapsed, it was unclear when the Hannigans would be indicted, brought in for questioning, or arrested, and whether they would be charged at all. The brothers were able to flee Arizona.[30] Rather than wait around for a trial and verdict, President Echeverría tried to get ahead of the situation. He and the Ministry of Foreign Affairs publicly pressed for the US and Arizona governments to investigate the case and prosecute the Hannigans. But they also saw an opportunity to hammer home the message they had been driving for years: Mexico needed to create outlets for Mexicans within Mexico. Absent that, there would be no solution to the string of abuses reported year in and year out from the United States.

President Echeverría began to unveil initiatives directed at increasing permanence among workers in nonagrarian fields. "We have to make a great collective economic effort" to "develop industrial, mining, fishing, and tourism activities," and not just small-scale agriculture, he said at a press conference in Chiapas. He was there to open a production plant for the eradication of a parasitic insect called Cochliomyia hominivorax. It infected the tissue of warm-blooded animals, including cattle, killing the animals and rendering their flesh unsellable.[31] By investing in science, Mexico could protect the industry and its jobs. The broader goal, he concluded, had to be for the government and social forces to come together to create opportunities for Mexicans in both urban and rural settings, until "not a single Mexican worker [from either place] leaves."[32]

His countermigratory messaging remained consistent when, a couple of weeks later, with the Hannigan controversy still lingering, he delivered his last state of the union address. He condemned the "flagrant violation of human rights" in the United States and affirmed that Mexico needed to economically support its nationals to keep them from risking their "life and dignity" in the United States. Finally, he proclaimed that Mexico should never enter a guest-worker agreement with the United States, or consider it an acceptable solution. Looking to history, he argued that guest-worker programs "never prevented the continued existence of undocumented migration." If anything, they just contributed to it by promoting the United States as a destination.[33] Echeverría's administration thus ended with a complete about-face on guest work.

What Echeverría left unstated is that his discourse and initiatives hardly slowed the migratory flow. The new administration of José López Portillo inherited a steady out-migration roiled in controversy because of abuses suffered by Mexicans in the United States. Portillo's initial posture was to call for "just and humane" treatment from US authorities.[34] But he quickly found the limits of such appeals to human decency, forcing him, like Echeverría, to call for countermigratory measures.

In April 1977, tensions flared in Ciudad Juárez, as locals and migrants claimed that Border Patrol agents were purposefully drowning migrants crossing the Rio Grande. María Jesús, a victim and witness, swam across with four friends, including twenty-year-old Camon Longoria. Border Patrol agents captured them on the US side and hurled them into the Franklin Canal in El Paso, an irrigation canal that draws water from the Rio Grande. Four of the migrants survived but Camon became stuck and pleaded with the Border Patrol for help. According to María, the officers pushed him back into the canal as he fought to make it out, resulting in his death.

Locals found out about the incident and were so incensed that 150 of them gathered to throw rocks at Border Patrol officers. The agents were attempting to apprehend a group of migrants who had crossed the Rio Grande. The crowd did not relent until the Border Patrol released the migrants in its custody. Two of the Border Patrol officers were injured. The Ministry of Foreign Affairs vowed to investigate the drownings. Cesar Chavez, meanwhile, wrote to the new US president, Jimmy Carter, asking for a US-led investigation into the "assassination of braceros at the border."[35] While investigations proceeded, Portillo ordered local police, local municipalities, and immigration personnel along the border to ramp up operations against human traffickers.[36]

Important campesino organizations argued that Portillo should follow in Echeverría's footsteps and emphasize agrarian uplift to calm out-migration. The CNC, Central Campesina Independiente, and Unión General de Obreros y Campesinos de México (General Union of Workers and Peasants of Mexico) declared that it was the responsibility of Mexico, not the United States, to solve the migration issue, by creating sources of subsistence within the country. The leader of the Unión General de Obreros y Campesinos de México declared, "[We] Mexicans have a responsibility of solving our issues internally." This did not imply the United States should escape criticism. As he stated, "It is paradoxical that a nation like the United States that publicly trumpets the defense of human rights, in this case tramples over those rights, . . . attacking our braceros and even assassinating them." Nonetheless, Mexico should be expected to lead the search for solutions.[37]

President Carter indeed underscored the importance of human rights in international affairs. So he was less dismissive of Mexico's concerns regarding migrant abuse than the Nixon and Ford administrations had been. In a direct response to the drowning of Camon, the INS publicly promised that it would curb the violent excesses of Border Patrol officers against Mexican migrants. The new commissioner, Leonel J. Castillo, declared, "The reports we have received about abuses to human beings in the frontier region are surprising, and we will do something about them." Following a meeting with political authorities in Tijuana, including the city's mayor and the director of the Mexican migration office there, Castillo said he looked forward to "entering all areas of cooperation possible with Mexico." Together, he predicted, they would institute "measures that will end the horrible abuse of humans in the frontier."[38]

Portillo believed a window of opportunity for migratory solutions opened up with Carter. He tried to figure out the depth of Carter's commitment to human rights. During the Interparlamentaria of 1977, he addressed the US delegation himself and argued before it that the only way to truly end migrant suffering was to find economic opportunities for them within Mexican territory. Notably, he did not use the apparent opening to advocate for a guest-worker program. Instead, he took up the mantle of economic reform that Echeverría had leaned on during his administration and asked for US assistance as an economic ally. Echeverría had similarly proposed that the United States could help Mexico catalyze its rural economy and slow out-migration, specifically by instituting a tariff relief program targeted to benefit zones of high out-migration. But after he was rejected by the United States, Echeverría had not pursued the matter further. Portillo would be far more insistent that the United States needed to help his country address Mexicans' economic precarity.[39]

Portillo's main proposal was for the United States to lower tariffs on the importation of Mexican goods to the United States. In his vision, this would result in increased sales of Mexican products in the United States and stimulate the Mexican economy. Mexicans would be able to increasingly remain in their homeland making or harvesting these goods. Unlike Echeverría, Portillo asked the United States for general national tariff relief rather than a microtargeted approach. Speaking to the press, Portillo accepted that it was Mexico's task to "create sufficient employment opportunities here, in our country." But he said the United States "would have to help us" if Mexico was to succeed. Once Americans purchased more goods from Mexico, employment in Mexico would rise, and "my people," he foresaw, "will not have to cross the border to search for jobs in the United States."[40] His go-to phrase, inherited from Echeverría, was that Mexico's wish was to "export products, not *brazos*."[41]

Other administration officials fell in line behind Portillo's assertion that "our desire is that Mexicans can achieve their maximum personal and social realization in our fatherland." They expressed faith that Mexico could curb the flight of campesinos by improving their economic outlook, and they emphasized that the US government had a pivotal role to play by facilitating the consumption of Mexican goods in the US market. The secretary of foreign affairs and Mexican ambassador to the United States were particularly central, as they negotiated with Carter's team.[42] The Mexican ambassador predicted that if Mexico was able to increase exports to the United States, within two years, more than 600,000 jobs would be created in Mexico, "raising the standard of living and preventing the exodus of Mexicans."[43]

There were encouraging signs for Mexico that Carter might join its efforts to confront migration at its source. Upon his appointment, the new US ambassador in Mexico, Patrick Joseph Lucey, promised his "special emphasis" would be to improve the "commercial relation that exists between the two countries." He promised to relay to Carter Mexico's concrete proposals for how the two countries could partner to control migration. After meeting with Portillo, he highlighted the potential for an agreement whereby the United States lowered tariffs on Mexican goods and thereby bolstered the Mexican economy.[44]

President Carter moved to solve the migratory dilemma but not in the way Mexico envisioned. News arrived in Mexico in early August that Carter was preparing a package for Congress that would include a partial amnesty for migrants who had lived in the United States since 1970, bolstered support for the Border Patrol to guard the border, and an unspecified amount of money for Mexico and other nations sourcing migration to the United States to help them create jobs.[45] The US ambassador later specified that the amount Carter had in mind was $2 billion, a large part of which would go to Mexico.[46] Carter's proposal failed to make it through Congress, ensuring that the migratory crisis would continue. Moreover, what Mexico had asked for was not a one-time injection of money but a consistent, long-term US policy of favoring Mexican imports in order to enduringly catalyze Mexican industries.

Mexico finally made some progress on its specific ask in November 1977. The Mexican and US secretaries of commerce announced that, thanks to ongoing talks between Portillo and Carter, the United States and Mexico were signing a three-year agreement whereby the United States would reduce duties on select Mexican products, including some fruits, vegetables, and artisanal products, in exchange for Mexico's doing the same on machinery and equipment exported by the United States. The Mexican secretary of commerce, Fernando Solana, calculated that this would lead to Mexico increasing its exports by 1.5 billion pesos. Solana argued that this was the type of partnership the United States and Mexico needed to partake in to "intelligently" address the "root cause" of migration. Though Mexico welcomed this partial reduction of duties for select products, it was not what it had envisioned. Portillo and his secretary of foreign affairs were interested in a longer, blanket reduction of tariffs across all Mexican exports. In their view, only that kind of wide, open encouragement to Mexican production would sufficiently stimulate the economy to keep Mexicans rooted. So they continued to lobby Carter for general tariff relief.[47]

Mexico occasionally deviated from its focus on enlisting US help to stimulate its economy and reduce out-migration. In 1978, for instance, Mexico secured a loan from the World Bank to stop the exodus of campesinos from the countryside to Mexican cities and the United States. The World Bank agreed to lend Mexico $469 million, in six installments, of which $256 million was earmarked for agriculture-related projects. "This is the largest operation the World Bank has attempted in Latin America," said the bank in its official report, "and the largest loan toward economic development."[48]

Nevertheless, what gripped Portillo's administration in 1978 and 1979 was obtaining special tariff relief from the United States for all, not just some, products originating in Mexico. Secretary of Commerce Solana said Mexico wanted the United States to exempt its products from the 10 percent tariff it ordinarily imposed on imports to protect American manufacturers from foreign competition.[49] The United States came close to accepting the proposal. In what became known as "Memorandum 41," the State Department and the National Security Council recommended that Carter enter a "special relationship" with Mexico. The United States needed an oil provider, amid instability in Iran and sharply rising oil prices, and Mexico had recently discovered massive reserves of oil within its territory. The State Department and the National Security Council argued that the United States should grant Mexico special concessions on its imports and support on the issue of migration in exchange for access to Mexican oil.

The idea, however, was opposed by the Treasury Department and Secretary of Energy James Schlesinger, who argued that the United States need not make preemptive concessions and rush in search of Mexican oil.[50] Schlesinger made three key arguments against establishing a long-term, open reliance on Mexican oil: one, the United States faced no critical short-term shortage of oil or gas; two, seeing as the problem was more in the medium and long term, the best solution was to encourage natural gas and oil production underway in Alaska, which would be discouraged if the United States entered a special relation with Mexico; and finally, Mexico's asking price for the oil was too high.

Meanwhile, the Treasury Department argued that the United States could not enter a special relationship for two reasons: first, the United States was actively negotiating a multilateral General Agreement on Tariffs and Trade in Geneva, and giving Mexico a unilateral concession would compromise its negotiating power; second, Treasury noted that any concession bestowed to Mexico would be sought by other Latin American nations. Carter decided to follow the advice of the Treasury and Energy Departments. He declined Portillo's invitation to enter a special relationship, reduce tariffs, and thereby tackle migration.[51]

Carter continued to want access to Mexican oil—just without reference to tariffs, migration, and long-term partnerships. He arranged a meeting with Portillo in Mexico to acquire oil. The visit offered Mexico an opportunity to use its oil reserves to cajole the United States into its desired tariff-reduction scheme. Carter's visit was condemned by some on the Mexican Left. They saw it as the arrival of an opportunistic "gold rusher." Students at the Universidad Nacional Autónoma de México tagged the walls of the university with slogans including "repudiate Carter."[52] President Portillo struggled to settle on a strategy leading up to the Carter visit. Originally, he maintained he would pursue a "package deal," in which the oil sale was negotiated alongside tariffs and migration relief. In the end, he decided not to "pit oil against braceros."[53]

Carter was consistent that he would only be discussing topics disentangled from one another, his priority being the acquisition of oil at a "fair price."[54] Portillo desisted from pressuring Carter into a "package deal," deciding not to risk the potential sale of Mexico's crude oil reserves.[55] In this way, the window of opportunity closed for Portillo to achieve an across-the-board tariff reduction conducive to Mexican production, job growth, and diminished out-migration. Portillo surmised that not all was lost. The oil sale could help "finance economic development, the creation of job sources, and the solution of the migratory problem."[56]

Incidents of migrant abuse continued despite Carter and INS commissioner Castillo's rhetorical commitment to human rights. In fact, the two Hannigan brothers were repeatedly acquitted between 1976 and 1981. Thomas Hannigan was acquitted three times. Patrick Hannigan was found guilty only in a third trial. He received a three-year sentence. In the midst of US-Mexican oil negotiations, another migrant was assassinated by a Border Patrol agent as he attempted to cross the border. Herman Baca, of the Committee on Chicano Rights, accused the Border Patrol of shooting detained migrants "execution style" while they were in handcuffs. The chief of the Border Patrol in San Ysidro admitted that the two migrants, Efren Reyes and Benito Rincón, were in handcuffs but claimed the gunshot was a result of a scuffle that took place between the handcuffed migrants and officer Daniel Cole, during which his officer mortally wounded Reyes in self-defense.[57]

This explanation was not satisfying to political leaders in Mexico, where members of Congress condemned the Border Patrol. President Portillo, meanwhile, bemoaned the persistent human rights abuses, dismissed guest work as a solution because it would only entrench out-migration, and pointed again to economic solutions as the only way to keep migrants from being abused.[58] As Santiago Roel, the secretary of foreign affairs, put it, the best approach was to lean into "great projects of economic development." However, given that the United States did not support Mexico's tariff relief scheme, he estimated it might take until the year 2000 for Mexican job growth to match the pace of its demographic growth.[59]

Not wishing to alienate Mexico, Carter issued a letter to the governors of all fifty states, following the execution of Rincón. He requested that they continue to follow their "responsibility" in policing undocumented migration but that they do so "justly and humanely," ensuring that each individual be treated with respect for their "basic rights."[60] He told the Department of Justice to be vigilant for abuse. This yielded what the Department of Justice celebrated as its first case charging US Border Patrol agents for physically assaulting migrants. In September 1979, the department brought charges against Bruce Brown, Daniel Charest, Dirk Dick, and Jeffrey Otherson, who brutalized at least five migrants, hitting them in their face, hands, and body before forcing them back to Mexico. The migrants were beaten after making an obscene gesture. Two of the agents were acquitted; the other two received community service and three years' probation.[61]

Yet even while the Department of Justice was trumpeting its intervention, more incidents of migrant abuse emerged. A chief of police in Louisiana, Ray Alford, held nine migrants hostage on his farm. He forced them to work for him and then stowed them away in "tiger cages" approximately one yard long for twelve hours a day. Under the lead of the Federal Bureau of Investigation, the Louisiana Department of Justice charged Alford for violating federal antislavery and peonage laws. The US Civil Rights Division announced it was the first time the laws had been used in a case involving Mexican, rather than Black, victims. The *New York Times* observed that "the case became notorious in Mexico" because it validated the long-standing analogy that "illegal aliens are slaves in the United States." Alford pled guilty and received a three-month prison sentence. The judge could have imposed a five-year sentence.[62]

Portillo's administration remained consistent in its positions—that guest work was not an answer and that economic reform offered the only solution to migration—until the end of his term. The Ministry of Foreign Affairs continued to argue that guest-worker programs catalyzed, rather than controlled, migration and in the past had operated "unilaterally," with the United States having a preponderance of control over migrants. In a meeting in the summer of 1981, Portillo expressed to the nascent Ronald Reagan administration that Mexico did "not desire to export workers." What it wanted was "to export goods." In this way, he still sought tariff relief from the United States. Such an approach, he continued to underscore, would provide a permanent stimulus to Mexico's economy, helping it to retain migrants.[63]

In line with his predecessors, Reagan was reticent on this point, so Mexico experimented with autonomous adjustments. Portillo created a new *fideicomiso* or trust fund, financed by the Banco Nacional de Crédito Rural (National Bank of Rural Credit). The trust would provide a variety of campesinos—ejido members, members of a colonia, and small rural landholders—perceived as most likely to leave as migrants, with financial resources if their average production declined over their last couple of harvests. The *fideicomiso de riesgo compartido* (trust fund for shared risk) was the only trust fund active under the aegis of the Mexican government. Successful campesino applicants could use the funds to cover basic inputs, including seeds and machinery.[64]

It was not until the 1980s, with the new presidential administration of Miguel de la Madrid and a series of shocks, including a debt crisis, the plunging of the Mexican peso, and devastating earthquakes, that Mexico nakedly adopted the position that the United States was a "safety valve" for Mexican migrants who would be otherwise stuck in a crisis situation at home. President de la Madrid would maintain this position even as migrants continued to experience mistreatment and abuse by the Border Patrol and US civilians. It was a marked shift born of acute conditions. A Mexican nation that had actively, if unsuccessfully, searched for ways to mitigate the migration and its adverse effects was to unreservedly tolerate it.

CONCLUSION

CAUGHT IN THE CURRENT

Mexico Surrenders to Out-Migration, 1980–Present

The politics of Mexican out-migration were transformed in the 1980s. In the three decades prior, Mexico monitored the migration and sought to slow or stop it when it undermined the ruling party's image, the country's social order, or its economic pillars. Beginning in 1982, Mexico largely abandoned precautions and refrained from trying to stem the migratory tide. Instead, it unabashedly embraced migration as a phenomenon necessary to the stability of the Mexican economy and shrugged off its downsides. President José López Portillo's successor in 1982, Miguel de la Madrid, was crucial in this transition.

De la Madrid and his team were public and explicit in their view that the United States was an indispensable outlet for Mexican labor, given the economic malaise that gripped Mexico as de la Madrid took office. The policies they advocated sought to ensure Mexicans' continued presence in the United

States and were not to any extent about keeping Mexicans in Mexico. Among other policies, they supported a possible mass amnesty of undocumented Mexican workers in the United States in the 1980s and opposed a possible mass expulsion.

De la Madrid thus abandoned Mexican leaders' historic pattern of hedging between promoting and constraining out-migration. This was a significant change. Most recently, Portillo, de la Madrid's predecessor, had tried to better position Mexican exports in the US market, thereby promoting job growth in Mexico and reducing out-migration, but hadn't been successful in getting US cooperation. Nonetheless, with scandals of migrant abuse constantly emerging from the United States, he had determined he could not simply send Mexicans to the United States and touted countermigratory measures.

While Mexico's mitigatory migratory policies certainly weakened after 1982, especially in the transition from Portillo to de la Madrid, ultimately they did not undergo a total collapse. Mexico embraced the idea of migration as a "safety valve," almost in those very words. Yet beginning with de la Madrid's two successors, Carlos Salinas de Gortari and then Ernesto Zedillo, Mexico evolved slightly, beyond a total surrender to out-migration. The de Gortari and Zedillo presidencies did not seek to retain Mexican nationals, but they realized that one aspect of the migration could still be tinkered with: remittances. Bending migrants back to their homeland was not palatable, but directing their US earnings back home certainly was.

Mexico's mitigatory migratory policies in the 1990s under de Gortari and Zedillo involved forging ties with its still-swelling diaspora, making migrants comfortable with emissaries of the Mexican state, and eventually launching programs to convince migrants to send more of their money home. These funds were depicted as crucial to stabilizing the economy following a severe economic crisis in the 1980s and to jolting development and modernization efforts in migrants' hometowns, including updates to their infrastructure and social services. The Mexican government, which for decades under PRI rule had displayed a belief that it could influence the physical movement of migrants, was now content with negotiating the abstract flow of money from migrants back to Mexico.

"PESO REFUGEES"

Shortly after President de la Madrid was inaugurated in 1982, American demographer Michael Teitelbaum sounded the alarm on an economic crisis gripping Mexico that he predicted would cause undocumented migration to the United States to mushroom. Mexico's economy was experiencing runaway inflation as indexed by the devaluation of the peso relative to the US dollar. With the worth of the peso plummeting, the gap between what Mexican wageworkers could earn in Mexico and what they could earn in the United States was expanding rapidly. Teitelbaum laid out the math. In 1981, prior to inflation, the US dollar was equivalent to twenty-five pesos. At that rate alone, the prevailing wage in the United States was ten times higher than that in Mexico. Following two major devaluations by 1982, the value of a US dollar tripled and then quadrupled relative to the peso.[1]

If Mexican migrants coveted US dollars before, warned Teitelbaum, they would seek them all the more now. They were "peso refugees" and could be expected to arrive in droves. Teitelbaum's plea was for the US government to take seriously the need for a proper immigration plan. He endorsed a congressional bill that would provide amnesty for undocumented workers, increase resources for border policing, and sanction employers who hired unauthorized entrants. In the absence of such a holistic measure, feared Teitelbaum, undocumented migration would grow unchecked, leaving the government with little recourse but to launch mass deportations.[2]

Teitelbaum's forecasts of a booming migration materialized with great speed. A year into Portillo's term, news outlets reported that, "predictably," undocumented migration from Mexico was escalating amid unemployment and peso devaluation crises there. It was estimated that, year over year, such migration had doubled. The economic crisis in Mexico was sufficiently dire that the administration of Ronald Reagan worried Mexico might suffer a severe political crisis, resulting in the rise of a left-leaning regime. As expressed by Reagan officials, Mexico was "the last domino" left for the Soviet Union to topple in its attempt to remake as much of the world as possible in a procommunist, anti-American image. US officials assured that "the money would be found" if the flailing Mexican economy had to be propped up in order to stabilize the rule of the PRI.[3]

The depth of Mexico's crisis hardly abated as the 1980s progressed. By late 1986, Reagan officials affirmed their continued worry that Mexico's deflationary spiral was so profound it might result in political instability. By 1986, US policy experts were concerned by not only the Mexican economy but also allegations of electoral fraud besetting the PRI. Prominent figures within the US government, including the assistant secretary of state for Inter-American affairs, the head of the Customs Service, and the head of the Drug Enforcement Administration's operations division, publicly rebuked Mexico for its corruption at a congressional hearing, abandoning their self-professed "normal caution." The Central Intelligence Agency also worried in official assessments that economic hard times and austerity in Mexico might produce a political tinderbox. John Gavin, the US ambassador to Mexico from 1981 to 1986, similarly felt Mexico verged on "doomsday" scenarios. The only bulwark to mass social uprisings, he postulated, was Mexicans' supposed aversion to the "kind of bloodshed and confrontation they experienced during their revolution." The US Army reported that "given the country's growing economic problems, the potential for social unrest is increasing."[4]

Operative in these dire prognostications of Mexico's future were predictions by the US Census Bureau of impending demographic growth in Mexico that would further aggravate Mexicans' ability to eke out a living in their homeland. The bureau's Center for International Research envisioned that with Mexican population set to expand from 81.7 million in 1986 to 112.8 million by the year 2000, Mexico would need to create 1 million jobs per year, a feat it had only approximated from 1978 to 1981 amid an oil boom. The Census Bureau predicted that, between inflation and exploding population, Mexico could only cope through out-migration.[5]

This is precisely what transpired. Amid a crisis that was partially economic and potentially political, and likely to worsen, President de la Madrid unapologetically embraced out-migration as a palliative. On the one hand, he lauded legislation passed by the US Congress in 1986 to grant amnesty to undocumented workers. The mass legalization offered lawful permanent residence to the undocumented, as long as they could prove they had lived continuously in the United States since January 1, 1982. Mexico welcomed this piece of US immigration reform. It meant that Mexicans, with their newfound legal status, would not have to fear deportations, and that the Mexican state would not have to fear their return to Mexico at a sensitive time.

On the other hand, Mexico opposed and was disconcerted by the other half of the US immigration reform package, namely, sanctions for employers who knowingly hired undocumented migrants. The Immigration Reform and Control Act (IRCA) required employees to verify all their workers were eligible for employment in the United States and to fill out a form, the I-9, attesting to their work eligibility. By making employers liable for their complicity in promoting undocumented migration, the US Congress hoped to avoid undocumented migration in the future. Indeed, President Reagan, at the signing of the amnesty act, framed it as the final US solution to the problem of undocumented immigration: forgiveness for migrants who had bypassed legal immigration channels and punishments for employers who might be tempted to abet their arrival in the future. The United States, in short, imagined it was creating a permanent clean slate for itself. Employers would be subject to civil penalties for initial offenses and criminal penalties if they were found to engage in repeated patterns of hiring unauthorized migrants.

The anti-immigration portion of the 1986 IRCA worried President de la Madrid's administration. The concern was that the United States had arrived at an effective policy to police and deter undocumented migration. Mexico imagined that with employers reticent to hire undocumented migrants, many of them would head back to Mexico, while others would never leave Mexico to begin with. Moreover, many Mexicans would not be eligible for the amnesty. Many were short-term, cyclical sojourners—periodically going back and forth between the United States and Mexico. To be eligible for the IRCA amnesty, migrants had to prove uninterrupted residence in the United States since 1982. Finally, Mexico feared the United States would supplement its legislation with massive deportations to clear out any remaining undocumented migrants and thereby achieve its clean slate.

President de la Madrid's administration decried the policing of undocumented migration through employer sanctions and sought assurances from the United States that mass expulsions were not in the offing. De la Madrid himself acknowledged that his government had become dependent on out-migration, irrespective of whether it was legal or not. "Any reduction in the flow of migration toward the United States can be a serious element in the development of Mexico," he stated, "since this factor has served as a mechanism of adjustment in regard to employment."[6] This technocratic wording made clear Mexico's position: under de la Madrid, Mexico embraced the United States a source of employment for Mexican nationals, flatly and without reservation. Mexico's secretary of agriculture, Eduardo Pesqueira, similarly conceded that Mexico had little to offer Mexicans who wished to migrate, saying it would take a "lot of imagination" and time for the government to find employment domestically for Mexico's growing population.[7]

The jobs Mexicans could find in the United States represented one part of the boon Mexico worried about losing following the signing of IRCA. The other element it feared might be in jeopardy were the remittances Mexicans sent home to support their families. This money represented not just a lifeline for struggling households but an infusion of dollars into a country suffering from a deflationary spiral. If indeed employers stopped hiring unauthorized migrants out of a fear of civil and criminal penalties, the migratory outflow might slow and so too might the backflow of remittances.

The Mexican government did not have a good grasp on how much money, precisely, migrants sent back to Mexico. But it knew it was significant. Its reliance on remittances was political common sense. As one Mexican official put it, "Nobody knows exactly how much the workers send back, but we know that it is a lot."[8]

Amid this context in the 1980s, President de la Madrid was not interested in exploring, planning, or implementing measures to slow the migration of Mexicans to the United States. President Cortines's notion of "the braceros of Mexico for the fields of Mexico," the almost decade-long IBP, and the emphasis Presidents Echeverría and Portillo put on exporting goods rather than workers were measures completely alien to de la Madrid. His concern was that Mexicans retain access to the United States. In choosing to allow Mexican nationals to leave, de la Madrid experienced minimal pushback. Church leaders were the only remaining force within Mexico actively calling for the internal rooting of Mexican peoples through job creation. They called for rural development "so that the countryside can retain its people."[9]

While President de la Madrid's administration largely concerned itself with endorsing and perpetuating out-migration, his two immediate successors, de Gortari and Zedillo, identified an area where the Mexican state could still intervene: remittances back to Mexico. Whereas de la Madrid had been content that Mexico should receive any infusion of US dollars during the height of Mexico's inflationary crisis, de Gortari and Zedillo believed Mexico should systematically tap into Mexican migrants' earnings. They thus moved to develop closer ties to the growing Mexican diaspora, establish trust with expatriate communities, and experiment with policies that encouraged a backflow of remittances.

The Mexican government's formal attempts to strengthen its ties with the Mexican diaspora began with the establishment in 1990 of a new office within the Secretariat of Foreign Affairs, called the Programa para las Comunidades Mexicanas en el Exterior (Program for Mexican Communities Abroad, or PCME). The PCME sought to align different Mexican federal agencies, state governments, and municipal governments behind initiatives to make Mexicans feel connected to the land they left behind. Its central mandate was ideological: to convince migrants that the Mexican nation was not defined by its formal borders but extended past them. Through that formulation, it hoped to convince Mexican migrants that they continued to belong to the imagined Mexican community, despite living in the United States.[10]

The PCME spearheaded various initiatives as part of its goal to make migrants feel included within the Mexican nation. Much of its work focused on Spanish-language education. The PCME sent 250 teachers to the United States to serve in areas that lacked bilingual teachers. It donated 300,000 books in Spanish to public and school libraries in the United States. And it carried out an adult learning program with 5,000 enrolled students to help them learn how to read and write in Spanish. The guiding presumption of these initiatives was that the Spanish language was a vehicle through which the Mexican state could help differentiate Mexicans from the Anglo society in which they lived and keep them connected to their ancestral land.[11]

Moreover, the PCME tried to bring Mexican immigrant communities into relief and connect them sentimentally to the Mexican nation and politically to the Mexican state. To help identify Mexican communities and leaders within them, the PCME sponsored soccer tournaments, envisioning that it could use these sites of leisure to acquaint itself with its diaspora. It also worked through Mexico's network of 42 consulates in the United States to promote ethnic pride. It sponsored folkloric activities, art exhibitions, campaigns to educate migrants about civic holidays, and friendly competitions, and tried to adapt these to migrants' region of origin. For instance, for immigrants from Zacatecas living in the United States, the PCME organized a rodeo.

Most critical, the PCME sponsored meetups between immigrant communities and political authorities from their places of origin. These face-to-face dialogues helped create familiarity between migrants and the Mexican government. In a preview of policies to come, the PCME used these meetups to encourage Mexicans to invest in their hometowns, especially in the building of infrastructure, such as roads, electrical wiring, and schools.[12]

Throughout the twentieth century, the Mexican government had gestured toward maintaining ties with its emigrant population. But the efforts of the 1990 reflected the first sustained, methodical, and institutionalized attempt to do so. Mexican officials themselves were aware of this policy change. Carlos González Gutiérrez, who worked as the consul for community affairs at the Mexican consulate in Los Angeles and by the late 1990s headed the Division of Hispanic Affairs at the Embassy of Mexico in the United States, recalled that "the systematic effort by Mexico to cultivate ties with . . . the organized [expatriate Mexican] community only began in the early 1990s."[13]

Mexico's attempts to build closer ties to its emigrant population were well timed. First, the passage of IRCA in 1986 meant that Mexicans who were legalized could come out of the shadows. No longer unauthorized immigrants, they could exist in the United States without a fear of impending removal and could move in society more openly. In practice, as González Gutiérrez noted, this meant Mexicans were able to participate in immigrant clubs and organizations without fear of making themselves vulnerable as outsiders and singling themselves out for deportation.[14]

Second, the Mexican government in the 1990s did indeed risk losing connection to Mexican migrants. The passage of IRCA led the Mexican diaspora to become larger and more permanent than in generations prior. Pre-IRCA, many Mexican migrants engaged in cyclical migration, staying in the United States for a few years and then returning home. Post-IRCA, Mexicans by and large became permanent immigrants. Mexicans' shift to long-term resettlement was partly fueled by the amnesty. It normalized the status of at least 2 million Mexican migrants, anchoring them to the United States. Over time, they were also able to sponsor their immediate family members for relocation and legal status, removing the incentive to return to their homeland. Finally, IRCA provided for strengthened border enforcement, driving up the costs and difficulty of border crossing. New generations of undocumented migrants who arrived in the United States in the post-IRCA period calculated that migrating cyclically was not practical. They began to live in the United States indefinitely.[15]

As the Mexican government bound itself to Mexican migrant communities, it began to experiment with ways to coax back a more pronounced, focused backflow of remittances. Its mitigatory migratory measures thus did not focus on retaining or retrieving Mexican migrants from abroad which no longer seemed feasible or compelling. Instead, the Mexican government's emphasis across federal, state, and municipal levels was to ensure that migrants shared their American wealth with their hometowns. Mexico's idea was to turn migrants into investors, who could catalyze the development of their hometowns with their remittances. Mexico built on the face-to-face interactions that migrants and officials had through PCME initiatives.

The Mexican government's first major effort to encourage remittances was the Two-for-One program in Zacatecas. Begun in 1992, the initiative promised that for every peso migrants sent back home to support a development project, the federal government and the state government of Zacatecas would each also contribute a peso. Because of its success, the initiative morphed by 1998 into the Three-for-One program, as municipal governments also joined the pledge to contribute a peso for each peso of investment sent back by diaspora members.

Migrants collected and sent money back to Mexico through a very particular kind of immigrant organization: the hometown association. As the name implies, these associations helped bring together migrants originating from the same town in Mexico. Zacatecas emerged as an attractive site for the launch of the Two-for-One program because it possessed the most robust network of hometown associations in the United States. In the 1990s, there were over 200 hometown associations, divided into 10 federations, including Southern California, Chicago, Denver, Dallas, Las Vegas, Atlanta, Houston, Waco, Florida, and North Carolina. Overall membership numbered around 40,000.[16]

Through the Two-for-One program, migrants from Zacatecas were able to support a variety of development projects. Whereas traditionally migrant remittances had largely supported individual households, with the government's intervention they were redirected toward the development of infrastructure projects, such as building irrigation wells and dams; "human resource development," such as funding for libraries, computer centers, and scholarships; and public health initiatives, such as modernizing wastewater plants. This was no marginal contribution. In the first eight years of the Two-for-One program, organized Zacatecan migrants financed a total of 429 projects in their hometowns, representing a total investment of $17 million. Moreover, the initiative gained buy-in from migrants as it matured and began to pay dividends. This can be inferred from the upward trends in projects sponsored by migrants each year: seven in 1993, thirty-four in 1995, seventy-seven in 1997, and ninety-three in 1999.[17]

A second formal initiative to encourage remittances grew out of the federal government's promotion of in-person meetings between migrants and authorities at the state level. Migrants from Guanajuato also had a robust network of hometown associations, mainly based out of California. Taking advantage of this grassroots organization, the Guanajuato government in 1996 launched a program known as Mi Comunidad (My Community). Whereas the Two-for-One program drew on remittances to fund general infrastructural development, Guanajuato's pilot drew on migrant money to promote industry and job creation. Specifically, it helped migrants pool their money together to open *maquilas* in their hometowns. Maquilas were factories that were exempted from taxes if they were oriented toward export production.

The maquilas created in Guanajuato with migrant remittances mainly dedicated themselves to the production of garments and textile products. They produced immediate results. In the town of Yuriria, Guanajuato, for instance, Mexican migrants sent $220,000 to invest in the opening of three maquilas. This led to the creation of 100 jobs in the town. This was significant because only 23 percent of Yuriria residents had full-time jobs. Amid such a dearth of economic opportunity, even the few jobs opened by remittance maquilas could make a significant difference at the microlevel.[18]

Overall, in its first four years of operation, the My Community program attracted $1.2 million in migrant investment, led to the creation of twelve maquilas across nine different municipalities, and resulted in the creation of 500 jobs. Migrants were the majority shareholders of the new factories. The Guanajuato government involved itself financially but only to cover the first two months of wages and training for new workers. Outside of that, it focused on technical support, such as the designs of facilities, the drafting of business plans, and the provision of low-interest loans. Based on the momentum it acquired in its first four years of operation, the My Community program continued to attract migrant interest. As of 2000, migrants had gathered another $980,000 and were poised to double the size of the program by opening nine more maquilas in nine municipalities, creating 420 jobs in their hometowns.[19]

Other states within Mexico with high rates of out-migration, such as Michoacán and Oaxaca, settled for more ad-hoc programs of collaborative investment with Mexican migrants. These states developed Oficinas de Atención a Oriundos en el Exterior (Offices of Attention to Citizens Abroad). These state-level agencies worked in collaboration with the federal Ministry of Foreign Affairs. They sponsored cultural events to establish a connection to migrants. Then they pitched specific, small infrastructure projects to migrants, as needed. They would invite migrants to contribute and offer varying amounts of state government support. Other states in Mexico, such as San Luis Potosí and Jalisco, followed a similar ad hoc strategy of recruiting migrant remittances only when needed for specific projects. However, those states did not establish formal Oficinas de Atención a Oriundos en el Exterior to recruit migrant investment.[20]

While the Mexican government sought to varying degrees to boost remittance flows, most remittances from migrants in the 1990s were sent independently from government initiatives. Contemporary estimates suggested that "migradollars" (money sent back home by migrants) accounted for an influx of $1.5 billion to Western Mexico and $2 billion to Mexico as a whole. Sociologist Douglas Massey helps capture the meaning of these sums. At $2 billion, remittances were equivalent to "90 percent of Mexico's earnings from agricultural exports, 78 percent of its direct foreign investment, 59 percent of its earnings from tourism, and 56 percent of its earnings from the maquila industry." Moreover, this money was spent on more than consumption and "family support." Migrants spent an estimated $84 million in entrepreneurial activities. As such, remittances were "an important source of its [Mexico's] investment capital."[21]

That said, as Massey points out, numbers do not capture the significance of remittances to Mexican society and the Mexican state. The wealth generated by tourism, maquilas, and agricultural exports generally tended to concentrate in the hands of economic elites, only partially trickling down to working people. By contrast, the money sent by migrants went "directly to the people concentrated at the lower end of Mexico's income distribution." As such, remittances represented a powerful infusion of capital to struggling families and communities. Remittances could stabilize them and forestall social or political conflict.[22]

Into the 2000s, PRI administrations continued to be wedded to outmigration without reservations. Indeed, the Mexican government's stance was lampooned by director and writer Luis Estrada in his 2014 film *La dictadura perfecta* starring comedian Damián Alcázar. In a scene that was used as the film's trailer, the Mexican president, played by Sergio Mayer, meets with the US ambassador in the national palace in Los Pinos. Mayer, bearing an intended resemblance to then-president Enrique Peña Nieto, candidly tells the US ambassador in front of cameras that "we actually have many problems in Mexico," some of which could be solved if the United States were friendlier to migration from Mexico. Mayer lays out his proimmigration argument through a racialized reading of the US political economy: "We [Mexicans] are waiting to do all the dirty jobs not even the *negros* [Black Americans] want to do." In the film, this sets off a social media firestorm of memes, with Mexicans lambasting Mayer's unabashed subservience and distasteful racial commentary.[23]

In the 2000s, the PRI lost its stranglehold on the federal government after more than seventy years of uninterrupted rule. Non-PRI presidencies deviated from straightforwardly stating they had accepted out-migration and were clinging to remittances. They resurrected the discourse that it was possible to root Mexicans internally. It was a useful way of distinguishing themselves from the PRI. However, their vision would not be like the one espoused by President Cortines that Mexico could moor Mexicans domestically by leaning on domestic policy, such as ejido support or colonia formation. They mirrored more the posture of José López Portillo: that Mexico could stanch the out-migration if the United States provided meaningful support.

During the presidency of Vicente Fox, a leader of the Partido Acción Nacional (National Action Party, or PAN) and the first non-PRI president in seventy years, Mexico's minister of foreign affairs, Jorge Castañeda, attempted to shape a migratory politics less defined by an unapologetic acquiescence to out-migration. In his various interfaces with US authorities, he proposed that the countries come together in a mutually fruitful "partnership for prosperity." At bottom, this would involve the United States substantially increasing direct investment in Mexico, to create economic opportunities for Mexicans in their homeland.[24] The partnership for prosperity failed to materialize to the degree needed to sustainably curb out-migration.

A similar stance to that of the PAN functioned as the official policy of recent non-PRI-affiliated president Andrés Manuel López Obrador of the left-wing Movimiento de Regeneración Nacional (National Regeneration Movement, or MORENA). In the face of continued migration from Mexico throughout his administration from 2018 to 2024, he too called for the United States to assist Mexico in instituting policies of economic development. The main difference is that Mexico, under Obrador, also became an advocate for other Latin American nations sourcing migration to the United States. President Obrador's arguments were not solely for US investment in Mexico but Latin America as a whole, understanding that no migrant "abandons his land on a whim; they do so because of necessity." For President Obrador, the United States was the country that provoked instability, migration, and a lack of peace in the hemisphere because it dedicated "too much of its resources on military spending" instead of guiding "its economic power to cooperation in projects of development."[25] Though Obrador promised he would "not desist" and would "keep hammering this theme with the government of the United States," he admitted "slow progress" in attempting to "convince them we have to work together." The hemispheric contramigratory economic collaboration he trumpeted as ideal proved elusive.[26]

Obrador's successor, Claudia Sheinbaum—also representing MORENA—is presently facing the unenviable position of contending with the volatile presidency of Donald Trump. His campaign was buttressed by a pledge to launch the largest mass deportation in US history. In response, Mexico has partly adopted a wait-and-see approach, given the difficulty inherent in determining how much of his discourse is bluster and to what extent his roundups will target Mexican migrants directly. As a baseline measure, Mexico has prepared shelters along its northern frontier to receive possible repatriates. And, beginning in January of 2025, it instituted a program called México te abraza (Mexico embraces you) to ease the reintegration of repatriated Mexicans. It promises to grant each deportee about 2,000 pesos (about 100 US dollars) to facilitate their trip back to their hometown, enroll them in the country's social services, and connect them with job opportunities.[27] Sheinbaum's policies are likely to evolve depending on the severity of the United States' expulsion campaign.

As it pertains to ongoing and future out-migration, Sheinbaum has begun to emphasize that the United States' own policies could contribute to an expanding exodus. In particular, she has warned against the imposition of tariffs on Mexico, arguing that they will undermine the Mexican economy and fuel undocumented migration. Taking a page from Obrador, she has argued that the only way for the United States to stem migration from Mexico and Latin America is to invest in the region's economic uplift, not "walls" and "soldiers." In a February 2025 meeting with Kristi Noem, the US secretary of Homeland Security, Sheinbaum conveyed her hope that the United States would join Mexico in creating a "pole of economic development" along the Guatemala-Mexico border to stimulate job opportunities for Mexicans and Guatemalans alike. She favors extending existing rail lines in Chiapas into Guatemala to facilitate trade and commerce. However, given Trump's predilection for governing via fiat and unilateral measures, such a collaboration seems unlikely. As with Obrador's, Sheinbaum's public assurances that migration can be "resolved" seem to be hollow proclamations.[28]

Despite twenty-first-century shifts in leadership between the PRI, PAN, and MORENA, the Mexican state seems to lack both the disposition and tools needed to alter the long-standing pattern of out-migration to the United States. With remittances widely thought of as a bulwark against economic and social turmoil, none of these modern parties has identified a compelling reason to truly counteract migration and, at long last, turn the tide. Perhaps the moment for such countermigratory policies came and went many decades ago, during and after the BP. In that era, Mexican mass migration was still an evolving process, and Mexican politics featured a wider array of ideas for how it could be slowed and even stopped. With Mexico effectively absent as a countermigratory force from the 1980s onward, the question of how to regulate migration has fallen, for now, to a punitive and draconian American right—relentless in its ploys to stem the migratory flow and indifferent to human rights, civil liberties, and posterity alike.

ACKNOWLEDGMENTS

Behold the power of endless repetition! After an incessant loop of thinking and typing, I am delighted this book has achieved its final form.

My journey—from sitting quietly in ESL classrooms, to completing a PhD program, to becoming a college professor—has been quite a trip. I want to issue a heartfelt thank-you to all of those who helped me along the way, whether by encouraging me, sharing their wisdom, or sharpening my thinking.

From the CUNY College of Staten Island, my alma mater, I want to thank Katie Geschwendt, Geoffrey Hemphill, Richard Lufrano, Charles Liu, and Calvin Holder, may he rest in peace. I was told Harvard University, my next stop, would be a far more hostile institution. My doctoral advisors made sure this was not the case. Thank you to Evelyn Brooks Higginbotham, Walter Johnson, Lisa McGirr, and Kirsten Weld for making time to mentor me.

I owe an enormous thank-you to the entire History Department at New York University. It has been the honor of my life to serve as a professor of history. I still remember being dazzled by Professors Lufrano and Holder at CSI and the way they narrated and explained history without any obvious script or PowerPoint behind them. Their mastery and cogency, more than anything, lured me to history as a career. My oratory skills will never be at their level, but I am thankful to New York University for letting me ply my craft and engage with a variety of gifted students. I want to extend a special thank-you to my esteemed colleagues Steven Hahn, Kevin Kenny, and Andrew Needham for their warm and persistent support over the years.

This book would not have materialized without the wise and warm stewardship of my editors at the University of North Carolina Press: Debbie Gershenowitz, Andrew Graybill, Catherine Hodorowicz, and Benjamin

Johnson, and project editor Valerie Burton. I came to them because of their enormous reputation and was still blown away by their care and execution.

On the personal front, I would like to apologize to all my friends and family who have had to put up with my fleeting attention. This book insisted on pulling me away from you all. I did my best to resist it so we could share happy moments together. I hope you will all continue to indulge my flights of contemplation with the same grace and love you have up to now. Writing would be horrific if you were not there as a reprieve. This goes out to my dear friends, David Bonilla, William Chiriguayo, Niya Huang, David de la Torre, Oscar de la Torre, Joan Matsalia, Frank Matsalia, and Peter Xu. And to my beloved family: my funny grandpa, Martín Cantoran; my equally hilarious uncle, Jimmy Cantoran; my caring grandma, Paula Lucero; my kind aunt, Mayra Cantoran; my blossoming cousins, Alex Cantero, Madeline Cantoran, Shannel Cantoran, and Jonathan Montas; my very Irish brother-in-law, Justin Williams; my charming nephews, Finn and Zyon Williams; my dauntless sister-in-law, Deneesha Lawrence; my beautifully cheerful mother-in-law, Rosslyn Lawrence; my ferocious mom, Lorena Lucero; my indefatigable dad, Alejandro Ibargüen; my shrewd little sis, Ashley Ibargüen; my blood but also spiritual brother, Brian Ibargüen; my steadfast friend and wife, Renelle Lawrence; and, above all, to my brilliant children, Abra and Hunter. Thank you for giving me resolve.

NOTES

ABBREVIATIONS

AGN   Archivo General de la Nación, Mexico City, Mexico
DGIPS   Fondo de la Secretaría de Gobernación, Dirección General de Investigaciones Políticas y Sociales
FARC   Fondo Adolfo Ruiz Cortines
FMAC   Fondo Manuel Ávila Camacho
OM-AHES   Oficialía Mayor, Archivo Histórico del Estado de Sonora, Hermosillo, Mexico

INTRODUCTION

1. Deborah Cohen, *Braceros: Migrant Citizens and Transnational Subjects in the Postwar United States and Mexico* (University of North Carolina Press, 2011), 21–47. Cohen emphasizes that Mexico also trumpeted other potential payoffs to the migration, including modernization and the improved technological savvy of migrants. Historian Mireya Loza, moreover, underscores how Mexico also found in the BP a way to de-Indigenize its peasant population and advance the racial ideology of *mestizaje*. See Mireya Loza, *Defiant Braceros: How Migrant Workers Fought for Racial, Sexual, and Political Freedom* (University of North Carolina Press, 2016).

2. For more on such precautions, see Alberto García, *Abandoning Their Beloved Land: The Politics of Bracero Migration in Mexico* (University of California Press, 2023). García shows that state and municipal authorities came to control the implementation of federal precautionary measures. He emphasizes that local authorities used their ability to grant and deny migrants contracts to augment their own political power and standing. A similar conclusion is reached in Michael Snodgrass, "The Golden Age of Charrismo: Workers, Braceros, and the Political Machinery of Postrevolutionary Mexico," in *Dictablanda: Politics, Work, and Culture in Mexico, 1938–1968*, ed. Paul Gillingham and Benjamin Smith (Duke University Press, 2014).

3. Diana Irina Córdoba Ramírez, "Los centros de contratación del Programa Bracero: Desarrollo agrícola y acuerdos político en el norte de México, 1947–1964" (PhD diss., Colegio de México, 2017).

4. For an excellent overview of the Bracero Program, the protections included in the contract, and their ultimate weakness, see Neil Foley, *Mexicans in the Making of America* (Harvard University Press, 2014), chap. 5.

5. The foundational literature on the BP is US-centric and features Mexico mostly as a facilitator of migration. See, for example, Kitty Calavita, *Inside the State: The Bracero Program, Immigration, and the INS* (Routledge, 1992); and Erasmo Gamboa, *Mexican Labor and World War II: Braceros in the Pacific Northwest, 1942–1947* (University of Washington Press, 2000). Subsequent studies, influenced by transnational and borderlands frameworks, have looked more deeply at Mexico, but still showcase it mostly as a facilitator. See Kelly Lytle Hernández, *Migra! A History of the US Border Patrol* (University of California Press, 2010); and Cohen, *Braceros*. Catherine Vézina, *Diplomacia migratoria: Una historia transnacional del Programa Bracero, 1947–1952* (Centro de Investigación y Docencia Económicas, 2017).

6. See Deborah Cohen, "Caught in the Middle: The Mexican State's Relationship with the United States and Its Own Citizen-Workers, 1942–1954," *Journal of American Ethnic History* 20, no. 3 (Spring 2001): 118.

7. Sociologist David Fitzgerald denies that Mexico contemplated measures to terminate out-migration. He argues that "conflicts within the Mexican state have not been whether about there should be any emigration at all." David Fitzgerald, *A Nation of Emigrants: How Mexico Manages Its Migration* (University of California Press, 2008), 38.

8. Among the key works in establishing and popularizing the safety valve theory are Manuel García y Griego, *The Importation of Mexican Contract Laborers to the United States, 1942–1964: Antecedents, Operation, and Legacy* (Program in United States–Mexican Studies, University of California San Diego, 1981); Cohen, "Caught in the Middle," 118; Fitzgerald, *Nation of Emigrants*, 38, 55; Alexandra Délano, *Mexico and Its Diaspora in the United States: Policies of Emigration since 1848* (Cambridge University Press, 2011), 9–10, 30, 89; Martha Menchaca, *The Politics of Dependency: US Reliance on Mexican Oil and Farm Labor* (University of Texas Press, 2016), 189; and Ana Raquel Minian, *Undocumented Lives: The Untold Story of Mexican Migration* (Harvard University Press, 2018), 16. Each describes Mexico as using migration as a "safety" or "release valve" for long stretches of its twentieth-century history. Jorge Durand has critiqued the applicability of this recurrent metaphor, arguing that it overstates the power of the Mexican state to discharge its population at will. It depicts Mexico as a master regulator of its migratory flow, as though it alone or even principally dictated when and how Mexicans moved abroad. Migration, he contends, has been contingent and predominantly determined by the US labor market. See Jorge Durand, *Más allá de la línea: Patrones migratorios entre México y Estados Unidos* (Consejo Nacional para la Cultura y las Artes, 1994), 67. This project concurs with Durand's assessment. It adds, furthermore, that the Mexican government's intent was inconstant across time, limiting the utility of adhering a definitive "safety valve" label to its emigration policy.

9. For an analysis of Eastern European emigration control, see Tara Zahra, *The Great Departure: Mass Migration from Eastern Europe and the Making of the Free World* (W. W. Norton, 2016), 6. According to Zahra, Eastern European states realized in the nineteenth century that "emigration could be managed like the steam valve on a teapot; that encouraging people to stay or go could be used as an instrument of policy, to serve both domestic and international goals." For an analysis of Italy's varying policies in the twentieth century, see Julie M. Weise and Christoph Rass, "Migrating Concepts: The Transatlantic Origins of the Bracero Program, 1919–42," *American Historical Review* 129, no. 1 (March 2024):

22–52; Paolo Tripodi, *The Colonial Legacy in Somalia: Rome and Mogadishu. From Colonial Administration to Operation Restore Hope* (MacMillan, 1999), 1–40; and Stefano Bellucci and Massimo Zaccaria, "Wage Labor and Mobility in Colonial Eritrea, 1880s to 1920s," *International Labor and Working-Class History* 86 (2014): 89–106. Italian leaders, such as Prime Minister Benito Mussolini, encouraged internal migration within the Italian Empire, to places such as Eritrea and Somaliland, including in the 1920s, when they soured on the racially motivated restrictions countries such as the United States were implementing against Italian labor migrants. For the case of India and China, see Sunil S. Amrith, *Crossing the Bay of Bengal: The Furies of Nature and Fortunes of Migrants* (Harvard University Press, 2013), 139, 178, 189, 192–93. Nationalists and political leaders in both countries saw the emigration of indentured workers as a humiliation. Recognizing that they could not effectively protect these workers from suffering and from contributing to perceptions of Indians and Chinese people worldwide as "coolies," they at times strategized to prevent their departure.

10. See Kevin J. Middlebrook, *The Paradox of Revolution: Labor, the State, and Authoritarianism in Mexico* (Johns Hopkins University Press, 1995); Jeffrey W. Rubin, *Decentering the Regime: Ethnicity, Radicalism, and Democracy in Juchitán, Mexico* (Duke University Press, 1997); Jonathan Schlefer, *Palace Politics: How the Ruling Party Brought Crisis to Mexico* (University of Texas Press, 2008); Tanalís Padilla, *Rural Resistance in the Land of Zapata: The Jaramillista Movement and the Myth of the Pax Priísta, 1940–1962* (Duke University Press, 2008); Alejandro Quintana, *Maximino Ávila Camacho and the One-Party State: The Taming of Caudillismo and Caciquismo in Post-revolutionary Mexico* (Rowman and Littlefield, 2010); Paul Gillingham and Benjamin Smith, eds., *Dictablanda: Politics, Work, and Culture in Mexico, 1938–1968* (Duke University Press, 2014); and Paul Gillingham, *Unrevolutionary Mexico: The Birth of a Strange Dictatorship* (Yale University Press, 2021).

11. Hernández, *Migra!*, 7–8. Hernández's periodization draws from John Mason Hart, *Empire and Revolution: The Americans in Mexico since the Civil War* (University of California Press, 2002).

12. Renata Keller, *Mexico's Cold War: Cuba, the United States, and the Legacy of the Mexican Revolution* (Cambridge University Press, 2015); Eric Zolov, *The Last Good Neighbor: Mexico in the Global Sixties* (Duke University Press, 2020).

13. Loza, *Defiant Braceros*; Ana Elizabeth Rosas, *Abrazando el Espíritu: Bracero Families Confront the US-Mexico Border* (University of California Press, 2014); Miroslava Chávez-García, *Migrant Longing: Letter Writing across the US-Mexico Borderlands* (University of North Carolina Press, 2018). Deborah Cohen shows migrants engaging in micropolitics by controlling their posture and callousing their hands to appear as docile and seasoned laborers to Mexican and US authorities. See Cohen, *Braceros*, 98.

14. The 1954 incident has served as compelling matter for book covers, chapter openings, and brief midchapter vignettes, but the analyses are marred by a superficial engagement with the Mexican state. Existing accounts emphasize US-Mexican diplomatic exchanges and how the BP breakdown played out on the ground in the borderlands. They fail to show how the international crisis prompted Mexico's executive branch to reappraise its domestic policies. See Mae Ngai, *Impossible Subjects: Illegal Aliens and the Making of Modern America* (Princeton University Press, 2004), 145–46, 153–54; Deborah Kang, *INS on the Line: Making Immigration Law on the US-Mexico Border, 1917–1954* (Oxford University Press, 2017), cover, 150–51; Fitzgerald, *Nation of Emigrants*, 1–2; Hernández, *Migra!*, 145–46;

Don Mitchell, *They Saved the Crops: Labor, Landscape, and the Struggle over Industrial Farming in Bracero-Era California* (University of Georgia Press, 2012), 232–40. To the extent that Mexico's countermigratory discourse and policies are acknowledged, they are cast as the "bluster" of a state merely posturing to gain BP concessions. See Cohen, "Caught in the Middle," 118. The content of Mexico's internal deliberations shows Mexico explored contramigratory solutions in 1954 and gravitated to them the more the United States spurned Mexico's proposed improvements to bracero labor protections.

15. For an argument of Mexico's increasing weakness and irrelevance in policing migration during the BP, see García y Griego, *Importation*, 31. He argues that Mexico's bargaining position and power over the migration underwent a "demise . . . as early as 1950," as World War II receded in significance. His temporal arc is reproduced in Cohen, "Caught in the Middle," 115; and Hernández, *Migra!*, 194. David Fitzgerald and Ana Minian date a related phenomenon: when Mexico began to unreservedly accept out-migration irrespective of its downsides. They single out the late 1960s and early 1970s for Mexico's adoption of an *ad extremum* safety valve policy. See Fitzgerald, *Nation of Emigrants*, 55; and Minian, *Undocumented Lives*, chap. 1. To the extent scholars push back on the narrative of Mexican declension, it is to suggest that Mexico was permissive from the get-go. For instance, Alexandra Délano argues that the deliberate allowance of migration was a "constant" feature of Mexican governance, even predating the PRI. Mexico, in that formulation, had no power to lose. See Délano, *Mexico and Its Diaspora*, 37, 89–95.

16. Growers are held responsible for the end of the IBP in Luis Aboites Aguilar, *El Norte entre algodones: Población, trabajo agrícola y optimismo en México, 1930–1970* (Colegio de México, 2013), chap. 4. The other existing account of the IBP focuses on the complex set of actors involved in it, not its collapse. See Sergio Chávez, "The Sonoran Desert's Domestic Bracero Programme: Institutional Actors and the Creation of Labour Migration Streams," *International Migration* 50, no. 2 (April 2012): 20–40.

17. María Patricia Fernández-Kelly, *For We Are Sold, I and My People: Women and Industry in Mexico's Frontier* (State University of New York Press, 1983); Altha J. Cravey, *Women and Work in Mexico's Maquiladoras* (Rowman and Littlefield, 1998); Alejandro Lugo, *Fragmented Lives, Assembled Parts: Culture, Capitalism, and Conquest at the US-Mexico Border* (University of Texas Press, 2008); Leslie Sklar, *Assembling for Development: The Maquila Industry in Mexico and the United States* (Routledge, 1989); Jefferson Cowie, *Capital Moves: RCA's Seventy-Year Quest for Cheap Labor* (Cornell University Press, 2019); Erik Loomis, *Out of Sight: The Long and Disturbing Story of Corporations Outsourcing Catastrophe* (New Press, 2016).

18. This argument is made most forcefully by Ana Minian, who posits that in Mexico a "political culture that acquiesced to and even supported citizens' emigration flourished during the 1970s." Minian, *Undocumented Lives*, 16. Délano similarly argues that the PRI operated with "a policy of no policy," because it was content with tacitly permitting undocumented migration. Délano, *Mexico and Its Diaspora*, 84.

19. Raúl Delgado Wise and Héctor Rodríguez Ramírez, "The Emergence of Collective Migrants and Their Role in Mexico's Local and Regional Development," *Canadian Journal of Development Studies / Revue canadienne d'études du développement* 22, no. 3 (January 2001): 747–64; Luin Goldring, "Family and Collective Remittances to Mexico: A Multidimensional Typology," *Development and Change* 35, no. 4 (2004): 799–840; Federico Torres and Yevgeny Kuznetsov, "Mexico: Leveraging Migrants' Capital to Develop Hometown

Communities," in *Diaspora Networks and the International Migration of Skills: How Countries Can Draw on Their Talent Abroad*, ed. Yevgeny Kuznetsov (World Bank Publications, 2006).

CHAPTER ONE

1. Fernando Saúl Alanís Enciso, *El primer programa bracero y el gobierno de México, 1917–1918* (Colegio de San Luis, 1999), 1–10.
2. Alanís Enciso, *Primer programa bracero*, 76–82.
3. Neil Foley, *Mexicans in the Making of America* (Harvard University Press, 2014), 48.
4. Terrence Haverluk, "The Changing Geography of U.S. Hispanics, 1850–1990," *Journal of Geography* 96, no. 3 (August 2007): 137.
5. Juan Ramón García, *Operation Wetback: The Mass Deportation of Mexican Undocumented Workers in 1954* (Greenwood University Press, 1980), 231.
6. D'Ann Campbell, *Women at War with America: Private Lives in a Patriotic Era* (Harvard University Press, 1984), 73.
7. N. Ray Gilmore and Gladys W. Gilmore, "The Bracero in California," *Pacific Historical Review* 32, no. 3 (August 1963): 272–73.
8. Gilbert Joseph, *Mexico's Once and Future Revolution: Social Upheaval and the Challenge of Rule since the Late Nineteenth Century* (Duke University Press, 2013), 12, 129, 150, 198.
9. Deborah Cohen, *Braceros: Migrant Citizens and Transnational Subjects in the Postwar United States and Mexico* (University of North Carolina Press, 2011), 201.
10. Cohen, *Braceros*, 92–95.
11. Deborah Cohen, "Caught in the Middle: The Mexican State's Relationship with the United States and Its Own Citizen-Workers, 1942–1954," *Journal of American Ethnic History* 20, no. 3 (Spring 2001): 112.
12. Friedrich Schuler, *Mexico between Hitler and Roosevelt: Mexican Foreign Relations in the Age of Lázaro Cárdenas, 1934–1940* (University of New Mexico Press, 2004), 1, 38, 100–138.
13. Javier Ibarrola, *El ejército y el poder: Impacto e influencia política en el México moderno* (Océano de México, 2003), 16–26.
14. Javier Flores Carrera, "Bracero: Historia de los trabajadores del Programa Bracero, 1942–1966" (PhD diss., Universidad de las Américas en Puebla, 2006), 19–20; Richard B. Craig, *The Bracero Program: Interest Groups and Foreign Policy* (University of Texas Press, 1971), 41.
15. Flores Carrera, "Bracero," 19–20; Richard B. Craig, *The Bracero Program: Interest Groups and Foreign Policy* (University of Texas Press, 1971), 41.
16. Howard Campbell, "Bracero Migration and the Mexican Economy, 1951–1964" (PhD diss., American University, 1972), 56.
17. F. D. Roosevelt, "Eight Hundred and Fifty-Third Press Conference from October 20, 1942," in *Public Papers of the Presidents of the United States: F. D. Roosevelt*, vol. 11 (Best Books on Corporation, 2013), 429.
18. Craig, *Bracero Program*, 40.
19. Natalia Molina, "Constructing Mexicans as Deportable Immigrants: Race, Disease, and the Meaning of 'Public Charge,'" *Identities* 17, no. 6 (December 2010): 641–66.

20. Kitty Calavita, *Inside the State: The Bracero Program, Immigration, and the INS* (Routledge, 1992), 19–24.

21. Robert C. Jones, *Los braceros mexicanos en los Estados Unidos durante el periódo bélico* (Unión Panamericana, 1946), 5–35; Jorge del Pinal, "Los trabajadores mexicanos en los Estados Unidos," *El Trimestre Económico* 12, no. 45 (April 1945), 1–45.

22. Emilio Zamora, *Claiming Rights and Righting Wrongs in Texas: Mexican Workers and Job Politics during World War II* (Texas A&M University Press, 2009), 78–89.

23. Calavita, *Inside the State*, 2.

24. Craig, *Bracero Program*, 41–42.

25. Ana Elizabeth Rosas, *Abrazando el Espíritu: Bracero Families Confront the U.S.-Mexico Border* (University of California Press, 2014), 21.

26. Cohen, *Braceros*, 22–23; Rodolfo O. de la Garza and Gabriel Szekely, "Policy, Politics and Emigration," in *At the Crossroads: Mexican Migration and U.S. Policy*, ed. F. D. Bean, R. de la Garza, B. R. Roberts, and S. Weintraub (Rowman and Littlefield, 2007).

27. Alan Knight, "The Rise and Fall of Cardenismo," in *Mexico since Independence*, ed. Leslie Bethell (Cambridge University Press, 1991), 241–320, 417–22.

28. Cohen, *Braceros*, 22.

29. Enrique Cárdenas, "Mexico's Industrialization during the Great Depression: Public Policy and Private Response," *Journal of Economic History* 44, no. 2 (June 1984): 603–5; Enrique Cárdenas, *La industrialización mexicana durante la Gran Depresión* (Colegio de México, 1987), 111–76.

30. Bianca Torres Ramírez, *Historia de la Revolución Mexicana, 1940–1952: Hacia la utopía industrial* (Colegio de México, 1984), 93–120.

31. Rosas, *Abrazando el Espíritu*, 21–22.

32. Roosevelt, "Eight Hundred and Fifty-Third Press Conference," 428.

33. Alicia Lemus Jiménez, "Migración en la Sierra P'urhépecha a los Estados Unidos de Norte América durante la primera y segunda etapa del programa bracero, 1942–1954" (PhD diss., Universidad Iberoamericana, 2012), 32–34, 66–67, 98. See also media coverage: "Braceros testarudos," *El Imparcial*, April 3, 1946; "Continúa el espectáculo de braceros," *El Imparcial*, August 9, 1949; "Comienza el registro de braceros," *El Imparcial*, August 16, 1949; "Como reses llevan a Mexicali a los braceros del sur," *El Imparcial*, September 11, 1951.

34. Peter L. Reich, *Mexico's Hidden Revolution: The Catholic Church in Law and Politics since 1929* (University of Notre Dame Press, 1995), 55–93; Leslie Bethell, ed., *Mexico since Independence* (Cambridge University Press, 1991), 255–56.

35. "Todos propietarios y no todos proletarios, pide la Iglesia," *Excélsior*, May 18, 1951. Unless otherwise noted, all translations are my own.

36. Eugenia de Lara Rangel, "De la dispersión a la unificación del movimiento obrero: La fundación de la CTM, 1933–1936"; Blanca Margarita Acedo Angulo, "En la construcción y consolidación del Estado cardenista, 1936–1940"; Virginia López Villegas, "En el periodo de la unidad nacional y de la Segunda Guerra Mundial, 1940–1946"; and Luisa Mussot López y Guadalupe González Cruz, "En la posguerra: Reestructuración de la CTM y formación de un nuevo proyecto sindical, 1947–1952," all in *Historia de la CTM, 1936–2006: El movimiento obrero y el Estado mexicano*, ed. Javier Aguilar García (Universidad Nacional Autónoma de México, 2009).

37. Gareth A. Jones, "Dismantling the Ejido: A Lesson in Controlled Pluralism," in *Dismantling the Mexican State?*, ed. Rob Aitken, Nikki Craske, Gareth E. Jones, and David E. Stansfield (Palgrave Macmillan, 1996).

38. "16,000 braceros rechazaron ofertas de trabajo en su patria," *Excélsior*, June 5, 1951.

39. "16,000 braceros rechazaron ofertas de trabajo en su patria," *Excélsior*, June 5, 1951.

40. Harvey Levenstein, "Sindicalismo norteamericano, braceros y 'espaldas mojadas,'" *Historia Mexicana* 28, no. 2 (December 1978): 153–84; Tasuku Todayama, "Transnational Labor Activism against Migrant Labor: The Post–World War II US-Mexican Labor Alliance for Border Control," *Japanese Journal of American Studies*, no. 23 (2012): 163–83.

41. Cynthia Hewitt de Alcántara and Félix Blanco, *La modernización de la agricultura mexicana, 1940–1970* (Siglo Veintiuno, 1978); Roger Bartra, *Estructura agraria y clases sociales en México* (Universidad Nacional Autónoma de México, Instituto de Investigaciones Sociales, 1974), 1–20; Susan R. Walsh Anderson, *Land Reform in Mexico, 1910–1980* (Academic Press, 1984), 51–102; Salomón Eckstein, *El ejido colectivo en México* (Fondo de Cultura Económica, 1966), 31–62.

42. "La CNC contra la salida de brazos," *El Nacional*, July 26, 1949.

43. "Se oponen a que salgan más braceros," *El Sol de León*, August 30, 1948.

44. María Teresa Fernández Aceves, "Política y ciudadanía: El liderazgo de María Guadalupe Urzúa en la Confederación Nacional Campesina, 1953–1957," *Relaciones Estudios de Historia y Sociedad* 38, no. 149 (March 2017): 88–92.

45. Elisa Servín, "A golpes de autoritarismo: La Unión de Federaciones Campesinas de México, un intento fallido de organización rural independiente," *Historia y Grafía*, no. 37 (July–December 2011): 23–24.

46. Catherine Vézina, "Consideraciones transnacionales sobre la gestión del Programa Bracero, 1946–1952," *Relaciones*, no. 146 (Spring 2016): 224–26.

47. David Yetman, "Ejidos, Land Sales, and Free Trade in Northwest Mexico," *American Studies* 41, no. 2–3 (Summer–Fall 2000): 217.

48. Catherine Vézina, "Consideraciones transnacionales," 226–28.

49. Telegram of the Asociación Agrícola del Valle de Mexicali to President Manuel Ávila Camacho, February 12, 1944, exp. 546.6/120-2, caja 793, FMAC, AGN; telegram of the Algodonera del Valle to President Ávila Camacho, February 20, 1944, exp. 546.6/120-1, caja 793, FMAC, AGN; telegram of the Asociación de Cosecheros Matamoros to President Ávila Camacho, April 9, 1944, exp. 546.6/120-1, caja 793, FMAC, AGN; telegram of the Asociación Nacional de Cosecheros to President Ávila Camacho, April 30, 1944, exp. 546.6/120-1, caja 793, FMAC, AGN; telegram from Regino and Bonifacio Avilés to President Ávila Camacho, exp. 548.1/19, caja 803, FMAC, AGN.

50. See note 49.

51. Letter from José Davalos Álvarez and José G. Sánchez Gutiérrez to President Ávila Camacho, July 8, 1943, exp. 546.6/120-1, caja 793, FMAC, AGN. The two were business leaders complaining about the loss of hundreds of men in Jalisco. See also letter from Damian López to President Ávila Camacho, September 3, 1944, exp. 546.6/120-1, caja 793, FMAC, AGN; "Los industriales no desean salgan ya braceros mexicanos para los EEUU," *El Nacional*, February 13, 1946.

52. Letter from Eduardo López to President Miguel Alemán, September 9, 1948; letter from Omar Medina to President Alemán, October 17, 1949; letter from Sebastián Arellano

to President Alemán, October 27, 1949; letter from Raúl Chávez to President Alemán, October 29, 1949; letter from Óscar Castro to President Alemán, November 2, 1949; letter from Julio Suárez to President Alemán, August 19, 1950; letter from Sebastián Martínez to President Alemán, August 24, 1950, 402.6/1, Fondo Miguel Alemán, AGN.

53. Letter from Rodolfo Sifuentes, Elario Vazques, and twenty-six undersigned migrants to President Alemán, November 2, 1949; follow-up letter with thirty-two undersigned migrants, November 17, 1949; letter from Severino Meza and thirteen undersigned migrants to President Alemán, November 7, 1949; letter from José Carranza, Heriberto Gonzales and sixty-two undersigned migrants to President Alemán, November 8, 1949; telegram from Javier Mendieta and eight undersigned migrants to President Alemán, November 8, 1949, 326.6/2, Fondo Miguel Alemán, AGN.

54. "Hasta en el país hay exceso de braceros," *El Informador,* June 19, 1951.

55. David Fitzgerald, "Inside the Sending State: The Politics of Mexican Emigration Control," *International Migration Review* 40, no. 2 (2006): 275.

56. Fitzgerald, "Inside the Sending State," 273.

57. Fitzgerald, "Inside the Sending State," 275.

58. David Skerritt, "Máscara contra cabellera: La migración de veracruzanos a Estados Unidos en perspectiva histórica," in *In God We Trust: Del campo mexicano al sueño americano,* ed. Rosio Cordova, María Cristina Núñez, and David Skerritt (Plaza y Valdés, 2007); David Skerritt, "Braceros veracruzanos durante la Segunda Guerra Mundial," *Ulúa: Revista de Historia, Sociedad y Cultura,* no. 9 (2015): 221.

59. Fitzgerald, "Inside the Sending State," 275.

60. Galarza details NAWU's work in this domain in Ernesto Galarza, *Farm Labor and Agri-business in California* (University of Notre Dame Press, 1977). Galarza's papers at Stanford University include an exhaustive collection of the articles he generated. See subseries A, box 1, folder 8.

61. Gabrielle Morris, *The Burning Light: Action and Organizing in the Mexican Community in California* (Berkeley Regional Oral History Office, 1982). This is a transcript of various recordings of Galarza, including an oral history.

62. Mexican newspapers became a sort of public logbook of abuses against migrants. Rather than attempt a chronology of all major Mexican periodicals, I provide here a sampling of articles from just one newspaper operating out of the major sending state of Jalisco. The abuses operative in the BP are made clear in the articles, sometimes by the title alone. See "La odisea de un bracero," *El Informador,* June 17, 1944; "Comentarios al día," *El Informador,* December 21, 1944; "Devaneos en Pepián," *El Informador,* December 23, 1944; "Contratos que no aceptan," *El Informador,* November 4, 1945; "Otro escandaloso fraude a los braceros," *El Informador,* March 12, 1945; "En espera de los braceros," *El Informador,* April 2, 1946; "Braceros defraudados," *El Informador,* May 1, 1946; "Reflexiones de un bracero," *El Informador,* March 22, 1947; "No entrará ni un mexicano más al Estado de Texas, EEUU," *El Informador,* September 27, 1947; "Deficiencias en los transportes de mexicanos," *El Informador,* October 7, 1948; "Mexicano discriminado," *El Informador,* October 7, 1948; "El asunto de los braceros," *El Informador,* August 10, 1949; "Vejaciones y trato de animales reciben los braceros," *El Informador,* June 7, 1951; and "El caso de Calexico, California," *El Informador,* May 18, 1950. The dog food story comes from "Carne de perro para nuestros braceros," *El Imparcial,* October 2, 1951.

63. Letter from Adela S. de Vento to President Adolfo Ruiz Cortines, June 8, 1953, exp. 548.1/122, FARC, AGN. See also Cynthia Orozco, *No Mexicans, Women, or Dogs Allowed: The Rise of the Mexican American Civil Rights Movement* (University of Texas Press, 2009), 201. Roberto Cintli Rodríguez, *Adela Sloss-Vento: Writer, Political Activist, and Civil Rights Pioneer* (Hamilton, 2017).

64. Telegram from the Mexican American Labor Committee to President Cortines, May 9, 1953, exp. 548.1/122, FARC, AGN.

65. Letter from Antonio Díaz Soto y Gama to President Cortines, June 12, 1953, exp. 548.1/122, FARC, AGN.

66. *El hombre sin patria*, dir. Miguel Contreras Torres (Mexico City: Producciones Contreras Torres, 1922).

67. *Adiós mi chaparrita*, dir. René Cardona (Mexico City: Central Cinematográfica Mexicana, 1939).

68. *El hijo desobediente*, dir. Humberto Gómez Landero (Mexico City: AS Films Producciones Grovas, 1944); *Hay muertos que no hacen ruido*, dir. Humberto Gómez Landero (Mexico City: AS Films Producciones Grovas, 1946); *El niño perdido*, dir. Humberto Gómez Landero (Mexico City: AS Films Producciones Grovas, 1947); *Músico, poeta y loco*, dir. Humberto Gómez Landero (Mexico City: AS Films Producciones Grovas, 1946).

69. *Primero soy mexicano*, dir. Joaquín Pardavé (Mexico City: Mitchell Camera, 1950); *Yo soy mexicano acá de este lado*, dir. Miguel Contreras Torres (Mexico City: Hispano Continental Films, 1951); *Acá las tortas*, dir. Juan Bustillo Oro (Mexico City: Cinematografía Grovas, 1951).

70. *Espaldas mojadas*, dir. Alejandro Galindo (Mexico City: ATA Films, 1955). See also Carlos Monsiváis, *Historia mínima: La cultura mexicana en el siglo XX* (Universidad Nacional Autónoma de México, 2012), 269.

71. Eduardo de la Vega Alfaro, *Cine, política y censura en la era del Milagro Mexicano* (Universidad de Guadalajara, Centro Universitario de Ciencias Sociales y Humanidades, 2017). Alfaro uses *Espaldas mojadas* as one of four film case studies to show how the Mexican state used censorship to exert its hegemony over the booming popularity of Mexican cinema in the 1950s.

72. Carlos González de León, *El cancionero de Pedro Infante* (Publirama, 2002). The memory of Pedro Infante's song as an "anthem" among migrants is from José Piedad Melgoza, *El bracero* (Universidad Autónoma de Nuevo León, 2003), 6.

73. See Ernesto Galarza, *Farm Workers and Agri-business in California, 1947–1960* (University of Notre Dame Press, 1977), 154–59.

74. For an account of interruptions to the BP prior to 1954, see Foley, *Mexicans*, 132–36.

CHAPTER TWO

1. Neil Foley, *Mexicans in the Making of America* (Harvard University Press, 2014), 132–36.

2. Mae Ngai, *Impossible Subjects: Illegal Aliens and the Making of Modern America* (Princeton University Press, 2004), 145–46, 153–54; Deborah Kang, *INS on the Line: Making Immigration Law on the US-Mexico Border, 1917–1954* (Oxford University Press, 2017),

cover, 150–51; David Fitzgerald, *A Nation of Emigrants: How Mexico Manages Its Migration* (University of California Press, 2008), 1–2; Kelly Lytle Hernández, *Migra! A History of the US Border Patrol* (University of California Press, 2010), 145–46; Don Mitchell, *They Saved the Crops: Labor, Landscape, and the Struggle over Industrial Farming in Bracero-Era California* (University of Georgia Press, 2012), 232–40.

3. Deborah Cohen, "Caught in the Middle: The Mexican State's Relationship with the United States and Its Own Citizen-Workers, 1942–1954," *Journal of American Ethnic History* 20, no. 3 (Spring 2001): 119–20. President Cortines is described as merely trying to "diffuse" the situation of angry migrants held up at the border.

4. Antonio García de León, "La otra guerra: La invasión norteamericana a Veracruz en 1914," *Jornadas de Historia de Occidente*, no. 36, 87–94; Charles C. Cumberland, "Huerta y Carranza ante la ocupación de Veracruz," *Historia mexicana* 6, no. 4 (1957): 534–47.

5. Enrique Krauze, *El sexenio de Adolfo Ruiz Cortines* (Clío, 1999), 7–9; John M. Hart, "U.S. Military Involvement in the Mexican Revolution," in *The Oxford Companion to American Military History* (Oxford University Press, 1999), 432.

6. Charles H. Weston, "The Political Legacy of Lázaro Cárdenas," *The Americas* 39, no. 3 (1983): 383–405; Ben Fallaw, *Cárdenas Compromised: The Failure of Reform in Postrevolutionary Yucatán* (Duke University Press, 2001), 1–5, 130–52.

7. Friedrich E. Schuler, "Francisco Múgica," in *Encyclopedia of Mexico*, vol. 2 (Fitzroy and Dearborn, 1997), 975.

8. María Soledad Loaeza, "Ruiz Cortines y Eisenhower: Diálogo de sordos," *Nexos*, October 1, 2014. Mugica's granddaughter recounted that the stain of collaboration with the United States never quite left Cortines. Meanwhile, for Mugica, the prospect of seeing Cortines in office was revolting, partly because he felt his moderateness represented the death-knell of the revolution, but also because he truly believed Cortines to be a traitor. This brought him close to staging a coup. He gathered thousands in a theater in Baja California, rallying to remove Cortines from office, after allegations spread that Cortines, on top of it all, had won through corrupt dealings. Calmer heads prevailed, though resentments endured. Daniel Blancas Magrigal, "Mugica, el constituyente que atemorizaba a los políticos tradicionales," *La Crónica de Hoy*, May 2, 2017.

9. Julio Moreno, *Yankee Don't Go Home! Mexican Nationalism, American Business Culture, and the Shaping of Modern Mexico, 1920–1950* (University of North Carolina Press, 2003).

10. Laura Moye, "The United States Intervention in Guatemala," *International Social Science Review* 73, no. 1–2 (1998): 44–52; Frederick W. Marks III, "The CIA and Castillo Armas in Guatemala, 1954: New Clues to an Old Puzzle," *Diplomatic History* 14, no. 1 (1990): 67–86.

11. Enrique Krauze, *Mexico: Biography of Power. A History of Modern Mexico, 1810–1996* (Harper Collins, 1997), 622–23; Frank Brandeburg, *The Making of Modern Mexico* (Prentice-Hall, 1964), 336–37. Brandeburg narrates how Mexico adopted an "absolutist" position on the matter of US intervention in the Americas and on the meaning of self-determination, seeing even the most minimal meddling as a serious violation. For records of the Mexican government tracking the situation in Guatemala, including the actions and opinions of Mexicans supportive of Guatemala, see exp. 583.1/3, FARC, AGN.

12. Loaeza, "Ruiz Cortines y Eisenhower."

13. "Vale más la Vida de un Animal que de un Bracero: Angustiosa Queja de Compatriotas," *El Heraldo*, June 29, 1953.

14. For more information on this story, and the general conditions of Mexicans in the United States and their relevance to diplomatic disputes between the United States and Mexico, see Brandenburg, *Making of Modern Mexico*, 336–37.

15. José Lázaro Salinas, "La emigración de braceros: Visión objetiva de un problema mexicano," in *Braceros: Las miradas mexicana y estadounidense, antología (1945–1964)*, ed. Jorge Durand (Universidad de Zacatecas, 2007), 287.

16. "Las puertas están abiertas para nuevas gestiones, pero sobre las bases fijadas por el Gobierno," *El Imparcial*, January 18, 1954.

17. "México suspende el envío de braceros," *La opinión*, January 17, 1954.

18. Enrique Krauze, *Mexico: Biography of Power. A History of Modern Mexico, 1810–1996* (Harper Perennial, 1998), 609. The radio show was called *Hora Nacional* (National hour) and began officially in 1937 under the Department of Press and Propaganda. The program aired on Sundays at 10 p.m.

19. Notification issued by the governor of Jalisco, Agustín Yáñez, to municipal presidents, January 19, 1954, leg. 8, 9, exp. 548.1/122, FARC, AGN.

20. These responses can be found in exp. 545.3/98, FMAC, AGN.

21. Alexandra Délano, *Mexico and Its Diaspora in the United States: Policies of Emigration since 1848* (Cambridge University Press, 2011), 72; Letitia Calderón Chelius, foreword to *They Should Stay There: The Story of Mexican Migration and Repatriation during the Great Depression*, by Fernando Saúl Alanís Enciso, translated by Russ Davidson (University of North Carolina Press, 2017), xix.

22. "Unificación nacional con el presidente: Todos los grupos sociales y políticos se solidarizan," *El Imparcial de Sonora*, January 18, 1954.

23. Telegram from José Cruz Contreras, president of the PRI's Regional Executive Committee, and Carlos Caballero, president of PRI's Municipal Committee, to Mexican president Adolfo Ruiz Cortines, January 18, 1954, leg. 1, 2, exp. 548.1/122, FARC, AGN.

24. Letter from Alberto Gómez Garduño to President Cortines, January 16, 1954, leg. 1, 2, exp. 548.1/122, FARC, AGN.

25. Letter from Celso Zacarías Daniel, General Secretariat of Council of Small Businesses Number 12 in Guadalajara, Jalisco, to President Cortines, January 23, 1954, leg. 6, 7, exp. 548.1/122, FARC, AGN.

26. Letter from Gaudencio Limón Segura, on behalf of Central Military Hospital, Urology Department, to President Cortines, January 19, 1954, leg. 3, exp. 548.1/122, FARC, AGN; letter from Jefatura, Mexican Air Force, to President Cortines, January 20, 1954, leg. 6, 7, exp. 548.1/122, FARC, AGN.

27. Letter from *Excélsior* journalists to President Cortines, January 18, 1954, leg. 1, 2, exp. 548.1/122, FARC, AGN.

28. Letter from *Novedades* journalists to President Cortines, January 18, 1954, leg. 1, 2, exp. 548.1/122, FARC, AGN.

29. Letter from Cadena García Valseca [newspaper company] journalists to President Cortines, January 18, 1954, leg. 1, 2, exp. 548.1/122, FARC, AGN.

30. Letter from Salvador Azuela to President Cortines, January 19, 1954, leg. 3, exp. 548.1/122, FARC, AGN.

31. Letter from Guillermo Ruiz V. to President Cortines, January 21, 1954, leg. 4, exp. 548.1/122, FARC, AGN.

32. Letter from Artemisa Xochitl Sáenz to President Cortines, January 20, 1954, leg. 3, exp. 548.1/122, FARC, AGN.

33. Letter from Juan Sánchez Terán and President Blas Freyre García, on behalf of Defensores de Veracruz, to President Cortines, January 22, 1954, leg. 5, exp. 548.1/122, FARC, AGN.

34. Telegram from Col. Aniceto López Salazar to President Cortines, January 21, 1954, leg. 4, exp. 548.1/122, FARC, AGN.

35. Telegram from Sociedad de Padres de Familia Escuela DF Sarmiento to President Cortines, January 17, 1954, leg. 3, exp. 548.1/122, FARC, AGN.

36. Telegram from Federación de Estudiantes de Guadalajara to President Cortines, January 16, 1954, leg. 3, exp. 548.1/122, FARC, AGN.

37. Telegram from Comité Nacional de la Confederación Jóvenes Mexicanos to President Cortines, January 16, 1954, leg. 3, exp. 548.1/122, FARC, AGN.

38. Telegram from student body at the Universidad Nacional Autónoma de México, to President Cortines, January 27, 1954, leg. 6, 7, exp. 548.1/122, FARC, AGN.

39. Telegram from Federación Organizaciones Populares Jalisco to President Cortines, January 19, 1954, leg. 3, exp. 548.1/122, FARC, AGN.

40. Hubert C. de Grammont, "Los empresarios también se organizan: La Unión Nacional de Cosecheros," in *Historia de la cuestión agraria mexicana: Política estatal y conflictos agrarios, 1950–1970*, ed. Julio Moguel (Impresa Siglo, 1989).

41. Telegram from Alberto Salinas Ramos, president of the Asociación Nacional de Cosecheros, to President Cortines, January 14, 1954, leg. 1, 2, exp. 548.1/122, FARC, AGN.

42. Letter from Alberto Salinas Ramos, president of the Asociación Nacional de Cosecheros, to President Cortines, January 15, 1954, leg. 1, 2, exp. 548.1/122, FARC, AGN.

43. Letter from municipal president José Zertuche to President Cortines, on behalf of Cámara Agrícola Ganadera del Norte de Coahuila, January 22, 1954, leg. 5, exp. 548.1/122, FARC, AGN.

44. Telegram from Confederación de Asociaciones Agrícolas del Estado de Sinaloa to President Cortines, January 20, 1954, leg. 4, exp. 548.1/122, FARC, AGN.

45. Telegram from Cámara de Comercio de Hermosillo to President Cortines, January 20, 1954, leg. 5, exp. 548.1/122, FARC, AGN.

46. Telegram from Trabajadores de Recursos Hidráulicos to President Cortines, January 21, 1954, leg. 4, exp. 548.1/122, FARC, AGN.

47. Telegram from Confederación de Trabajadores de Tabasco to President Cortines, January 20, 1954, leg. 4, exp. 548.1/122, FARC, AGN.

48. Telegram from Federación Regional de Trabajadores de Soconusco to President Cortines, January 25, 1954, leg. 6, 7, exp. 548.1/122, FARC, AGN.

49. Telegram from Sindicato Minero to President Cortines, January 22, 1954, leg. 5, exp. 548.1/122, FARC, AGN.

50. Letter from Federación Revolucionaria de Obreros y Campesinos to President Cortines, January 21, 1954, leg. 6, 7, exp. 548.1/122, FARC, AGN.

51. Telegram from Federación de Trabajadores de Sinaloa to President Cortines, January 19, 1954, leg. 3, exp. 548.1/122, FARC, AGN. For other examples that illustrate these themes, see letters from Federación de Agrupaciones Obreras y Campesinas de Tijuana;

Sindicato Nacional de Trabajadores de la Educación; Comité Nacionalista Frente Único de Trabajadores del Volante; Sindicato Nacional de Azucareros de Tala, Jalisco; Local Sindicato de Petroleros; Sindicato de Plomeros y Ayudantes de Nuevo Laredo; Sindicato de Electricistas de Nuevo Laredo; Sindicato de Pintores y Ayudantes de Nuevo Laredo; Sindicato de Trabajadores Talleres Gráficos de la Nación; Trabajadores de Limpia y Transportes; Unión de Trabajadores Electricistas Federales; Alianza de Tranviarios; Trabajadores de Asistencia Puerto Veracruz; Sindicato de Pepenadores del D.F.; Manuel Segura León on behalf of Comité Nacionalista Frente Unido de Trabajadores del Volante; and Sección de Técnicos y Manuales del Sindicato de la Producción Cinematográfica to President Cortines, January 18–20, 1954, leg. 3, 4, 5, exp. 548.1/122, FARC, AGN.

52. Telegram from Comité Ejecutivo CTM to President Cortines, January 19, 1954, leg. 3, exp. 548.1/122, FARC, AGN.

53. Letter from CTM Nuevo León to President Cortines, January 18, 1954, leg. 3, exp. 548.1/122, FARC, AGN.

54. See, for instance, telegrams from CTM Sonora, CTM Tamaulipas, CTM Jalisco, CTM Sindicato Terraceros, and CTM Agrupación Sindical de Trabajadores y Empleados de los Centros Deportivos, to President Cortines, January 17–20, 1954, leg. 3, 4, exp. 548.1/122, FARC, AGN.

55. Telegram from Comité Ejecutivo, Confederación Regional Obrera Mexicana, to President Cortines, January 19, 1954, leg. 4, exp. 548.1/122, FARC, AGN.

56. Letter from CROM Puebla to President Cortines, January 25, 1954, leg. 6, 7, exp. 548.1/122, FARC, AGN.

57. Following John Womack, I generally refer to Mexicans living outside of cities as campesinos rather than peasants. As he argues, the category of peasant raises "abstract questions of class," "generally sounds exotic and suggests a creature . . . from a society essentially foreign." See John Womack, *Zapata and the Mexican Revolution* (Vintage, 1970), x.

58. Michael J. Gonzales, *The Mexican Revolution, 1910–1940* (University of New Mexico Press, 2002). Ejidos were especially hard-pressed to perform against domestic firms with financial and technological advantages, and which tended to monopolize fertile lands for themselves.

59. For an example of the Mexican state narrating the ejido and its enduring importance, see *Despertar lagunero: Libro que relata la lucha y triunfo de la Revolución en la comarca lagunera* (Sindicato y el Consejo Técnico de los Trabajadores de los Talleres Gráficos de la Nación, 1937). This photo book, with an initial publication run of 40,000 copies, narrates campesinos' move from semibondage under latifundios to "freedom" under the ejido.

60. For an example of ejidatarios' enduring idealism, see Frederick Praeger, *People in Ejidos: A Visit to the Cooperative Farms of Mexico* (International Council for Research in the Sociology of Cooperation, 1954), 127–29. The book consists of interviews with ejidatarios who extol the ejido's value. The personnel at the Banco Ejidal were supportive too, though they expressed doubts about the ejido's long-term viability. People in cities, and some high-level officials in the government, however, dismissed communal land cultivation, seeing the ejido as obscure, antiquated, and merely symbolic.

61. Telegram from Acción Política Ganadera Mexicana to President Cortines, January 19, 1954, leg. 1, 2, exp. 548.1/122, FARC, AGN.

62. Telegram from Campesinos Mexicanos Confederados to President Cortines, January 19, 1954, leg. 3, exp. 548.1/122, FARC, AGN.

63. Telegram from Liga Nacional Campesina de México to President Cortines, January 17, 1954, leg. 3, exp. 548.1/122, FARC, AGN.

64. Telegram from Campesinos Mexicanos Confederados to President Cortines, January 18, 1954, leg. 1, 2, exp. 548.1/122, FARC, AGN.

65. Telegram from Confederación Nacional de Campesinos to President Cortines, January 19, 1954, leg. 3, exp. 548.1/122, FARC, AGN.

66. Telegram from Confederación Nacional de Campesinos de Puebla to President Cortines, January 19, 1954, leg. 3, exp. 548.1/122, FARC, AGN.

67. Telegram from Confederación Nacional de Campesinos de Veracruz to President Cortines, January 19, 1954, leg. 3, exp. 548.1/122, FARC, AGN.

68. Telegram from Confederación Nacional de Campesinos de Sinaloa to President Cortines, January 20, 1954, leg. 3, exp. 548.1/122, FARC, AGN.

69. Telegram from Confederación Campesina de República Mexicana to President Cortines, January 20, 1954, leg. 3, exp. 548.1/122, FARC, AGN.

70. Telegram from Federación Nacional de Granjeros to President Cortines, January 19, 1954, leg. 3, exp. 548.1/122, FARC, AGN.

71. Telegram from Liga Nacional Campesina to President Cortines, January 17, 1954.

72. Telegram from Coalición de Agrupaciones Revolucionarias to President Cortines, January 21, 1954, leg. 6, 7, exp. 548.1/122, FARC, AGN.

73. Telegram from Ejidos Confederados to President Cortines, January 20, 1954, leg. 5, exp. 548.1/122, FARC, AGN.

74. Letter from the Federación Nacional de Agrupaciones Campesinas de México to President Cortines, January 18, 1954, leg. 1, 2, exp. 548.1/122, FARC, AGN.

75. Letter from the Comité Municipal de Defensa Revolucionaria of La Barca, Jalisco, to President Cortines, January 23, 1954, leg. 6, 7, exp. 548.1/122, FARC, AGN.

76. Armando Gonzales Santos, *Estructura económica y social de México: La agricultura* (Nacional Financiera, 1957), 138–39.

77. Letter from the Coalición de Grupos Revolucionarios to President Cortines, January 19, 1954, leg. 3, exp. 548.1/122, FARC, AGN.

78. Letter from Comité Regional Campesino to President Cortines, January 23, 1954, leg. 8, 9, exp. 548.1/122, FARC, AGN.

79. Letter from Ignacio Sánchez Ruiz, Antonio Ruiz Castellanos, and Enrique Rosado to President Cortines, January 19, 1954; internal memo, Office of the Presidency, regarding the Ruiz, Castellanos, and Rosado letter, January 20, 1954; letter from Undersecretary to the President Benito Coquet to Secretary of Foreign Affairs Luis Padilla Nervo, January 22, 1954, leg. 4, exp. 548.1/122, FARC, AGN. See also letter from Melitón Cabrera to President Cortines, January 20, 1954; letter from José Pérez to President Cortines, January 20, 1954; and letter from Antonio Vizcarra Espinosa to President Cortines, January 23, 1954, leg. 6, 7, exp. 548.1/122, FARC, AGN.

CHAPTER THREE

1. Letter from Deputy (Representative) Jacobo Aragán Aquillón to President Adolfo Ruiz Cortines, January 19, 1954, leg. 3, exp. 548.1/122, FARC, AGN.

2. Letter from Deputy Jesús María Suárez to President Cortines, January 18, 1954, leg. 1,2, exp. 548.1/122, FARC, AGN.

3. Letter from Deputy Emmanuel Palacios to President Cortines, January 17, 1954, leg. 3, exp. 548.1/122, FARC, AGN.

4. Letter from Deputy Pedro Ayala Fajardo to President Cortines, January 17, 1954, leg. 3, exp. 548.1/122, FARC, AGN.

5. Letter from Senator Miguel Osorio Ramírez to President Cortines, January 16, 1954, leg. 3, exp. 548.1/122, FARC, AGN.

6. Telegram from Congreso del Estado de Campeche to President Cortines, January 20, 1954, leg. 4, exp. 548.1/122, FARC, AGN; telegram from Poder Legislativo de Tlaxcala to President Cortines, January 20, 1954, leg. 4, exp. 548.1/122, FARC, AGN.

7. Letter from Comité Ejecutivo Regional del PRI, Mexico City, to President Cortines, January 18, 1954, leg. 1, 2, exp. 548.1/122, FARC, AGN.

8. Letter from Comité Ejecutivo Regional del PRI, Culiacán, Sinaloa, to President Cortines, January 18, 1954, leg. 1, 2, exp. 548.1/122, FARC, AGN.

9. Letter from Román Cepeda Flores, governor of Coahuila, to President Cortines, January 19, 1954, leg. 3, exp. 548.1/122, FARC, AGN.

10. Letter from Ignacio Soto, governor of Sonora, to President Cortines, January 19, 1954, leg. 5, exp. 548.1/122, FARC, AGN.

11. See telegram from Agustín Yáñez, governor of Jalisco, to President Cortines, January 18, 1954, leg. 1, 2, exp. 548.1/122, FARC, AGN.

12. Letter from Melchor Ruiz, president of the Consejo Municipal of San Juan Evangelista, to President Cortines, dated January 18, 1954, leg. 1, 2, exp. 548.1/122, FARC, AGN.

13. Letter from Efraín Aranda Osorio, governor of Chiapas, to President Cortines, January 20, 1954, leg. 5, exp. 548.1/122, FARC, AGN.

14. Letter from Víctor Meno Palomo, governor of Yucatán, to President Cortines, January 19, 1954, leg. 5, exp. 548.1/122, FARC, AGN.

15. Letter from Manuel Bartlett Bautista, governor of Tabasco, to President Cortines, January 20, 1954, leg. 5, exp. 548.1/122, FARC, AGN.

16. Telegram from Braulio Maldonado, governor of Baja California, to President Cortines, January 19, 1954, leg. 1, 2, exp. 548.1/122, FARC, AGN.

17. Telegram from Col. Manuel Durán to President Cortines, January 19, 1954, leg. 3, exp. 548.1/122, FARC, AGN.

18. Telegram from Gen. Eduardo G. García to President Cortines, January 20, 1954, leg. 3, exp. 548.1/122, FARC, AGN.

19. Telegram from Pacheco Iturribaria to President Cortines, January 18, 1954, leg. 1, 2, exp. 548.1/122, FARC, AGN.

20. Telegram from Gen. Valle Jordán to President Cortines, January 19, 1954, leg. 3, exp. 548.1/122, FARC, AGN.

21. Telegram from Partido Popular to President Cortines, January 19, 1954, leg. 4, exp. 548.1/122, FARC, AGN.

22. Telegram from Partido Social Integralista to President Cortines, January 20, 1954, leg. 4, exp. 548.1/122, FARC, AGN.

23. Telegram from Partido Político Nacionalista de México to President Cortines, January 19, 1954, leg. 4, exp. 548.1/122, FARC, AGN.

24. Abraham Pérez López, *Diccionario biográfico hidalguense*, vol. 3 (Gobierno del Estado de Hidalgo, 2010), 177–78.

25. Letter from Bartolomé Vargas Lugo to President Cortines, January 13, 1954, leg. 1, 2, exp. 548.1/122, FARC, AGN.

26. Letter from Bartolomé Vargas Lugo.

27. María del Carmen Zetina Rodríguez, Rutilio García Pereyra, and Efraín Rangel Guzmán, "Administración del agua y los recursos de la nación: La Junta Federal de Mejoras Materiales, Ciudad Juárez, Chihuahua, 1931–1936," *Región y sociedad* 29, no. 70 (September–December 2017): 103–32.

28. Letter from Eliseo L. Cespedes, president of the Junta Federal de Mejoras Materiales, Nuevo Laredo, Tamaulipas, to President Cortines, January 16, 1954, leg. 1, 2, exp. 548.1/122, FARC, AGN.

29. Letter from A. N. Molina Enríquez to President Cortines, January 16, 1954, leg. 11, 12, exp. 548.1/122, FARC, AGN.

30. Pedro de Alba, "Siete artículos sobre el problema de los braceros," in *Braceros: Las miradas mexicana y estadounidense, antología (1945–1964)*, ed. Jorge Durand (Universidad de Zacatecas, 2007).

31. Internal memo, Office of the Presidency, white paper for proposed Colonizing Commission, January 21, 1954, leg. 1, 2, exp. 548.1/122, FARC, AGN.

32. White paper for proposed Colonizing Commission.

33. "México suspende el envío de braceros," *La Opinión*, January 17, 1954.

34. Braulio Maldonado, *Baja California: Comentarios políticos y otras obras selectas* (Universidad Autónoma de Baja California, 2006), 196.

35. Maldonado, *Baja California*, 212.

36. Maldonado, *Baja California*, 213.

37. Maldonado, *Baja California*, 214.

38. Maldonado, *Baja California*, 214.

39. Telegram from Braulio Maldonado, governor of Baja California, to President Cortines, January 19, 1954, leg. 1, 2, exp. 548.1/122, FARC, AGN.

40. See telegram from Agustín Yáñez, governor of Jalisco, to President Cortines, January 18, 1954, leg. 1, 2, exp. 548.1/122, FARC, AGN; notification issued by Agustín Yáñez, governor of Jalisco, to municipal presidents, January 19, 1954, leg. 8, 9, exp. 548.1/122, FARC, AGN.

41. "La fuerza militar vigila," *El Informador*, January 24, 1954.

42. Letter from US acting secretary of labor to US assistant secretary of state John Cabot, October 1, 1953, file 18, box 1, RG 154, National Archives and Records Administration, College Park, Maryland. The letter summarizes the DOL's disagreements with Mexico. Its insights are important because the box pertaining to the DOL's handling of the 1954 BP lapse was disposed of "erroneously" in 1973.

43. The system of joint deliberations is described in Richard B. Craig, *The Bracero Program: Interest Groups and Foreign Policy* (University of Texas Press, 1971), 71, 80, 88–89, 106.

44. Letter from US acting secretary of labor to Cabot, October 1, 1953.

45. Letter from US acting secretary of labor to Cabot, October 1, 1953.

46. Letter from US acting secretary of labor to Cabot, October 1, 1953.

47. Letter from US acting secretary of labor to Cabot, October 1, 1953.
48. Letter from US acting secretary of labor to Cabot, October 1, 1953.
49. Letter from US acting secretary of labor to Cabot, October 1, 1953.
50. Letter from US acting secretary of labor to Cabot, October 1, 1953.
51. Letter from US acting secretary of labor to Cabot, October 1, 1953.
52. "Dos aspectos de un problema," *La Opinión*, January 26, 1954.
53. "Estados Unidos quiere a braceros mexicanos a como dé lugar," *La Opinión*, January 13, 1954.
54. "Retención de braceros," *El Informador*, January 22, 1954.
55. "Mexicans Hold Labor Recruiters," *Oxnard Press Courier*, February 4, 1954.
56. "EE.UU. abrió," *El Informador*, January 24, 1954.
57. "La fuerza militar vigila," *El Informador*, January 24, 1954.
58. "El nuevo 'contrato,'" *El informador*, January 22, 1954.
59. "Mexico suspende el envío de braceros," *La Opinión*, January 17, 1954.
60. "Ha perjudicado la emigración de los braceros," *El Informador*, January 24, 1954.
61. "Causa impresión lo de la entrada libre de braceros," *La Opinión*, January 24, 1954.
62. "Planes para la industrialización," *La Opinión*, January 23, 1954.
63. "Una labor de convencimiento," *La Opinión*, January 23, 1954.
64. "No debe salir ni un campesino," *La Opinión*, January 23, 1954.
65. "Impedirán la emigración," *La Opinión*, January 23, 1954.
66. "Evitarán la emigración de braceros a E.U. con amplios créditos y trabajos," *La Opinión*, January 25, 1954.
67. "Evitarán la emigración."
68. "Evitarán la emigración."
69. "Solución de grave problema," *La Opinión*, January 25, 1954.
70. "Dos aspectos de un problema."
71. "Braceros contratados," *El Informador*, January 24, 1954.
72. Maldonado, *Baja California*, 212.
73. Gabriela Cardoso Morayla, "El Programa Bracero en el municipio de Uruapan y su impacto socioeconómico, 1942–1964" (PhD diss., Universidad Michoacana de San Nicolás de Hidalgo, 2010), 142.
74. Adolfo González, interview by Rochelle Garza, May 24, 2006, "Interview no. 1295," Institute of Oral History, University of Texas at El Paso, http://digitalcommons.utep.edu/cgi/viewcontent.cgi?article=2307&context=interviews.
75. Alfonso Ceja, interview by Adriana Sandoval, May 20, 2006, "Interview no. 349," Institute of Oral History, University of Texas at El Paso, http://braceroarchive.org/es/items/show/349?view=full.
76. Adolfo González interview.
77. Maldonado, *Baja California*, 210.
78. Morayla, "Programa Bracero," 145.
79. "La fuerza militar vigila," *El Informador*, January 24, 1954.
80. "Baja California puede dar acomodo a miles y miles de trabajadores agrícolas," *La Opinión*, January 24, 1954.
81. "No hubo paso por Calexico," *El Informador*, January 24, 1954.
82. "Braceros contratados," *El Informador*, January 24, 1954.

83. "Border in Riot as Braceros Fight Troops," *Victoria Advocate*, January 24, 1954.

84. Bob Porter, interview by Beth Morgan, March 6, 2003, "Interview no. 1565," Institute of Oral History, University of Texas at El Paso, https://scholarworks.utep.edu/interviews/1565.

85. Bob Porter interview.

86. "Demanda braceril," *Excélsior*, January 24, 1954.

87. "Detienen la emigración de braceros," *La Opinión*, January 25, 1954.

88. Loret de Mola, "El feudalismo nuevo," *La Opinión*, January 23, 1954.

89. "Pero pasó" *La Opinión*, January 27, 1954.

90. "Pero pasó."

91. Juan Sánchez Abasta, interview by Violeta Mena, May 28, 2005, "Interview no. 67," Institute of Oral History, University of Texas at El Paso, http://braceroarchive.org/items/show/67.

92. "Border Guard on Alert," *Prescott Evening Courier*, January 28, 1954.

93. "La avalancha braceril," *La Opinión*, February 2, 1954.

94. "Otro tumulto de braceros en Mexicali," *La Opinión*, February 2, 1954.

95. "9,000 asaltaron la frontera con EEUU," *La Opinión*, February 3, 1954.

96. Note from US ambassador Francis White to Undersecretary of Foreign Affairs José Gorostiza, March 10, 1954, box 1, file 5, RG 174, National Archives and Records Administration, College Park, Maryland.

CHAPTER FOUR

1. Max Paul Friedman, "Reciprocity in Mexican Relations with the United States: Past Indicators of Future Dilemmas," *Mexican Law Review* 6, no. 2 (January–June 2014): 314–15; Max Paul Friedman, "Fracas in Caracas: Latin American Diplomatic Resistance to United States Intervention in Guatemala in 1954," *Diplomacy & Statecraft* 21, no. 4 (December 2010): 669–89.

2. Piero Gleijeses, *Shattered Hope: The Guatemalan Revolution and the United States, 1944–1954* (Princeton University Press, 1992); Greg Grandin, *The Last Colonial Massacre: Latin America in the Cold War* (University of Chicago Press, 2004).

3. Letter from Ambassador Francis White to US president Dwight D. Eisenhower, August 29, 1955, MS 194, box 11, series III, Francis White Papers, Sheridan Libraries Special Collections, John Hopkins University, Baltimore, MD. The letter summarizes private conversations between Ambassador White and Mexican president Adolfo Ruiz Cortines.

4. Kelly Lytle Hernández, "The Crimes and Consequences of Illegal Immigration: A Cross-Border Examination of Operation Wetback, 1943 to 1954," *Western Historical Quarterly* 37, no. 4 (Winter 2006): 421–44; Adam Goodman, *The Deportation Machine: America's Long History of Expelling Immigrants* (Princeton University Press, 2020), 56–72; Deborah S. Kang, *INS on the Line: Making Immigration Law on the US-Mexico Border, 1917–1954* (Oxford University Press, 2017), 158–63.

5. Manuel García y Griego, *The Importation of Mexican Contract Laborers to the United States, 1942–1964* (Program in United States–Mexican Studies, University of California San Diego, 1981), 31. His temporal arc for the "demise" of Mexico's power as a migratory regulator is reproduced elsewhere. See Deborah Cohen, "Caught in the Middle: The Mexican

State's Relationship with the United States and Its Own Citizen-Workers, 1942–1954," *Journal of American Ethnic History* 20, no. 3 (Spring 2001): 115; Kelly Lytle Hernández, *Migra! A History of the US Border Patrol* (University of California Press, 2010), 194; and Mireya Loza, *Defiant Braceros: How Migrant Workers Fought for Racial, Sexual, and Political Freedom* (University of North Carolina Press, 2016), 3–4.

6. For books that show how the one-party state adapted to challenges to its absolutist, centralized rule, see Kevin J. Middlebrook, *The Paradox of Revolution: Labor, the State, and Authoritarianism in Mexico* (Johns Hopkins University Press, 1995); Jonathan Schlefer, *Palace Politics: How the Ruling Party Brought Crisis to Mexico* (University of Texas Press, 2008); Tanalís Padilla, *Rural Resistance in the Land of Zapata: The Jaramillista Movement and the Myth of the Pax Priísta, 1940–1962* (Duke University Press, 2008); Alejandro Quintana, *Maximino Ávila Camacho and the One-Party State: The Taming of Caudillismo and Caciquismo in Post-revolutionary Mexico* (Rowman and Littlefield, 2010). Paul Gillingham usefully characterizes Mexico as a "dictablanda," or soft dictatorship, in which negotiation with social groups was paramount but accompanied by the threat of state violence and punitive measures. See preface to *Dictablanda: Politics, Work, and Culture in Mexico, 1938–1968*, ed. Paul Gillingham and Benjamin Smith (Duke University Press, 2014); and Paul Gillingham, *Unrevolutionary Mexico: The Birth of a Strange Dictatorship* (Yale University Press, 2021).

7. Luis Aboites Aguilar, *El Norte entre algodones: Población, trabajo agrícola y optimismo en México, 1930–1970* (Colegio de México, 2013), 188. A recent comparative study of contracting centers within Northern Mexico, including in Sonora, likewise underlines the ascendant power of elite growers over the Mexican government in the mid-twentieth century. This narrative fails to reckon with the government's eventual decision to abandon the IBP. See Irina Córdoba Ramírez, *Desarollo agrícola y acuerdos políticos en el norte de México: Los centros de contratación del Programa Bracero, 1947–64* (Universidad Nacional Autónoma de México, 2023), 9, 159, 161, 165. Similarly, an earlier study on the IBP is focused more on understanding its mechanisms than its undoing; it is an analysis of the function, not dysfunction, of the IBP. See Sergio Chávez, "The Sonoran Desert's Domestic Bracero Programme: Institutional Actors and the Creation of Labour Migration Streams," *International Migration Review* 50, no. 2 (April 2012): 20–40.

8. Aboites Aguilar, *El Norte entre algodones*, 186.

9. Letter from Enrique Mazón on behalf of the Comité de Control de Pizcadores de Hermosillo to Treasury General of the State of Sonora, September 27, 1955, tomo 2144, exp. 321.45 "55"/5, OM-AHES. The other members of the committee included representatives from the Unión de Crédito Agrícola de Hermosillo, the Unión de Crédito Ganadero y Agrícola, the Asociación Agrícola de Hermosillo, the Asociación de Pequeños y Medianos Comerciantes de la Costa de Hermosillo, the Unión de Colonos de la Costa de Hermosillo, and one for independent growers not affiliated with any particular organizational body.

10. Letter from Sonora Industrial S.A. Planta Despepitadora "King" to Treasury General of the State of Sonora, September 24, 1955; letter from Empresas Honenberg to Treasury General of the State of Sonora, September 24, 1955; letter from Producers McFadden S.A. de C.V. to Treasury General of the State of Sonora, September 24, 1955, tomo 2144, exp. 321.45 "55"/5, OM-AHES.

11. This system is described most thoroughly in letter from Anderson, Clayton & Co., S.A. de C.V., to Treasury General of the State of Sonora, November 6, 1955, tomo 2144, exp. 321.45 "55"/5, OM-AHES.

12. Letter from Álvaro Obregón, governor of Sonora, to Treasury General of the State of Sonora, September 30, 1955, tomo 2144, exp. 321.45 "55"/5, OM-AHES; letter from Treasury General of the State of Sonora to Empresas Honenberg, July 26, 1956, tomo 2144, exp. 321.45 "55"/5, OM-AHES.

13. Letter from Anderson, Clayton & Co., S.A. de C.V., to Treasury General of the State of Sonora, November 6, 1955, tomo 2144, exp. 321.45 "55"/5, OM-AHES; letter from Sonora state fiscal agent Jesús V. Rojal to Treasury General of the State of Sonora, June 29, 1955; letter from agricultural production inspector José Abitia to Treasury General, December 5, 1955, tomo 2144, exp. 321.45 "55"/5, OM-AHES.

14. This list of activities and the money dedicated to each is described in detail in letter from Enrique Mazón, Comité de Control de Pizcadores, to Sonora governor Luis Encinas, August 1, 1962, tomo 2144, exp. 321.45 "55"/5, OM-AHES. It details how much was spent on transporting migrants, offering food to them, and printing materials to provide them with a special pass.

15. Letter from Enrique Mazón on behalf of the Comité de Control de Pizcadores to the Treasury General of the State of Sonora, September 27, 1955, tomo 2144, exp. 321.45 "55"/5, OM-AHES.

16. "Reunión entre Secretaría de Gobernación y comisión mixta de pizcadores," *El Imparcial*, September 22, 1955; "Apertura de oficina de braceros en Empalme," *El Imparcial*, September 22, 1955.

17. "Departamento de trabajo hospeda a braceros," *El Imparcial*, March 17, 1951; "Organismos privados y centrales de la región piden a Gobernación resolver el problema braceros," *El Imparcial*, March 20, 1951; "Gobernación se responsabiliza por 7,000 braceros en Hermosillo," *El Imparcial*, March 24, 1951; "Viaja Gob. Soto a CD México para atender asunto de braceros," *El Imparcial*, March 27, 1951; "Aumento de salario para pizcadores y formación de 'Comité Pro-ayuda a Braceros,'" *El Imparcial*, March 28, 1951; "Anuncio de contrataciones próximamente," *El Imparcial*, March 29, 1951; "Suspensión de cocinas públicas," *El Imparcial*, April 4, 1951; "Protesta violenta de braceros," *El Imparcial*, April 6, 1951; "Reapertura de cocinas públicas," *El Imparcial*, April 9, 1951; "Se contratan 500 braceros pero se derrumba una pared del estadio donde estaban alojados," *El Imparcial*, April 10, 1951; "Proceso de elegir braceros y quejas de migrantes," *El Imparcial*, April 11, 1951; "Se queja unión de trabajadores del valle de Mexicali por sistema de contratación," *El Imparcial*, April 12, 1951; "Sexto día sin contratación de braceros," *El Imparcial*, April 17, 1951; "Se contratan 200 hombres," *El Imparcial*, April 19, 1951; "Pelotón de soldados agrede a braceros y lesiona a tres gravemente," *El Imparcial*, April 20, 1951; "Gobierno federal paga pasaje de vuelta a migrantes que no han sido contratados," *El Imparcial*, May 3, 1951; "Escándalo por reporte en 'Novedades' que policía cobra a migrantes por darles paso," *El Imparcial*, May 8, 1951; "Contratación de braceros por agricultores sonorenses," *El Imparcial*, May 10, 1951; "Permanecen 2,500 a 3,000 aspirantes en Hermosillo," *El Imparcial*, June 21, 1951; "Fin de temporada de contratación: Quedan 1,000 aspirantes en Sonora," *El Imparcial*, July 20, 1951.

18. "Gob. Soto anuncia que Hermosillo ya no será sede de contrataciones," *El Imparcial*, July 16, 1951.

19. "Gob. Soto explica el porqué del centro de contratación en Hermosillo," *El Imparcial*, February 16, 1955; "Es muy agudo el problema de los braceros," *Heraldo del Yaqui*, March

14, 1955; "Culpan a Gobernación por concentración de braceros en Sonora," *El Imparcial*, March 17, 1955; "Pasan por angustiosa situación seis mil braceros en Hermosillo," *Heraldo del Yaqui*, March 31, 1955; "Protesta de braceros y concesión de Gob. Soto," *El Imparcial*, April 2, 1955; "Dice Ordaz no ser responsable por concentración de braceros en Hermosillo," *El Imparcial*, April 4, 1955; "Los braceros tienen una gran ayuda del gobierno," *Heraldo del Yaqui*, April 6, 1955; "E. Unidos regresa a los braceros no contratados," *Heraldo del Yaqui*, April 7, 1955; "Quince mil braceros están en Hermosillo," *Heraldo del Yaqui*, April 22, 1955; "José T. Rocha pide se traslade la oficina de contratación a otro poblado del estado," *El Imparcial*, April 30, 1955; "Fue suspendida la contratación de braceros," *Heraldo del Yaqui*, May 2, 1955; "Empalme, concentración para los braceros," *Heraldo del Yaqui*, May 3, 1955; "Funcionario de Gobernación José T. Rocha casi linchado por cierre de centro de contratación," *Heraldo del Yaqui*, May 2, 1955.

20. Letter from Sonora secretary of government Gerardo Loustaunau to municipal president of Colorado, Sonora, February 14, 1958; letter from Sonora secretary of government Gerardo Loustaunau to municipal president of Colorado, Sonora, March 10, 1958; letter from interim municipal president Enrique Islas to Governor Obregón, May 7, 1958; Nacozari, Sonora, municipal president Edmundo Perra Montaño, to Governor Obregón, March 10, 1958; memorandum from Juan Jordán, chief of contracting center in Empalme, to Sonora secretary of government, June 27, 1958, tomo 2144, exp. 321.45 "55"/5, OM-AHES.

21. "Pizcadores ya pizcan en Hermosillo bajo nuevo sistema," *El Imparcial*, January 25, 1956.

22. Telegram from Empalme municipal president Horacio Morales Apodaca to Sonora secretary of government Guillermo Acedo Romero, January 31, 1956; telegram from Empalme municipal president Horacio Morales Apodaca to Sonora secretary of government Guillermo Acedo Romero, February 6, 1956; letter from Sonora general secretary of government Rafael Moreno Enríquez to Mexican undersecretary of the interior Fernando Román Lugo, with a copy to Governor Obregón, February 8, 1956, tomo 2144, exp. 321.45 "55"/5, OM-AHES.

23. Letter from Guillermo Soberanes, head of Servicios Coordinados de Salubridad y Asistencia en el Estado de Sonora, to Governor Obregón, March 6, 1956, tomo 2144, exp. 321.45 "55"/5, OM-AHES.

24. Letter from Empalme municipal president Horacio Morales Apodaca to Sonora secretary of government Guillermo Acedo Romero, with copy to Governor Obregón, April 18, 1956, tomo 2144, exp. 321.45 "55"/5, OM-AHES.

25. Letter from Empalme municipal president Horacio Morales Apodaca to Governor Obregón, May 24, 1956, tomo 2144, exp. 321.45 "55"/5, OM-AHES.

26. Letter from Morales Apodaca to Obregón, May 24, 1956.

27. Telegram from Empalme municipal president Horacio Morales Apodaca to Governor Obregón, July 8, 1956; letter from Empalme municipal president Horacio Morales Apodac to Mario Boneta, representative of the Mexican Ministry of the Interior at the Empalme contracting center, with copy to Governor Obregón, the Sonora secretary of government, and Griffor Burr, US representative at the Empalme contracting center, July 30, 1956, tomo 2144, exp. 321.45 "55"/5, OM-AHES.

28. Letter from Empalme municipal president Horacio Morales Apodaca to Mexican secretary of the interior Ángel Carvajal, with copy to Mexican secretary of health Guillermo

Moronas Prieto, Governor Obregón, and Mario Boneta, representative of the Mexican Ministry of the Interior at the Empalme contracting center, August 7, 1956, tomo 2144, exp. 321.45 "55"/5, OM-AHES.

29. Letter from Morales Apodaca to Carvajal, August 7, 1956.

30. Letter from Morales Apodaca to Carvajal, August 7, 1956.

31. Letter from Morales Apodaca to Carvajal, August 7, 1956.

32. Letter from Morales Apodaca to Carvajal, August 7, 1956.

33. "Quejas de trabajadores en Empalme," El Imparcial, September 6, 1956; "Contratiempos en el uso de mano de obra migrante," El Imparcial, October 2, 1956.

34. Aboites Aguilar, El Norte entre algodones, 403–5.

35. Telegram from Jesús de Saracho to Governor Obregón, October 30, 1958, tomo 2144, exp. 321.45 "55"/5, OM-AHES.

36. Letter from Salomé Trujillo, Juan Limón, Guadalupe Cuevas, and other signatories [names illegible] to President Cortines, July 18, 1956, 565.4/91, FARC, AGN. Letter is accompanied by newspaper clippings referenced below.

37. "Como animales tratan a los braceros que se contratan para ir a trabajar a Estados Unidos: Capataces con armas y palos tienen confinados detrás de alambras erizadas de púas," newspaper in Monterrey, Nuevo León, July 17, 1956, transcribed by Mexico's Office of the Presidency, 565.4/91, FARC, AGN.

38. Letter from Trujillo et al. to Cortines, July 18, 1956.

39. Letter from Sebastián F. Domene, president of the Comisión Coordinadora para la Contratación de Trabajadores Agrícolas, to President Cortines, July 24, 1956, exp. 546.6/46, FARC, AGN.

40. Letter from subchief of the Departamento de Tránsito Federal to Sebastián Domene, president of the Comisión Coordinadora para la Contración de Trabajadores Agrícolas, August 31, 1956, exp. 546.6/46, FARC, AGN.

41. Pedro Benítez, interview by Perla Guerrero, May 13, 2006, "Interview 260," Bracero Oral History Project, Brown University, http://braceroarchive.org/items/show/260.

42. Rigoberto García Pérez, interview by David Bacon, January 2, 2001, http://dbacon.igc.org/TWC/b01_Bracero.htm.

43. Eusebio Hernández, interview by Grisel Murillo, May 20, 2006, "Interview no. 1226," Bracero Oral History Project, University of Texas at El Paso, Institute of Oral History, https://scholarworks.utep.edu/cgi/viewcontent.cgi?article=2248&context=interviews.

44. Isidro de Jesús Pérez, interview by Mireya Loza, July 3, 2008, "Interview no. 1448," Bracero Oral History Project, University of Texas at El Paso, Institute of Oral History, https://digitalcommons.utep.edu/cgi/viewcontent.cgi?article=2545&context=interviews.

45. José González, interview by Dr. Priscilla Falcón, February 11, 2008, Bracero Oral History Project, University of Colorado, www.unco.edu/colorado-oral-history-migratory-labor-project/bracero-project/meet-braceros/gonzalez.aspx.

46. Aguileo Namba, interview by Mario Sifuentes, February 11, 2008, "Interview 178," Bracero Oral History Project, Brown University, http://braceroarchive.org/items/show/178?view=full.

47. "Empalme será el centro de contratación," El Imparcial, February 14, 1957.

48. "Reanudaran la contratación de braceros," El Imparcial, January 10, 1957.

49. "Hasta marzo habrá contratación de nuevos braceros en Empalme," El Imparcial, January 20, 1957.

50 "Hasta marzo habrá contratación."
51. "Justas quejas en Empalme de braceros," *El Imparcial*, April 6, 1957.
52. "Empalme: Tumba de la dignidad nacional," *El Imparcial*, June 1, 1957.
53. "Agentes de Sra. de Gobierno a Empalme Sonora," *El Imparcial*, June 1, 1957.
54. "Agentes de Sra. de Gobierno."
55. "Juicios a los que engañan a los braceros," *El Imparcial*, August 22, 1957.
56. "Conviene que no muevan a los braceros," *El Imparcial*, August 22, 1957.
57. "Pizcadores para Hermosillo," *El Imparcial*, August 21, 1957.

CHAPTER FIVE

1. "Como país algodonero México está a la cabeza del mundo," *El Imparcial*, June 1, 1957.
2. "Acelera la pizca de algodón en Hermosillo," *El Imparcial*, September 3, 1957.
3. "Abrieron las oficinas para pizcadores," *El Imparcial*, September 13, 1957; "Constante envío de gente a las pizcas en la costa," *El Imparcial*, October 3, 1957; "Terminaran la pizca con éxito," *El Imparcial*, November 28, 1957.
4. "Otra vez el espectáculo de famélicos braceros en Empalme," *El Imparcial*, February 21, 1958; "Clausuraron el centro de contratación en Empalme," *El Imparcial*, April 14, 1958.
5. Correspondence from Guadalupe Huerta Córdova, Javier Huerta Hernández, Salvador Ramos Sánchez, Sipriano Ramos Montes, Leopoldo Ramos Montes, Abel Montango Vargas, Vicente Montano Vargas, Jesús Mendoza Sánchez, Roberto Ibarra Solorzano, Felipe Madrueno Ayal, Antonio Rosales Gómez, Miguel Arteaga Cortez, David Llamas Guerrero, Arnoldo Sandoval Magana, Jesús Sandoval Magana, Manuel Vargas Anaya, José Valencia Alcaraz, and Francisco Valencia Alcaraz, to Sonora secretary of the interior Francisco Enciso, with copy to Mexican secretary of the interior Gustavo Díaz Ordaz, February 27, 1959, tomo 2144, exp. 321.45 "55"/5, OM-AHES.
6. Correspondence from Huerta Córdova et al. to Enciso, February 27, 1959; "Coyotaje y corrupción en contratación de migrantes," *El Imparcial*, March 1, 1959.
7. "Crítica situación de los braceros en Empalme," *El Imparcial*, March 14, 1959.
8. "Reanudan la contratación en Empalme," *El Imparcial*, March 19, 1959.
9. "Más de 12,000 braceros hay en Empalme: Robos, escándalos, y desde luego, coyotes," *El Imparcial*, April 16, 1959.
10. "Empalme: Emporio del delito—Millones de pesos hacen los estafadores de braceros, tahúres y otros hampones," *El Imparcial*, May 18, 1959.
11. "Empalme: Emporio del delito."
12. Letter from Alianza de Braceros Nacionales de México to Sonora governor Álvaro Obregón, May 15, 1959, tomo 2144, exp. 321.45 "55"/5, OM-AHES.
13. Letter from Guadalupe Pérez to Governor Obregón, May 20, 1959, tomo 2144, exp. 321.45 "55"/5, OM-AHES.
14. Letter from Pablo Valenzuela to Sonora secretary of the interior Francisco Enciso, June 15, 1959, tomo 2144, exp. 321.45 "55"/5, OM-AHES.
15. "Atendieron la queja de los braceros," *El Imparcial*, August 19, 1959. These accusations are echoed in letter from migrant [name illegible] to Governor Obregón, September 2, 1959; letter from Erasto López, Emilio Cortez Pérez, Fidel Herrera, Manuel López, Lucio Castellanos Gomes, Rogelio Zarate Gomes, Juan Castellanos López, Felipe Santos

Villanueva, Marcelino Castellanos, and Ernesto Lopes to Governor Obregón, September 26, 1959; letter from migrant to Obregón, September 2, 1959, tomo 2144, exp. 321.45 "55"/5, OM-AHES.

16. "Auto de formal prisión para los estafa braceros," *El Imparcial*, September 2, 1959.

17. "Posible fin de programa de braceros," *El Imparcial*, January 25, 1960.

18. "600,000 braceros se contratan en Empalme en 1960," *El Imparcial*, January 25, 1960.

19. "Reanudan la contratación de braceros en marzo pxmo. en el centro de Empalme: Mientras dura el receso, agentes de la procuradora general llegan a investigar fraudes," *El Imparcial*, January 27, 1960.

20. Letter from group of migrants to President Adolfo López Mateos, with copies to the Mexican secretary of the interior, the Mexican secretary of foreign affairs, the governor of Sonora, and the newspaper chain García Balseca, February 18, 1960, tomo 2144, exp. 321.45 "55"/5, OM-AHES. Page with signatories is cut off.

21. Letter from migrants to President Mateos, February 18, 1960.

22. Letter from migrants to Governor Obregón, with copies to the chief of the contracting center in Empalme, the mayor of Empalme, President Mateos, and the director of *El Diario del Yaqui*, March 31, 1960, tomo 2144, exp. 321.45 "55"/5, OM-AHES. The migrants did not list their names but signed as "Braceros del Control del Valle de Guaymas."

23. Letter from Máximo García and Víctor Bedalla to Governor Obregón, May 13, 1960, tomo 2144, exp. 321.45 "55"/5, OM-AHES.

24. Letter from Félix Mora Martínez to Governor Obregón, October 10, 1960, tomo 2144, exp. 321.45 "55"/5, OM-AHES.

25. "Arqueo de Caja de los Fondos del Comité de Control de Pizcadores," June 30, 1962, accompanied by letter from Enrique Mazón, president of the Comité de Control de Pizcadores, to Governor of the State of Sonora, Luis Encinas, August 1, 1962, tomo 2144, exp. 321.45 "55"/5, OM-AHES.

26. Report from Joaquín Lozano Corona, agent of the Servicios Coordinados de Salubridad y Asistencia en el Estado de Sonora to Governor Encinas, August 1, 1960, tomo 2144, exp. 321.45 "55"/5, OM-AHES.

27. Letter from Secretary of the Interior Francisco Enciso, on behalf of Governor Luis Encinas, to Enrique Mazón, president of the Comité de Control de Pizcadores, October 19, 1960. See also correspondence from municipal president of Hermosillo, César Gandara, to Governor Encinas, October 17, 1960, tomo 2144, exp. 321.45 "55"/5, OM-AHES.

28. "600,000 braceros se contratan en Empalme."

29. Memorandum regarding the problem of braceros, from Governor Encinas to Mexican secretary of the interior Gustavo Díaz Ordaz, November 25, 1961, tomo 2144, exp. 321.45 "55"/5, OM-AHES.

30. "Gran Labor de Sanidad en el Yaqui," *El Imparcial*, June 4, 1960.

31. Letter from Governor Encinas to Mexican secretary of the interior Díaz Ordaz, December 1, 1961, tomo 2144, exp. 321.45 "55"/5, OM-AHES.

32. Letter from Asociación de Productores de Algodón del Noroeste, A.C., to Governor Encinas, April 24, 1962; letter from Confederación de Organismos Agricultores del Estado de Sonora to Mexican secretary of the presidency Donato Miranda Fonseca, March 8, 1962, tomo 2144, exp. 321.45 "55"/5, OM-AHES.

33. "También salen de Empalme los braceros," *El Imparcial*, August 7, 1961.

34. "7 mil braceros reunidos en Empalme," *El Imparcial*, September 14, 1961.

35. Letter from Francisco Aguilar Figueroa, Humberto Márquez, Alfonso Cobián López, Javier Flores Espino, Vicente Layna Navarrete, Librado Contreras Molina, Rufino Delgadillo Mendiola, and Rafael Medina Gutiérrez to Governor Encinas, December 30, 1961, tomo 2144, exp. 321.45 "55"/5, OM-AHES.

36. Letter from Sonora state judicial police agent Rodolfo Cuevas Montoya to state judicial police chief Guillermo Cajigas, September 13, 1961, tomo 2144, exp. 321.45 "55"/5, OM-AHES.

37. Letter from Montoya to Cajigas, September 13, 1961.

38. "Arqueo de caja de los fondos del Comité de Control de Pizcadores," June 30, 1962, accompanied by letter from Enrique Mazón, president of the Comité de Control de Pizcadores to Governor Encinas, August 1, 1962, tomo 2144, exp. 321.45 "55"/5, OM-AHES.

39. "Garantías a pizcadores en el Yaqui," *El Imparcial*, August 8, 1961.

40. Personal note, Sonora secretary of the interior Enrique Fox Romero, "Informe del Lic. Gustavo Vásquez Romo," April 18, 1962, tomo 2144, exp. 321.45 "55"/5, OM-AHES.

41. Personal note, Romero, April 18, 1962.

42. Memorandum regarding the problem of braceros in Sonora by Mexican secretary of the presidency Donato Miranda Fonseca. Fonseca wrote this brief following a meeting between the Asociación de Productores de Algodón del Noroeste, A.C., and President Mateos. It details their conversation of February 3, 1962, during which the association expressed to the president its concerns over the ending of the IBP. See also letter from Governor Encinas to Sonora secretary of the interior Encinas, instructing him to meet with growers to "formulate the measures that ought to be taken regarding the problem of cotton pickers," tomo 2144, exp. 321.45 "55"/5, OM-AHES.

43. Letter from Asociación de Productores de Algodón del Noroeste, A.C., to Governor Encinas, April 24, 1962, tomo 2144, exp. 321.45 "55"/5, OM-AHES.

44. Letter from Asociación de Productores de Algodón del Noroeste to Encinas, April 24, 1962.

45. See letter from Confederación de Organismos Agricultores del Estado de Sonora to Mexican secretary of the presidency Donato Miranda Fonseca, March 8, 1962, tomo 2144, exp. 321.45 "55"/5, OM-AHES.

46. Notification issued by Sonora secretary of government Refugio Bernal to municipal presidents of Sonora, July 20, 1962; telegram from Enrique Mazón to Sonora governor Luis Encinas, September 1, 1962; personal note, Romero, April 18, 1962, all in tomo 2144, exp. 321.45 "55"/5, OM-AHES.

47. Notification by Bernal to municipal presidents of Sonora, July 20, 1962.

48. "Arqueo de Caja de los Fondos del Comité de Control de Pizcadores," August 1, 1962, tomo 2144, exp. 321.45 "55"/5, OM-AHES.

49. "Importante junta de algodoneros en Guaymas," *El Imparcial*, July 3, 1962; "Pizcarán . . . si pueden salir a los EE.UU.," *El Imparcial*, July 16, 1962; "Pedirán más pizcadores a Adame," *El Imparcial*, July 17, 1962.

50. "Acompaña Encinas a los agricultores a sus entrevistas," *El Imparcial*, July 21, 1962; "Insistirán los agricultores en un aumento de brazos," *El Imparcial*, July 21, 1962.

51. Letter from Cámara Nacional de Comercio of Ciudad Obregón, Sonora, to Governor Encinas, August 2, 1962, tomo 2144, exp. 321.45 "55"/5, OM-AHES.

52. Telegram from Enrique Mazón to Governor Encinas, September 1, 1962, tomo 2144, exp. 321.45 "55"/5, OM-AHES.

53. "Usará máquinas pizcadoras en su algodón el Sr. Antonio Haro," *El Imparcial*, July 21, 1962.

54. "El algodón: Sus problemas y su futuro en Hermosillo," *El Imparcial*, September 4, 1962.

55. "El algodón."

56. "Llegan pizcadores constantemente a la zona agrícola," *El Imparcial*, September 5, 1962.

57. "Revela bracero secretos del oficio," *El Imparcial*, September 5, 1962.

58. "Sin escasez de brazos termina la pizca," *El Imparcial*, September 12, 1962.

59. División de Comercio Internacional y Desarrollo de la Comisión Económica para América Latina y el Caribe, *América Latina y la economía mundial del algodón* (United Nations, 1985), 80–85, https://repositorio.cepal.org/bitstream/handle/11362/8527/S8500024_es.pdf?sequence=1&isAllowed=y.

60. A public report from the Mexican national bank estimated the drop in cotton prices from the 1950s to the 1960s was as sharp as 60 percent. Miguel Álvarez Uriarte and Teresa Herrera Lavín, "Las fluctuaciones de los precios internacionales del algodón y sus repercusiones en la economía mexicana," *Comercio Exterior Bancomext*, February 1979, 224, http://revistas.bancomext.gob.mx/rce/magazines/428/14/RCE13.pdf.

61. Telegram from interim governor of Sonora Enrique Fox Romero to municipal presidents of Huasabas, Granados, Fronteras, Saric, Aconchi, Huepac, Onavas, and Cumpas, Sonora, September 1, 1964, tomo 2144, exp. 321.45 "55"/5, OM-AHES.

62. Lori A. Flores, "A Town Full of Dead Mexicans: The Salinas Valley Bracero Tragedy of 1963, the End of the Bracero Program, and the Evolution of California's Chicano Movement," *Western Historical Quarterly* 44, no. 2 (Summer 2013): 124–43.

CHAPTER SIX

1. Quote is from Ana Raquel Minian, *Undocumented Lives: The Untold Story of Mexican Migration* (Harvard University Press, 2018), 16. See also David Fitzgerald, "Inside the Sending State: The Politics of Mexican Emigration Control," *International Migration Review* 40, no. 2 (2006): 259–93. Fitzgerald calls the 1970s a period of "unregulated exit."

2. "Detuvieron en Tijuana a un enganchador que metía braceros clandestinos en EU," *Excélsior*, January 26, 1968; "Mujer acusada de pasar 'braceros' ilegalmente," *El Universal*, March 19, 1968; "Detienen al jefe de una banda de enganchabraceros," *Excélsior*, October 15, 1968; "Batida en la frontera contra los enganchadores de braceros," *Excélsior*, March 6, 1969; "Los denunciaban tras pasarlos ilegalmente," *La Prensa*, March 7, 1969; "Larga condena para los estafadores de braceros," *La Prensa*, March 8, 1969; "Ocultos en camiones se llevan a braceros," *La Prensa*, March 10, 1969; "Formal prisión para el enganchador de braceros," *La Prensa*, March 12, 1969; "Acusación contra un embaucador de presuntos braceros," *Excélsior*, March 13, 1969; "Engatusadores de braceros presos en Nuevo Laredo," *Excélsior*, March 26, 1969; "Aumento la inmigración ilegal a EU," *Novedades*, October 5, 1970; "Preocupan al gobierno los braceros," *El Diario de México*, June 17, 1971.

3. Mexican Ministry of the Interior, "Información de Tepic," June 10, 1971, exp. 10, caja 1675b, DGIPS, AGN.

4. "Amparo negado a 4 que estafaron a 'braceros,'" *El Sol de México*, July 27, 1971.

5. Report from chief of Dirección General de Población to the Mexican Ministry of the Interior, September 30, 1971, exp. 10, caja 1675b, DGIPS, AGN.

6. Mexican Ministry of the Interior memo summarizing case against Alianza de Braceros as a human smuggling group, October 20, 1971, exp. 10, caja 1675b, DGIPS, AGN.

7. Mexican Ministry of the Interior, "Información de Tijuana," internal report, February 3, 1971, exp. 10, caja 1675b, DGIPS, AGN.

8. Letter from Oficialía Mayor to Dirección General de Asuntos Jurídicos, January 6, 1972, exp. 10, caja 1675b, DGIPS, AGN.

9. Mexican Ministry of the Interior, "Información de Piedras Negras," internal report, June 22 and July 9, 1971, exp. 10, caja 1675b, DGIPS, AGN; "Los traficantes de braceros tienen comprados a policías y autoridades fronterizas," *Ovaciones*, June 7, 1973; "500 dls. cuesta una tarjeta autentica para trabajar en EU," *Excélsior*, June 12, 1973.

10. "Ambos gobiernos reprueban cruel actitud de agentes fronterizos," *La Prensa*, June 20, 1971.

11. Mexican Ministry of the Interior, "Información de Tijuana," internal report, September 15, 1971, exp. 10, caja 1675b, DGIPS, AGN.

12. Mexican Ministry of the Interior, "Información de Baja California," May 6, 8, 10, 1971; "Información de Baja California," internal report, May 7, 1971; "Información de Mazatlán," May 9, 1971; "Información de Mexicali," May 9, 11–15, 19–22, 24–29, 31, June 1, 1971; "Información de Culiacán," May 10, 12–15, 22, 24, 27–28, 31, June 2, 1971; exp. 10, caja 1675b, DGIPS, AGN.

13. Jorge A. Bustamante, "Maquiladoras: A New Face of International Capitalism on Mexico's Northern Frontier," in *Women, Men, and the International Division of Labor*, ed. June C. Nash and María P. Fernández-Kelly (State University of New York Press, 1983); Leslie Sklar, *Assembling for Development: The Maquila Industry in Mexico and the United States* (Routledge, 1989); María Patricia Fernández-Kelly, *For We Are Sold, I and My People: Women and Industry in Mexico's Frontier* (State University of New York Press, 1983).

14. "Pasan ilegalmente para trabajar como braceros," *Últimas Noticias*, May 24, 1971.

15. Mexican Ministry of the Interior, "Información de Culiacán," internal report, June 26, 1971, exp. 10, caja 1675b, DGIPS, AGN.

16. "Negociaciones entre EU y México para proteger a los braceros," *Ovaciones*, June 7, 1971.

17. "Estafaba a braceros con documentos falsos," *La Prensa*, June 17, 1971; "México tratará de concertar un nuevo convenio de braceros," *El Heraldo de México*, June 23, 1971; "Evitarán se exploten a nuestros braceros," *Universal Gráfico*, June 23, 1971; "Urge solucionar el grave caso de espaldas mojadas," *La Prensa*, June 24, 1971; "280 mil mexicanos deportados de EU; Protección legal para los braceros," *El Diario de México*, June 24, 1971.

18. Mexican Ministry of the Interior, "Información de Guadalajara," internal report, July 5, 1971, exp. 7, caja 1689b, DGIPS, AGN.

19. Mexican Ministry of the Interior, "Estado de Sonora, información de Villa Juárez," internal report, August 12, 1971, exp. 7, caja 1689b, DGIPS, AGN.

20. Mexican Ministry of the Interior, "Estado de Sonora, información de Villa Juárez."

21. Mexican Ministry of the Interior, "Estado de Sonora, información de Cd. Obregón," internal report, August 14, 1971, exp. 7, caja 1689b, DGIPS, AGN.

22. Mexican Ministry of the Interior, "Estado de Sonora, información de Cd. Obregón," August 14, 1971; "Información de Cd. Juárez," internal report, August 31, September 3, 10 1971, exp. 10, caja 1675b, DGIPS, AGN.

23. "Nuevo impulso a las regiones fronterizas a causa de la creciente mano de obra inactiva," *El Heraldo de México*, November 4, 1971; "A nivel de gobernantes debe resolverse el problema de la emigración ilegal de braceros a EU," *El Heraldo de México*, January 12, 1972; "Nada saben hacer los braceros: Alfonso Charles," *La Prensa*, June 9, 1973.

24. "Los funcionarios protegen a braceros: Relaciones," *Excélsior*, April 19, 1973; "De Zacatecas, Michoacán y Jalisco es de donde van más braceros a trabajar ilegalmente en EU," *El Sol de México*, April 19, 1973.

25. "Fallo de una comisión: La mayoría de los braceros son trabajadores rurales," *Ovaciones*, April 21, 1973.

26. "Los funcionarios protegen a braceros: Relaciones," *Excélsior*, April 19, 1973.

27. Mexican Ministry of the Interior, "Trabajadores migratorios," internal report, May 15, 1973, exp. 1, caja 1676a, DGIPS, AGN.

28. "La tragedia de los braceros," *El Heraldo de México*, July 21, 1972.

29. "Garrotadas, patadas, gases, a mexicanos que entran ilegalmente a EU," *Excélsior*, August 28, 1972.

30. "El problema de los 'mojados' mexicanos es latente en E.U.," *El Universal*, October 12, 1972.

31. "Quinientos mexicanos purgan condenas en Estados Unidos por entrada ilegal," *El Universal*, October 23, 1972.

32. "Como en campos de concentración hacinan a los mexicanos llegados ilegalmente a EU," *Últimas Noticias*, October 17, 1972; "Braceros hacinados como ganado en las barrancas de arresto en EU," *El Heraldo de México*, October 17, 1972.

33. "México y EU en tratos para el posible envió de braceros," *Últimas Noticias*, September 23, 1972.

34. "Solicitud de Texano Price: Entrada de braceros mexicanos por falta de mano de obra," *Excélsior*, September 23, 1972.

35. "Estados Unidos requiere la mano de obra mexicana para la agricultura," *El Día*, October 27, 1972.

36. "Nuevo convenio de braceros proponen 3 estados de EU: Reunión de LE con los gobernadores," *Novedades*, January 29, 1973.

37. "Defender a mexicanos emigrantes, labor principal de consulado en Houston, Texas," *Novedades*, October 19, 1972; "A siete mil pesos vendían falsas tarjetas migratorias," *El Heraldo de México*, July 26, 1972; "Declaración de dos falsificadores falsos de micas para trabajar en los EU," *El Día*, July 26, 1972; "Vendían tarjetas migratorias a dos mil pesos," *Últimas Noticias*, August 8, 1972; "Se pasó de listo y cayó," *Novedades*, August 9, 1972; "Tráfico humano descubierto en Los Angeles," *Novedades*, August 29, 1972; "Atraparon 24 falsificadores," *La Prensa*, September 15, 1972; "Golpe definitivo a la falsificación de las credenciales de burócratas," *El Universal*, October 23, 1972; "Capturan una banda que traficaba con braceros," *La Prensa*, February 12, 1973; "Falsificaban documentos en gran escala," *El Universal*, February 13, 1973; "Descubren una banda que falsificaba documentos para braceros," *Últimas Noticias*, February 23, 1973; "Falsificación de documentos migratorios

en Tijuana B.C.," *Ovaciones*, February 23, 1973; "Falsificación de pasaportes," *La Prensa*, February 24, 1973.

38. "Ousted Mexicans Pay Off to Stay Close to US Jobs," *New York Times*, April 1, 1973.

39. "Ousted Mexicans Pay Off."

40. "Declara el líder de la CNC: Autoridades migratorias de EU principales responsables de la deportación ilegal de braceros," *El Nacional*, April 17, 1973; "Las autoridades migratorias de EU son responsables del tráfico con braceros," *El Diario de México*, April 17, 1973; "CNC contra el tráfico de los braceros," *La Prensa*, April 17, 1973; "Exigen que se proteja al campesino," *El Universal*, April 18, 1973; "Acusa Fidel Velázquez: De Estados Unidos nuevas pruebas de saña en su trato a braceros," *El Día*, April 19, 1973.

41. "La criminal trata de braceros," *Avance*, April 17, 1973; "Responsabilidad yanki: La situación migratoria de braceros," *El Heraldo de México*, April 17, 1973; "Responsabilidad nuestra: Bajar la producción de braceros," *Excélsior*, April 18, 1973; "La miseria: Causa fundamental del bracerismo," *El Día*, April 18, 1973.

42. "Que las autoridades mexicanas han actuado con toda honestidad," *Ovaciones*, April 18, 1973; "Explica el Sr. Barona Lobato la situación de los braceros," *Excélsior*, April 17, 1973; "Las noticias sobre braceros son originadas por grupos políticos en oposición al actual gobierno de EU," *El Heraldo de México*, April 19, 1973; "Niegan falta de honradez de autoridades mexicanas en el caso de los braceros," *El Nacional*, April 19, 1973.

43. "Una mafia trafica con los braceros reconoce Allan L. Gerhardt: Ningún funcionario en ella, dice," *Excélsior*, April 18, 1973.

44. "No desplazan a nadie los braceros mexicanos," *El Universal*, April 21, 1973.

45. "Una de tantas soluciones para el problema de los braceros," *Avance*, April 21, 1973.

46. "Fuentes de trabajo y salarios decorosos contra el bracerismo," *Sol de Medio Día*, April 25, 1973.

47. "El problema de los braceros solo se resolverá mediante medidas bilaterales: Declaración de la Comisión Intersecretarial," *El Nacional*, April 19, 1973; "Aun sin convenio, los braceros deben de contar con garantías," *El Día*, April 21, 1973; "Regularizarán la contratación de braceros," *La Prensa*, April 21, 1973; "Estudian el convenio sobre braceros con EU," *El Diario de México*, April 21, 1973; "Se podrá negociar la contratación de braceros, dice la Secretaría de Trabajo," *El Sol de México*, April 21, 1973; "Probable conferencia especial México-EU sobre los braceros," *Universal Gráfico*, April 21, 1973; "La ausencia de un convenio entre EU y México impide proteger al bracero," *El Día*, April 28, 1973.

48. "Ninguna ley proteccionista contra México," *Excélsior*, March 27, 1973; "Reunión interparlamentaria," *El Heraldo de México*, March 30, 1973.

49. Mexican Ministry of the Interior, "Información de Guanajuato," internal report, May 24, 1973, exp. A, caja 1506, DGIPS, AGN.

50. "La delegación mexicana terminó ya su preparación sus preparativos para la Interparlamentaria," *El Día*, May 21, 1973.

51. "Recepción presidencial a los legisladores norteamericanos," *El Heraldo de México*, May 25, 1973.

52. "'Operación Guayabera' de los interparlamentarios," *Excélsior*, May 25, 1973.

53. Transcript of interparliamentary meeting, May 25, 1973, exp A, caja 1506, DGIPS, AGN.

54. "Los problemas deben resolverse conforme a derecho, dijo Echeverría," *El Heraldo de México*, May 25, 1973.

55. "Es inaceptable no dar protección a los braceros, sean ilegales o no, acuerda la Interparlamentaria," *El Sol de México*, May 15, 1973; "Años tardará en resolverse el problema de los braceros: J. J. Jova, embajador de EU," *Excélsior*, May 15, 1973; "Comité con EU para resolver lo de los braceros," *La Prensa*, May 15, 1973; "Buen trato a trabajadores migratorios," *El Diario de México*, May 15, 1973.

56. "Inmigrantes ilegales capturados en los primeros meses: Pretexto para encubrir la corrupción," *El Heraldo de México*, May 25, 1973.

57. "Doble de mexicanos ilegales esperan durante 1973 en EU," *Novedades*, May 5, 1973; "Con tácticas de la Gestapo detienen a mexicanos," *Ovaciones*, May 24, 1973; "600 braceros detenidos: Realizan en Estados Unidos una gran redada que es típica de Gestapo," *La Prensa*, May 25, 1973; "Redada contra los braceros ilegales en EU: Activistas chicanos tachan la acción de típica de la Gestapo," *Novedades*, May 25, 1973; "Gigantesca redada contra mexicanos ilegales en EU: La policía usa métodos prohibidos," *El Sol de México*, May 25, 1973; "Redada de ciudadanos latinoamericanos que se encuentran ilegalmente en EU," *El Nacional*, May 25, 1973; "Gigantesca redada de braceros en EU: Miles de detenidos," *El Heraldo de México*, May 25, 1973; "Detenidos en Estados Unidos," *El Crucero*, May 30, 1973; "EU intensifica la campaña contra entradas ilegales," *Excélsior*, May 31, 1973.

58. "Volcó un camión con obreros mexicanos," *Sol de Medio Día*, August 1, 1973; "Mueren 9 braceros," *Novedades*, August 2, 1973; "Mueren 9 trabajadores agrícolas en EU," *El Día*, August 2, 1973; "9 braceros muertos," *El Universal*, August 3, 1973.

59. "Cementerios clandestinos de braceros en el sur de California," *Sol de Medio Día*, August 11, 1973.

60. "México fortalece los consulados en la zona fronteriza del norte," *Ovaciones*, July 9, 1973; "Ordena Gobernación una campaña contra enganchadores de braceros," *Últimas Noticias*, May 16, 1973; "Fortalecerán todos los consulados fronterizos," *La Prensa*, July 10, 1973; "Alto al bracerismo," *Últimas Noticias*, July 10, 1973; "Se frenará el inhumano tráfico de los braceros," *La Prensa*, July 11, 1973; "Campaña permanente contra los enganchadores de braceros," *El Día*, July 11, 1973.

61. "Trato digno y humano, exigirá México a EU para los braceros," *El Sol de México*, April 26, 1973; "Abordarán el problema de los braceros," *Diario de la Tarde*, April 26, 1973; "Braceros, salinidad y Nixon: Temas de Roger," *Diario de la Tarde*, May 12, 1973; "Debe resolver con equidad EU el problema de braceros ilegales," *Novedades*, June 4, 1973; "Para ello será la colaboración entre México y Estados Unidos," *Ovaciones*, June 5, 1973; "EU obligado a dar justa solución a los braceros," *La Prensa*, June 13, 1973; "México demanda protección y mejor trato a braceros," *El Heraldo de México*, June 13, 1973; "México demanda que se proteja al bracero," *El Universal*, June 13, 1973; "Igualdad jurídica y económica en EU para los braceros," *El Sol de México*, June 13, 1973; "Los patrones de EU se oponen a un convenio sobre braceros," *Universal Gráfico*, June 13, 1973; "El problema de los braceros es económico y no político," *El Día*, June 16, 1973.

62. "Gigantesca redada de mexicanos en Los Angeles," *Ovaciones*, June 20, 1973; "Estados Unidos nos devuelve cada mes a cincuenta mil braceros," *Ovaciones*, August 9, 1973; "Deportados de EU declaran en Piedras Negras," *Novedades*, July 31, 1973; "Drama de emigrantes," *La Prensa*, July 24, 1973; "Expulsan a 5 mil mexicanos por semana en Los Angeles," *La Prensa*, June 21, 1973; "Diez veces más detenciones que hace ocho años," *Excélsior*, September 3, 1973; "Veinte braceros por hora detuvieron en EU en dos días," *El*

Sol de México, September 4, 1973; "La detención de los ilegales en EU suele terminar en tragedia," *El Universal*, November 29, 1973.

63. "EU marca con un sello a trabajadores deportados," *La Prensa*, June 22, 1973; Mexican Ministry of the Interior, "Información de Tijuana," internal report, June 22, 1973, exp. 1, caja 1676A, DGIPS, AGN.

64. "La valla fronteriza se instalará, reafirma el subjefe de patrulla," *Excélsior*, July 17, 1973; "La canija frontera electrónica," *Universal Gráfico*, July 28, 1973; "Los técnicos estadounidenses esperan 'cazar' este año a no menos de 150 mil mexicanos," *El Día*, July 27, 1973.

65. "Una comisión de México y EU estudia el lacerante problema de los braceros: Rabasa," *El Nacional*, July 19, 1973; "El muro electrónico no es solución," *Universal Gráfico*, July 17, 1973; "Necesitamos soluciones profundas contra el bracerismo," *El Heraldo de México*, July 19, 1973; "Con medidas apresuradas y unilaterales no se resolverá jamás el problema de los braceros, declara Mora Picarte," *El Día*, June 21, 1973.

66. "Pláticas con EU para lograr un acuerdo sobre los braceros," *El Heraldo de México*, September 1, 1973; "Un millón de mexicanos ilegales, desprotegidos en EU: Olloqui," *Excélsior*, September 1, 1973; "Acepta EU que necesita trabajadores mexicanos," *La Prensa*, September 1, 1973; "Se busca dar seguridad jurídica a un millón de mexicanos: De Olloqui," *El Sol de México*, September 1, 1973.

67. "México negociará con EU el problema de los braceros," *El Heraldo de México*, September 28, 1973.

68. "México propone a EU un acuerdo sobre braceros," *Últimas Noticias*, October 4, 1973; "Propone México un nuevo acuerdo de braceros," *Excélsior*, October 5, 1973; "EU resolverá en dos meses el problema de los braceros," *La Prensa*, October 12, 1973; "Convenio sobre braceros con EU, dentro de dos meses," *El Diario de México*, October 12, 1973.

69. "Miopía cíclica migratoria en EU," *El Diario de México*, October 17, 1973; "El nuevo convenio sobre braceros garantizará el trato justo para mexicanos," *Crucero*, October 17, 1973.

70. "Proyecto de solución al problema de los trabajadores migratorios," *El Heraldo de México*, November 10, 1973; "Braceros, principal problema entre México y EU, declara Joseph John Java," *El Heraldo de México*, December 6, 1973; "No se abandona a los braceros dijo Rabasa," *Avance*, January 23, 1974; "El de los braceros, asunto bien complicado, dice Jova," *Ovaciones*, January 30, 1974; "Rabasa pedirá hoy a Kissinger un convenio oficial para la contratación de braceros," *El Sol de México*, February 2, 1974; "Inconformidad absoluta de México con el trato de braceros en EU," *El Heraldo de México*, June 20, 1974; "Invita Rabasa a EU a firmar un convenio sobre braceros, similar al celebrado con Canadá," *El Sol de México*, June 20, 1974; "Desecha Washington la posibilidad de elaborar un nuevo convenio sobre braceros," *Ovaciones*, June 21, 1974.

71. "No hay perspectivas de otro contrato sobre braceros," *El Universal*, December 12, 1973; "Convenio de braceros, cuando disminuya el desempleo, se dice en Washington," *Excélsior*, December 12, 1973.

72. "Los sindicatos, un obstáculo para un acuerdo sobre los braceros," *El Diario de México*, March 22, 1974; "Declara Rabasa: Los sindicatos de EU persiguen a los braceros," *Últimas Noticias*, March 22, 1974; "Los sindicatos, obstáculo para un acuerdo sobre los braceros," *El Heraldo de México*, March 22, 1974; "Los sindicatos de EU contra los braceros,"

Avance, March 23, 1974; "La AFL-CIO contra braceros," *La Prensa*, March 23, 1974; "Habla Cesar Chavez, líder de la UFWOC," *Ovaciones*, January 28, 1974.

73. "Falso que los sindicatos norteamericanos se opongan a los mexicanos," *El Heraldo de México*, February 25, 1974; "El embajador de México en EU, señala el problema de los braceros como el más grave entre nuestro país y los EU," *El Día*, February 26, 1974.

74. "Cónsules mexicanos en centros de detención de braceros en EU," *El Día*, March 9, 1974; "México solicitará la legalización de trabajadores en EU," *Excélsior*, April 19, 1974; "Pide México a EU legalizar nuestros trabajadores migratorios," *Universal Gráfico*, May 14, 1974.

75. "Áspera y fuera de protocolo se juzgó en medios diplomáticos la respuesta de EU; México revisará sus relaciones tras la negativa de Washington de firmar un convenio sobre braceros," *El Sol de México*, August 8, 1974.

76. "Propone México un pacto de braceros, gobierno a gobierno," *Últimas Noticias*, August 6, 1974; "Basta de 'palabrería y protocolos,'" *El Sol de México*, August 6, 1974; "Un tratado como el que quiere México no resolverá el problema de los inmigrantes ilegales, responde EU," *El Sol de México*, August 7, 1974; "No quiere EUA celebrar el tratado sobre los trabajadores migratorios," *El Universal*, August 7, 1974; "Confiá de Olloqui que Ford procure solución al problema de braceros," *Excélsior*, August 7, 1974.

77. "Piden 'inutilizar el imán de atracción,'" *El Sol de México*, August 20, 1974; "Blanden la Ley Rodino," *La Prensa*, August 20, 1974.

78. "Colonización, remedio al bracerismo," *La Prensa*, August 8, 1974.

79. "Poco interés de EU en un convenio braceril 'por temor al desempleo allá,' dice Rabasa," *Excélsior*, August 24, 1974; "'Casi imposible' un pacto sobre braceros," *Últimas Noticias*, October 17, 1974.

80. "Bracerismo, problema que los mexicanos debemos resolver, dando créditos y técnica al campesino para que no vaya a trabajar a EU," *El Sol de México*, October 5, 1974.

81. "Solo, México afrontará el problema de los braceros: LE," *El Sol de México*, October 21, 1974.

82. "No se hará un nuevo convenio de braceros," *La Prensa*, October 22, 1974.

83. Mexican Ministry of the Interior, internal report, May 15, 1973, exp. 1, caja 1676a, DGIPS, AGN.

CHAPTER SEVEN

1. "Manifestó Echeverría: Firmar un compromiso sería reconocer que la inmigración de braceros es necesaria," *Ovaciones*, October 23, 1974.

2. "El bracerismo, por falta de agua y tierra, dijo LE," *Excélsior*, October 23, 1974; "México no aceptará una cuota sobre braceros: LE; Sería tanto como reconocer que es un problema inevitable, dijo el presidente ante los campesinos," *El Día*, October 23, 1974; "Muro de progreso contra bracerismo," *La Prensa*, October 23, 1974; "Hay que despojar a los funcionarios del egoísmo para evitar el bracerismo," *El Heraldo de México*, October 23, 1974.

3. "Debe apoyarse a LEA en su política respecto al problema de los braceros," *Crucero*, October 25, 1974.

4. Letter from Congreso Permanente Agrario to Mexican president Luis Echeverría, October 25, 1974; Mexican Ministry of the Interior, "Información de Distrito Federal," internal report, October 25, 1974, exp. 8, caja 1676c, DGIPS, AGN.

5. "Repudian convenio sobre braceros," *La Prensa*, October 28, 1974; "Un convenio sobre braceros sería humillante y dañino," *El Universal*, October 28, 1974.

6. "Efectos de plan presidencial: En el campo aumentará la producción y se combatirá el desempleo y el bracerismo," *Sol de Medio Día*, November 15, 1974; "Mayores fuentes de trabajo, única solución al problema de los braceros, afirma LE," *El Heraldo de México*, November 27, 1974; "Puerta falsa al bracerismo," *El Diario de México*, November 27, 1974; "Baja California crea fuentes de trabajo para arraigar a los que pensaban irse de braceros," *Sol de Medio Día*, November 19, 1974.

7. "Señala semillero de braceros, la banca," *Diario de la Tarde*, April 15, 1975.

8. "Colonización, positiva," *La Prensa*, April 26, 1975.

9. "Colonización, positiva."

10. "Emigra a EU la juventud," *Diario de la Tarde*, July 26, 1975; "Jóvenes el 61.4% de braceros que van a EU," *La Prensa*, July 26, 1975; "61.4% de los mexicanos que ingresan a los EU tienen entre 18 y 29 años," *El Sol de México*, July 26, 1975; "Ahí más de 1,400,000 mexicanos ilegales en EU: Informe ante LE," *Últimas Noticias*, May 13, 1976.

11. "Aunque sean ilegales tienen derecho a un trato humano, dice el jefe del Senado," *Últimas Noticias*, September 17, 1974; "Reclama México en la ONU trato digno para las espaldas mojadas," *El Sol de México*, October 10, 1974.

12. "Respeto a los derechos de los braceros: ONU," *Excélsior*, November 7, 1974.

13. "40 ilegales muertos en 6 meses; Bandas neonazis en EU los atacan," *Sol de Medio Día*, June 25, 1976.

14. "Plan mexicano para evitar la emigración ilegal a EU," *Excélsior*, May 24, 1976.

15. "Cacería de espaldas mojadas," *Universal Gráfico*, August 5, 1976.

16. "Hambrientos, duermen en la calle 150 mexicanos deportados de EU," *La Prensa*, August 5, 1976; "Humillados y sin un centavo, 60 deportados buscan que comer," *Sol de Medio Día*, August 5, 1976.

17. "'Problema artificial para armar una crisis': Líder chicano," *Ovaciones*, July 28, 1976; "Campaña de terror y represión contra mexicanos en EU: CASA," *Excélsior*, July 28, 1976; "Dicen los 'espaldas mojadas': Si para las transnacionales de EU no hay fronteras, que no las haya para el trabajo," *Ovaciones*, July 28, 1976; "Para evitar repatriaciones apelará la hermandad hasta la violencia," *El Universal*, July 27, 1976; "Quieren esclavos y no trabajadores en EU," *Universal Gráfico*, July 28, 1976; "La cacería del 'espaldas mojada': Moda política en Estados Unidos," *El Día*, July 29, 1976.

18. "Firme postura del gobierno de México," *Excélsior*, July 30, 1976.

19. "Urge crear más empleos para ellos: JLP," *Últimas Noticias*, August 3, 1976.

20. "Ayuda a los trabajadores migratorios deportados," *Ovaciones*, August 6, 1976.

21. "No todos los braceros deportados podrán ser acomodados en el SE: Algunos de ellos no son campesinos sino obreros," *El Heraldo de México*, August 10, 1976.

22. "Fuentes de trabajo para los repatriados," *El Universal*, July 29, 1976.

23. "Es imperativo crear empleos para evitar el bracerismo," *El Día*, July 30, 1976.

24. "Se agrava problema de desempleo," *Heraldo de México*, August 4, 1976; "Propone presidente de la Conaco una emergencia ante deportación de ilegales," *Excélsior*, August 5, 1976.

25. "No hay tal deportación masiva, H. Smith," *Excélsior*, August 9, 1976.

26. "Las relaciones con EU sobre braceros, 'en la Edad de Piedra,' dice un coordinador del Colegio de México," *Excélsior*, August 6, 1976.

27. "Nos quemaron, colgaron: Los braceros torturados," *Excélsior*, August 23, 1976; "Pide México todo el rigor de la ley contra los que torturaron a 3 aspirantes a braceros," *El Día*, August 23, 1976; "Jamás olvidaré el hierro en mis carnes: Eleazar," *Excélsior*, August 23, 1976; "Torturaron a 3 mexicanos en EU," *La Prensa*, August 23, 1976; "Exige México castigo para los agresores de los 3 braceros," *El Sol de México*, August 23, 1976; "Saña con los 3 mexicanos," *Últimas Noticias*, August 23, 1976; "La ley obliga EU a hacer justicia," *El Sol de México*, August 24, 1976; "Indignada reacción nacional: Opinan 12 senadores que el grave atentado contra 3 mexicanos en EU amerita castigo," *El Día*, August 24, 1976.

28. "Indignada reacción nacional."

29. "Condena la Cámara el trato brutal a braceros mexicanos," *El Día*, August 25, 1976.

30. "'No se burlará a la justicia': Raúl H. Castro, gobernador de Arizona," *Ovaciones*, August 27, 1976; "Huyeron de Arizona los ricos 'caza-braceros,'" *El Sol de México*, August 27, 1976; "Nula justicia texana," *La Prensa*, August 28, 1976; "Aplicaré la justicia para asegurar que lo de Douglas no volverá a ocurrir, declaró Bobbit, procurador de Arizona," *Excélsior*, August 28, 1976.

31. "El respeto a los derechos humanos en el caso de los braceros, pide LE," *El Día*, August 26, 1976.

32. "Castigo para los agresores, exige LE," *El Sol de México*, August 26, 1976.

33. "Rechazó a un nuevo convenio de braceros," *El Sol de México*, September 2, 1976; "'Flagrante violación de derechos humanos con nuestros braceros,'" *Últimas Noticias*, September 2, 1976; "Condeno el mal trato que se da en EU a braceros," *La Prensa*, September 9, 1976; "Mientras falte empleo habrá brazos," *El Universal*, September 11, 1976.

34. "Pide JLP trato justo y humano de EU para los braceros mexicanos," *Ovaciones*, February 8, 1977.

35. "150 mexicanos atacaron a la Patrulla Fronteriza," *La Prensa*, April 21, 1977; "Ahogan a braceros," *Últimas Noticias*, April 21, 1977; "Clamor contra los mata-braceros," *Ovaciones*, April 21, 1977; "Autoridades mexicanas investigan el caso de los braceros ahogados," *Últimas Noticias*, April 21, 1977; "Mas de 150 personas, 'en plan de guerra,' por un mexicano que se ahogó al intentar cruzar la frontera con EU," *Heraldo de México*, April 21, 1977; "Investiguen los asesinatos de braceros en la frontera: Chavez," *Últimas Noticias*, April 23, 1977.

36. "Gobernación ordena una supervigiliancia," *Últimas Noticias*, May 2, 1977.

37. "Corresponde a México la solución al problema de los braceros, señalan centrales campesinas," *Excélsior*, April 26, 1977.

38. "Promete EEUU tratar como seres humanos a los ilegales," *Ovaciones*, May 19, 1977.

39. "Con más fuentes de trabajo se evitarían los braceros," *Diario de México*, June 1, 1977.

40. "Las medidas policiacas son inútiles: JLP," *Excélsior*, June 27, 1977.

41. "No son delincuentes los braceros, dijo LP," *La Prensa*, September 2, 1977.

42. "Pláticas EU-México para un arreglo sobre braceros," *Diario de México*, July 2, 1977; "Como resolver el problema de los braceros," *La Prensa*, July 15, 1977; "Braceros, punto medular," *Últimas Noticias*, August 8, 1977; "Crear empleos en México, forma de acabar con los braceros: De Olloqui," *Universal*, August 30, 1977; "Problema mutuo: Braceros," *Prensa*, September 7, 1977; "El desempleo, es problema principal," *Novedades*, February 8, 1979.

43. "Crecimiento industrial, un freno al bracerismo," *Ovaciones*, August 11, 1977.

44. "Propuestas concretas sobre braceros este año," *El Sol de México*, July 20, 1977; "Amnistía total a ilegales con siete años en EU pedirá Carter," *Excélsior*, July 21, 1977.

45. "Propondrá Carter ayudar a México a crear más empleos," *El Sol de México*, August 1, 1977.

46. "Plan de EU contra el bracerismo," *Diario de México*, September 29, 1977.

47. "Convenio entre iguales firman EEUU y México," *Novedades*, December 3, 1977.

48. "Frenaran el éxodo de braceros," *El Diario de México*, July 10, 1978.

49. "EU viola acuerdos concretos al gravar la importación mexicana," *El Sol de México*, February 3, 1979; "México pagará el 10 por ciento de impuestos, por exportación," *Heraldo de México*, February 8, 1979.

50. "Planeaban abrir las puertas de EU a inmigrantes y productos mexicanos," *Heraldo de México*, February 2, 1979.

51. "Ni productos mexicanos, ni más braceros: Carter," *La Prensa*, February 2, 1979; "Carter negó a México un 'trato especial,'" *El Diario de México*, February 1, 1979.

52. Mexican Ministry of the Interior, "Información de Distrito Federal," internal report, February 5, 6, and 7, 1979, exp. 6, caja 1575b, DGIPS, AGN; "Información del Distrito Federal," internal report, February 7, 1979, exp. 13, caja 1676d, DGIPS, AGN.

53. "Gas, petróleo y braceros; temas a tratar por JLP y Carter," *Heraldo de México*, January 29, 1979; "Sí pretende EU gas y petróleo de México," *Excélsior*, February 8, 1979; "Amenaza a EU su dependencia petrolera," *Uno Más Uno*, February 9, 1979; "Carter, Gambusino en busca de oro negro, si tratara el tema con JLP," *Heraldo de México*, February 9, 1979; "Nunca hacen visitas desinteresadas a México los presidentes de EEUU," *Sol de Medio Día*, February 12, 1979; "El petróleo solo servirá el interés de México, no de EU," *Heraldo de México*, February 12, 1979; "Dique a chantajes; no vincularemos petróleo y braceros: JLP," *Excélsior*, February 10, 1979.

54. "'Las pláticas con López Portillo serán difíciles': Carter," *Ovaciones*, February 13, 1979.

55. "Japón y EU se disputarán el petróleo mexicano," *Heraldo de México*, February 12, 1979.

56. "Dique a chantajes."

57. "Un indocumentado mexicano fue asesinado por un policía fronterizo en California," *Uno Mas Uno*, March 23, 1979.

58. "Un indocumentado mexicano"; "Las autoridades migratorias de EU violan los derechos humanos," *El Universal*, March 27, 1979; "Otro bracero fue asesinado," *Sol de Medio Día*, March 27, 1979; "Condenan el maltrato a braceros las 2 cámaras," *Diario de México*, March 27, 1979; "Sigue la matanza de los indocumentados," *Heraldo de México*, April 23, 1979; "Urge velar por los indocumentados," *El Sol de México*, May 15, 1979; "Se evitará la salida de braceros," *Diario de México*, October 1, 1979; "Debe lucharse por un trato humano a los trabajadores mexicanos," *El Día*, October 8, 1979; "Busca la ONU mecanismos para defender a braceros," *Excélsior*, November 29, 1979.

59. "Hay que mejorar el trato a los braceros: Roel," *El Sol de México*, May 5, 1979; "Roel en contra de un convenio sobre braceros," *Avance*, April 18, 1979.

60. "Aboga la Casa Blanca por los indocumentados," *Uno Más Uno*, May 8, 1979.

61. "Enjuician a patrulleros en EU por haber golpeado a mexicanos," *El Heraldo de México*, September 26, 1979.

62. "Encadenó, esposó y encerró en una jaula un juez policial de EU a indocumentados mexicanos," *El Nacional*, September 28, 1979.

63. "México y EU no han firmado un convenio bilateral sobre la migración de trabajadores desde 1965," *Uno Más Uno*, June 1, 1981; "El programa de braceros no es solución," *Últimas Noticias*, May 21, 1981; "Trabajadores huéspedes?," *Uno Más Uno*, June 15, 1981.

64. "Ordena JLP recursos adicionales para apoyar al campo," *Universal*, March 4, 1981.

CONCLUSION

1. Michael S. Teitelbaum, "Peso Refugees," *New York Times*, September 28, 1982.

2. Teitelbaum emphasized the scale of the ongoing Mexican migration in academic writings as well. Michael S. Teitelbaum, "Immigration, Refugees, and Foreign Policy," *International Organization* 38, no. 3 (Summer 1984): 429–50.

3. "Washington Drops in on 'the Last Domino,'" *New York Times*, April 17, 1983.

4. "Hard Times in Mexico Cause Concern in the US," *New York Times*, October 19, 1986.

5. "Hard Times in Mexico."

6. "Immigration Policy; Mexico Fears the Loss of America as a Safety Valve," *New York Times*, March 15, 1987.

7. "Mexico Moves to Assist Returning Immigrants," *Washington Post*, May 6, 1987.

8. "Mexico Moves to Assist."

9. "Immigration Policy."

10. Carlos González Gutiérrez, "Fostering Identities: Mexico's Relations with Its Diaspora," *Journal of American History* 86, no. 2 (September 1999): 545.

11. González Gutiérrez, "Fostering Identities," 546.

12. González Gutiérrez, "Fostering Identities," 546, 560–61.

13. González Gutiérrez, "Fostering Identities," 562.

14. González Gutiérrez, "Fostering Identities," 562.

15. An analysis of the transformation of Mexican migration patterns pre- and post-IRCA is provided in Douglass Massey, Jorge Durand, and Nolan Malone, *Beyond Smoke and Mirrors: Mexican Immigration in an Age of Economic Integration* (Russell Sage Foundation, 2002). See also Zai Lang and Douglass Massey, "Effects of the Immigration Reform and Control Act of 1986: Preliminary Data from Mexico," in *Illegal Immigration to the United States: The Experience of the 1980s*, ed. Frank D. Bean, Barry Edmonston, and Jeffrey S. Passel (Urban Institute Press, 1990); Katharine Donato, Douglass Massey, and Jorge Durand, "Stemming the Tide? Assessing the Deterrent Effects of the Immigration Reform and Control Act," *Demography* 29, no. 2 (May 1992): 139–57.

16. Raúl Delgado Wise and Héctor Rodríguez Ramírez, "The Emergence of Collective Migrants and Their Role in Mexico's Local and Regional Development," *Canadian Journal of Development Studies / Revue canadienne d'études du développement* 22, no. 3 (January 2001): 13.

17. Delgado Wise and Rodríguez Ramírez, "Emergence of Collective Migrants," 13–14.

18. Federico Torres and Yevgeny Kuznetsov, "Mexico: Leveraging Migrants' Capital to Develop Hometown Communities," in *Diaspora Networks and the International Migration of Skills*, ed. Yevgeny Kuznetsov (World Bank Institute, 2006), 101–3.

19. Torres and Kuznetsov, "Mexico," 112–13.

20. Torres and Kuznetsov, "Mexico," 114–15.

21. Douglass Massey and Emilio Parrado, "Migradollars: The Remittances and Savings of Mexican Migrants to the United States," *Population Research and Policy Review* 13 (1994): 23, 25. See also Douglass Massey and Emilio Parrado, "International Migration and Business Formation in Mexico," *Social Science Quarterly* 79, no. 1 (March 1998): 1–20.

22. Massey and Parrado, "Migradollars," 25.

23. *La dictadura perfecta*, dir. Luis Estrada (Mexico City: Bandidos Films, 2014).

24. "When He Talks for Mexico, Washington Pays Attention," *New York Times*, March 19, 2002.

25. "Presidente plantea crear oportunidades para contrarrestar fenómeno migratorio y garantizar bienestar en países de América Latina y el Caribe," Sitio Oficial de Andrés Manuel López Obrador, October 22, 2023, https://lopezobrador.org.mx/2023/10/22/presidente-plantea-crear-oportunidades-para-contrarrestar-fenomeno-migratorio-y-garantizar-bienestar-en-paises-de-america-latina-y-el-caribe.

26. "Presidente plantea crear oportunidades," October 22, 2023.

27. "México te abraza," Portal del Gobierno de México, January 28, 2025, www.gob.mx/cms/uploads/attachment/file/971337/28enero25_M_xico_te_abraza.pdf.

28. "México Propone Desarrollo en la Frontera Sur: Alternativa a la Militarización de EEUU," *El Ciudadano*, April 2, 2025, www.elciudadano.com/noticias-mexico/mexico-propone-desarrollo-en-la-frontera-sur-alternativa-a-militarizacion-de-eeuu/04/02; "Conferencia de prensa de la presidenta Claudia Sheinbaum Pardo del 1º de abril de 2025," Portal del Gobierno de México, April 1, 2025, www.gob.mx/presidencia/es/articulos/version-estenografica-conferencia-de-prensa-de-la-presidenta-claudia-sheinbaum-pardo-del-1-de-abril-de-2025?idiom=es.

INDEX

Page numbers in italics refer to illustrations.

activism, civic, 26, 48; and discourse of indignity, 33, 34, 35; and labor unions, 34, 41, 133; and 1954 BP suspension, 45, 46, 52, 53, 54, 56, 88. *See also* IBP: and migrant narratives and protests; migrants: protests by

agricultural industry, Mexican: competence of, 105, 106, 114; crop and regional diversity of, 30, 31; and exports, 204, 205; impact of migratory restrictions on, 11, 24, 104, 106, 107, *108*, 112, 119, 129; labor demands of, 21, 22, 30, 31, 32, 33, 57, 58, 87, 145, 235n42; and modernization as countermigratory instrument, 21, 29, 78, 181, 185, 190; self-serving antimigratory discourse of, 32, 57–60. *See also* Asociación Nacional de Cosecheros (ANC); Bracero Program (BP); Bracero Program, 1954 suspension of; colonization; cotton industry, Mexican; ejidos; internal Bracero Program (IBP)

agricultural industry, US, 17; against worker protections, 9, 82, 83, 84; and blacklisting of employers, 50, 83, 84, 86, 101; and Mexican countermigratory policies, 85, 214n16; on timing of migratory chain, 1, 2, 14, 17, 22, 99, 113, 114. *See also* Imperial Valley, CA; migrant mistreatment

Alemán, Miguel, 25, 29, 30, 57

Arizona, 39, *108*, 162, 172, 184, 185

Asociación Nacional de Cosecheros (ANC), 57, 67; white paper on migration by, 58–59

Ávila Camacho, Manuel, 8, 20, 21, 22, 25

Baja California, 10, 31, 94, 166, 185, 220n8; and coercive countermigratory measures, 73, 95; and IBP, 12, 104, 105, 106, *108*, 112; and migratory flow, 30, 31, 73. *See also* agricultural industry, Mexican; Maldonado, Braulio; Mexicali, Baja California; Northern Mexico

border, Mexico-US, 22, 26, *108*, 181; militarization of, 15, 31, 42, 44, 79, 82, 91, 155, 168, 169, 175, 189, 197, 202; opened by US, 41, 70, 71, 74, 82–90; transcendence of, 33, 34, 37, 200. *See also* Baja California; Border Patrol, US; Mexicali, Baja California

Border Industrialization Program (BIP), 109, 110; and migrant unemployment, 156, 159; and scholarship, 13, 14

249

Border Patrol, US, 153, 212n5; critics of, in cinema and press, 38, 39, 161, 164; and militarized border, 15, 189; overwhelmed by migrant stream, 99–101; post-BP brutality by, 15, 155, 156, 157, 162, 167, 168, 182, 186, 187, 191, 192, 193; and US open-border policy, 86, 95, 97, 99. *See also* border, Mexico-US

BP. *See* Bracero Program (BP)

Bracero Program (BP): as anti-Nazi endeavor, 21, 22, 25; and bilateral negotiations, 1, 2, 8, 9, 10, 11, 19, 22, 23, 43, 44, 45, 68, 101; and corruption, 124, 125, 128, 130, 132, 133, 135; dissatisfaction and exclusion of ejidos from, 24, 25, 26, 28, 29, 30; and formal migrant protections, 2, 19, 22, 25, 50, 101; limited to Central Mexico, 24, 25, 26, 31, 112; Mexican growers' use of, 104, 114, 128, 129, 130, 133, 135, 136, 143, 144, 146; Mexico's risk-benefit assessment of, 2, 20–25; 1948 suspension of, 40, 41, 43; as program of migrant humiliation, 19, 20; termination of, 13, 149, 152, 156; uneven synchronicity with IBP of, 128. *See also* Bracero Program, 1954 suspension of; internal Bracero Program (IBP); migrant mistreatment

Bracero Program, internal. *See* internal Bracero Program (IBP)

Bracero Program, 1954 suspension of, 43; aroused by US intervention in Guatemala, 45, 48, 49, 50, 51; and countermigratory repression, 10, 42, 44, 51, 70, 73, 81, 82, 91, 95, 96; despite US open-border policy, 70, 82–90; migrant resistance to, 80, 91–98; and optimism of ejidos, 45, 52, 62–67, 223n58, 223n59, 223n60; as patriotic defense, 45–55, 81, 221n18; supported by Mexicans, 45, 46, 52–60, 61, 63, 64, 71–82, 106, 235n42; as transition to pro-permanence platform, 44, 45, 68, 71–78, 82, 89–91; US noncompliance with, 10, 82–87. *See also* Bracero Program (BP); countermigratory measures, coercive; Mexicali, Baja California; Ruiz Cortines, Adolfo

Bracero Program of 1917, 17, 18

"Braceros of Mexico for the Fields of Mexico" initiative, 10, 89–91

Calexico, CA, 30, 35; border crossing at, 79, 86, 99

California, 35, 168, 201; establishment of Mexican settlements in, 18; and migratory flow from Baja California, 30, 73, 79, 108. *See also* Calexico, CA; Imperial Valley, CA

Camacho, Manuel Ávila. *See* Ávila Camacho, Manuel

campesinos: and CI, 160, 164, 165; dependence of ejidos on, 28, 29; and Luis Echeverría's reform initiatives, 165, 177, 178, 179, 180, 183; as objects of countermigratory discourse, 72, 75, 76, 89; and José López Portillo's reform initiatives, 188, 189, 193; and white paper on migration, 58, 59. *See also* campesinos, organizations of; Confederación Nacional Campesina (CNC)

campesinos, organizations of, 60; agrarian reform advocated by, 62–67, 176, 177, 178, 187. *See also* campesinos; Confederación Nacional Campesina (CNC)

Cárdenas, Lázaro, 47, 75; and corporatism, 19, 47; and land redistribution, 24, 48, 177; and oil, 21, 53

Carranza, Venustiano, 18, 19, 46

Carter, Jimmy, 15, 187, 188, 189, 190, 191, 192

Catholic Church: and BP, 20, 26, 44; in defense of workers, 26, 27, 200

Central Mexico, 87, 140; post-BP crisis of idle labor in, 157, 158, 159; as principal guest-work labor pool, 24, 25, 26, 112

Chavez, Cesar, 169, 187

Chiapas, 60, 73, 186, 207

Chihuahua. *See* Juárez, Ciudad

Coahuila, 24, 59, 72, 87, 90, 179

colonization, 29, 30, 33; and "Braceros of Mexico for the Fields of Mexico" initiative, 10, 89–90; and Comisión Colonizadora para Trabajadores Emigrantes, 77, 78, 90; and DAAC, 170, 171, 174; in pro-permanence rhetoric and policies, 66, 67, 68, 70–72, 77, 78, 81, 89, 90, 94, 95, 106, 171, 175–79, 183, 193. *See also* ejidos

Comisión Intersecretarial (CI), 160; proposals to solve out-migration by, 161, 164, 165, 168, 171

Comisión Mixta de Control de Trabajadores (CMCT), 107, 141, 146, 229n9; finances and logistics of, 109, 110, 116, 125, 126; and grower-government collaboration, 129; and overcrowded migrant depot, 137, 138. *See also* internal Bracero Program (IBP)

Confederación de Trabajadores de México (CTM), 28, 44, 74; against out-migration, 61, 183; braceros shamed by, 27, 28, 31; on US-Mexico bribery campaign, 163–64. *See also* Confederación Nacional Campesina (CNC); unions, labor

Confederación Nacional Campesina (CNC), 28, 31, 44, 163; advocacy for agrarian reform and colonization, 29, 30, 164, 165, 176, 177, 178, 187; in support of 1954 BP suspension, 63, 64. *See also* campesinos; campesinos, organizations of; Confederación de Trabajadores de México (CTM); ejidos

Congress, of Mexico, 49, 71, 72, 153, 180; and agrarian reform, 177, 179; condemnation of migrant mistreatment by, 185, 191; and renewal of guest-worker program, 168, 169. *See also* Mexican government; Mexico

Congress, US, 13; and amnesty legislation for undocumented workers, 197, 198, 199, 201, 202; and hyper-criminalization of migration, 170, 184; migration reform opposed by, 162, 166, 189; opposition to Mexican countermigratory measures, 10. *See also* United States

Constitution, Mexican, 18, 120; on land distribution, 24, 47, 62, 179

consuls, 7, 52, 80; and antimigrant brutality, 155, 163, 167; and BP of 1917, 17; and bracero working and living conditions, 40, 41; and strengthening diaspora ties, 201

corruption: and BP, 124, 125, 128, 130, 132, 133, 135; as cause of public anger, 105, 106, 124, 125, 126, 129, 130, 131, 132, 133, 134, 135, 136, 140, 141, 155; and ejidos, 66, 75; and IBP, 12, 105, 106, 122–26, 129–36, 138, 140, 141, 143; and media exposé of US-Mexico bribery campaign, 163, 164

Cortines, Adolfo Ruiz. *See* Ruiz Cortines, Adolfo

cotton industry, Mexican, 12, 24; antimigration entreaties of, 30; and IBP, 104, 105, 107, *108*, 109, 111–14, 116–23, *119*, 129, 133, 136–44, 146–49; labor demands of, 2, 11, 12, 156, 158

countermigratory measures, coercive, 5, 10; and growers, 31, 106; and IBP, 112, 114, 118, *118*, 119, *119*, 130, 132, 133, 135, 140, 141; and 1954 BP suspension, 10, 42, 44, 51, 70, 71, 73, 74, 76, 81, 82, 89, 91, 94, 95, 96, 97, 98. *See also* border, Mexico-US: militarization of; Border Patrol, US; deportations; Immigration and Naturalization Service (INS)

countermigratory policies, economic, 15, 152, 173; and lump-sum payments, 97, 98; and public works programs, 10, 73, 76; and tariff relief, 15, 181, 188, 189, 190, 191, 192, 193; and World Bank loan, 189, 190. *See also* agricultural industry, Mexican; Border Industrialization Program (BIP); colonization; economy, Mexican; ejidos; permanence, policies and rhetoric for

coyotaje. *See* human smuggling

de la Madrid, Miguel, 193; surrender to out-migration of, 16, 195–96, 198, 199, 200
Departamento de Asuntos Agrarios y Colonización (DAAC), and pivot to pro-permanence policies, 170, 171, 174, 175, 176, 177, 179, 180
Department of Justice, US, 85, 86, 163, 192
Department of Labor, US (DOL), 23, 51; and efforts to control migrant stream, 99; and efforts to derail Mexican pro-permanence policies, 10; and efforts to resume BP, 101; and Mexican interventionism, 82–86, 226n42, 103
deportations, 163, 164; and "peso refugees," 197; and post-BP antimigrant brutality, 156, 160, 161, 167, 168, 182, 184; in 1930s, 18, 22; and Operation Wetback, 103, 104; and Donald Trump, 206

Echeverría, Luis: and BIP, 159; and CI, 160, 164; and CNC, 164, 165, 175, 176, 178; crisis-driven policymaking of, 152, 153; and crisis of idle labor, 157, 158, 159; and DAAC, 175, 177, 179; and economic reform initiatives, 15, 159, 169, 171, 174, 180, 183, 185, 186; and Gerald Ford, 170, 171, 172, 174, 175; guest-worker program sought by, 14, 153, 157, 160, 162, 163, 166, 169; and migrant mistreatment, 181, 182, 185, 186; and Richard Nixon, 160, 166, 169, 173; and pivot to pro-permanence policies, 14, 15, 153, 170, 171, 172, 173, 174, 175, 186; tariff relief sought by, 15, 181, 188; and United Nations, 180, 181, 185. *See also* human smuggling: Mexican policing of
economy, Mexican: and demographic boom, 16, 192, 198; and government manipulation of remittance flow, 16, 196, 199, 202, 203, 204, 205, 207; and industrial development, 13, 19, 25, 62, 58, 87, 88, 89, 176, 183, 185; and inflation, 16, 184, 197, 198, 200; and oil, 21, 191; and peso devaluation, 16, 25, 193, 197. *See also* Border Industrialization Program (BIP); colonization; ejidos
ejidos: and "Braceros of Mexico for the Fields of Mexico" initiative, 89–91; opposition to BP of, 24, 25, 26, 28, 29, 30; and optimism during 1954 BP suspension, 45, 52, 62–67, 106, 223nn58–60; in policies and visions for permanence, 67, 74, 75, 76, 78, 89, 90, 106, 165, 171, 174, 178, 179, 193; and social change, 62; as underfunded and corrupt, 75. *See also* campesinos, organizations of; Confederación Nacional Campesina (CNC)
Empalme, federal contracting center, 107–17, *108*, 121–28, 130–41, 143, 144, 147; and military and police force, 112, 114, 132. *See also* internal Bracero Program (IBP)
employers, US, 10; as abusive, 2, 9, 20, 34, 35; blacklisting of, 50, 83, 84, 86, 101

Ford, Gerald: and Luis Echeverría, 170, 171, 172, 174, 175; on Mexican efforts to renew guest-worker program, 170, 173; opposition to tariff relief of, 15, 181

Gortari, Carlos Salinas de, 196, 200
Guadalajara, Jalisco, 54, 56, 71, 140
Guanajuato, 88, 157, 178, 179, 183; and opposition to BP migration, 29, 30, 32, 33; and remittance flow, 203, 204
Guatemala, 104, 220n11; Mexican defiance of US intervention in, 41, 48, 49, 50, 51, 102, 103; and Claudia Sheinbaum's jobs creation proposal, 207
guest-worker program. *See* Bracero Program (PB)

Hermosillo, Sonora: BP processing center in, 110, 111; CMCT in, 109, 110, 125, 126, 129, 137, 138, 139, 146, 229n9; and IBP growers, *108*, 117, 126, 129, 138, 140, 143, 148 human smuggling, 31, 37; and IBP, 124, 125, 126, 129–35, 138, 140, 141, 143; Mexican policing of, 153, 154, 155, 156, 173; in post-BP era, 153–56, 161, 163, 167, 173, 187, 237n6. *See also* migration, undocumented

IBP. *See* internal Bracero Program (IBP)
Immigration and Naturalization Service (INS): and Mexico-US open border, 41; and post-BP deportation surge, 184; and raids, 103, 167, 168; and US Border Patrol brutality, 187
Immigration Reform and Control Act (IRCA), 198, 199, 201, 202, 246n15
Imperial Valley, CA, 30, 51; and lettuce industry labor demand, 79, 80, 83, 85, 93; reputation for hazardous labor of, 92
Infante, Pedro, 39, 40, 56, 219n72
internal Bracero Program (IBP), 12; and antimigrant use of force, 112, 114, 118, *118*, 119, *119*, 130, 132, 133, 135, 140, 141; centrality of Northern Mexico to, 104, 105, 106, 107, *108*, 109, 128, 129, 130, 143, 145, 146, 147; and chronic government incompetence, 12, 106, 114, 117, 122, 126–32, 134–39, 141–47; and growers' competence, 106, 107, 109, 110, 111, 114, 117, 120, 121, 122, 126, 132–41, 148; and growers' reckless management, 120, 121, 136, 137, 138; and human smuggling, 124, 125, 126, 129, 130, 131, 132, 133, 134, 135, 138, 140, 141, 143; and migrant narratives and protests, 12, 13, 106, 111, 117–22, 128–36, 140, 141, 142; termination of, 12, 142, 143, 147, 148; as transition to pro-permanence solutions, 105. *See also* Comisión Mixta de Control de Trabajadores (CMCT); corruption; Empalme, federal contracting center; Hermosillo, Sonora; López Mateos, Adolfo; migrant mistreatment: and domestic exploitation; Obregón Tapia, Álvaro; Ruiz Cortines, Adolfo

Jalisco, 66, 218n62; high rates of out-migration from, 32, 160, 166, 183, 204; and IBP, 113, 121, 122, 136, 140; and opposition to BP migration, 32, 33, 217n51; post-BP crisis of idle labor in, 157; in support of Adolfo Ruiz Cortines's anti-US stand, 54, 56, 60, 61, 72; and US open-border policy, 87
Juárez, Ciudad, 38, 163; and BIP, 13; in cinema, 38, 39; migrant protests in, 158, 159, 186; and migratory flow, 41, 161, 182

Kissinger, Henry, 168, 169

labor unions. *See* unions, labor
landholders, large, 24; dispossession of, 28, 57, 62, 176, 223n59
latifundistas. *See* landholders, large
López Mateos, Adolfo: and IBP disfunction, 12, 13, 128, 139; migrant letters to, 135; and termination of IBP, 142, 143, 144, 145, 147
López Obrador, Andrés Manuel, 206, 207
López Portillo, José: and Jimmy Carter, 187, 188, 189, 190, 191; and countermigratory coercion, 186, 187; and economic reforms, 188, 192, 193; and pivot to pro-permanence policies, 174, 191, 192, 200; US help enlisted by, 15, 188, 189, 190, 191, 192, 193, 205; and World Bank loan, 189, 190
Lugo, Bartolomé Vargas. *See* Vargas Lugo, Bartolomé

Maldonado, Braulio, 89; and coercive countermigratory measures, 89, 96; and colonization policies, 81, 95; and IBP overcrowding, 112; as migrant in US, 80, 92; opposition to migration of, 73; pro-permanence rhetoric of, 81, 85. *See also* Baja California
Mateos, Adolfo López. *See* López Mateos, Adolfo

Index

Mexicali, Baja California, 43, 79, 85; concentration of migrants in, 73, 80, 81, 85, 86; migrant insurgency in, 10, 11, 91, 94–101, 97, 98, 100, 220n3; and migratory flow, 30, 51, 89; post-BP economic reform in, 175. *See also* Baja California

Mexican Americans: and Hermandad de Trabajadores, 182; migrant mistreatment by, 38, 92, 93, 161

Mexican government: as conduit of cheap labor, 101; and economic subordination to US, 13, 14, 104; equivocal search for migratory policies by, 3, 4, 5, 6, 8, 20, 26, 44, 71, 152, 153, 174, 181; and illusion of domestic autonomy over migration, 4, 5, 8, 10, 11, 15, 70, 71; and symbiosis between Mexican labor and US policy, 5, 6, 102, 103, 114, 123, 128. *See also* Congress, of Mexico; corruption; economy, Mexican; Maldanado, Braulio; Mexico; Partido Revolucionario Institucional (PRI); *and names of specific Mexican presidents*

Mexican Revolution, 17, 19, 121; and dispute between Adolfo Ruiz Cortines and Francisco Mugica, 46, 47, 48, 55, 220n8; and ejidos, 24, 62; and Lázaro Cárdenas, 47; in patriotic rhetoric, 63, 77, 80

Mexico: and "autonomous flexibility" toward migration, 8, 9, 10, 11, 17–20, 42–46, 69–71; and "dependent channeling" of migration, 11–15, 103–26, 128, 129, 151, 152, 153, 173, 174; and "disembodied manipulation" of migration, 15, 16, 193, 195–207; and "safety valve" migration trope, 3, 4, 53, 193, 151, 152; and scholarship on guest-worker programs, 2, 3, 6, 9, 44, 104, 105, 151, 211nn1–2, 212nn4–5, 212nn7–8, 213n14, 214nn15–16, 214n18, 219n74; vs. other migrant-sending countries, 3, 4, 212n9. *See also* Mexican government; Partido Revolucionario Institucional (PRI); United States

Mexico-US border. *See* border, Mexico-US

Michoacán: high rates of out-migration from, 87, 154, 160, 166, 178, 179, 183, 204; and IBP, 113, 121, 122, 136; and opposition to BP migration, 32, 33

migrant mistreatment, 221n14; and BP, 5, 9, 13, 49, 107, 149, 150, 218n62; and domestic exploitation, 10, 12, 13, 102, 105, 106, 107, 111, 114–25, 118, 119, 127–43; and Mexican government's reputation, 2, 9, 22, 35, 39, 49, 51, 186; in Mexican popular culture, 36–40; post-BP proliferation of, 14, 152, 153, 154, 182, 184, 185, 186, 191, 192, 193, 196. *See also* employers, US; human smuggling; migrants; press, Mexican

migrants, 94, 213n13; from industrial sector, 183; micropolitics of, 7, 8, 12, 70; mobility rights of, 6, 7, 8, 10, 11, 29, 80, 85, 91–99, 97, 98; and mutual conflict and solidarity, 99–101, 100; protests by, 12, 13, 106, 111, 117, 118, 119, 120, 122, 128–37, 140, 141, 142, 158, 159, 186; and remittance flow, 16, 196, 199, 202, 203, 204, 205, 207; and stain of disloyalty, 26, 101; statistics on, 59, 74, 180, 184. *See also* human smuggling; migrant mistreatment; migration, undocumented

migration, undocumented, 2, 12, 13, 20, 84; and hyper-criminalization of migration in US, 170, 184; impact of guest-worker program restrictions on, 29, 31, 33, 106, 152, 153; post-BP proliferation of, 152, 153, 162, 167, 168, 180, 181, 184; US amnesty for, 86, 197, 198, 199, 201, 202. *See also* human smuggling

migration and out-migration, promises of: and closer Mexican-US political ties, 1, 2, 7, 19, 21, 22, 23, 25; and modernization, 19, 22, 25; and "safety valve" migration trope, 3, 4, 53, 193, 151, 152; and well-compensated agricultural work, 1

254 *Index*

military and police, of Mexico, 86; and IBP, 112, 114, 118, 119, *119*, 132, 133, 140, 141; investigation of human smuggling, 130, 154, 167, 187; involvement in corruption and human smuggling of, 132, 141, 153, 155; and migrant insurgency in Mexicali, 10, 91, 95, 96, 97, 98; and 1954 BP suspension, 10, 42, 44, 51, 70, 71, 73, 74, 81, 82, 89, 91, 97. *See also* border, Mexico-US: militarization of

Movimiento de Regeneración Nacional (MORENA), 206, 207

Nixon, Richard, 15, 187; on Mexican efforts to renew guest-worker program, 160, 166, 169, 173

Northern Mexico: and BIP, 13; BP enrollment restrictions for, 24, 31; as central to IBP, 104, 105, 106, 107, *108*, 109, 128, 129, 130, 143, 145, 146, 147; labor shortages in, 31, 32, 57, 58, 87, 145; post-BP idle labor and overcrowding, 156, 157. *See also* agricultural industry, Mexican

Oaxaca, 33, 71, 122, 204
Obrador, Andrés Manuel López. *See* López Obrador, Andrés Manuel
Obregón Tapia, Álvaro: and IBP disfunction, 114, 115, 117, 125, 133, 135; and IBP problems, 112, 113; migrant letters to, 135, 136, 233n15; role in creating IBP, 11, 12, 106, 107, 109
Ordaz, Gustavo Díaz, 77, 130, 138, 144; disinterest in improving IBP of, 125, 139, 146

Partido Acción Nacional (PAN), 205–6, 207
Partido Revolucionario Institucional (PRI): authoritarian logic of, 4, 5, 10, 68, 229n6; and corporatism, 19, 47; end to political monopoly of, 205; peasant-centric rhetoric of, 9, 26, 89, 176, 179. *See also* Mexican government; Mexico

permanence, policies and rhetoric for: in citizens' letters, 52–56, 67, 68; government pivot to, 14, 20, 68, 81, 88, 89, 106, 152, 153, 170, 171, 172, 173, 174, 175, 179, 180, 186, 191, 192, 200; and individual and national dignity, 33–40, 44, 45, 52, 53, 54, 56, 60, 61, 63, 64, 72, 74, 77, 124, 172, 174; and masculinity, 20, 34, 60; and national self-reliance, 171, 172, 175, 176, 178, 186, 187; and strengthening families, 76. *See also* Bracero Program, 1954 suspension of; colonization; Echeverría, Luis; ejidos; López Portillo, José; Maldonado, Braulio; Ruiz Cortines, Adolfo
police. *See* military and police, of Mexico
Portillo, José López. *See* López Portillo, José
press, Mexican: on BP migrant mistreatment, 9, 14, 20, 26, 34, 35, 36, 39, 49, 107, 152, 218n62; on domestic labor exploitation, 32, 96, 105, 106, 114, 117, 118, 122, 123, 124, 126, 130, 131, 135; on Guatemala-US relations, 48, 50; and migrants' micropolitical strategies, 7, 12; and "Operación Guayabera," 166; on post-BP migrant mistreatment, 152, 161, 162, 163, 164, 168, 184; and Adolfo Ruiz Cortines's anti-US stand, 53, 54, 63, 73, 77, 81, 84, 85, 88, 90, 91; as stigmatizing migrants, 101
press, US, 53; on BP migrant mistreatment, 35; on Mexicali migrant insurgency, 96, 97, 101; on post-BP migrant mistreatment, 14, 162, 163, 164, 192
Programa para las Comunidades Mexicanas en el Exterior (PCME), and strengthening diaspora ties, 200, 201
public works programs, 10, 73, 76

racial discrimination, 23, 93, 101, 161; and nativism in US, 18; and racist tropes about Black workers, 165, 168; in US, 49, 50; and US white supremacist groups, 181

Reagan, Ronald, 192, 193
Roosevelt, Franklin Delano, 21, 22, 25
Ruiz Cortines, Adolfo: and "Braceros of Mexico for the Fields of Mexico" initiative, 10, 89–91; and capitulation to new BP, 11, 101; and coercive countermigratory measures, 10, 51, 52, 70, 71, 82, 87, 89, 91, 96, 97; and Comisión Colonizadora para Trabajadores Emigrantes, 77, 78, 90; failed efforts to protect braceros by, 50, 51, 82; decision to suspend BP by, 46, 50, 51, 52, 69, 84; and IBP, 11, 12, 107, 109, 110, 117, 118, 119, 120, 121; and migrant insurgency in Mexicali, 10, 80, 81, 85, 91, 94, 96; and pivot to pro-permanence policies, 68, 81, 88, 89, 106; pliability toward US of, 103, 104; and policymaking during 1954 BP suspension, 70, 71, 77, 220n3; supportive letters from public to, 52–56, 67, 68; tainted by past pro-US collaboration, 46, 47, 48, 49, 51, 55, 220n8. *See also* Bracero Program, 1954 suspension of

Sheinbaum, Claudia, 206, 207
Sinaloa, 64, 72; and IBP, 12, 106, 121, 125
Sonora, 24, 61; as key state in IBP, 12, 106–7, 108, 109–17, 120–26. *See also* Obregón Tapia, Álvaro
State Department, US, 23, 41, 84, 101, 103

Tamaulipas, 24; and countermigratory discourse, 61, 76, 88; and IBP, 12, 104, 106, 120, 121, 129, 136; in support of Adolfo Ruiz Cortines's anti-US stand, 53, 54
Texas, 18; and labor demand, 162; and migrant mistreatment, 23, 35, 38, 39, 49, 92, 159, 161, 182, 184; and migratory flow, 41, 92, 155

Tijuana, 79, 187; and BIP, 13; and migratory flow, 73, 168

undocumented migration. *See* migration, undocumented
unions, labor, 73; as advocates for migrant rights, 34, 41, 133; and dissatisfaction with BP, 20, 25, 26, 27, 34; overpowered by big business, 183, 184; in support of Adolfo Ruiz Cortines's anti-US stand, 45, 53, 56, 60. *See also* Confederación de Trabajadores de México (CTM); Confederación Nacional Campesina (CNC)
United States: draconian tactics of, 15, 168, 170; as indispensable outlet for Mexican labor, 195, 199; as Mexican workers' desired site of employment, 5, 7, 15, 71, 94, 147; open-border policy of, 10, 70, 71, 82–87, 94, 99; opposition to Mexican countermigratory policies, 7, 10, 41, 82–87; as place of migrant suffering, 14, 33–40, 45, 49, 152, 173, 196; and power over Mexican labor, 6, 7, 11, 45, 88, 101, 102, 164, 168, 170, 182, 192. *See also* agricultural industry, US; Department of Labor, US
US Border Patrol. *See* Border Patrol, US
US Congress. *See* Congress, US
US Department of Justice. *See* Department of Justice, US
US Department of Labor. *See* Department of Labor, US
US-Mexico border. *See* border, Mexico-US
US State Department. *See* State Department, US

Vargas Lugo, Bartolomé, 74–76
Veracruz, 33, 64, 72, 81; US military intervention in, 46, 48, 55

women: discouraged from BP enrollment, 23, 24; and gendered ethics, 148; and gendered organization of labor, 13, 18, 19, 159; in support for Adolfo Ruiz Cortines's anti-US stand, 53

World War I, 18; and US labor demand, 17, 19

World War II, 1–2, 6, 40; and closer Mexico-US political ties, 19, 21, 22, 25; and German-Mexican-US relationship, 21; and US labor demand, 18, 19

Yaqui Valley, Sonora, 108, 122, 133, 139, 140, 143, 146, 148, 158

Yucatán Peninsula, 159, 178, 179, 180

Zacatecas: and crisis of idle labor, 157; high rate of out-migration from, 160, 179, 201; and remittance flow, 202, 203

Zedillo, Ernesto, 196, 200